Beyond Aesthetics

Beyond Aesthetics

Art and the Technologies of Enchantment

Edited by
Christopher Pinney and Nicholas Thomas

Oxford • New York

First published in 2001 by
Berg
Editorial offices:
150 Cowley Road, Oxford, OX4 1JJ, UK
838 Broadway, Third Floor, New York, NY 10003-4812, USA

Berg is an imprint of Oxford International Publishers Ltd.

Library of Congress Cataloging-in-Publication Data
A catalog record for this book is available from the Library of Congress.

British Library Cataloguing-in-Publication Data
A catalogue record for this book is available from the British Library.

ISBN 13: 978-1-85973-464-3
ISBN 1 85973 464 2 (Paper)

Printed in the United Kingdom

Contents

Contents

Preface

Is it useful to see art objects, not as bearers of meaning or aesthetic value, but as forms mediating social action? This book addresses a range of issues in the anthropology of art in relation to this thesis, in relation to a theory proposing that former emphases upon significance and aesthetics in the anthropology of art have proved unproductive, and that art should instead be seen as a special kind of technology that captivates and ensnares others in the intentionalities of its producers. This is one of the arguments of Alfred Gell's posthumously published *Art and Agency: an Anthropological Theory* (1998), which this collection uses as a departure point, to re-assess questions of agency and meaning in art.

Most of the chapters of this book are based on drafts presented at a conference which took place in Canberra in August 1998. This event was intended in part as a commemoration of the work of Alfred Gell, who had died in January 1997, but the participants were nevertheless committed to debating Alfred's work with the kind of impartial vigour that characterized his own seminar engagements and writings. Among a number of people who made stimulating contributions and helped make the conference a success, but who are not represented in this volume, we must thank Eric Hirsch, Howard Morphy, and especially Simeran Gell.

The conference was supported by the Wenner-Gren Foundation for Anthropological Research and the British Academy, and hosted by the Centre for Cross-Cultural Research at the Australian National University. We are very grateful to those institutions for making the event possible, and must particularly thank Hilary Ericksen and Ian Bryson, research assistants at the Centre for Cross-Cultural Research; Hilary put a great deal of work into the organization of the conference and supported the initial phases of editorial work; Ian Bryson, who provided further editorial assistance and co-ordination, has helped us bring the project to fruition. Thanks also to Kathryn Earle at Berg for her patience and support.

Introduction

Nicholas Thomas

In 1973, Anthony Forge observed that the position of the anthropology of art was 'curious'. He was remarking on the field's marginality within the discipline, that seemed incommensurate with the level of interest in 'primitive art' outside it. Nearly thirty years later, the anthropology of art remains 'curiously' situated, for different reasons. Forge's work helped draw research on art away from antiquarian museology and into the anthropological mainstream by embedding it within ethnography; over the 1970s and 1980s, ethnographic studies of indigenous arts became well-established, and typically focused on questions of communication, meaning, and the distinctiveness of indigenous ways of seeing and aesthetic systems. These concerns were still central in *Anthropology, Art and Aesthetics* (Coote and Shelton 1992), which reflected the state of play in the field, at least within British anthropology.

What became 'curious' was an apparent lack of dialogue between work which effectively analysed art practices within local ethnographic settings, and emerging preoccupations with the politics of art, cross-cultural relations, and representation – debates that for a time had centred upon the famous or notorious 1983 'Primitivism' show at the Museum of Modern Art, New York (Rubin 1983; McEvilley 1984; Clifford 1988). It was also odd that while anthropologists in every other possible field within the discipline were addressing social and cultural phenomena in most imaginable cultural settings, the Coote and Shelton volume suggested that work on art remained, like Forge's 1973 collection, confined not merely to 'non-Western' societies but more particularly to certain tribal or formerly tribal peoples, in other words to those formerly identified as 'primitive'. In other words, the 'anthropology of art' seemed to have no body of theory, no perspective, that could be disembedded from the ethnography of indigenous art and applied to art in general. Anthropologists, certainly, could and did embrace issues around representation and cultural politics (Marcus and Myers 1997; MacClancy 1997; Phillips and Steiner 1998), but when they did so they generally drew upon methods of textual critique and upon issues raised in cultural studies and related fields. While, in 1994 Morphy was able to provide a coherent (and very valuable) synthesis of the 'anthropology of art', this meant largely an anthropology of style and meaning in indigenous art.

The present volume does not aim to provide a new synthesis which draws the semiotic and ethnographic perspectives on art together with those associated with anthropological postmodernism. It is instead concerned to debate a highly original intervention in the field, which may challenge both. In the 1960s and 1970s Herbert Cole (1969) argued for Igbo 'art as a verb' and Robert Faris Thompson (1974) made more general claims for the processual dimension of African art. Questions of agency were also alluded to by Robert Layton, who addressed art objects as 'agents of an ideology [impacting] upon the form of social relations' (1981:43). Alfred Gell's 1998 book, *Art and Agency*, could be seen as a radical elaboration of this interest in foregrounding process in the analysis of art works. Gell's work is not a study of material culture, but an argument that insists on the agency of things, at least on the agency they are taken to exercise. Its arguments against linguistic and semiotic interpretation are, in the opening if not the closing sections of the book, so categorical that they surely have at least the merit of establishing the limits of this rejection of the preoccupation with meaning that has dominated the anthropology of art since Lévi-Strauss. Gell here develops the art historian David Freedberg's exploration of the 'powers' of art and his analysis echoes with W.J.T. Mitchell's consideration of what pictures 'really want'. The premise of this volume is the belief that Gell's drastic reformulation of the anthropology of art is of major importance. Our collection provides a wide-ranging review of the field, addressing music and performance as well as diverse art genres from various parts of the world, but it is a review that is anchored in an engagement with his challenging text. Some contributors are concerned to adapt and elaborate on certain of Gell's concepts; others are more concerned to dissent from his arguments; all take *Art and Agency* as a key point of reference. The first part of this introduction attempts to distil the arguments of Gell's complex and demanding book.

The arguments of *Art and Agency* were foreshadowed in a number of essays, notably 'The Technology of Enchantment and the Enchantment of Technology' (1992), which is worth reviewing briefly here. In that article, Gell provocatively claimed that the anthropology of art had got virtually nowhere thus far, because it had failed to dissociate itself from projects of aesthetic appreciation that do for art what theology does for religion. He argued that if the discipline was instead to adopt the position analogous to that of the sociology of religion, it needed a methodological philistinism equivalent to sociology's methodological atheism. This required disowning the 'art cult' to which anthropologists, as cultured middle-class intellectuals, generally subscribe. Gell was not, however, advocating a demy-stifying sociological analysis, that would identify the role of art in sustaining class cultures, or in legitimizing dominant ideologies: Gell suggested that approaches of this kind – exemplified by Bourdieu's *Love of Art,* and *Distinction*, failed to engage with art objects themselves, with their specificity and efficacy. More particularly, he was relatively uninterested in the questions raised by art-world institutions, believing instead that the anthropology of art should address the workings of art in general. He therefore acknowledged but bypassed the much-debated issues of the fetishization and devaluation of the 'primitive', together with a host of other questions around collecting, appropriation, exhibitions, and representation that have preoccupied many recent scholars writing about indigenous art (Price 1989; Clifford 1988; Coombes 1994; Thomas 1999). Parenthetically, it is worth noting that Gell's address was to scholars in anthropology, rather than in the wider field of those engaged in art practices; it is fair to say that those concerned with these practices, particularly in South Africa, Australia, New Zealand, and Canada would perhaps find it hard to produce a sustained discussion that passes over the range of currently hot political issues, concerning the definition and representation of indigenous art, the relations between traditional and contemporary practices, and the repatriation of museum objects. Gell was not personally indifferent to these questions, which are in fact alluded to in passing, but it was not necessary for him, as it may be unavoidable for others of us, to connect theorizing with the wider field of political contention, and several of the chapters in this book test, challenge, and extend Gell's arguments in the contexts of contemporary debate. Close parenthesis.

In 'The Technology of Enchantment', Gell proposed that it was possible to address questions of the efficacy of the art object, without succumbing to the fascination and aura of those objects, by taking art as a special form of technology, and especially by regarding art objects as devices 'for securing the acquiescence of individuals in the network of intentionalities in which they are enmeshed' (1992: 43). For example, brilliantly involuted and captivating forms such as those of Trobriand prow-boards (of the Massim region, Papua New Guinea) work a kind of psychological warfare, in a situation of competitive exchange. These boards confront the hosts of exchange partners, ideally dazzle them, beguile them, and confuse them, leading them to surrender their valuables – anthropology's famous kula shells – for less than their value. The claim here is not reductive, however: it is not suggested that in some sense the object *by itself* does this, or would do it, independently of a field of expectations and understandings, which in this case envelope the artefact with magical prowess, which is known to have entered into its making. Technology is enchanting because it is enchanted, because it is the outcome of some process of barely comprehensible virtuosity which exemplifies an ideal of magical efficacy that people struggle to realize in other domains. This is also the point at which Gell somewhat qualified his exclusion of the aesthetic from the domain of analysis, at least to the extent that judgements of what is strong and weak (rather than beautiful or ugly) are central to efficacy: to work its magic on enemies, exchange-partners, or prospective buyers, a shield, a prow-board, or a painting must be a compelling example, and if that adjudication is to be analysed, we need to know something of cross-cultural aesthetics, and we may even need to license ourselves to engage in a little art theology, to recognize brilliance as we trace the work that brilliance does.

There was a minor inconsistency in the 1992 article, in the sense that it seemed to be assumed that the anthropology of art remained the study of 'primitive' art (1992: 62). (Gell rejected the euphemistic term 'non-western' on the grounds that this included high Oriental art and other traditions, which clearly possessed an entirely different social location to the canonical tribal art forms.) However, the examples he proceeded to use, in pointing to the 'halo effect of technical difficulty' and other aspects of the art objects, included the paintings of the American illusionist J.F. Peto, and of Picasso. The implication that his theory might in fact be a theory of the workings of all art, rather that that supposedly characteristic of particular populations, becomes a premise of *Art and Agency*.

The first chapters of *Art and Agency* amount to a dramatic elaboration of the arguments of the 1992 article. Gell begins by deferring to the desirability, in broader cultural and political terms, of acknowledging the distinctness of non-western aesthetic systems, but asserts that this cannot constitute an 'anthropological' theory, on the grounds that anthropological theories are essentially concerned with social relations, over the time-frame of biographies. As he acknowledges, this definitional orientation may be contentious, but it arguably provides a productive departure point for this particular inquiry. There are two linked arguments for a shift away from cross-cultural aesthetics. The first is that many canonical pieces of tribal art, such as the Asmat shields of southwest New Guinea, are plainly not intended to elicit 'aesthetic' appreciation in the conventional sense – they rather had a part to play in the deadly psychological warfare of headhunting that was so fundamental to Asmat sociality before pacification. The second is a categorical rejection of the linguistic analogies that have been mobilized by so many semiotic and symbolic theories of art. And this is perhaps the sense in which his book is most radical. For many scholars, and indeed in much commonsense thinking about art, it is axiomatic that art is a matter of meaning and communication (although among art historians there have been some prominent exceptions such as David Freedberg). His book suggests that it is instead about *doing*.

'Doing' is theorized as agency, as a process involving indexes and effects; the anthropology of art is constructed as a theory of agency, or of the mediation of agency by indexes, understood simply as material entities which motivate inferences, responses or interpretations. Indexes stand in a variety of relations to prototypes, artists, and recipients. Prototypes are the things that indices may represent or stand for, such as the person depicted in a portrait – though things may be 'represented' non-mimetically, and non-visually. Recipients are those whom indexes are taken to effect, or who may, in some cases, be effective themselves via the index. (A view of a country estate commissioned by the landowner may be a vehicle of the recipient's self-celebrating agency, more than that of the artist.)

Artists are those who are considered to be immediately causally responsible for the existence and characteristics of index, but as we have just noted, they may be vehicles of the agency of others, not the self-subsistent, creative agents of Western commonsense ideas and art-world theory. In this respect, it is worth noting that despite the notable differences between the style and orientation of his book, and the Melanesianist deconstructionism of Marilyn Strathern (1988; see also Wagner 1992), Gell could be seen to fully embrace Strathern's notion of the 'partible' or 'distributed' person, and indeed to make explicit the ways in which it follows from this concept that actions and their effects are similarly not discrete expressions of individual will, but rather the outcomes of mediated practices in which agents and patients are implicated in complex ways. On the one hand the agency of the artist is rarely self-sufficient; on the other the index is not simply a 'product' or end-point of action, but rather a distributed extension of an agent. Gell offers us the chilling example of one of Pol Pot's soldiers, who distributes elements of his own efficacy in the form of landmines.

The theory receives more sustained exemplification in his chapters six and seven, which address forms of 'decorative' and 'representational' art respectively. Chapter six discusses apotropaic patterns, involuted designs intended to entrance and ward off dangerous spirits; with examples such as the Asmat shield, these perhaps manifest most obviously one of his book's larger theses, namely that art objects mediate a technology to achieve certain ends, notably to enmesh patients in relations and intentionalities sought or prescribed by agents. Lest this appear a reductive approach to art, one that takes objects essentially as vehicles of strategies, it is important to emphasize that the formal complexity, and indeed the technical virtuosity, exhibited in works of art is not incidental to the argument but absolutely central to it. It is crucial to the theory, in fact, that indexes display 'a certain cognitive indecipherability', that they tantalize, they frustrate the viewer unable to recognize at once 'wholes and parts, continuity and discontinuity, synchrony and succession' (1998: 95).

His long chapter seven ranges widely over idolatry, sorcery, ritual, and personhood, drawing on a bewildering range of south Asian and Polynesian source material, but is fully consistent with the claims of his previous sections. Idols are indeed of special relevance for *Art and Agency*, because they stand for an agent or patient (in the case of sorcery), for persons or deities, in manifest and powerful ways. They are indices that may be animated in a variety of ways, that enable transactions in lethal effect, fertility, auspiciousness, and the like. The larger point is that there are multiple implications of agency in objects, 'an inseparable transition' between them and actual human agents. Once appreciated as indexes of agency, iconic objects in particular can occupy positions in the networks of human social agency that are almost equivalent to the positions of humans themselves.

Up to this point, Gell's theorizing and exemplification focus upon the work of particular objects or indexes in particular actions, on specific processes rather than entire repertoires of art works. He concludes chapter seven by acknowledging that there are many vital respects in which art works do not appear as singular entities, but rather as ensembles. The remainder of *Art and Agency* appears to take a sharp turn away from the paradigm of the agent and index that has received such concerted attention thus far. It tackles the question of familial relations among art works, and seems to shift back to conventional ground, in engaging with the concept of style.

He is again concerned to avoid linguistic models such as 'a grammar of style' and instead seeks rather to identify axes of coherence through a strictly formal analysis of generative relations among motifs. He proceeds to offer (1998: ch. 8) a richly visual analysis of these relations. The point that Janus figures (which are almost pervasive in Oceanic art) indexed invulnerability had already been made in Gell's study of Polynesian tattooing, *Wrapping in Images* (1993); it was not simply that the figure could see in all directions, but that the face was itself an expression of power, and, in sculptural form, was canonically the face of a deity rather than that of a human. One of the central claims of *Wrapping in Images* was that eastern Polynesian tattooing was a technology that reinforced the body, and in the highly competitive, unstable and violent societies of the Marquesas, it is not unexpected to find that tattooing entailed the multiplication of the body's faces. These themes are highly salient to Gell's discussion of Marquesan forms (1998: 168–220) such as the famous *u'u* clubs, described here as 'the ultimate double-double tiki', but the discussion goes well beyond the earlier commentaries on the arts of empowerment in these societies. The real object, in this case, is the diagnosis of the formal principles that give Marquesan art its singularity, and these are identified, not at the level of appearance, but through the types of transformations that link Marquesan art works.

At the most abstract level, the principles that govern these transformations can be connected to the cultural milieu. Gell suggests that the most basic principle to be detected in the Marquesan corpus is a principle of 'least difference': 'the forms taken by motifs and figures are the ones involving the least modification of neighbouring motifs consistent with the establishment of a distinction between them'. This trend can in turn, he claims, be connected with the most basic feature of identity-formation in Marquesan society, which was characterized by acute status competition; this was not simply a matter of political jockeying, but rather a ritually-saturated process of inter-individual contact and commensality. Personal integrity was continually threatened by dispersal and de-differentiation; many Marquesan artefacts amounted, individually, to devices that wrapped the body and protected particular orifices, or the body as a whole in situations of crisis; in the ensemble as a whole, the principle of least difference resonated with a preoccupation with a continually prejudiced effort of differentiation, of differentiation in the midst of dissolution. 'There was an elective affinity between a *modus operandi* in the artifactual domain, which generated motifs from other motifs by interpolating minuscule variations, and a *modus operandi* in the social realm which created "differences" arbitrarily against a background of fusional sameness' (1998: 218–19).

It is worth underlining the distinction between this effort and that of Allan Hanson, which Gell finds to be worthy but misconceived. Whereas Hanson attempted to identify one-to-one correspondences between formal properties in Maori art (such as disrupted symmetry) and properties of Maori culture (competitive reciprocity), Gell points out that the stylistic elements that are singled out are universal, or at least commonly encountered, and cannot therefore be determined by singular features of Maori culture. Although the 'elective affinity' that he seeks to identify between Marquesan style and culture could be seen to be similar to the relation of recapitulation that Hanson postulated between Maori aesthetic form and culture, for Gell the affinities will emerge not at the level of characteristic relations in particular bodies of material but at that of 'relations between relations'; at the level, in other words, of meta-properties that demonstrably render that style peculiar to itself.

The final chapter of *Art and Agency* makes a further, equally ambitious step, onto ground that has often been unsatisfactorily traversed, the problem that has been conventionally posed in terms of what collective counterparts individual minds and consciousnesses possess. Gell's approach to the issue may be fresh and rewarding precisely because it does not start from the usual departure points, but rather builds on several preceding arguments – 'inner' and 'outer', internal and external, have already been shown to be relatively rather than absolutely contrasted. Inspired both by Peer Gynt's onion, by Strathern's fractal conception of personhood, and by the extraordinary exemplification of fractal and distributed personhood in Polynesian and especially Marquesan art, Gell evokes the notion of a 'distributed mind' through an argument that 'the structures of art history demonstrate an externalised and collectivised cognitive process'. The famous malanggan of New Ireland and the kula transactions of the Massim region of Papua New Guinea are invoked to advance this argument, demonstrating, with the support of the work of Nancy Munn in particular, that the kula operator 'is a spatio-temporally extended person' (1998: 221–30). At this point two of the book's key themes, that of the distributed mind and that of efficacious agency, are drawn together. Efficacy is founded on a comprehensive internal model of the outside field. One becomes a great kula operator, in other words, by modelling a working simulacrum, a dynamic spacetime map, of the play and history of kula in the world. Internal mental process and external transactions in objectified personhood are (ideally) fused. Mind, therefore, can exist objectively as well as subjectively, as a pattern of transactable objects.

Gell does not conclude with this large claim, but proceeds to vindicate the concept of the distributed mind through the more familiar instance of the individual (canonically western) artist's work, turning also to engage with questions of continuity over time, and foreshadowing the concluding discussion of questions of tradition. His key terms here are 'protention' and 'retention', which advert to the ways in which art works at once anticipate future works and hark back to others. His key example is the oeuvre of Duchamp, and particularly the very striking notion of 'the network of stoppages' which inspired not only Gell's understanding of the issue, but the diagrammatic form in which he presents it. The final section of *Art and Agency* reverts to the collective register, arguing that a similar pattern of protentions and retentions can be identified in the history of Maori meeting houses, therefore understanding this historical corpus as 'a distributed object structurally isomorphous to consciousness as a temporal process' (1998: ch. 9).

A number of the chapters in our book challenge Gell's attempt to exclude linguistic or quasi-linguistic meaning from the interpretation of art. This is one of the points of James Weiner's Chapter One, which aims also to situate Gell's arguments within an anthropological Romanticism that Weiner argues is unavoidable and in fact desirable in the anthropology of art. Weiner moreover argues that Gell is over-hasty in casting aside the aesthetic, on the grounds that there is more to the aesthetic than narrow considerations of taste and beauty. His chapter points toward the broader field of sensory response to conventional forms, which, it is argued, must be seen in communicative terms that are explored through the imbrication of language and music. Weiner's European and Melanesian examples are framed in relation to Gell's earlier Umeda ethnographic work, which reveals interpretative dimensions that, for Weiner are somewhat repressed in *Art and Agency.* Ian Keen's Chapter Two also deals with music, and discusses the transposition of Gell's theory of agents, patients, and indices from the material to the musical domain, focusing particularly on the movement to create historically authentic performances. This chapter draws attention to the complex relations of agency and prototype that pertain to cultural creations that are understood in explicitly museological terms. Susanne Küchler's Chapter Three begins with a useful positioning of Gell's arguments relative to the aesthetics of Kant and Schiller, and proceeds to outline a novel investigation into the mathematics of art, engaging topology, decentred spatial conceptions, and particularly knotting. Knotting emerges as a particular technology of knowledge, which (in the Pacific) provides spatial and material counterparts to notions of kingship and sorcery. Cords and bindings at once exemplify logical and mathematical conundra, and processual and performative values, in linking the visible and the invisible, as well as past and present. Though Küchler's chapter ranges over many examples, those most proximate to Gell's arguments are associated with effects of the body politic and specifically of kingship in Oceania.

These themes are effectively taken up in Anne D'Alleva's Chapter Four, which again engages Gell's exclusion of metaphor and metonymy in favour of the 'presented object'. Working from Polynesian examples that are central to *Art and Agency*, D'Alleva argues that symbolic meaning is too extensively attested to, to be set aside in this fashion. Yet she demonstrates that Gell's theme of captivation can be addressed more fully if these imaginative elements of the index are more properly acknowledged. Captivation also provides the focus of Lissant Bolton's discussion in Chapter Five of textiles from Ambae (Vanuatu); Bolton explores the roles and significance of various textiles in Ambae rank systems, and supports Gell's view that Melanesian aesthetics is more concerned with accomplishment and power than with beauty. She suggests that the licence he accords the object – to index, mediate, embody and transmit status – enables in this case a richer understanding of indigenous notions of power and the empowerment of material forms. This cluster of chapters on indigenous Pacific art forms concludes with Shirley Campbell's Chapter Six on Vakutan canoe art, of value here both because it is so richly evoked, and because Gell's 1992 paper on 'The Technology of Enchantment and the Enchantment of Technology' used Campbell's material as a key case, to justify his broadly instrumental analysis of these art forms. Campbell acknowledges the art forms' efficacy, but argues, along similar lines to those of D'Alleva, that the meaning and symbolism of the forms must be acknowledged.

It was noted earlier that the anthropology of art had long been oddly restricted to tribal art. Many of the essays in this volume shift beyond that domain, and it is certainly true that Gell's theme of captivation is salient to many forms of cultural expression in very diverse contexts. This is demonstrated in Daniel Miller's valuable Chapter Seven on Trinidadian web sites. Miller suggests that these possess various affinities with the kula exchange system of the Massim, in which exchange-practitioners sought to spread fame, extend their networks, and draw others into their own intentionalities. In the same way, the internet now functions as a domain through which 'Trinis' can expand their fame and express their social efficacy.

Of the last five chapters in this volume, four focus on the politics of art. Although the theory of the 'technology of enchantment' could be seen to be inherently political – focusing as it does on the efforts of certain agents to use art works to entrap other agents in their intentionalities – *Art and Agency* is largely unconcerned with the political manipulation of art in a more concrete sense, and it likewise passes over the vigorous contemporary debates concerning representation, authenticity, appropriation and authority in contemporary indigenous art. Christopher Pinney's Chapter Eight lends support to Gell's interest in the agency of images, and contextualizes this issue in a wider juxtaposition (following Fried, Buck-Morss and others) between modernist 'absorption' and a 'corpothetic' 'theatricality' characteristic of diverse art practices, notably the mass production of Hindu images. In his case material, the various modalities of divine embodiment do not exemplify either the Melanesian construct of 'fractal personhood' or the 'concentric idols' emphasized in Gell's discussion of south Asian art in *Art and Agency*. Rather, they reveal and are produced by fields of conflict. Similarly, Clare Harris's discussion in Chapter Nine acknowledges the values of Gell's perspective on the person- and god-like properties of images, particularly in the ritual context, but finds in the Tibetan case that images of the Dalai Lama, like many other art forms, are highly determined by the politics of neo-nationalism. The conditions of political rupture produce not only conflicted but highly mutable responses to these icons of distributed personhood.

Francesca Merlan's Chapter Ten, on 'Aboriginal Cultural Production into Art', returns to the terrain of the indigenous and ethnographic, or rather, reveals the contemporary workings of indigenous art in the colonial/postcolonial interface of settler Australia. Merlan points out that 'indigenous aesthetics' can not be seen merely as an academic issue that is either addressed or not, but is rather also an issue that surfaces in many social locations, in which art works are recast and revalued, from radically opposed perspectives. This is also the domain tackled in Charlotte Townsend-Gault's Chapter Eleven, which takes a particular object, a baton, of significance in the Northwest Coast aboriginal cultures, and in a variety of adapted and appropriated forms, and traces what it indexes, in this equally conflicted field. Marilyn Strathern's Chapter Twelve draws Gell's arguments concerning technologies into another domain of debate, that surrounding intellectual property rights. She examines the underpinnings of ideas of efficacy and creativity in Western discourses of new technology and in New Ireland malanggan, which otherwise loom large both in *Art and Agency* and in Susanne Küchler's Chapter Three in this volume.

This collection suggests three things. The first is that the 'anthropology of art' will always occupy 'curious' situations because it is irretrievably eclectic. There can arguably be no synthesis of formal enquiries into the properties of art form and their logics in a universal sense, of historical work on the functioning of old indigenous genres, of interpretive ethnographies, of comparative studies of western and indigenous images and performances, and of political interventions in the politics of representation. There is a frustrating sense in which debates about art and especially about 'ethnographic art' go around in circles, reworking tired definitional debates and questions of how indigenous work should be exhibited. The interplay between the variety of intellectual agendas in comparative studies of art, and the interplay between these primarily academic enquiries and public and political debate, make it inevitable that anthropologies of art will remain provisional and insecure. The value of notions such as captivation may lie in the extent to which they enable a break from older debates that have become circuitous. The second is that most though perhaps not all contributors would feel strongly that debate about art practices cannot be pursued without engagement with art's politics. Such engagement is, in part perhaps, a response of academics anxious to position themselves in some appropriate way, in relation to indigenous peoples with whom they have worked. But it is not just that. The political may enrich and may be enriched by an anthropology 'beyond aesthetics'. Third, and finally, if most contributors find Gell's arguments overstated in certain respects, there is no doubt that they are productive, in focusing attention on the agency of objects, on the work of art within the projection of the distributed person, and on the conflicted workings of technologies of enchantment.

References

Clifford, J. 1988. *The Predicament of Culture*. Cambridge, Mass.: Harvard University Press.

Cole, H.M. 1969. 'Art as a Verb in Iboland', African Arts III, I.

Coombes, A.E. 1994. *Reinventing Africa*. New Haven: Yale University Press.

Coote, J. and A. Shelton (eds) 1992. *Anthropology, Art and Aesthetics*. Oxford: Oxford University Press.

Forge, A. 1973. 'Introduction', in Forge (ed.), *Art in Primitive Society*. New York: Oxford University Press.

Freedberg, D. 1989. *The Power of Images*. Chicago: University of Chicago Press.

Gell, A. 1992. 'The Enchantment of Technology and the Technology of Enchantment', in Coote and Shelton (eds), *Anthropology, Art and Aesthetics*.

—— 1993. *Wrapping in Images: Tattooing in Polynesia*. Oxford: Oxford University Press.

—— 1998. *Art and Agency: an Anthropological Theory*. Oxford: Oxford University Press.

Layton, R. 1981. *The Anthropology of Art*. Cambridge: Cambridge University Press.

MacClancy, J. (ed) 1997. *Contesting Art*. Oxford: Berg.

McEvilley, T. 1984. 'Doctor, Lawyer, Indian, Chief', *Art Forum,* November 1984.

Marcus, G.E. and F.R. Myers (eds) 1997. *The Traffic in Culture*. Berkeley: University of California Press.

Mitchell, W.J.T. 1996. 'What Do Pictures Really Want?' October 77, Summer.

Morphy, H. 1994. 'The Anthropology of Art', in T. Ingold (ed.), *Companion Encyclopaedia of Anthropology*. London: Routledge.

Phillips, R.B. and C. Steiner (eds) 1998. *Unpacking Culture*. Berkeley: University of California Press

Price, S. 1989. *Primitive Art in Modern Places*. Chicago: University of Chicago Press.

Rubin, W. 1983. *'Primitivism' in 20th Century Art*. London: Thames and Hudson.

Strathern, M. 1988. *The Gender of the Gift*. Berkeley: University of California Press.

Thomas, N. 1999. *Possessions: Indigenous Art/Colonial Culture*. London: Thames and Hudson.

Thompson, R.F. 1974. *African Art in Motion: Icon and Act in the Collection of Katherine Coryton White*. Berkeley: University of California Press.

Wagner, Roy 1992. 'The Fractal Person', in M. Godelier and M. Strathern (eds), *Big Men and Great Men: Personifications of Power in Melanesia*. Cambridge: Cambridge University Press.

Romanticism, from Foi Site Poetry to Schubert's *Winterreise*

James F. Weiner

In the last pages of *Art and Agency*, Alfred Gell turns to a painting by Marcel Duchamp, *The Network of Stoppages* (1998: 246). It was painted on a used canvas, on which Duchamp had already put sketches of previous and planned works (*Young Man and Girl in Spring*, and *Large Glass* respectively). The figure in the foreground, notes Gell, 'looks rather like a map of some railway-system . . . Each "branch" seems to come to an end in a "terminus" of some kind' (ibid.). Gell quite brilliantly goes on to draw a relationship between the foregrounded figure of a map of lines and termini, and what he infers to be Duchamp's own perceived intervals or interruptions between three of his works he wished to show as linked; as Gell put it, he 'allows us to see his "sinking" past as a transformable component of his present . . .' (1998: 250).

Gell adduces these observations towards the point with which he concludes his volume: that the art-work is 'a place where agency "stops" and assumes visible form . . . Duchamp's subjectivity, his inner *durée* is concretely instantiated, as a series of moments, or "delays" or "perchings", in the objective traces of his agency . . .' (ibid.). By way of comparative support for this hypothesis anthropologically, Gell refers to Lévi-Strauss's own Bergsonian meditations on the metaphysics of the Dakota Indians (as reported by Durkheim):

> Everything as it moves, now and then, here and there, makes stops. The bird as it flies stops in one place to make its nest, and in another to rest in its flight. A man when he goes forth stops when he wills. So the god has stopped . . . (Lévi-Strauss 1963: 98, cited in Gell 1998: 248).

Gell uses this Dakotan theory of the intervallic property of life to move to a consideration of the Maori Meeting House, the last 'object' he considers in his book. By the time we have come to the end of *Art and Agency*, we are left with the notion of the art-work as a nexus of movements, stoppages, redirections and contrived intervals, all centred around its most explicit manifestation, the moving properties of the enhoused human body.

Given my own predilections with regard to art, which will become apparent shortly, I would like to hazard a guess that Gell, had he not been the victim of the tragic foreshortening of his life, might at this point have gone on to talk about music – perhaps in Part Two of *Art and Agency* – as the quintessential art of movement, rest and interval. For as I have suggested (Weiner 1991), the longhouse of the Foi of Papua New Guinea is not only a similarly structured field of spaces and borders, but provides an architectural setting within which these and other social spaces are iconically contoured out through the media of dance, song and poetry. Insofar as the Foi possess no decorative graphic art apart from the dubiously labelled art of bodily self-decoration, the ceremonial fusion of music, dance and poesis is where we must look for the Foi art-work.

However, to do so, we must bring a very different set of considerations to what we mean by the art-work. Music, dance and poetry – which, as I will show shortly, I find it difficult to disentangle – unlike graphic and plastic art, only partially reside in the act of composition: they are primarily manifest in their performance, as human activity, as *ergon* and *energeia*, 'the activity of work', and as *melea*, 'the limbs in their muscular strength'. Hence, by Gell's own Strathernian terms, they are always already socially and relationally constituted as human action, they are in their own 'vicinity', in his words. Paradoxically, by Gell's lights, that most form-dominated art achieves its social impact through the most empirically observable of social responses and elicitations.

We might also say that although internal and external relations are present in both media, the art of objects compels us, as it did Gell, to locate its primary mediatory effects external to the work, whereas the pragmatic domination of music and language by form focuses our attention on mediatory relations *within* the artwork. This seems to be the case, at any rate, for Western art-work, and is certainly true of Western 'art' music in general and Schubert's songs which I will examine shortly.

The kinds of mediation we want to consider, and the nature and content of their social effects, are closely related to the kinds of resemblance and representative efficacy we look for in artistic productions. Because of the more overt formal properties of musical systems, our Western inclination is to see patterns of tone, rhythm and phrasing as a matter of the development of musical convention per se, while visual art has a more primary iconic and representative function. But as anthropologists who have worked with less visually-dominated people such as Steven Feld and myself have maintained, with respect to the relationship between song, music and landscape among certain non-Western people like the Foi, we find that the opposite is the case: Primary resemblance flourishes in the realm of the auditory, while what little graphic imagery they have is far more conventional and non-representational. I will try to suggest some implications for the form that sociality takes in these two different cases at the end of this chapter.

Language, Poetry and Music

I want to focus, as I have in the past with respect to the Foi and to whom I will return now, on the imbrication of language and music. But first I want to create a framework which, in direct contrast to that of Gell, places language, and the quality of being related to languaging functions, at the centre of the art work in any medium. Let us first recall that Lévi-Strauss drew a close association between myth, language and music, an association which nevertheless accorded a logical and ontological priority to language itself. Lévi-Strauss noted that language consisted of phonemes, the units of relation and opposition, words, and sentences. Myth and music were alike in resembling language while otherwise missing one of the levels. In the case of myth, there were no phonemes, only words and sentences, and this spurred Lévi-Strauss to deduce the presence of analogous 'mythemes' in the structuring of myths. In the case of music, there were phonemes, that is, tonal relations, and sentences, but no 'words'. And so he concludes:

> If we try to understand the relationship between language, myth, and music, we can only do so by using language as the point of departure, and then it can be shown that music on the one hand and mythology on the other both stem from language but grow apart in different directions, that music emphasizes the sound aspect already embedded in language, while mythology emphasizes the sense aspect, the meaning aspect, which is also embedded in language (1978: 53).

Roy Wagner links myth, drama, music and graphic art even more comprehensively in a total consideration of symbolic articulation. He turns to Nancy Munn's *Walbiri Iconography*, where Munn notes that 'Songs are in a sense symbols of oral language, and ancestral designs are symbols of visual or graphic "language"' (1973: 146). The Walbiri visual or graphic language is composed of a series of conventional iconographs of line, circle and dot which have polysemic but conventionally understood referents. Wagner then contrasts the 'macrocosmic' expansion of human 'microcosmic' iconographs into 'myths, songs, designs and "country"' (Wagner 1978: 23), and goes on to speculate about the relationship between these artistic modes of imagistic expansion. He suggests that these larger-frame expansions are not derivatory or evolutionarily more recent but are part of the most basic articulatory terrain of the system. Wagner then concludes that: '. . . because macrocosmic image is neither primitive nor derivative, we can conclude that forms such as graphic art, poetry, music, and ritual are not either – they must be as old, as basic, and as important as language, for they are part of the same condition' (Wagner, 1978: 26).

In other words, 'the arts themselves must be understood as "speech media"' (Kramer 1984: 4) which, as Nietzsche maintained, serve 'the desire to speak on the part of everything that knows how to make signs' (1968: 428), which argues, I think, for a somewhat broader view of language than Gell himself would have countenanced, at least in this manuscript (though not, I think, in other writings of his). So it is not a matter of separating language off from the rest of the human imagistic capacity, but determining the particular relation to language that each form of macrocosmic expansion embodies. For if language had no relation to art, music and drama, its own functionality would be rendered provocative and we would be hard-pressed to restore its expressive properties which as anthropologists we come to learn about so forcefully in the field.

Gell linked the preoccupation of a 'bad' anthropology of art with aesthetics with its insistence that were such a thing as 'artistic meanings' that were immanent in the artworks themselves. I think this linkage on Gell's part was tendentious at best. For we can easily jettison a consideration of autonomous or discrete artistic meaning, a task with which I am in entire agreement and have said so in print (1996), without throwing out the bath water of aesthetics or language or signs. Aesthetics is not restricted to a consideration of how a notion of beauty or sensory fitness is achieved in any given tradition. The notion of such sensory appro-priateness is just one part of a more general process by which a community gives cognizance to its own conventional forms – and we can take that statement to apply very generally. These can be grammatical forms or 'rules', which in turn link very directly to what we call social forms, such as manners, politenesses, modes of address, and the like. They also include forms that are for the most part tacit (until glossed by the anthropologist as a 'rule'), such as the notion of what constitutes a proper marriage, or the suitable dimensions and size of dwellings. When we consider these varying manifestations of social form, the pattern of discriminations that people make on a continuous basis, as Bourdieu argues, we realize that the elicitation and judgement of proper form is a constant preoccupation, even if, as I have said, it is tacit, in the social and communicative life of people. In other words, we don't have to decide what beauty is in the realm of the artistic, but we do have to confront the manifest ways with which a social entity produces conventions of all sorts for itself. These conventions do not just order specific expressive modalities but function in a more comprehensive communicative and annotative manner, as I think Gell was trying to say in the last two chapters of *Art and Agency*.

Romanticist Anthropology

Once we have allowed considerations of form and convention to re-enter the analysis of the art-work, we are led to another theme with which any treatment of art, anthropological or otherwise, must invariably come to terms, and that is Romanticism. I don't mean merely the nineteenth century's dominant literary and artistic *genre*, though I will consider that with respect to Schubert's songs. I also mean the inevitable tendency of any humanities or social science analysis to come to grips with the issue of *form* and *content* in the expressive and affective life of humans, and to see the identification of style as a function of culture that is emergent with respect to such form. Especially in North America, cultural anthropology as it came to be called became much more firmly wedded to the original German Romantic project of revealing the *geist* of a particular culture through its artistic, stylistic and expressive forms rather than through its 'secondary elaborations', as Boas called them, of technology, economy and politics (see Yengoyan 1997).

'Romantic' has recently been unfortunately invoked in a pejorative sense by those seeking to discredit anthropology's residual interest in cultural difference unrelated to the effects of colonialism. But Romanticism is more than a vapid modernist nostalgia; it is a label for a complex nexus of cultural, literary and historical themes which shaped nineteenth-century Europe and the human sciences, including anthropology, which were engendered during that period. I want to make a simple point: anthropology, and most certainly the anthropology of art, cannot avoid Romanticism, and I certainly couldn't in my confrontation with Foi song poetry. I had reason to remark to Steve Feld early in 1998 that it is almost impossible for anthropological analyses of lyric expression to avoid lyricism in the form of its analysis, and we find this put to admirable effect in Feld's, Basso's, Scoditti's, and if the reviewers are to believed, my own analysis of non-Western poetic forms. More than that, anthropological Romanticism will always, as did Gell in his article 'The Umeda Language Poem' (1979), find something stylistically salient in 'naive' or 'folk' poetry which is a function of communality and its communicative imperatives, and the attachment to place and landscape that is the common preoccupation of landed people. Anthropological Romanticism sees the human relation with that world as one of mutuality rather than mere appropriation and the mimicry of artifice; it strives to downplay the contrast between human artifice and nature in art, and tends to focus its artistic attention on poetry. More importantly, it refuses to detach meaning and expression from the sensuous world of embodied being and perception and thus locates itself prominently within the contribution that phenomenology makes to human science in the nineteenth and twentieth centuries.

Let us then not try to repress our Romanticism, or denature it, as I think Gell tried to do quite unnecessarily in places in *Art and Agency* (though I think we will all agree that fortunately he quite failed to eliminate it altogether, and it was given far more central expression in his 'Vogel's Net' paper [1996]). Let us instead see Gell's approach to artistic meaning in general as quintessentially Romanticist. I want then to consider what most commentators consider not only the first but the most enduringly perfect example of the German *lieder* to have been created during the early nineteenth century, Franz Schubert's *Winterreise*, 'Winter Journey'. Of course, Schubert and Gell were both victims of a tragically early death and it was a fact that at one point Schubert was Gell's favourite composer, whom he even defended to a hostile music reviewer in a letter to the *Canberra Times* when he was a lecturer at the Australian National University (so Don Gardner tells me). But more importantly, both were responsible for a critical synthesis of sound, music and language which had far-reaching effects on the development of their respective art (if you don't mind me calling anthropology an art).

To begin with, let me despatch as quickly as I can any lingering suspicions that might be held by the readers of this volume (given that prima facie, the contributors are at risk of dividing themselves into two armed camps, the anthropologists vs the art historians) that a fundamental difference exists between 'folk' art forms and 'high' art forms, and indeed between the Western and non-Western artwork. This is one of the powerful contributions that Gell's book does make, for he moves back and forth between talking about West African fetishes to High Enlightenment painting without noticeably batting any ontological or theoretical eyelashes. If we have made a case for dissolving a factitious separation between representation and imagery, then this contrast which is related to the first cannot long sustain a purchase on our analysis of the artwork. Because the reason I have chosen the German *lieder* as one of the subjects is precisely because it marked the dramatic re-entry of folk song into the composition of 'art music'. The very term 'Romantic' goes back to the Latin term 'Romanus' which was

> extended first to the peoples of the Roman Empire, then to their various dialects of vulgar Latin, and in the Middle Ages to those literary forms which were most commonly written in the popular dialects instead of literary Latin . . . (Immerwahr 1970: 35).

In other words, 'romantic' was, among other things, a gloss applied to a demo-cratizing ethnological sensibility in Europe before the birth of Anthropology proper. In Germany, Johann Gottfried Herder, who is receiving more serious attention these days from a variety of linguists and anthropologists (not to mention other humanities scholars of contemporary bent who have no qualms at all about their own Romanticism, even though they euphemize it as 'phenomenology' or a fascination with the 'sensuous corporeality of embodied perception'), most effectively brought to public attention in Germany the immanent and irretrievable loss of German folk language and folk songs in the late eighteenth century.

But this was the challenge to art music composers of the late eighteenth century: 'How does a song achieve . . . "the appearance of the spontaneous, the artless, the familiar, in a word: *the folk idiom*", if the composer is schooled in the art system' (Feil 1978: 13). The 'Great Transformation' between the Classical and Romantic period involved, among other things, the emerging superiority of melody and its expressive and sensuous properties over polyphony and the formal properties of music in general (Rousseau hated Bach's music for the way it sacrificed melody to counterpoint [an opinion that nowadays is at the least contentious]). But it was Schubert, one of the first of the great Romantic precursors, 'who succeeded in maneuvering this new form to a central position in musical thinking and creativity; and who realized "lyric poetry as musical structure"' (Georgiades 1967: 17). He successfully composed music in the polyphonic mode as song, that is, he developed 'one setting that combined a lyrical voice part with an instrumental part' (Feil, 1978: 18), an observation to which I'll return at the end of this chapter.

What features of nineteenth-century Romanticism are germane to our anthropological project? Barzun identifies them succinctly:

> As against poetic diction and 'noble' words, the romanticists admitted all words; as against the exclusive use of a selected Graeco-Roman mythology, they took in the Celtic and the Germanic; as against the uniform setting and tone of classical tragedy, they studied and reproduced the observable diversities known as 'local color.' As against the antique subjects and the set scale of pictorial merits prescribed by the Academy, they took in the whole world, seen and unseen, and the whole range of colors. As against the academic rules prohibiting the use of certain chords, tonalities, and modulations, they sought to use and give shape to all manageable combinations of sound . . . (1961: 59–60).

An altogether admirable and democratic programme which we would not hesitate to endorse in the face of the oppressiveness of Official Forms. Let us see what leverage this broader anthropological Romanticism gives us in the comparison of Western and non-Western song forms.

The Wanderer

For those unfamiliar with the origin of Schubert's song texts, the original set of poems were written by Wilhelm Müller (1794–1827), like Schubert the victim of an early death, and who also provided Schubert the poetry for his other major song cycle *Die Schöne Müllerin* as well. They detail the winter wandering of a young man, mourning the death of a young women whom he loved and who loved him. The barrenness of the winter landscape, the homelessness and aimlessness of the wanderer, and the inner desolation of his spirit, all reference each other in the imagery which the wanderer notices in his grief-stricken journeying.

What makes it possible to compare Schubert's *Winterreise* with Foi song poetry are: (1) the dominant strophic structure of each; (2) the theme of human movement through a landscape punctuated by recognizable landmarks which serve as markers of human movement and its stoppage and for the progress of both the plot and the composition; (3) the manner in which both musical forms articulate both primary and secondary forms of linguistic and musical iconism in support of their primary lyrical imagery. The major difference is that, as strophic as *Winterreise* is (and indeed the songs of *Die Schöne Müllerin* as well), compositionally, each song has a beginning and end. Therefore, although in the plot, the protagonist doesn't get anywhere, and the music does its best to convey the sense of someone wandering aimlessly in a circle, closure is achieved musically in each song. In a Foi 'song cycle', on the other hand, there is no musical closure at all, only the endless fugal layering of the basic strophic couplet, yet each song brings the subject, a dead man's life, to a complete closure. When I say it is fugal I mean that it is so 'numerically' rather than musically: the Foi song cycle expands by the addition of different men's memorial songs, rather than the contrapuntal development of a polyphonic theme. What the Foi songs do not do musically, they do in terms of subject matter and the inherent 'contrapuntality' of social and territorial identities, whereas the reverse is true for Schubert's great song cycles. The Foi songs are also 'cyclical' in another important literal sense, in that each group of men comprising a song group moves from one end of the longhouse to the other and back again during the night as they complete their series of songs (see Weiner 1991).

What grips me about *Winterreise* is the way Schubert has used the essential moving quality of the musical form to render the image of the winter wanderer. It is important to note that this embodiment of the poetic moving image in Müller's original poem is not just an 'expression of feeling', but a far more concrete synthesis of two manifestations of human movement. Indeed, Schubert's two great song cycles were precursors of a general theme of nineteenth-century German song, the *wanderlieder*, which places a journey at the centre of musical and poetic development (see Smeed 1987: 113). In the song 'Das Wandern' from *Die Schöne Müllerin*, Schubert uses a 2/4 time to suggest the walking movement, coupled with the repetitive use of eight notes in the bass and then by the sub-division into sixteenth notes.

In Müller's poetry we find distilled much of what nineteenth-century Romantic imagery was all about. Take the most oft-selected song from the cycle, 'Der Lindenbaum' ('The Linden Tree'), for example:

Am Brunnen vor dem Tore	At the gate, by the fountain
Da Steht ein Lindenbaum;	stands a linden tree,
Ich träumt' in seinem Schatten	in whose shade I dreamt
So manchen süßen Traum.	So many a sweet dream.
Ich schnitt in seine Rinde	In whose bark I carved
So manches liebe Wort;	so many a word of love;
Es zog in Freud' und Leide	in joy and sorrow I was drawn
Zu ihm mich immer fort.	to it again and again.

Ich mußt' auch heute wandern	Today, too, I had to pass it,
Vorbei in tiefer Nacht,	at dead of night.
Da had' ich noch im Dunkeln	and though it was dark
Die Augen sugemacht.	I closed my eyes.
Und seine Zweige rauschten,	And its boughs rustled,
Als riefen sie mir zu:	as if calling:
Komm her zu mir, Geselle,	Come, friend, here to me.
Hier find'st du deine Ruh'!	here you shall find peace. . . .[1]

A feature of both Schubert's songs and Foi songs is the way they textually invoke the sounds of their ambient landscape as metaphors for the very activity of singing itself. First of all, Foi singing is always accompanied by various percussive sounds, whether it is the thud of women's sago mallets pounding sago pith in time to their singing, or the rapping of weapon and axe butts on the floor of the longhouse as men sing. Interestingly, on the one occasion when men's dancing employs a sound-producing instrument as such, the drum, that is, the *Usane habora* ceremony, men do not sing at all.

But the imagery of the drum speaking for men, as it were, in the context of the *Usane*, re-enters the *sorohabora* song poetry textually. When Foi men beat the drums during the *Usane habora* night-time dancing, women are supposed to be irresistibly drawn sexually to the male performers. Women, as they make sago, very commonly sing to their husbands, 'don't come around with your sweet-talking drum and try to entice me away from work'.

1. *ira tengo so'a nomo*
   tree tengo drum to me
   odibihamone
   do not call out
   ira sugu so'a nomo
   tree sugu drum to me
   odobobareo
   shouldn't call out

2. *ira sugu sa'o nomo*
   tree sugu drum to me
   odibihamone
   do not call out
   ira suabo sa'o nomo
   tree suabo drum to me
   odobobarebe
   shouldn't call out

3. *yiya amena sorofigi tono*
   we men Sorofigi Ridge
   dawabo
   dawabo
   yiya amena yabagamu
   we men Yabagamu
   ibudawabo
   ibudawabo

4. *amena yabagamu*
   men Yabagamu
   dawabo
   dawabo
   amena kana derege
   men stone side
   dawabo
   dawabo

1. Your *tengo* tree drum
   Don't call out to me
   Your *sugu* tree drum
   You shouldn't call to me

2. Your *sugu* tree drum
   Don't cry out to me
   Your *suabo* tree drum
   Don't call out my name

3. We are the men of Sorofigitono
   Dawabo
   We are the men of Yabagamu
   Ibu Dawabo

4. We are the men of Yabagamu
   Dawabo
   We are the men of the mountain side
   Dawabo

It is very difficult to appeal to how multiplex is the imbrication of text, sound, and sound-image in a song such as this, where the appeal to *sound imagery* is made in at least three different ways: first, the naming and renaming of the sound-producing object, that is the drum; second, the song itself, in which a woman is singing of the drum (because to sing of the drum is to not hear the drum itself, which must not be accompanied by the human voice); and third, in the percussive accompaniment, either by man or woman, which mimics the beating of the drum described in the text of the song.

The 'sonorous appearance' of a material trace, a track of intentional movement as exposed to the Foi *audit* rather than the Western *gaze*, is what we find in this imagery. In the song 'Auf dem Flusse' ('On the Stream') from *Winterreise* we find this unmistakably auditory Foi-like or Kaluli-like synthesis, though it uses more conventional western musical and linguistic conventions for evocation. First, Schubert returns to the rhythm with which he opens the cycle in 'Gute Nacht': we are back on track with the walking 2/4 time of the opening song:

Der du lustig rauschtest	You who chattered so merry,
Du heller, wilder Fluß,	bright, wild stream,
Wie still bist du geworden,	how silent you are now;
Gibst keinen Scheidergruß	you bid me no farewell
Mit harter, starrer Rinde	A stark, hard crust
Hast du dich überdeckt,	you have spread over you;
Liegst kalt und unbeweglich	still and cold you lie
Im Sande ausgestreckt	stretched out in the sand. . . .[2]

From a purely musical perspective, *Winterreise* is perfused with rhythmic iconism, according to Gerald Moore, noted piano accompanist of the twentieth century. In 'Rückblick' ('Looking Back'), 'Rustling leaves and the flash of water are softly pictured in the piano . . . treble' (Moore 1975: 108); in 'Die Wetterfahne' ('The Weather Vane'), the verse announces, 'the wind plays with the weather vane on my beautiful Love's house . . .', and Moore suggests that the inconstant rhythm produced by the use of tempo *rubato* in these passages 'contributes to the prevailing turbulence' (1975: 81). And in 'Rast' ('Rest'):

> The Introduction wearily drags one foot after the other. By his stresses on the second beats, by his *staccato* on each quaver in the bass the composer, short of writing the actual word '*rubato*' . . . is surely indicating that some empathy is needed. The performers ask themselves how they would walk if they were dog-tired (1975: 114).

The next Foi song converges on the imagery of 'Auf dem Flusse'. This one also makes use of the polysemy of the Foi word *hua*, which means 'struck' (from the verb *hu-*, to strike, kill, hit); 'planted' (from the same verb, *mohu-*); and 'mother'. Crashing, rushing water strikes the stones in creek and river beds. Also, men must plant the stakes with which they construct fish dams across the mouths of small creeks. Finally, large bodies of water, like the Mubi, Baru, Yo'oro Rivers, and Lake Kutubu, are called *ibu hua*, the 'mother' of waters, as in any particularly large specimen of any category (hence *a hua*: 'mother of houses', i.e. the longhouse).

Hemomo'o is a detritus and flotsam collects as it flows downstream. It also means, 'froth, scum', etc. The verb *hubagia-* means two things: (1) to push aside logs and flotsam as one paddles a canoe; (2) to spread fish poison in dammed water. This fine verse thus compresses the image of spreading fish poison in still water, with that of the man threading a canoe through debris-laden water. Like the phrase in Müller's poem, it contrasts, albeit more implicitly, the noisy movement of water and life, with the absence of sound and movement that is implied by death.

1. *ibu dufu hua yibumena*
   creek dam planted sleep-man
   uaha yiboba'ae
   go-live sleeps
   ibu dufu hua yibumena
   creek dam planted sleep-man
   uaha yiboba'ae
   go-live sleeps

2. *ibu dufu hua yibumena*
   creek dam planted sleep-man
   uaha yiboba'ae
   go-live sleeps
   ibu dufu hua yibumena
   creek dam planted sleep-man
   uaha yiboba'ae
   go-live sleeps

3. *ibu dimani hua yibumena*
   water rushing strikes sleep-man
   uaha yiboba'ae
   go-live sleeps
   ibu a~gu hua yibumena
   water swiftly strikes sleep-man
   bereboba'ae
   is lost

4. *ibu hua yibumena*
   water mother sleep-man
   uaha yiboba'ae
   go-live sleeps
   ibu ka'asubagedia yibumena
   water crashing sleep-man
   bereboba'ae
   is lost

5. *ibu hemomo'o hubagia yibumena*
   water flotsam remove sleep-man
   uaha yiboba'ae
   go-live sleeps
   ibu a~gu hua yibumena
   water swiftly mother sleep-man
   bereboba'ae
   is lost

6. *nami ko'onomo yo aba-o*
   pig Ko'ono its father, oh!
   dawabo
   dawabo
   gesa sawa yo aba-o
   dog Sawa its father, oh!
   dawabo
   dawabo

7. *nami duni yo aba*
   pig many their father
   dawabo
   dawabo
   gesa sawa yo aba
   dog Sawa his father
   dawabo
   dawabo

1. Near the fish dam where you habitually sleep
   There you have gone to rest
   Near the fish dam where you are wont to stay
   There you have gone to sleep the night

2. Near the fish dam where you habitually sleep
   There you have gone to rest
   Near the fish dam where you are wont to stay
   There you have gone to sleep the night

3. He who sleeps near the rushing water
   There he silently sleeps
   Near the rushing hissing water
   Only the river's sound we hear

4. The man who sleeps near the sibilant water
   He has gone to rest there
   The soft crash of rushing water
   But he is lost

5. He who removed the flotsam as he paddled
   He has gone there to sleep
   Near the splashing rushing water
   He is lost

6. The father of the pig Ko'onobo
   Dawabo
   The father of the dog Sawa
   Dawabo

7. The man who cared for many pigs
   Dawabo
   He who cared for the dog Sawa
   Dawabo

Through both the combination of Müller's verse with Schubert's melodies and Foi song poetry, we come around to the realization that Stefan Georg was to make the centre of his poetic theory at the end of the 19th century: 'poetic form is realized as a kinetic aspect of meaning' (Kramer 1984: 7).

'Lift-up-over-Wording'

The last point I want to make about the relation between language and music concerns the issue of complexity raised by Peter Kivy, which I have raised elsewhere (Weiner 1997). Kivy acknowledges that an opera like *Faust* or *Hamlet* cannot do justice to the complexity of language and spoken dialogue upon which as drama they first depended. The dialogue must make way for the music and the music must, as it were, introduce its own register of expression that retains the drama's complexity but polarizes it into another form. But if we consider the sparseness of *lieder* form – a voice and solo piano accompaniment – we must understand that the opposite might also be the case: that the sonorous form of *lieder* may enhance the original poetic language upon which it is built. If, as Vollman suggests, we consider Müller's original poem, *Winterreise*, what strikes us is the almost appalling childishness of these images and visions. To be able to say to a frozen river, 'You lie cold and motionless, stretched out in the sand' (1978: 162) requires an eye that still sees the ordinary as alien or that has alienated itself from all that is ordinary.

We might then want to consider the reverse: Mendelssohn,

in a letter of October 15, 1842, . . . said that the thoughts which good compositions express are not too vague to be contained in words, but too definite. Good music, he says, does not become more significant or intelligible through 'poetic' interpretations; instead, it becomes less significant, less clear (Einstein 1947: 6).

Schubert, on the other hand, made the piano a far more dynamic counterpoint to the voice, and here we see conjoined the question of harmonies between incommensurate parts, and of a 'German' style in music: many of Schubert's most abrupt and mysterious progressions involve enharmonic changes, often via the German sixth.[3] It should not be forgotten that this device is a notational convenience, but one which, since it provides a means of linking two remote chords or keys, nearly always produces some sort of uncertainty or shock effect, changing the meaning and function of a note in mid-stream, as it were (Smeed 1987: 11).

We have already noted that the Foi make distinct the functions of the percussive drum, as an alternative male voice which, because of the resemblances that are manifest in its shape, production and sound, cannot accompany or compete with the actual voice of men: Hence, in the *Usane habora* performance, when men beat the drums, there is no singing. Georg Knepler, in his 1995 book on Mozart, gives a warmer example of this, using Zerlina's aria 'Vedrai carino' from Act Two of *Don Giovanni*. When Zerlina says to Masetto, 'it's a certain balm which I have with me; do you know where I keep it? . . .', the orchestra is playing the beating of her heart. And when she finally directs Masetto: *toccami qua*, 'touch me there' and places his hand on her heart, the orchestra can now cease to mimic the sound to which Zerlina has given a name and a gesture. In this way, Mozart and those who came after him (in particular Beethoven) 'semanticized' music through opera, just as Schubert and others who followed him in the German *lieder* tradition 'tonalized' poetry through song while maintaining the distinctness of the forms that make their combination possible. Just as Feld (1994) maintains for that central Kaluli aesthetic, 'lift-up-over-sounding', we can say more generally, the components of sung poetry 'are subject to an interweaving and overlapping of their *presences* which does not at all depend on a blurring or running-together of their immediate shape or meaning' (Kramer 1984: 8; see also Weiner 1995).

Kramer has described the complementary figure-ground relations by which music and poetry mirror each other:

> Music achieves its unique suggestiveness, the power . . . to embody unique states of mind as they might arise pre-verbally in consciousness, by resting its tacit connotations on an explicit combinatory structure that is highly charged with complexity, expectancy, and tension. In poetry, this expressive balance is reversed: poetic meaning . . . is a virtually limitless play of explicit connotative relationships . . . Supporting this is a combinatory structure that varies to the degree of formality with different styles, but that manifests itself in the rhythm and sonority of the verse (Kramer 1984: 6).

Conclusion: Alfred Gell, Romantic Rationalist

There are numerous contemporary anthropologists of the artistic and the expressive who deserve, in the positive sense, the appellation Romantic: Fernandez, Friedrich,

Feld, Basso, Wagner, Guss, Morphy, and Jackson to name a just few out of many I could have. What do they have in common which identifies them as Romantics? I suggest that three traits[4] are salient in the work of each: (1) a serious critique, in one form or another, of the dualisms of subject and object, self and world, and/or conscious and unconscious; (2) a focus on those social institutions, techniques or occasions through which a heightened state of self-consciousness, including social or communal consciousness, is achieved. These occasions or techniques are, in anthropological exercises, usually ritual or artistic in nature; and (3) the replacement, in an ontological, cultural and/or ethical sense, of objects by subjects and in general, a siting of subjectivity as one of the core problems and phenomenon of investigation of anthropological science, a feature that applies to all those who subscribe to one version or another of interpretational anthropology.[5]

If we were to judge *Art and Agency* by these three criteria, Alfred Gell was a much more watered-down Romanticist that many of his contemporaries, as it is only the second I feel comfortable about applying to him whole-heartedly. First of all, he took objects much more seriously, as his last manuscript attests to, and was much more classicist in his approach to their appearance, manufacture and display, a veritable Couvier of tattoos. Secondly, his realism and cognitivism made him only mildly hostile to the dualisms listed under the first rubric. Only in the second, in his fascination with Umeda pageant and ritual and with the forms of Polynesian High Art, did Gell make clear his preoccupation with the great institutions of social self-consciousness.

Yet Gell's earlier work on primary iconism in the Umeda language is one of the most forthrightly Romanticist pieces in the anthropological repertoire: it located language as the site of a fusion of feeling, subjectivity and cognition, which in turn had to be seen as components of communicative, that is social relational, process. Viewing *Art and Agency* against the background of his larger preoccupations with language, art and representation demonstrates Gell's life-long positioning between Romanticism and Rationalism which served as the only succinct rubric for his extraordinarily eclectic range of interests within anthropology.

Notes

1. Translated by George Bird and Richard Stokes, *The Fischer-Dieskau Book of Lieder*, p. 183.
2. *The Fischer-Dieskau Book of Lieder*, p. 183.
3. See for example Schubert's piano sonata in B D.960.
4. See Kramer (1984: 22).

5. There is one other broader nexus that I think needs to be identified with the integral Romanticism of anthropology's project, and that is the linking of music, and expressive vehicles in general, with the project of national or ethnic self-consciousness. Another way of identifying this more simply is: how do we come to terms with anthropology's Wagnerianism (see Wagner 1993; Boon 1972)? I must unfortunately leave the treatment of this large subject for another time.

References

Barzun, J. 1961. *Classic, Romantic, and Modern*. Chicago: University of Chicago Press.

Boon, J. 1972. *From Symbolism to Structuralism: Lévi-Strauss in a Literary Tradition*. Oxford: Basil Blackwell.

Einstein, A. 1947. *Music in the Romantic Era*. London: J.M. Dent and Sons, Ltd.

Feil, A. 1978. *Franz Schubert: Die Schöne Müllerin; Winterreise*. Portland, Oregon: Amadeus Press.

Feld, S. 1994. 'Aesthetics as Iconicity of Style or: "Lift-up-over-sounding": Getting into the Kaluli Groove'. In S. Feld and C. Keil, *Music Grooves*. Chicago: University of Chicago Press.

Fischer-Dieskau, D. 1976. *The Fischer-Dieskau Book of Lieder*. London: Victor Gollancz Ltd.

Gell, A. 1979. 'The Umeda Language Poem'. *Canberra Anthropology* 2(1): 44–62.

—— 1996. 'Vogel's Net: Traps as Artworks and Artworks as Traps'. *Journal of Material Culture* 1(1): 15–38.

—— 1998. *Art and Agency: An Anthropological Theory*. Oxford: The Clarendon Press.

Georgiades, G. 1967. *Schubert Musick und Lyrik*. Göttingen.

Immerwahr, R. 1970. 'The Word *Romantisch* and its History'. In S. Prawer (ed.) (v. *infra*).

Knepler, G. 1995. *Wolfgang Amadé Mozart*. Translated by J. Bradford Robinson. Cambridge: Cambridge University Press.

Kramer, L. 1984. *Music and Poetry: The Nineteenth Century and After*. Berkeley: University of California Press.

Lévi-Strauss, C. 1963. *Totemism*. Boston: Beacon Press.

—— 1978. *Myth and Meaning*. New York: Schocken Books.

Moore, G. 1975. *The Schubert Song Cycles*. London: Hamish Hamilton.

Munn, N. 1973. *Walbiri Iconography*. Ithaca: Cornell University Press.

Nietzsche, F. 1968. *The Will to Power*. Translated by W. Kaufmann and R.J. Hollingdale. New York: Vintage Books.

Prawer, S. (ed.) 1970. *The Romantic Period in Germany*. New York: Schocken Books.

Smeed, J. 1987. *German Song and its Poetry, 1740–1900*. London: Croom Helm.

Sychrava, J. 1989. *Schiller to Derrida: Idealism in Aesthetics*. Cambridge: Cambridge University Press.

Vollman, R. 1978. 'Wilhelm Müller and Romanticism', in Feil 1975 (v. *infra*), pp. 153–63.

Wagner, Richard 1993. *The Art-Work of the Future and other Works*. Translated by W. Ellis. Lincoln: University of Nebraska Press.

Wagner, Roy 1978. *Symbols that Stand for Themselves*. Chicago: University of Chicago Press.

Weiner, J. 1991. *The Empty Place*. Bloomington: Indiana University Press.

—— 1995. 'Introduction and Allegro', in *Too Many Meanings: A Critique of the Anthropology of Aesthetics. Social Analysis* 38: 6–17.

—— 1996. 'Aesthetics is a Cross-Cultural Category', in T. Ingold (ed.), *Key Debates in Anthropology*. London: Routledge, pp. 251–93.

—— 1997. 'Televisualist Anthropology: Representation, Aesthetics, Politics'. *Current Anthropology* 38(2): 197–235.

Yengoyan, A. 1997. 'Reflections on Ideas of Culture, Civilization, Politics and Aesthetics . . .' in J. Boddy and M. Lambek (eds), *Culture at the End of the Boasian Century. Social Analysis* 41(3): 24–41.

Zuckerkandl, V. 1956. *Sound and Symbol: Music and the External World*. Princeton, NJ: Bollingen Series XLIV.

−2−

Agency, History and Tradition in the Construction of 'Classical' Music: The Debate Over 'Authentic Performance'
Ian Keen

Introduction

Art and Agency poses a challenge for a discussion of music, for Alfred Gell's interpretive framework specifically addresses visual art rather than performance. The figures in his landscape of 'agents' and 'patients' involved in 'art-situations' include artist, recipient, art object, and prototype which the object represents. In 'Western' classical music, however, there is a differentiation of artist roles between composer and performer. Gell's scheme finds no obvious place for patron, publisher, or impresario, either; it is the relationship between composer, performer and audience with which this chapter is particularly concerned. As well as invoking Gell's framework for an analysis of the social relations of art, my topic invokes the subject of another of his major works, *The Anthropology of Time* (Gell 1992), for the debate about the authentic performance of classical music using period instruments and contemporary performance styles is about the construction of time, history, and the museum.[1]

This study centres around several themes. First, my interest lies in what the debate about authenticity in classical music has to say about Western concepts of time, history, and our relations to the past. Second, is the idea of 'classical' music. Third, classical music in general and the historical performance movement in particular are manifestations of the museum culture, the musical aspect of which Lydia Goehr (1992) calls 'the imaginary museum of musical works'; the historical performance movement is a logical extension of that structure. Fourth is agency, creativity and the work, and my starting point for this aspect is Alfred Gell's scheme for an anthropology of art.

Adapting Gell on Art

How might Gell's very interesting programme for an anthropology of art fare if adapted to musical performance? Two aspects of his framework relate to the analysis of the authenticity debate that follows: relations among agents and patients, and the indexical relations between work and artist.

Gell constructs variants of agent/patient relations among artist, index, prototype and recipient, in a variety of cultural contexts. 'Art-like situations' are those in which the material index (the visible, physical thing) permits a cognitive operation, namely the 'abduction of agency'. Indexes are not part of a calculus such as mathematics, or like the component of an artificial language, nor are indexical inferences made by induction or deduction. Rather the term abduction, used in semiotics and logic, is the appropriate one, defined by Boyer as 'an induction in the service of explanation, in which a new empirical rule is created to render predictable what would otherwise be mysterious' (Boyer 1994). The minimal definition of the visual art situation therefore involves the presence of some index from which abductions of many kinds can be made. To narrow the field, the category of indexes relevant to his theory 'are those that permit the abduction of "agency" and specifically "social agency"' (Gell 1998: 15). The index is itself seen as the outcome and/or instrument of social agency. Indeed, we approach art objects as if they had physiognomies like people, so that the inferential schemes of abduction that we bring to indexical signs are frequently very like, if not identical to, those that we bring to bear on other people. That 'smiling means friendliness' is a perspicuous example of abduction (1998: 15).

Gell ties this account of abduction to agency. An agent is one who causes events to happen by acts of mind, will or intention, and is the source or origin of causal events, 'independent of the state of the physical universe' (1998: 16). (It is evident from what follows that Gell means this to be a universal human construct.) 'Social agency' (by which he seems to mean the agency exercised by persons or things accorded the agentive properties of persons) can be exercised relative to 'things', and it can be exercised by 'things' and animals (1998: 17–18). Primary agents are distinct from secondary ones. Things, such as a soldier's gun or a mine that he or she lays, are a person's instruments, and are secondary agents. A mine is a component of a particular type of social identity and agency, an 'objective embodiment of the *power or capacity to will their use*, and hence moral entities in themselves' (1998: 21, emphasis in original). Such artefacts are 'agents' in being 'fragments' of primary agents.

Gell's approach to agency is contextual and relative. For every agent there is a patient, and for every patient an agent. The family car can momentarily be an agent in relation to the person as patient, and vice versa (1998: 22); an artist is an agent with the picture as patient; the picture as caricature is an agent with the victim as patient. The concept of patient is not a simple one, for an object may 'resist' the artist's actions in some way. Being a patient may be a 'derivative form of agency' (1998: 23).

Art objects are made by their maker, and so are *indexes of* their maker. Many such objects are made by humans yet are believed not to have been so made, for example those of divine origin, and so are indexed to their purported maker (1998: 23). An art object is also indexed to its intended reception by a public or recipients, whether active or passive, intended or unintended (1998: 24). For Gell, contra Goodman (1976: 231), iconic representation is based on the actual resemblance in form between depictions and the entities they depict or are believed to depict. The prototype 'causes' the image to assume a particular appearance (Gell 1998: 25).

A potential problem with Gell's framework is the structuralist assumption that 'agency' is constructed in fundamentally similar ways in all cultures, and imposes a dualism about intentional/mental and causal/material that other cultures may not share; variation lies in beliefs about what kinds of person-like agents do and do not exist, and how they interact among themselves and with other entities. This is not an obvious source of difficulty for this chapter, which is concerned with agency in an aspect of Gell's own cultural world, from whence his framework originates. There is another source of difficulty, however.

In this discussion of the debate about authenticity in the performance of classical music I am particularly concerned with indexical relations among artists as agents/patients and musical works. But the dimension of time needs to be added, in particular historical time, for there are further indexical relations between work, author, and their historical location. And because a musical work comes into being only when performed, the performer/interpreter must be added as an agent/patient. The existence of a 'prototype' of which the musical work is an iconic representation is problematic. Some 'classical' music is indeed intended to represent something; furthermore, vocal music usually incorporates language. Much classical music, however, is not intended to represent anything.[2] I am not going to discuss the issue of representation here, however.

The Historical Performance Movement

James Young states the ideals of the historical performance movement succinctly:

> Members of the early music movement tend to regard the quest for authentic performance as a process of solving musicological difficulties of a practical nature. They begin by compiling scores which are faithful to composers' manuscripts or to early editions. Performers of early music pay particular attention to scoring. They perform on authentic instruments and do so with an ensemble of the authentic size. Having determined a score and selected their instruments, performers of early music proceed to perform in accordance with authentic performance techniques, the techniques contemporary with a piece's composition. They also ensure that their instruments are tuned as they would have been at the time of composition (1988: 228–9).

The idea of a systematic and informed return to our musical past is relatively recent, and the drive to reinstitute old instruments and performance practice is even more recent (Godlovitch 1988: 260). The 'historical performance' movement began with the revival of Renaissance works, but then set out to play pre-Romantic works followed by Romantic works on 'original instruments', following, as far as is known from historical-musicological research, performance practices current at the time of composition. This was in reaction to changes during the nineteenth century in instruments and orchestration, and the application of what the enthusiasts saw as an anachronistic Romantic tradition of playing and interpretation that was suitable for the music of composers such as Wagner and Rachmaninov, but not Bach and Mozart.[3] The pioneers were figures such as Arnold Dolmetsch in the early twentieth century, Raymond Leppard (see Leppard 1988), and more recently performers such as Brüggen, Hogwood, Norrington and Wallfisch.[4] The movement has involved the cooperation of musicological and historical researchers and performers – roles that are in some cases united in the same person. The debate over 'authenticity' in the performance of musical works has involved a wide range and number of academics, musicians and critics, and is often impassioned. As Kerman (1985: 197) remarks, it has a strongly moral dimension; musicians are said to have an ethical 'responsibility' to composer and score. Certainly positions in the debate involve strong moral commitments to their respective doctrines and criticism of opposing ones.

As Kenyon remarks, it is ironic that most of the artefacts of the 'authenticity business' are in 'the extremely inauthentic form of recordings without audience which sound the same every time one plays them' (1988: 4). The recording industry, especially with the advent of the long-playing vinyl record and later the CD, has been deeply involved in the spread of the historical performance movement, vigorously marketing 'authentic' performances on 'original instruments' (McGegan 1992: 130; Taruskin 1995: 354).

The historical performance movement is of course an aspect of the 'classical' genre of music that was an aspect of the cultures of Europe, North America and European colonies, but which has since diffused more widely.

The Constitution of the Classical

The genre of 'classical music' implies a number of values: recreating canonical musical works by named composers (European in the early part of the period), comprising a single, though multi-stranded tradition; the composition of new works aspiring to be of eternal value for the concert hall and record; performing, recording and broadcasting performances of those works for the public. The category 'classical music' has widened, at least in the context of radio if not of the concert hall, to include a wide range of music composed or arranged for the symphony orchestra, and other 'classical' instruments and combinations of instruments. The classical canon, drawn originally from sacred and court music converted for concert hall performance, and later from art music composed especially for the concert hall, comprises the content of what Lydia Goehr calls 'the imaginary museum of musical works' (Goehr 1992).

What is so peculiar about the 'classical' genre of 'Western' music is its predominant (though not exclusive) orientation to the past. In Taruskin's analysis, with Romanticism came the idea of transcendent and autonomous art, primarily for contemplation, and made 'for the ages, not for you and me' (Taruskin 1995: 354). From the late eighteenth century, as music became a commodity produced by independent composers and marketed by publishers and impresarios rather than being composed and performed for patrons and employers, the discrete 'work' became more clearly defined as a 'regulatory' concept (Goehr 1992). At the same time, the musical work became to a greater degree the 'original' production of an individual, and strongly identified with that person. Makers were 'creators', and became objects of reverence.

From the time of Mozart and Haydn there developed the idea of a classical canon of works that were to be preserved and reperformed as 'masterpieces that had to be preserved in the permanent repertory' (Kerman 1985: 195), an idea of the Romantic rather than of the Medieval, Baroque or Modern eras (Ruf 1991). This was dependent on the printing, publishing and marketing of musical scores for performance by amateurs and professionals alike. The musical work became to a greater degree the 'original' production of an individual, and strongly identified with that person (reflected in changes in copyright law) (Goehr 1992). To a great extent the *oeuvre* of the (dead) composer is identified with the person, indeed *as* the person.

With recording a whole new category of music-object came into being, and hence a whole new category of passive music consumers. Consequently music could be commercialized to an extent previously unimaginable, 'yet it could be more completely classicised and secularised than ever before' (Taruskin 1995: 354).

Art, Science, and the Museum Culture

The museum culture, of which the virtual museum of musical works is but one aspect, links art to science. Though often opposed, fine art and science in 'the West' are closely related as institutions. They share structures such as the museum (or gallery) as a place; practices of storage and curation of objects, materials and documents; research concerning these; and their display for the benefit of the public. The 'museum culture' that links art, science, and public education, edification and recreation, bears a particular relationship to Western concepts of time and history. Museums bring together, preserve, store, and display objects and materials from a variety of times and places, classifying them according to geographical and temporal provenance. Zoological and botanical gardens do the same with representatives of living species; classifying, labelling, and concentrating a broad diversity into a single locale, sometimes recreating types of habitat in miniature (see Outram 1996).[5] Like scientific specimens, art objects too are collected, classified, stored and curated. They are the objects of research and scholarly publication into their significance, history, and social contexts. Some (but only some) works in a gallery collection go on public display for public appreciation and edification.

'Works of art' are objects, events or event-types, displayed or performed in a dedicated space, for the purpose of contemplating and appreciating qualities of the works which are described as 'aesthetic'. While works of art do 'work' of a variety of kinds (Thomas n.d.), the primary function of works of art is to be 'beheld' – looked at, listened to, and 'appreciated' for their own sake. Objects taken into the museum or gallery from other times and places are stripped of their former functions, as funerary urn, or memorial to an ancestor, to become objects for contemplation and appreciation (Fisher 1991). Much modern art, Fisher argues, is museum or gallery art, painted *for* that kind of space and that kind of gaze, and playing with the context, 'moving toward' the visitor. By the same token, 'art music' including 'classical' music of the European tradition, consists of 'works' authored by 'composers', performed in the dedicated space of the concert hall (or more frequently the virtual space of the CD), to be 'beheld' and 'appreciated' by an audience (Taruskin 1995: 393; Thom 1993: 73). As with art objects, many musical 'works' have been taken from very different contexts in order to be reconstituted as musical works for concert performance or recording. The classical canon comprises an imaginary museum of musical works.

The Imaginary Museum of Musical Works

Lydia Goehr (1992) quotes Franz Liszt, who thought that he had found the perfect way to treat the temporal art of music as a truly fine art:

> In the name of all musicians, of art, and of social progress, we require . . . the foundation of an assembly to be held every five years for religious, dramatic, and symphonic music by which all the works that are considered best in these three categories shall be ceremonially performed every day for a whole month in the Louvre, being afterwards purchased by the government, and published at their expense.

In other words, he concluded, 'we require the foundation of a musical Museum' (Walker 1987, cited in Goehr 1992: 205). Others had deployed the gallery metaphor: public performance of Bach's works would 'raise a worthy monument to German art' said Forkel in 1802, as well as 'furnish the true Artist with a gallery of the most instructive models' (Goehr 1992: 205).

In various places musical works had begun to be performed regularly, and the hope was that works would be played every so often in perpetuity. In a musical museum, Goehr suggests, works did not need to be heard every day; it was enough that they be on semi-permanent display, performed by respectful members of a musical meeting just as often as paintings and sculptures were viewed by gallery visitors. Stored away, they were always ready for exhibition (1992: 205–6). What were 'displayed' were musical 'works'. However, unless the work is identified with the score, the museum of musical works is a virtual museum, not physically bound to a particular archive or set of archives.[6]

The virtual museum of performed works depends, of course, on the existence of scores – written instructions for a musical performance. Taruskin (1995: 353) sees the differentiation of art music to be 'gazed at or bought and sold' from music as a practical activity, as in part a product of literacy. When written down, music had a kind of physical reality independent of the people who made it up and repeated it. Music could outlive those who remembered it, and could be silently reproduced and transmitted from composer to performer, so distinguishing their roles.

In Europe the *neumes* system of notation was current from the seventh to the fourteenth centuries, but notation that indicated the time values of notes did not come into use until the tenth century. Bar-lines were added in the sixteenth and seventeenth centuries (Kennedy 1994; see also Goodman 1976). It is only from Haydn and Beethoven's time that composers have added more specific and elaborate instructions as to tempo, dynamics and expression. The invention of printing made reproduction easy and cheap. Music could take the form of books, for which there was a market (Taruskin 1995: 353).

It is just because a musical work is an event-type – what Goodman (1976: 113) refers to as an allographic as opposed to an autographic work of art, that when 'visited', the virtual museum of musical works begins to lose focus, its objects shift and fragment before our eyes.[7]

Time and the Museum

The idea of the museum depends on the particular way in which 'time' is constituted in Western societies. Because the anthropology of time was another of Alfred Gell's interests (Gell 1992), I had hoped to include a discussion of his approach to the anthropology of time here, but it would be too much of a diversion. However, I do want to say something about temporal constructions that are particularly relevant to the idea of the museum of musical works. These are the time-line of history, evolution and progress, and tradition.

The idea of 'time' as an objective phenomenon that 'flows' or 'passes' independent of events but within which events occur, and that can be measured, saved and wasted, is *constituted* by means of numerical clock, calendar and time-line. By that I mean that the possibility of imagining 'time' as an objective phenomenon, the substrate of history, derives from these three inter-related numerical devices. As Adam (1990: 25) points out, 'As a mechanical model of the universe the clock expresses time as distance travelled in space'. The time-line, I suggest, also provides a spatial representation of temporality, making it possible to imagine *travelling* in time, as if the past and future were distant places.

The concept of evolution links the history of art and music to science, and hence to the fundamental conceptual structure of the museum. Modernism brought the scientific and artistic enterprises together in evolutionist terms – artists and critics alike understood Western art to be progressive like science: a matter of innovation and discovery led by the avant-garde. Even where the modernist conception of evolutionary progress (in any field) is rejected, the unifying conceptual structure remains one of processes, courses of events, or of the succession of forms following particular trajectories through time.

The matrix upon which works are placed in the imaginary museum of musical works, like built and printed museums of paintings and sculptures, is the time line – a virtual space across which the distribution of forms and the processes linking them is mapped, similar to the mapping of distributions in physical space. A composer has a 'biography' which also has its place in the imaginary museum, by means of which the composer can be situated historically, on the time line of history, as well as in relation to place, to be matched with the authored work. Contributors to the debate on the historical performance movement also deploy the image of a virtual museum of musical works. Peter Kivy (1988: 282) thinks that an imaginary journey on H.G. Wells's time-machine to eighteenth-century Leipzig just in time to hear the *St Matthew Passion* under the direction of Bach represents the kind of conceptual ideal that many 'perpetrators' of 'authentic historical performance' hold. Godlovitch (1988) characterizes the fundamental idea as that of 'a systematic and informed return to our musical past' (1988: 260). The authenticity movement is, I suggest, a logical elaboration of the concept of a museum of musical works. It involves the attempt to recreate a musical work as it would have been heard at the time of composition or first performance, the better to place the work on the time line by recreating the original event, or something like it, just as a work of art is (supposedly) better appreciated when restored it to its 'original' condition, erasing the work of time.

The authenticity project generates a number of problems and conundrums. They include problems of the coherence of the work; the question of what counts as an 'authentic' performance; the question whether an authentic performance is possible at all; the relative roles of performer and composer; and the relationship between scholarly and artistic values, or put in another way, the balance between historical authenticity and musical expression.[8] What follows reviews some positions taken by participants in the debate, including academics, critics, performers and composers.

What is the Work?

While recognizing the possibility of anachronism, participants in the authenticity debate tends to take the 'work' concept for granted. It is inconceivable that within the 'classical' genre a performer or a group of performers might, for example, play a medley of tunes from different works of the same composer, or works of different composers; let alone, as in the music for the film *Grease*, make a new performance out of themes from Beethoven's Fifth Symphony. The work is inviolate, and where the sources are scores of performances that did not constitute a finalized 'work', as in the case of Handel's *Messiah* (Westrup 1971), then an editor creates one.

What is required for authentic performance depends on what is taken to be constitutive of the musical work. It is not a physical object (although some would argue that it is identical with the score: see Ruf 1991), but must be 'realized' in performance. The score is a set of instructions for performance, and is in the nature of things incomplete (Thom 1990: 275, 1993; Ruf 1991: 172). (The LP or CD is also incomplete, but as a record of a performance, not as a set of instructions.) For the most part I shall skip philosophical discussions of the ontological status of the musical work.[9] However, this question is relevant to performance; for Davies (1987: 39) the 'composition' is identified with 'event-specifications' which in the case of the Western cultural tradition take the form of musical scores, but the composer's score underdetermines the sound of a 'faithful' performance, implying a degree of interpretive freedom.

Godlovitch (1988: 260) questions whether musical works are merely sequences of pitch and rhythm: 'Wouldn't it be true to say that what identifies the piece for its maker is not only its note sequence but also its instrumental and technical setting given the conditions of its creation'. If the notes matter, so should all those qualities of successful performance taken for granted by the composer (1988: 272). In this view the performer must take these other factors into account.

One of the practical issues is anachronistically rendering a set of scores for varied performances (such as *Messiah*) into a unique and definitive 'work'. If this is done, how can a performance be authentic (Sumikura et al. 1991).

What counts as an 'Authentic' Performance?

What is it that a historically informed performance is trying to capture?[10] Is the performance to be one that sounds like a performance which the composer directed?

But perhaps the circumstances were less than ideal: the performers were not up to scratch, the instruments were in bad repair, or other circumstances were less than ideal (Young 1988: 230; Kaufman 1990; Taruskin 1995: 162). Is it the way in which contemporaries of the composer may have performed the work? But perhaps they did not follow the composer's intentions. Schulenberg contends that it is now generally agreed (this was in 1990) that an authentic performance cannot resurrect a specific performance of the past, nor is it likely to give more than a general idea of how a composer might have presented his work (1990: 465). For him, authenticity has to do with the expressive aspects of music; the character of a musical work is structural – it has to do with relations between successions of notes.[11]

But is an authentic performance of a work one that follows the composer's intentions? How are we to have access to the composer's intentions? Clark (1991) thinks that one way of looking at authenticity is to discover the composer's intentions, of which the written form is only an approximation. Menachim Brinker distinguished determinate aspects of a work which convey the author's intentions, from indeterminate aspects which require a performer to 'concretize' (Burstyn 1995: 721; cf. Thom 1990).

We cannot know the composer's intentions, or rather we cannot know that we know them, in Taruskin's view, for composers do not always express them. If they do express them they may do so disingenuously, or they may be honestly mistaken, changing their mind with the course of time, as did Stravinsky (Taruskin 1995: 97). Perhaps composers before Beethoven did not have 'final thoughts' – while Mozart was concerned that tempi markings be observed, his scores show evidence of last minute changes of mind (Le Huray 1990: 137). I think it is mistaken to think of a composer as having wholly clear and comprehensive 'intentions' as regards performance, regardless of the freedom giving to the performer in conventions of performance practices. Does a composer have a perfect and final sound in his mind at the time of composing a work?

Perhaps an 'authentic' performance is one that realizes the composer's ideal of how the work would have sounded under optimal conditions, a kind of distillation of the style of performance of that and related works at a particular time and place, but how widely or narrowly should the conditions be defined (Davies 1988a; Young 1988: 229–32)? Even if historical verisimilitude is an impossibly distant goal, then with the Baroque violinist Marie Leonhardt, one might settle for playing pieces 'in such a way that the composer, or a contemporary, would recognize them; at worst, without bewilderment, and at best, with pleasure' (quoted in Kerman 1985: 203).

Davies (1987: 39) regards an authentic performance as one that is recognizable as a performance of the composition. A performance is more rather than less authentic 'the more faithful it is to the intentions publicly expressed in the score by the composer', but the fact that the score underdetermines the performance implies that the authenticity of any particular performance is judged against the appropriate member or members of a *set* of ideally faithful performances. This position allows for the creative nature of the performer's role in realizing, in a number of possible ways, the composer's intentions, whereas that of Godlovitch (1988) implies greater constraints. Thom (1990) takes a related position: an authentic performance is one which complies with the composer's explicit instructions (given in the score) and implicit instructions (that the performer will follow shared performance practices located in the culture in which the work is located). A performer's interpretation concerns matters for which 'the work' contains no prescription, so that two perfectly authentic performances may differ on questions of interpretation, and differ aesthetically from one another. All the definitions of authenticity discussed by Young (1988), Thom argues, treat authenticity solely as a feature of the sounds produced in a performance; however, a performance may sound authentic yet not *be* authentic, for example when the performer plays a left-hand trill with the right hand where the score specifies the left (Thom 1990: 273).

In practice, various authenticity-producing features are mutually incompatible. Kivy argues that the quest for authenticity is vain if performers aim for a performance that is exactly like a performance we would hear if we travelled in Kivy's time machine to the time of Bach.[12] We can only approximate, and so must choose in what respects we want a performance to be like the one we heard (Kivy 1988: 285). A performance of a Mozart concerto by Serkin on a Steinway is more authentic – more Mozart-like – than a musicologist's performance on Mozart's fortepiano in that it brings to bear his musical imagination using a familiar instrument, and comes out of a 'living tradition'. However, the musicologically correct performance by a musicologist on a period fortepiano is historically authentic in ways in which Serkin's is not (in its sonority for example). Thus historically authentic performance involves a trade-off; no one 'owns' authenticity (Kivy 1988: 286–7, 289).

For Leppard (1988: 33) authenticity means 'the clearest possible revelation of that music so that its intrinsic qualities, vitality and values are presented again as vividly as they may conceivably ever have been'. This requires compromise; the translation of music 'into our own time'. For critics such as Taruskin (1995), 'authentistic' performances are indeed 'authentic' but not in the way intended – they are authentic expressions of late twentieth-century taste, and are consonant with general trends in classical music, as well as continuous with trends in 'mainstream' performances of the classical canon. Claims to historical verisimilitude are spurious.

The idea of a virtual museum of musical works in the strong sense of recreating past events thus entails difficulties of agreeing just what is being re-enacted. These difficulties arise in part from the concept of 'the work' as an event-type, performances of which are 'realizations' of the work. The question is whether 'the work' as intended by the composer is being authentically realized, in which case it is a question of what counts as a legitimate token of the type, or whether a unique event (such as the first performance) is being re-enacted. The extreme of verisimilitude imagined by some participants in the debate is a logical extension of the museum idea – reconstructing a past event in every conceivable detail.[13] Literally re-enacting a unique event in all its particulars is imaginable but not possible in practice.

It is argued that a performance cannot be 'authentic' in every way. Is it enough to capture the sound if the context, including the dispositions of the audience, is left modern?

The Problem of Reception

Authenticity in performance is an impossible goal, the argument goes, if only because the effect of music depends on the hearer as much as the performers (see Kenyon 1997). Modern audiences come to music from earlier times with a very different mind-set from that of the original audience. This is most marked in the case of the sacred music of Bach, for example, which was an act of worship and an evocation of Lutheran values. Modern audiences do not bring similar experiences to bear on the music as did congregations in Bach's time, or share the same values and religious beliefs (Butt 1998: 106; Godlovitch 1988: 262; Sadie 1990). Young points to the difference between 'hearing', and 'hearing as'; a modern audience may *hear* sounds similar to those of a performance in the composer's time, but they may *hear* them *as* different things. Some intervals that were heard as dissonant in the Middle Ages (e.g. the third) are now heard as consonant (Young 1988: 233). Butt (1998: 100) comments that 'the correct scoring with the wrong sound attitude and a sense of alienation is hardly more correct than the wrong scoring together with a ready fluency and identification with an established practice'. Against this, Davies (1988b: 375) is committed to the view that the dissonance of an interval is style-relative; many listeners are able to make the appropriate adjustment in expectations.

Some commentators believe that the hermeneutical circle can be completed; while others contend that since not all of the original functions of the music and dispositions of the participants can be recaptured, the authenticity enterprise founders. The response to these arguments from the point of view of hermeneutics is that on these grounds the relevant features of Ozarks Bluegrass and *a fortiori* Balinese music could not be appreciated by the same listener. No one can doubt that the use of old instruments and former interpretive directives allow us to get closer to the spirit of the past than if these were altogether neglected. If this is denied the Modernist seems to eschew any way of understanding the past

(Godlovitch 1988: 262). Like Davies (1988a), Godlovitch (p. 264) embraces the possibility of the modern listener re-educating him- or herself.

There are other practical difficulties: the imaginary museum requires professional players of immense technical prowess who can play in a wide variety of styles and genres. How is a performer to take on the habitus of a wide variety of periods and styles with conviction? I turn now to the relative roles of composer and performer.

The Role of the Performer

'Ever since we have had a concept of "classical" music', Taruskin argues, 'we have implicitly regarded our musical institutions as museums and our performers as curators.' Curators do not own the artefacts in their charge, and are not free to dispose and use them at their own pleasure; rather they are 'pledged to preserve them intact' (1995: 149).

In realizing music of the past, objectified in the form of scores, performance manuals and the like, the performer has to 'interpret' the composer's (and editor's) instructions (Thom 1993). It is a question of the relative 'agency' of composer and performer; a musical work is indexically related to the composer and his or her time and place; and a performance is indexically related to the performer and the occasion as well as the composer and the composer's time. But what of the relation between the composer, the performer and the work? Is the performer to be a mere vehicle for faithfully conveying the composer's intentions, or a creative interpreter? Alternatively, is the score merely to form a ground on which the performer elaborates?

How can creativity be reconciled with authenticity? There has been a movement from creative 'interpretation' of the Romantic tradition to a conception, in the historical performance movement, of the performer as a self-effacing vehicle for the composer and work. Performers such as Hogwood practice a high degree of self-effacement, implying that performers should follow only the historical evidence, withhold their own personalities, and avoid overlaying the music with any 'present-day gloss' (Kenyon 1988: 6). 'Cautious correctness' or 'austere understatement' overcomes 'creative imagination' (O'Dea 1994).

Performers theorize their creative roles in various ways, such as finding the 'spirit' of the work or the personality of the composer. Mid-twentieth-century conductors such as Furtwängler interpreted this duty in a distinctive way. While loyal to the ideal of *Werktreue*, Furtwängler sought to bring out the inner spiritual meaning of the music through a degree of freedom from a literal reading of the musical text, while more recent construals of this role are more narrowly 'textualist', and identify the work with the text (Taruskin 1995: 12).[14]

Wanda Landowska, the pioneer of modern harpsichord playing, anticipated Barthes' doctrine of the death of the author:

> If Rameau himself would rise from his grave to demand of me some changes in my interpretation of his *Dauphine*, I would answer, 'You gave birth to it; it is beautiful. But now leave me alone with it. You have nothing more to say: go away!' (Landowska 1981: 407, cited in Taruskin 1995: 98)

However, Landowska claimed to be able to enter the composer's thoughts and 'penetrate his spirit' through familiarity with the works: 'The goal is to attain such an identification with the composer that no more effort has to be made to understand the slightest of his intentions or to follow the subtlest fluctuations of his mind' (1981: 406, cited in Taruskin 1995: 99). Landowska cared little that she used means other than those available to Bach to achieve those effects.[15] Taruskin suggests that a creative authenticist performer such as Roger Norrington, has to hide the fact of his or her creativity through the pretence of authenticity, in order to appear to be a better curator rather than 'a revamper' (Taruskin 1995: 169).

How can Aesthetic and Scholarly Goals be Reconciled?

Musicological scholarship has been deeply implicated in the debate over authenticity. The relationship between scholarship and performance appears to have been a dialectical one, as performers have drawn on research to support a developing convention governing 'authentic' period performance of eighteenth and early nineteenth century music (lower pitch, original or reproduction period instruments, gut strings, reduced vibrato, less attack at the beginning of a bow stroke, a relatively small band, and so on), followed by scholarly critique questioning that convention (e.g. Neumann 1977, 1993; Dreyfus 1983).

What are the trade-offs between scholarly authenticity and vital musical expression? The main contrast drawn in the debate is between, on the one hand, the concern for historical verisimilitude in the museum project of recreating the past and that hamstrings creativity and, on the other, the artistic endeavour of creating an expressive work, and the lively creativity which is truly 'authentic'. These aims are hardly compatible, for unlike the record-player or CD player, living performers are not reproduction machines. If a musician gives him or herself over entirely to the archaeological reconstruction of Mozartian performance then he or she must renounce the musically imaginative spontaneity of a 'living tradition', and bow to 'scientific' historical judgement (Kivy 1988: 287).

Improvisation and embellishment present particular problems in the case of Baroque music. How can a performer authentically improvise in a past style that is only incompletely and indirectly known in the form of written exemplars (Kaufman 1995)? Zaslaw (1996) points out that the average modern violinist is singularly ill-equipped to improvise in an appropriate way: 'Most modern violin instruction is so strongly orientated to the literal reproduction of fixed pieces of music that it may not be amiss to remind ourselves of possible advantages of a type of training that stressed freely improvised ornamentation' (1996: 96).

Agency and the Work

Classical music and the imaginary museum of musical works constitutes the musical work as a unique, integral object that is (primarily) the original work of a 'composer' as (usually) sole author. This is the outcome of the commodification of music. Too liberal an interpretation of a work is seen by some as threatening the identity of the work and its indexical relation to the composer. Does it matter if the player turns a Haydn allegro movement into andante – 'Yes, if you want to play *Haydn*', Godlovitch remarks (1988: 267). He adds:

> Authorship seems to matter a great deal, and not merely to allow us to pay our respects to the chap who made the prototype which we all subsequently fashioned after our own ideas. On the contrary. The authorship matters for exactly those reasons, whatever they are, that it matters when we trace a painting to Rembrandt or a sonnet to Donne. Who adds figures to Rembrandt? Who alters metaphors in Donne?

This is a contestable view: for example Janet Wolff, the Marxist theorist of art, argues (1981) that works of art are in fact communal creations, so that the idea of a sole author is a construction resting on a particular conception of agency and responsibility. The causal sequence that results in the work begins not in the mind of the composer, but with events and actions that had effects on the composer.

Be that as it may, classical music gives rise to a kind of contest between composer and performer. In the eighteenth century, the score often provided a foundation for a creative, innovative performance full of embellishment and improvisation, especially in slow movements, and in the form of *doubles* – improvisations on a movement (Zaslaw 1996). The relation of 'work' to performance, then, was more like the relation of a 'standard' popular or show song to a jazz performance in which improvisations are woven around the chord sequence. For Taruskin, a performance by Mozart bore a stronger resemblance to a modern pop concert than to a modern 'classical' one.[16]

With the construction of the classical repertory of commodified 'works', composers from the time of Mozart, Haydn, and especially Beethoven, increasingly demanded fidelity to their instructions, and indeed, scores became more detailed and specific in the instructions they provided (e.g. in the form of metronome markings). During the Romantic era performers asserted themselves by changing the score, or ignoring the markings, changing instrumentation, and perhaps with Furtwängler and Landowska they claimed to reveal the 'spirit of the work' in spite of (or because of) such changes.

Taking the extreme opposite position was Igor Stravinsky, who demanded that performers be completely self-effacing, rigidly adhering to the composer's instructions. He went so far as to record 'definitive' performances conducted by himself, although he later conceded that with time he had revised his approach to his own works (Taruskin 1995). The 'authentic' performer of the Hogwood type is indeed self-effacing, conceiving of his or her role as a mere vehicle for the music, pretending not to impose a personal 'interpretation' (although that stance just *is* an interpretation). Leech-Wilkinson (1984) regards the authenticity movement as an assault on personal freedom. The liberal middle-way, recognized by Taruskin (1995: 237), but not as 'authentic', reconciles the creativity of the performer with informed historical/musicological scholarship, resulting in a satisfying and revealing new *Gestalt*. O'Dea (1994) develops a doctrine of 'personal authenticity' from existentialist philosophy, that integrates creativity with historical authenticity; the performer should aim to be true to him- or herself, and to embrace musical interpretation as a way of being by cherishing the musical work as encoded in the score.

It seems that the tension between the value of the performer as creative 'artist', and the work as an expression of the composer's being, came about with the commodification of music and the emergence of the institutions of fine art and art music. Since a work in the classical *genre* must be performed to be realized (with the exception of electronic compositions), and since the composer can be the sole performer only in the case of solo works and where he or she is still alive and capable of performing, the tussle between the agency of the composer and the performer is inevitable.

These, then, are some of the arguments in the debate over authenticity in the historical performance movement. I turn now to relationships with the past implied by the imaginary museum of musical works.

Time and Tradition

The authenticity debate reveals a number of contrasting stances about the relation of the composer, performer and audience to the past. First is the recreation of the past in the present.

Recreating the Past in the Present

This is the museum of musical works' conception of time. The performers attempt (ostensibly) to recreate the sound, or the kind of sound, that would have been heard in the time of the composer, or follow the composer's explicit and implicit instructions. Rejecting the Romantic tradition, the attempt is made to strip away the accumulated detritus of anachronistic performance practice. Harnoncourt wrote that, 'The attempt must be made today, with Bach's masterpieces in particular, to hear and perform them as if they had never been interpreted before, as though they had never been formed nor distorted' (Harnoncourt 1982, cited in Kenyon 1988: 4). According to one diagnosis, however, the present creates illusory pasts. Taruskin cites Nietzsche: 'we try to give ourselves a new past from which we should have liked to descend instead of the past from which we actually descended' (1995: 178).

Living Tradition

The main alternative conception of musical time is that modern performers and audiences alike belong to a living, dynamic tradition connecting the present to the past. Performance practices, like instruments, evolve; works of the past are interpreted for present audiences. Neal Zaslaw (1996) points out that each generation modified what it had received from its teachers' generation, a point readily conceded by Taruskin (1995: 182), for the adherent to the living tradition accepts, even welcomes, this dynamism as a sign of life as against the dead hand of the scholar and curator. In a genealogical conception of this relation to the past, performers who have only recently died, such as Horowitz, were the pupils of men who heard, and were even taught by, Beethoven. This point may be conceded by the authenticists, but they say that links to the time of Mozart and before have been broken. In a variant of the living tradition argument, Hans Keller (1984) insists that the understanding of great music – and his example is Beethoven's late string quartets – may follow long after the time of composition, so that the modern player, who is in a much better position to understand such works, is the 'authentic' performer.

The idea of the living tradition can be used against the authenticists: Taruskin argues that much of what passes for historically informed performance in fact continues the classical tradition. What one usually hears from Frans Brüggen performing Beethoven 'authentically' is 'a very comfortable old Bruno Walter performance with old instruments' (1995: 127).

The 'living tradition' thus implies a chain of genealogical connections linking the present to the past, each successive generation modifying what went before but not rejecting it. This attitude to the past is compatible with modernism.

The Past as Burden to the Avant-garde

The acceptance of the idea of progress and evolution of the natural world, of society and culture in general, and of music in particular, has problematized the relation of the living composer to works of the past. Some, such as Brahms, studied and incorporated older structures in their work in a way that some have seen as 'postmodern'. While Schoenberg found his roots in the music of the past and saw his work as building on the past (Dreyfus 1983: 314), the avant-garde of the early twentieth century nevertheless broke with tonality, in effect rejecting the musical language of the past. Some avant-garde composers and performers reject tradition; Pierre Boulez writes that we are faced 'with the fear of being imprisoned by a history which continues unceasingly to accumulate treasures of knowledge', and asks, 'is it really necessary to retrace the whole course of history, to understand its complete trajectory?' (Boulez 1990: 358). By all means let there be a library (he uses this image rather than the museum), he concludes, but it 'must be a "library in flames", one which is perpetually reborn from its ashes in an always elusive, unforeseeable form' (1990: 358). Here, the relation of the present to the past is discontinuous, and in the strong version of modernism, the past is a burden to be sloughed off.

Sounds for the Times: the Rejection of Modernism

One diagnosis of the historical performance movement is that it has replaced the avant-garde, largely rejected by the listening public: partly because of rejection of the concept of progress in art, partly because of the 'difficulty' of avant-garde works. 'Authentic' performances are appealing because they defamiliarize the standard works of the canon, and mine the archive for 'new' experience of old music. In doing so they 'coopt' the avant-garde (Dreyfus 1983; Kenyon 1988; Kosman 1992). Authentic performance had its appeal by contrast with what Charles Rosen depicted as the 'deadening uniformity' of the conventional concert world, in which the same kinds of phrasing and vibrato were applied to all periods (O'Dea 1994: 365).

In another diagnosis, an apparently 'authentic' performance is valuable not because it bears a close relationship to past performance but just because it is 'artistically appealing' to a modern audience (Young 1988; Mellers 1992). As Taruskin puts it, 'what we call historical performance is the sound of now, not then. It derives its authenticity not from historical verisimilitude, but from its being for better or worse a true mirror of late twentieth-century taste' (1995: 166; see also Leech-Wilkinson 1984).[17]

The Timeless World

In the imagination of at least one commentator on authenticity, it is not a matter of recreating the past in the present or of rejecting the past, but of transcending time and space:

The beauty of it is that when past music, or any music, really comes to us in the here and now, it catches us up into a world where, in a certain manner, time is not. There is a magic in that world whereby, in some important although not of course literal sense, the borders of space and time dissolve, so that we become in our feelings at once of the twentieth century and of other centuries. (Donington 1974: 50)

This vision represents time-travel in the virtual museum at its freest.

Conclusions

The above review of the debate over authenticity in the historical performance movement has shown that two kinds of indexical relationship are of fundamental importance in the genre of 'classical' music: between composer and the work as a timeless type, and between the performer and the work as instantiated in performance.[18] Moreover, works and composers, and indeed performers and performances, are indexed to space on the time-line of history. The work as a type originates with the composer as agent, by virtue of his or her special ability. The work belongs to the composer not, or not only, in the proprietorial sense of 'ownership' but as in an inalienable possession.[19] The performer or performers, as soloist, conductor, or less strongly as a group (chamber ensemble, orchestra or choir), owns not the work but a performance.

The authenticity movement tends to privilege the relation of the work to its temporal position in the imaginary museum, underplaying the relation of the work to the composer. While the latter is important, what counts most is to realize the work in the appropriate period style. The performer remains the author of the performance in a weaker way than in the Romantic tradition, for the performer's role is ideally characterized (in strong authenticism) as that of a mere vehicle for the realization of the work and not as a creative interpreter. Paradoxically perhaps, the Romantic search for the spirit of the work undervalues the temporal position of the work and overvalues both the composer as author, whose intentions, or more strongly whose 'soul' is to be revealed, and the performer who, while purporting to reveal the spirit of the work, enjoys a degree of creative freedom.

The contrast with the relation between the composer of a jazz 'standard', such as George Gershwin, and jazz musicians who improvise on its chord sequence as ground, is striking. Here the imaginary museum of musical works consists not of scores realized in performance, but of recordings of singular and unique performances to be reproduced by a machine. An equivalent museum of recorded performances exists in the classical genre, parallel to the imaginary museum of musical works.[20]

Notes

1. I thank Klara Hansen for her enthusiastic and assiduous assistance with the research for this chapter, and Chris Pinney, Nicholas Thomas, and other participants in the conference for their comments.
2. Any music may be interpreted by a performer or listener as representing objects, actions, events, moods, etc., for example in Paul Tortelier's commentaries on the Bach solo works for cello.
3. Kenyon (1988: 2–3) points to two rather distinct movements: the revival of forgotten repertories played on now unfamiliar instruments (such as the work of David Munrow's Early Music Consort in the 1960s), and the performance of familiar repertories from the past in a radically different manner.
4. Raymond Leppard's approach was not so very authentic by current standards. In seeking to make seventeenth-century opera palatable to the masses – and to the Glyndebourne picnickers – he too cut and pasted, rearranged, transposed, and 'modernized' the orchestral sound, beefing up the continuo with harps and other instruments, adding string accompaniments at random, and so on (Rosand 1992: 124).
5. Phillip Fisher (1991) relates how the museum culture came about historically. What Andre Bazin called the 'Museum Age' began when princely and papal collections were opened to the public, and displayed in new ways. During the French Revolution and Napoleonic Wars the great European collections were plundered, scattered, reassembled and transferred to private and national collections. The Vatican collection, Sloane Collection (later to become the British Museum), and collections of Viennese Court-owned pictures, were opened to the public in the mid-eighteenth century; the Louvre was founded in 1793. A new collectivity called 'the public' visited zoos, libraries, parks, museums and concert halls, that had formerly been private game reserves, book collections, grounds of large estates, royal forests and reserves. What had been forms of wealth and display became tied to public education and enlightenment. Curators classified objects in private collections that were a hodge podge of curios, cut stones, medals, coins, specimens, statues, pots and paintings, ordering 'works of art' by provenance, period, school and artist. Works of art were gathered together, and displayed as national culture representing the spirit of the age and the nation.
6. Of course, we find in museums and archives collections of musical manuscripts and instruments. Like art galleries, there are spaces dedicated to the performance of music – though not usually linked to a particular archive. But then, while there is one and only one *Irises* by Van Gogh, there is a multitude of scores of Bach's Brandenburg Concerti. It is not necessary – in fact for the modern player it would be more difficult – to play the work from the original score. Musical

scores can be, and routinely are, copied without loss. A copy of Van Gogh's *Irises* is not the original work, but a copy (Goodman 1976).

7. Kuckerts (1991) believes that 'authenticity' has a particular meaning in the Western tradition, where music is notated, without equivalents in other cultures.

8. Lockwood (1991: 504), for example, values good scholarship as to note-text, articulation, dynamics, and placement and grouping of ideas, over intuition.

9. Some philosophers characterize the musical work as 'timbreless, ahistorical sound structures', others as closely connected to the means of performance, composer, and time and place of composition. Most agree that authenticity involves the use of instruments and performance practices from the time of the work's compositions. Davies (1991) argues that this favours the view that historically founded conventions determine the identity of the musical work.

10. The authenticity movement has been applied not just to performance, but to musical analysis as well: musical analysts such as Meier purport to carry out musical analysis in such a way as to be comprehensible to contemporaries (Schubert 1994).

11. This argument is supported by the point that below a certain tempo an ornament becomes too prominent.

12. The time-travel model, suggests Kivy, 'throws the doors wide open to every kind of historical research into the way music was performed in any given period, and the kinds of physical means at the disposal of performers. It sanctions the use of old and reconstructed instruments, the following of instructions about how to phrase, ornament, articulate, and so forth, that can be culled from treatises and documents of the period' (1988: 285).

13. Sadie (1997) wishes to extend the experience by visiting the places where the composers of the past lived and worked.

14. According to Taruskin's diagnosis, these musicians construed intentions in spiritual, metaphysical or emotional terms, understanding their realization to be through the effects of a performance, while the authenticists construe intentions in terms of empirically ascertainable facts, and their realization purely in terms of sound (1995: 99). Interestingly, Arnold Dolmetsch, the pioneer of historical reconstruction who was neglected in his own time by the mainstream, railed against the 'modernism' of the late nineteenth century, but was a vitalist in his emphasis on what the Old Masters *felt* about their own music, and what was the 'spirit of their art' (Taruskin 1995: 145; Dolmetsch 1915).

15. Similarly, Bruno Walter spoke explicitly of the performer's responsibility to gain intimate knowledge of 'the spiritual content of Bach's compositions'. He emphasized his endeavours to be faithful to Bach's intentions, often, Taruskin (1995: 99) adds, 'as a justification for his departures from eighteenth-century performance practice'. Charles Rosen described composing as 'the

act of fixing those limits within which the performer may move freely; although the performer's freedom is limited also by the order, syntax and meaning of the work, which the performer brings out'. Yet 'there is no reason to assume that the composer and his [sic] contemporaries always knew with certainty how best to make the listener aware of that significance' (quoted in Kerman 1985: 216). These arguments are reminiscent of legal doctrines about judges grounding their interpretations of law in the 'intention of Parliament' in days before they were permitted to refer to reports of Parliamentary debates.

16. Taruskin complains of an anachronistic notion of textual fidelity or *Wertkreue* in the authentic performance movement, limiting the freedom of performers, as well as anachronistic notions of form. 'Classical' concert decorum is projected back on to a repertory that in the case of Mozart 'actually embodied an aesthetic closer to that of today's pop culture' (1995: 188). Mozart reported in a letter how his listeners 'went into raptures' at a particular passage, applauding spontaneously, prompting Mozart to introduce the passage again toward the end of the movement (Taruskin 1995: 282). 'The performer was not there to serve the work; the work was there to serve the performer' (1995: 281). Taruskin recommends bringing the 'classical' and 'pop' canons together.

17. Citing the modernist composer John Cage, Taruskin goes so far as to say that the expressive or communicative purpose of musical performance has been discredited under modernism 'in the name of dehumanization, which is transcendence in its maximal phase' (1995: 23). Cage wrote, 'One of us is not trying to put his emotions into someone else. That way you 'rouse rabbles'; it seems on the surface humane, but it animalizes, and we're not doing it' (Cage 1966: 250; cited in Taruskin 1995: 23).

18. The *New Harvard Dictionary of Music* (Randel and Apel 1986) equates authenticity in the context of Western art music with 'the nature of the link between a composer and a work that bears his or her name' (cited in Sumikura 1991).

19. Marx's conception of the essence of what it is to be human, and of alienation, expresses this ethos: to be fully human is to 'actualize' the self, especially through labour.

20. Telling contrasts can also be drawn with debates over authenticity in other genres. During discussion of the paper on which this chapter is based, Nick Thomas asked why a similar debate had not occurred in the theatre. I have just been listening to the director of the new Globe Theatre in London talking about authenticity in performances of Shakespeare (ABC Radio National, 11 October 1998). A literal reproduction of a performance as it was in Shakespeare's time would be 'materialist'; to capture authentically one of the kinds of effect that a Shakespeare play had on his audience, the Director intends to commission new plays which are about intrigue in the City of London, just as

some of Shakespeare's plays were. Libby Keen suggested to me that the script of a play provides only the dialogue and bare stage directions; much more has to be filled out by director, actors, set designer and the rest than in the case of classical music. Furthermore, it is a dramatic narrative that is being communicated, and here the potential cultural, historical, and temporal gap between the play and the audience is potentially much greater (or just more obvious, perhaps). Perform Hamlet in the accents of Shakespeare's London, and a modern audience will understand very little. The closest parallel in the Western visual arts is restoration. The idea of all that cleaning and repainting is to remove the ravages of time and to 'restore' the work to a state that is as close to its original condition as possible. This too reveals a museological ethos rather than, say, a theological one.

References

Adam, B. 1990. *Timewatch: The Social Analysis of Time*. Oxford: Polity Press.

Boulez, P. 1990. 'The Vestal Virgin and the Fire-Stealer: Memory, Creation and Authenticity'. *Early Music* 18(3): 355–8.

Boyer, P. 1994. *The Naturalness of Religious Ideas: A Cognitive Theory of Religion*. Berkeley: University of California Press.

Burstyn, S. 1995. 'Authenticity in Interpretation'. *Early Music* 23(4): 721–3.

Butt, J. 1998. 'Bach's Vocal Scoring: What Can It Mean'. *Early Music* 26(1): 99–106.

Cage, J. 1966. 'Where are We Going, and What are We Doing?' *Silence*. Cambridge, Mass.: MIT Press.

Clark, A.E. 1991. 'Authenticity Problems of Music', in Y. Tokumara et al. (eds), *Tradition and its Future in Music*, 184. Tokyo and Osaka, Japan: Mita Press.

Davies, S. 1987. 'Authenticity in Musical Performance'. *The British Journal of Aesthetics* 27(1): 39–50.

—— 1988a. 'Transcription, Authenticity and Performance'. *The British Journal of Aesthetics* 28(3): 216–27.

—— 1988b. 'Authenticity in Performance: A Reply to James O. Young' *British Journal of Aesthetics* 28(4): 373–6.

—— 1991. 'The Ontology of Musical Works and the Authenticity of Their Performances'. *Nous* March 1991: 21–41.

Dolmetsch, A. [1915] 1969. *Interpretation of the Music of the Seventeenth and Eighteenth Centuries*. 3rd edn. Seattle: University of Washington Press.

Donington, R. 1974. *The Interpretation of Early Music*. London: Faber and Faber.

Dreyfus, L. 1983. 'Early Music Defended Against its Devotees: A Theory of Historical Performance in the Twentieth Century'. *Historical Quarterly* 69(3): 297–322.

Fisher, P. 1991. *Making and Effacing Art: Modern American Art in a Culture of Museums*. Oxford: Oxford University Press.

Gell, A. 1992. *The Anthropology of Time: Cultural Constructions of Temporal Maps and Images*. Oxford: Berg.

—— 1998. *Art and Agency: An Anthropological Theory*. Oxford: Clarendon Press.

Godlovitch, S. 1988. 'Authentic Performance'. *Monist* 71: 258–77.

Goehr, L. 1992. *The Imaginary Museum of Musical Works: An Essay in the Philosophy of Music*. Oxford: Clarendon Press.

Goodman, N. 1976. *Languages of Art: an Approach to a Theory of Symbols*. Indianapolis: Hackett Publishing Company.

Harnoncourt, N. 1982. *Mass in B Minor by Johann Sebastian Bach: Concentus Musicus Wien*. Telfunken 4840AZ. (Sleeve notes to sound recording.)

Kaufman, L. 1990. 'Aspects of Authenticity'. *The Strad* October 1990: 810.

Keller, H. 1984. 'Whose Authenticity?' *Early Music* 12(4): 517–19.

Kennedy, M. 1994. *The Oxford Dictionary of Music*. 2nd edn. Oxford: Oxford University Press.

Kenyon, N. 1988. 'Introduction: Authenticity and Early Music: Some Issues and Questions', in N. Kenyon (ed.), *Authenticity and Early Music: A Symposium.*, 1–18. Oxford: Oxford University Press.

—— 1997. 'Time to Talk Back to Treatise!' *Early Music* 25(4): 555–6.

Kerman, J. 1985. *Contemplating Music: Challenges to Musicology*. Harvard University Press, Cambridge.

Kivy, P. 1988. 'On the Concept of the "Historically Authentic" Performance'. *Monist* 71: 278–90.

Kosman, J. 1992. 'The Early Music Debate: Ancients, Moderns, Postmoderns'. *The Journal of Musicology* 10(1): 113–14.

Kuckerts, J. 1991. 'Authenticity Problems of Music', in Y. Tokumara et al. *Tradition and its Future in Music*, 180–1. Tokyo and Osaka, Japan: Mita Press.

Landowska, W. 1981. *Landowska on Music*. ed. D. Restout. New York: Stein and Day.

Le Huray, P. 1990. *Authenticity in Performance: Eighteenth Century Case Studies*. Cambridge: Cambridge University Press.

Leech-Wilkinson, D. 1984. 'The Limits of Authenticity: A Discussion'. *Early Music* 12(1): 3–25.

Leppard, R. 1988. *Authenticity in Music*. Portland, Oregon: Amadeus Press.

Lockwood, L. 1991. 'Performance and "Authenticity"'. *Early Music* 19(4): 501–7.

McGegan, N. 1992 . 'The Early Music Debate: Ancients, Moderns, Postmoderns'. *The Journal of Musicology* 10(1): 129–30.

Mellers, W. 1992. 'Present and Past: Intermediaries and Interpreters'. *Companion to Contemporary Musical Thought*. Volume II: 920–30.

Neumann, F. 1977. 'The Dotted Note and the so-called French Style'. *Early Music* 5: 311.

—— 1993. *Performance Practices of the Seventeenth and Eighteenth Centuries*. New York: Schirmer Books.

O'Dea, J. 1994. 'Authenticity in Musical Performance: Personal or Historical'. *British Journal of Aesthetics* 34(4) October: 363–77.

Outram, D. 1996. 'New Spaces in Natural History', in N. Jardine and J.A. Secord (eds), *Cultures of Natural History*, 249–67. Cambridge: Cambridge University Press.

Randel, D.M. and Apel, W. 1986 (eds). *The New Harvard Dictionary of Music*. Cambridge, Mass: Belknap Press.

Rosand, E. 1992. 'The Early Music Debate: Ancients, Moderns, Postmoderns'. *The Journal of Musicology* 10(1): 124–6.

Ruf, W. 1991. 'Authenticity Problems of Music', in Y. Tokumara et al. (eds), *Tradition and its Future in Music: Report of SIMS* (International Musicological Society, Fourth International Symposium, Osaka 1990), 171–2. Tokyo and Osaka, Japan: Mita Press.

Sadie, J.A. 1990. *Companion to Baroque Music*. New York: Schirmer Books.

—— 1997. 'A Sense of Place'. *Early Music* 25(4): 561–2.

Schubert, P. 1994. 'Authentic Analysis'. *The Journal of Musicology* 10(1): 3–18.

Schulenberg, D. 1990. 'Expression and Authenticity in the Harpsichord Music of J.S. Bach. *The Journal of Musicology* 8(4): 449–76.

Sumikura, I. 1991. 'Authenticity Problems of Music', in Y. Tokumara et al. (eds), *Tradition and its Future in Music Report of SIMS* (International Musicological Society, Fourth International Symposium, Osaka 1990), 172–3. Tokyo: Mita Press, 1991.

Taruskin, R. 1995. *Text and Act: Essays on Music and Performance*. Oxford University Press, New York.

Thom, P. 1990. 'Young's Critique of Authenticity in Musical Performance'. *British Journal of Aesthetics* 30(3): 273–6.

—— 1993. *For an Audience: a Philosophy of the Performing Arts*. Philadelphia: Temple University Press.

Thomas, N. n.d. 'The Work of Art'. Seminar delivered at the Joint Anthropology Seminar Series, Australian National University, 1997.

Walker, A. 1987. *Franz Liszt: Vol. 1 The Virtuoso Years, 1811–1847*. New York: Knopf.

Westrup, J. 1971. *Musical Interpretation*. London: British Broadcasting Corporation.

Wolff, J. 1981. *The Social Production of Art*. London: Macmillan.

Young, J.O. 1988. 'The Concept of Authentic Performance'. The British Journal of Aesthetics 28(3): 228–38.

Zaslaw, N. 1996. 'Ornaments for Corelli's Violin Sonatas, op. 5'. *Early Music* 24(1): 95–115.

–3–

Why Knot? Towards a Theory of Art and Mathematics

Susanne Küchler

Just as mathematics provides us with a primary mode of cognition, and can therefore enable us to apprehend our phsyical surroundings, so too, some of its basic elements will furnish us with laws to appraise the interactions of separate objects, or groups of objects, one to another. Again since it is mathematics which lends significance to these relationships, it is only a natural step from having perceived them to desiring to portray them. This in brief is the genesis of a work of art

(Max Bill 1949, repr. 1994)

One of the most endearing qualities of Alfred Gell was his ability to reveal the plot within which anthropologists find themselves ensnared when approaching the hot and emotive subject of art. Like Sherlock Holmes's detective novels, his writings have a forensic and simultaneously timeless quality, being at once strikingly novel and yet working like a 'burial place of memory' in making all pasts equally present (cf. MacDonald 1987). In 'Art and Agency', the plot is framed by a question whose validity is as evident now as it was when it was asked at the beginning of Western writings on art. Shedding the chassis of logocentricism, the question he puts to us is not 'how can art be the object of discursive thought?' but how can art be 'thought-like', or 'how can thought conduct itself in art'.

It is instructive to consider the positions towards this question as prefigured in the aesthetics of Kant and Schiller. What could be included within the order of art, and how that order could be related to other concerns resonates with a problem fundamental to Kant's theorem. Yet while Kant saw art as an essential part of contemplative life, Schiller saw art as part of active life – one seeing the conception of art as tied primarily to thought, while the other saw it as primarily tied to social relations.[1] Schiller's 'Letters on the Aesthetic Education of Man' redefined what constitutes the judging self in ways that were intended to overcome Kant's formalism. Schiller alleged that the self cannot be handed over to any rule or system of belief which we already have, any more than it can be regarded as the mere locus of urgencies and sensations. 'The mind,' to Schiller (letter XIX), 'is neither matter nor form, neither sense, nor reason, but a constructive activity pre-eminently exemplified in works of art through which we weave together elements from the worlds, by analogy, by suggestion, and by relations which are not those of literal connection.' The activity of the mind is no longer Kant's ordering unconcerned with – abstracted from – the character of things ordered, but is comprehensive in its attention. Schiller's conception of aesthetic constitutes the theoretical framework for our contemporary understanding of 'art education' in that it centred on social behaviour rather than on theoretical reflection in accounting for the cognitive impact of art.[2]

The divergent aesthetics of Kant and Schiller pointed towards the development of distinct institutional concerns with art – of modernist art practice advocating a transcendental theory of cultural form and of anthropology which devoted itself to a contextualization of art in culture and society. The most poignant insight of Alfred's latest work was that by re-embedding the anthropology of art within modernist practice one can reveal a new perspective on art which throws away the trappings of the eighteenth-century separation between the noumenal and the phenomenal which divided the aesthetics of Kant and Schiller (cf. Stafford 1991). The thought-like quality of objects which come to figure as art is once again subjected to scrutiny as modernist practice is revealed as a pre-eminently anthropological project, itself long having broken with the legacy of the industrial economy and enlightenment in ways which anthropology began to consider only recently.

Alfred cites Duchamp's project of the 'Ready-Mades' as achieving the most radical and poignant break with notions of artistic creativity and style that had informed artistic practice and scholarship to this time. While it appears that 'anything goes' in constituting Duchamps' ready-mades and its many contemporary echoes, artworks are in fact only apparently arbitrary, being carefully selected and working because they have complex historic and iconographic resonances (Gell 1996). They are objects that are scrutinized as vehicles of complicated ideas which are difficult, allusive, and hard to bring off. 'Such objects', to Alfred, 'thus embody intentionalities that are complex, demanding of attention, and perhaps difficult to reconstruct fully' (1996: 36).

Even without realizing it, anthropology by nature is drawn to the modernist critique of the object's participation in intentionality and relationality. Yet by working from within a quasi premodernist frame of the romantic preoccupation with distinguishing arts from crafts, anthropology, to Alfred, has failed to realize the potential of participating in the agenda set by modernism.

In this chapter I will critically address some of the fall-out springing from the modernist preoccupation with mathematics and the visualization of spatial cognition which was born out of the nineteenth-century rediscovery and popular acceptance of axiomatic representation. An overview of the relation between art and mathematics will be followed by an exploration of topology, also known as knot-theory, and its implication for an anthropological theory of art. Knot-theory models the behaviour of systems that have the capacity for self-organization, for generativity and autonomy – of systems, that is – whose behaviour cannot be explained by simple and identifiable laws and of which image-systems outside of the Renaissance are as much an example as the weather. Knots are, as Alfred showed, prone to become artworks for reasons which are pointed out by mathematics, yet which support Alfred's theory of 'abduction': it is binding which exemplifies the coming together of affective and cognitive processes, enabling 'syntonic' learning and the ability to think with objects. Knot-theory, moreover, promises to offer a model which can help us to get away from the dated mechanical model of reproduction, often associated with the term 'template', which has hindered anthropology from recognizing that style may indeed be independent of culture (Gell 1998: 160). The chapter concludes with an excursion into the ethnography of the knot of which the best example is arguably to be found in contemporary architecture. Anthropological theory never quite got hold of topology as it never quite understood why it should concern itself with the look of things, yet thanks to Alfred it may yet be able to catch up.

Geometry and Relationality

It was axiomatics which had opened the doors for mathematics to branch into innumerable logical 'paper worlds' of its own construction, thus implicitly questioning Euclidean geometry with its assumption of the anthropomorphic, relative and egocentric conception of space. Euclidean geometry, which had remained unchallenged for centuries, finally received a dramatic denouncement in 1915 when Einstein founded his new theory of gravitation upon the premise that our physical space possesses a non-Euclidean geometry that is created by the presence of mass and energy in the Universe.

While, as Alfred suggests, modernism arose out of the exploration of the implications of the reality of n-dimensional worlds for representation, anthropology held on fast to the belief of the universality of the conception of space as proceeding from the human body, constrained by the nature of the phenomenal world and by human physiology with its visual system and upright posture (Wassmann 1994: 646). The failure to recognize the implications of non-Euclidean geometry was only recently rectified with Wassmann's (1994) study of the Yupno of Papua New Guinea who, as he shows, use different reference systems at the same time in ways that are only comprehensible when apprehending spatial conception as decentred from the body in everyday life. Anthropology's delayed reaction to the demise of Euclid's world is even more surprising given the importance ascribed to spatial conceptualization as central to human cognition.

Modernist art, however, was born out of advanced mathematical and scientific thinking of the time. Impressionism and still more Cubism brought painting and sculpture much closer to what were the original elements of each: painting as surface design in colours; sculpture as the shaping of volumes to be informed by space. It was notably Kandinsky whose work suggested a fresh conception of art which liberated painting from romantic and literary associations. In his 'Spiritual Harmony in Art' published in 1912, he invoked a substitution of the artist's imagination by a mathematical approach to visualization, an idea carried forth by Klee, Brancusi and Mondrian. Their works portray elemental forms and visualise without representing objects that have an existence in ordinary life. Duchamp's work likewise originated in a mathematical parable on the fourth-dimension which for him 'as for certain of his contemporaries – was an essentially "real" but strictly unrepresentable domain beyond, or encompassing, the ordinary world we live in and perceive in the normal way' (Gell 1998: 243).

In anthropology, one may point to the late nineteenth-century writings of Rivers and collections made by Haddon in the Torres Straits as testifying to an equal preoccupation with knowledge technologies which are responsible for the externalization of spatial cognition (cf. Eastrop n.d.). Among such technologies, string-figures received unique attention in the collections and documentations of the time. Though they count among the forgotten exemplars of the Torres Straits collection today, more articles were published about string-figures in the first fifty years of the twentieth century than about any other item in ethnographic museums. Haddon's collection consisted of eight string figures which he had presented to the British Museum in 1889 after his first visit to the Torres Straits in 1888. Sewn onto sheets of card, the string-figures are quite small and it appears that each loop of string was used to form a cat's cradle and was then lifted from the maker's hand and sewn 'flattened' onto a sheet of card to preserve a two-dimensional form of the original three-dimensional string-figure. Haddon's cat's cradles did not exist only as strings sewn onto card, but also as figures, as text and as drawings. About fifty were published as figures with additional textual descriptions and illustrations and many more were collected as texts and diagrams in Haddon's second expedition, with many publications documenting the songs and actions accompanying the figures following in the first decades of the century. However, with the rise of the linguistic model in the 1950s, the interest in the visualizing of spatial cognition, and thus also in string figures, waned in anthropology and has even today not been fully rediscovered in the new branch of cognitive anthropology. Driven by logocentrism, anthropological thinking on art has been oblivious to contemporary developments in art and mathematics to an extent that has condemned its studies and even its exhibitions to be hopelessly out-of touch with contemporary theories of the visual.

Visualization, on the other hand, has always played an important role in mathematics, with new visual techniques resulting from the availability of new visual tools. More recently, a new branch of mathematics developed which uses computer modelling as imaging technology. In developing computer-driven visualization, mathematicians have for long drawn on art to enrich the awareness of visualization techniques. Artists likewise have visualized 'intuitions' which are the result of abstract reasoning, sometimes surprisingly paralleling mathematical constructs made visible in computer-generated imagery (cf. Emmer 1993).

The common interest of art and mathematics has been the visualizing of the fourth dimension which became possible only at the end of the nineteenth century with the development of a graphic system known as 'hypersolids'. The full impact of the visualization of the fourth dimension, however, was realized in mathematics only with the advent of computer modelling. Its rediscovery by mathematics was inspired by works such as those produced by the American artist David Brisson who developed the concept of hypersolids in the 1950s by producing perspective and orthogonal projection drawings as well as three-dimensional models of four-dimensional polytopes (cf. Brisson 1978). His *Hyperanaglyph*, a four-dimensional form projected onto three dimensions, established him as the leader in the visualization of higher solids. In 1975, he coined the term *hypergraphics* which came to denote both concept and technical process which transcended traditional methods of making image by methods of visualization that could blend con-temporary thinking in art and science. Much of the hypergraphic art work is mathematically precise and enhanced by materials, colours, surfaces, textures, methods of construction and so on (Banchoff 1990).

Like most mathematically inspired work which came to represent the modernist spirit, the imagery of hypergraphics is generative and multiple. What came to be known as 'mathematical recreations' celebrated the 'generate and test model of creativity' as the new way of doing mathematics (cf. Barrow 1992). Fun-sounding explorations such as 'how to tile a space with knots' became the hallmark of applied mathematics capable of constructing innumerable logical 'paper worlds', leading to radically new ideas as to the nature of mathematics itself. Observations derived from applied mathematics confirmed the predictions of Einstein's non-Euclidean theory of space – the real world was non-Euclidean after all and geometry no longer just logical systems on pieces of paper, but multiple perspectives reflecting a 'decentred' spatial cognition which fully realized the possibility inherent in the pictorial equivalent of the fourth dimension. As foreshadowed by Cubism's multiple perspective, the new mathematical visualization techniques realize a quasi-cinematic evocation of dynamic motion and change.

It was, however, only computer modelling, aided by mathematics, which was able to visualize spatial conception as decentred as it allowed transformation of the same object from a reference system in two space, to one in three space and four space. The spatial properties of an object now were no longer confined to the perceptual and relative relationship to the human body, but had become the material remains of mental arithmetic. Computer-generated visualization in mathematics led to the rediscovery and rethinking of topology in the form of 'knot-theory' which for long had provided the mathematical tool for tracing the behaviour of solids in shifting reference systems. Re-discovered by mathematics in the 1950s, the visualization of knots became one of the most dominant tools for the conceptualization of n-dimensional space.

Knot-theory and the Topology of Cultural Form

The fact that geometric objects retain their properties under deformation was known already by D'Arcy Wendthworth Thompson (1961[1902]) and applied to an understanding of organic systems and their capacity for self-organisation and generative transformation in his work 'on Growth and Form'. Thompson turned topology into an analytical tool, known as the 'Wen-Diagram', whose usefullness in tracking the generative capacity inherent in the formal properties of objects was aptly demonstrated by Alfred in his analyses of Umeda dance styles and Marquesan art (Gell 1986; 1998: 206).

The revolutionary impact of topology upon science, leading to the New Biology and New Genetics, however, was made possible only by the ability to model the behaviour of organic systems using powerful computers. Now the buzz word in the emerging science of topology is a new paradigm known as 'nonlinearity' whose impact is felt beyond science in architecture and art. Nonlinear systems were known to exist already for some time, but were proven to be relevant only as computing allowed for the modelling of such systems which do not behave according to sets of laws, but are perpetually self-organizing (Saunders 1997: 52). To see how self-organization, leading to the spontaneous creation of order, arises is one of the most profound problems facing science today as are the consequences of two allied features of nonlinear systems known as their autonomy and constitution in terms of generic properties.

The world of cellular systems and of systems of cultural form may still appear unconnected and thus of no consequence for those concerned primarily with the latter, yet those days are disappearing as visualization techniques in computing bridge the gap between mathematics and art. Three-dimensional modelling and the creation of viral life-forms is made possible by what computing calls the 'manifold', the identification of the generative element inherent in form which enables to be elicited transformations that increasingly become spontaneous and self-governing, allowing as much for the creation of computer-generated viral forms as for the animation of computer imagery.

Beyond its implication for a conception of spatial cognition and representation, knot-theory harbours yet other insights that are of relevance for anthropology: mathematics has for long recognized the knot as a unique artefact in that it 'both embodies mathematical principles and has a tendency to evoke a range of emotional, personal sorts of thoughts' (Strohecker n.d. 31). It was the evocative capacity of the knot which in science proved vital for an understanding of the nature of concrete thinking and its importance in the learning of mathematics. Mathematics found itself thinking of the knot as this kind of object that is likely to touch people's lives in connecting with personal and 'affective' aspects of thought and thus as forming the springboard for associations that are both abstract and concrete in their mnemic capacity. Like Proust's famous Madeleine cake, the knot had begun to exemplify the ability to remember by chance something previously experienced and connect it into strings of associations without which thought itself would not be possible.[3]

For long, the understanding of how objects carry abstract ideas into the head has been obscured by what has been labelled the 'projectionist fallacy' which proposed that objects are the product of the externalizing of concepts that are pre-existent to these objects (cf. Davis 1986). The assumption that concepts are projected into visual representations found support in the theory of *'memoria'*, the conscious recollection of forgotten experiences, which was rediscovered for the humanities by Frances Yates's (1966) work on the 'Art of Memory'. The theoretical contexts in which this happened can be easily described with notions which developed out of post-structuralist readings of Freud and Benjamin, Bergson and Proust, which claim an underworld of consciousness and subject-centred philosophy: a supra-human memory whose mechanism is used but not controlled by subject-centred remembering, internalized perhaps, but in a forgetting, self-forgetting special meaning.

As collective, unconscious memory, *memoria* was of merely practical interest: it was recommended for the reckoning with the past, as a programme for museums, as a legitimization for Archives. Reserved as a 'black box' for brain physiology and belittled as a 'hobby horse' for historians, *memoria* became of broader interest only with the rise of artificial intelligence and the use of computers for the storage of data – when the accessibility of the memory store and thus the individual con-nection to collective memory came into question. Long before the full impact of technology led to a re-examination of the theory of the unconscious and its impli-cation for an understanding of memory (cf. Rosenfield 1992), the mathematician Papert (1980: vi) offered a new approach to the cognitive validity of representations. He reminded us that we do not start with concepts, but think with objects, both in childhood and in everyday experience – by using them as image in thought, and maintaining in thinking the properties that these objects would demonstrate in the physical world. Papert describes how the properties of a particular object played a role in his development as a mathematician:[4]

Before I was two years old I had developed an intense involvement with automobiles. The names of car parts made up a very substantial part of my vocabulary: I was particularly proud of knowing about the parts of the transmission system, the gearbox, and most especially the differential. It was, of course, many years later before I understood how gears work; but once I did, playing with gears became a favourite pastime. I loved rotating circular objects against one another in gear-like motions and, naturally, my first 'erector set' project was a crude gear system . . .

I believe that working with differentials did more for my mathematical development than anything I was taught in elementary school. Gears, serving as models, carried many otherwise abstract ideas into my head (Papert 1980, vi).

Work at MIT carried out during the 1980s by Carol Strohecker put Papert's theory of 'syntonic learning', describing the correspondence between the child's experience and the behaviour of things, to test in what she called 'the Knot Lab'. The Knot Lab, situated in an American inner city elementary school, was created as a place where children were encouraged to have dialogues and debates about different ways to think about knots (and eventually other issues in life, too). Strohecker's research showed how children engaged in 'dialogues' with themselves as they developed a form of critical thinking in which they would launch an interpretation of a knot and then retract or modify it as they continued their exploration.

It is this capacity of the knot, made visible as apparently inextricably entangled pattern covering the surface of things (from mazes to Celtic script), to become the object of affect-driven thought which for long may have led to its exclusion from science. Yet it is precisely its embeddedness in the mundane and relational texture of the everyday which appears to suggest the pertinence of an ethnography of the knot.

Towards an Ethnography of the Knot

Alexander the Great knew how to deal with knotty issues: as legend has it, the Macedonian king decided to try his luck with the fabled Gordian knot, a tough length of cornel bark wrapped tightly around the pole of an ox cart. It was said that the person who succeeded in untying this knot was destined to rule. A man of action, rather than dexterity, Alexander unsheathed his sword – and the rest, of course, is history. The legacy of the Gordian knot is the perception of its gendered nature which is still largely with us today. The concern with the knot thus appears embedded in the microcosm of the household and its intricate web of social relations and work, in a world, in other words, from which those who strive for clarity of thought aim to escape.

Yet it is this quality of the knot, its embeddedness in the everyday, its tendency to suggest the fluid mechanics of persons and things, that renders the knot into a unique object for anthropology. In this second part of the chapter, I will sketch the pertinence of an ethnography of the knot for continuing Alfred's quest into uncovering the 'abductive' quality of objects. The knot may appear as a purely functional aspect of the design of things such as Papua New Guinean netbags, as a means of recording information such as the Andean Quipu, or as the representational property of ritual artefacts such as the Tahitian *to'o* or the New Ireland *malanggan*. Its mundane, function-oriented appearance led to the knot being overlooked by anthropologists even when it constitutes the materiality of artefactual form and when the ritual associated with the artwork is known to be significantly associated with acts of 'binding' (cf. Babadzan 1993; Gell 1998: 111). In fact, however, the knot behaves like the trap – the most unlikely thing to be art, and yet the most successful of all.

While I have already outlined why mathematicians finds knots fascinating, the mathematical definition of a knot opens ones eyes to the possibility that a knot may be more than a mere useful thing in that it is good to think with. A mathematical knot, as Adams summarizes succinctly in his introduction to knot-theory, is a *knotted loop of string*, except that we think of the string as having no thickness, its cross-section being a single point.[5] The knot is then a closed curve in space that does not intersect itself anywhere. This minimal definition of the knot entails an implicit qualisign that differentates the knot from the loop. For in contrast to the loop, the working thread in the knot is not pulled through the body of the work as in the construction of each loop with the consequence that knotted string will unravel when broken, while looped string will effectively seal each break and thus retain its flexibility (cf. MacKenzie 1991: 2). Furthermore, the original closed knotted curve can be deformed without undoing the original knot, a fact which has led mathematicians to think of the knot as being made of easily deformable rubber.

There are two insights developed in knot-theory that warrant mention here. The first fact worth mentioning is that, while there are a large number of distinct knots, such as the so-called un-knot, the trefoil knot or the figure 8 knot, each knot can undergo deformations known in knot-theory as *projections*. The second fact lies in the observation that essential for understanding and distinguishing knots is the *surface* or the space around the knot. The space around the knot is everything but the knot, with the knot lying within or beneath the surfaces which make it visible to the eye. Mathematically speaking, therefore, all the surfaces that we look at live in the complement of the knot. In plain English, this just means that the knot usually appears to us as a planar surface which, when aligned in a series, constitutes a visually impenetrable plane. This projectable surface-pattern of the knot distinguishes it most clearly from the looped string for which it is most frequently mistaken (cf. MacKenzie 1991; Hauser-Schaublin 1996).

As the knot is contained within the negative space created by patterned surfaces, it lends itself to be applied to the conceptualization of sculptural form. And, as it is prone to retaining its geometric properties under deformations, the sculpted knot enables intellectual economies to unfold around a polity of images. Within the Pacific, the tightly knotted cordage of the Tahitian *to'o* and the richly incised and hollowed out curvilinear planes of *malanggan* carvings represent two logical applications of knotting in the creation of the figural. But, whereas the *to'o* (Figure 3.1) visually celebrates impenetrability of the plane as evidence of completed containment , the *malanggan* (Figure 3.2) renders the contained negative space of the knot visible in the hollows of its surface thus acknowledging the merely partial and temporal nature of containment (cf. Babadzan 1993; Küchler 1997).

That the knot can be discovered in the surface of figural space is shown by the work of the American artist Brent Collins who has created a series of sculptures which amplify the rather unusual explicit application of knot theory to wood (Figure 3.3). Wood is a rigid substance, so much so that it is difficult to imagine a surface carved from wood as having the quality of stretchable rubber. Yet many of his pieces display invariant symmetrical relations and uniform thickness from which one can abstract closed, knotted and linked ribbons curving through space (Francis with Collins 1995: 59). The mathematical surface depicted by his artworks indeed constitutes a knot-spanning surface or a 'framed link', with the knot literally being carved out of the wood and constituting the hollow, negative space of the sculpture. In a recent paper Francis (1995) analyses Collins's sculpture as 'spanning an "unlinked link", which looks like a figure-8, and Listing's knot, which is also called a figure-8 knot after the shape of the isotopic deformation of it' (1995: 61). Variations in sculptural form are carried out by Collins in tracing the six possible different surfaces spanning the Listing's knot.

What may have been in Collins's case a rather abstract application of topology to a given material artefact is based in Celtic knotwork on the practice of pleating. Knot illuminations such as the King Solomon's knot, still popular in medieval times, were thought of as vehicles of wisdom, as a resource of knowledge restricted to scribes who held proprietary claims in visualizing plaits. Celtic knot design was based on three overlapping grids which defined the path of the knot as a series of geometrically arranged dots. The way in which the square (the primary grid) and its centre (the secondary grid) provide the co-ordinates for the division of the sides of the square (the tertiary grid) may, according to Meehan (1995: 16), have been seen by early monks as a symbol of tri-unity, three in one. 'To the monks of early Christianity,' according to Meehan, 'the geometry of the square symbolised the creation of the manifold universe, and it was important to them to contemplate how the Two – the infinite and the finite, indeed all opposites – could be engendered by the One' (1995: 17). The unity of the grids is effected through the woven line, as all grid-points ultimately are to disappear into the background of the knot. With this principle in mind, all knot patterns covering the illuminated Gospel books of Celtic Art could be created.

Figure 3.1 To'o, God image of wood with Sennit. Found in the Society Islands, Tahiti, 1881. British Museum Q81.OC.1550

It is in Meehan's (1995: 114) recent work on the secret method of Celtic scribes that I came across a depiction of a Kells bird with a spiral knot neck whose visual similarity with a *malanggan* carving from the northern part of New Ireland formed in part the motivation for this chapter (Figure 3.4). This visual similarity between

Figure 3.2 Sketch of Malanggan, New Ireland, 1888 British Museum XXXVI

these two forms, while not significant in itself, points to the possibility of generating both the surface of figural space and two dimensional pattern through binding. The space thus created is strictly self-referential in that it does not represent spaces of imaginary or past experience. As virtual space, the knot-spanning surface acts synthetically in bringing together, like the mathematical formula or the architectural plan, experiences from a number of domains; rather than just articulating already existing knowledge, the knot as artefact is thus capable of creating something 'new' – a momentary integration of distinct domains of experience which may be a reason for the symptomatic use of the knot as contractual object.

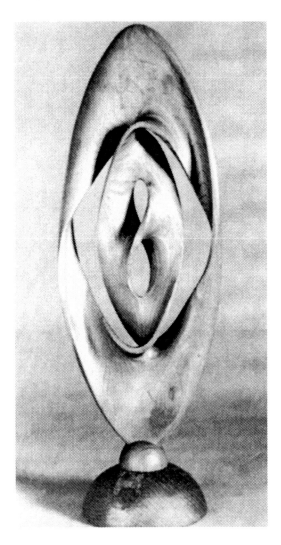

Figure 3.3 Brent Collins, One Sided Surface with opposed Cheiralities, oiled cedar, 30 × 12 × 4 in, 1984. Copyright G. Francis.

No one has brought out this significance of the knot more clearly than Andy Goldworthy whose landscape sculpture utilizes walls to bring existing forms in the landscape to a higher pitch. The 'Give and Take Wall' he constructed at Stone Wood was made in accordance with a contract to mark the boundary with a neighbour's land. The wall, as stated in a recent interview with Goldworthy, 'appears almost knotted, emphasising contract, a monument to practical property relations'.

Figure 3.4 Malanggan, New Ireland, 1932, Museum der Kulturen basel, Vb 10579

The cross-over between mathematics and art alluded to in the figural knot is of course nothing new and is also not restricted to the explicit application of mathematical theories, let alone knot-theory (Francis 1995: 57). We are mostly familiar with explicit mathematical art in a quite traditional sense through the application of symmetry, platonic solids and optical illusions, and of subjects that are rather conventional such as cubes, spheres, Mobius bands and the like. Michael Baxandall's study of fifteenth-century Italian painting exquisitely pointed to the fact that the surface of a painting was conditioned by the application of mathe-matical and geometric riddles whose emplacement in visual form excited the wit of the patrons of art for whom the capacity to achieve mathematical conversions of any kind was key to their social and economic position (Baxandall 1976).

Interestingly, it was this shared apparatus of mathematics and geometry, transmitted and popularized through painting, which transcended the diversity of value systems that effectively separated towns into virtual economic islands by facilitating conversions on a regional basis.

Such examples give credence to the suggestion that the knot epitomizes what Levinson (1991) called 'knowledge technology' responsible for externalizing non-spatial, logical problems in a distinctly spatial manner. Associative or inferential thought provoked by the knot may thus condition spatial cognition because of the textured and deformative properties of the knot. The translation of a non-spatial conceptual problem into a spatial one has been studied hitherto primarily as a symptom and material artefact of mapping. Navigators, hunters, ocean fishers, trackers and traders must operate with complex mental maps, and with various systems of dead reckoning to locate current positions on the map. Less practical spatial models are cosmologies, mental models of the universe, where spirits, ancestors, moral and spiritual qualities, together with terrestrial and celestial phenomena are conceived of as all having their proper place in some three-dimensional scheme. Such holistic spatial models may be expressed in ritual, myth, art and architecture; yet do artefacts conceived as knot-spanning surfaces or as aggregates of one or more knots really work to externalize knowledge acquired through experience as do diagrams, maps, charts or the like?

Such an assumption, I believe, would neglect the intrinsic spatial and trans-formative properties of the knot which exist in a self-evident and most importantly non-ego-centred manner. To understand the knot, or artefacts made as a composite knot, let alone realize its 'abductive' qualities which provoke non-random associations, one has to understand the physical properties of knots and conceive of the knot in relation to its possible, logical deformations (cf. Gell 1998; Bateson 1979). Indeed, it might be said that the problem rendered spatially in the knot is not a problem that can be conceived experientially at all other than on the basis of binding itself; that is, it is unlikely that the knot is the result of a projection of pre-existing concepts derived from social-cultural experience, but that it evidences a complex relational and transformational field which can be discovered simply by doing it and looking at it.

Following mathematics we may thus conclude that a knot is not referential but synthetic, in relating inextricably the texture of its surface to the logic of binding. Unlike the open mesh of the looped string, the knot does not hint at what lies beneath its surface, but is itself to be discovered beneath its own surface. The knot is all that is to be seen.

The knot is the knowledge, a knowledge of the linking of things, material and mental, that may as well exist apart. It may be this feature of the knot which allows it to be linked to sorcery across the Pacific. No one has as yet better revealed the importance ascribed to binding and to the cord as representation of binding than

Valeri in his work on the king's sacrifice in Hawaii (1985: 296–300). In Hawaii, a sacred cord (*'aha*) acted as reference point of genealogy – representing not just the king's relationship with the gods, but also the connecting force of genealogy that 'binds together all other genealogies, since it is their reference point and the locus of their legitimacy and truth' (Valeri 1985: 296). The cord of Hawaiian kingship was not inherited – the undoing of the King's sacred cord dissolving the social bond embodied by the king. The strands obtained from the undoing of the cords were woven into caskets in which the bones of the king are enshrined (Valeri 1985: 298).

During the king's reign, the weaving of the cord which celebrated his installation was re-enacted repeatedly as the central organizing rite of the sacrifice of the king. The metaphoric or real 'twisting' of the strands that make up the *'aha* cord enclosed and thereby removed from sight the space where the knot resides, containing and thus arresting the divine powers which come to form the mystical body of kingship.

The Hawaiian sacred cord thus effected a contiguous relation with divinity, insofar as it does not represent through resemblance, but associative or contiguous link. As recently pointed out by Ginzburg (1991), we have become unaccustomed to such a kind of representation which, rather than effecting a substitution through resemblance with something or someone we know and can see, recalls what is rendered absent. Ginzburg examines this latter kind of representation using Kantorowitcz's (1957) classic study of the 'King's Two Bodies' which described the historical development of the concept in European thought epitomized in the ritual sacrifice of funerary effigies made for French and English kings in the fourteenth and fifteenth centuries. Made to represent the natural and mortal body of the king, the sacrifice of the effigy also fashioned the mystical body of kingship whose powers were thought eternal.

The cord offers an extreme solution to image such representation in that it renders perceptible only the surface which embraces, yet hints at the knot itself which will become apparent only with the death of the king and the unravelling of the cord. As undifferentiated as the knots are that make up the cord, so kingship in Hawaii seen in the light of the cord appeared to possess a unifying force. In Valeri's words 'the king's "cord" (*'aha*) is in fact also the 'association' or 'congregation' (*'aha*) of nobles. The cord becomes the community; the link that connects the king with the social bond itself' (Valeri 1985: 296–7). In braiding his sacred cords the king braids social relationships, or, as Valeri puts it, 'binds men with his cords' (1985: 298). The king's title reflects the idea that he is the 'binder', as *'haku'* or 'ruler' means 'to weave', 'to put in order', 'to compose a chant'. Valeri extends the political function ascribed to weaving or binding to the poetic function of chants which are collectively composed by those whom the king tied to himself, thus becoming a bond that, bound in the memory of all, binds them all (1985: 299).

The 'weaving' of the chants, like the weaving of the cords, is thus 'also an intellectual weaving, since social relations are reconstituted by the reproduction of the ideas that are their correlate and justification' (1985: 299). The cord thus evokes, according to Valeri, social bond, memory, but also transformation as it can be used to tie and untie, as made evident in string games which are used, according to Valeri, 'to represent mythical transformations or even to produce ritual ones' (1985: 299). The unvarying element of two opposing states (tied and untied) represented by the cord, permits thus the representation of the passage from one to the other – from the inaccessibility of divine nature to its desacrilized state in myth and ritual, or from sickness to healing in medical rites.

The Hawaiian sacred cord is thus given *processual value* in being assigned a temporal and performative role responsible for linking the invisible and the visible. The capacity of the knot to fashion decentred spatial cognition is of paramount importance for understanding how knotted effigies can visually and conceptually effect a 'body politic' that appears at once phenomenal and yet also mystical in nature. The images that appear in and around the space of the knot both mirror a society comprised of relations and constitute simultaneously a system of reference for spatial cognition that is independent of particular points of view. Alternatingly formed and dissolved in processes of tying and untying, knotted effigies recall the spatio-temporal conception of a body politic which mediates the contradictory nature of gods whose powers need to be arrested while being kept at a safe distance. Activated by binding, ancestral power appears in continuous motion – being conceived as a flow that is activated through its periodic arrest and release from the space where the knot resides. Yet binding is not just metaphorically setting into motion the processes that condition the body politic, it is also effecting a visualization of these processes as a series of stoppages. While all taking the form of a knot, such stoppages are visualized in manifold ways, their varying appearances mirroring relationality. Ranked polities of images emerge from within the space of the knot whose visual and conceptual differentiation grounds the articulation of social rank not in ritual context or discourse, but in the mundane matters of binding.

Yet it is indeed not necessary for an ethnography of the knot to take as its subject artworks such as the Andean Quipu, Papua New Guinean netbags or other such exotic items that anthropology has found in its preoccupation with the 'Other'. This is because much of contemporary architecture aspires to the new aesthetic of continuous surface and wrapping imagery, such as the Guggenheim museum in Bilbao. It is, however, Neil Denari's work, while more obscure perhaps than that of any of his contemporaries, which articulates most eloquently the implications of topology for architecture.

Denari's technique rests upon a critique of the map, reflecting upon the resonance of the map with the sheet and the ribbon – the mapping impulse, itself synonymous with capitalism, being reformulated into a technical key called GALLERY-MA SPACE – visualized as as an interrupted 'worldsheet or ribbon-like, 2-D surface'. According to Denari,

> In the contemporary world, it seems as if architecture should not function as a vessel or container of knowledge or the social. Such a fixed/closed idea of function retards the processes, filtrations and overcodings that a supple architectural system could provide. Instead, it should operate more like an extrapolation machine, a device capable of re-spatialising the dramatic currents and flows of culture, not merely a mirror held up to reflect it. By BLENDING UP (OR DOWN) the worldsheet, architecture is a sudden spatialising and transforming third dimensional phenomenon which actualises and sets into motion the intertextualised codes. My scheme for the Gallery-Ma space is an overcoded diagram of this concept (1996: 47).

Denari's architecture puts into practice a topological understanding of spatial conception to created architectural spaces which are generative and transformative, rather than singular and unique. His buildings evoke the momentous texture of a surface-spanning knot which can be simultaneously viewed from multiple perspectives.

The ethnography of the knot , if executed in ways that could only be paraphrased in this chapter, would enable one to show the link between the first part of 'Art and Agency' and its concern with patterning and its last chapter entitled 'the Extended Mind' in which Alfred returned to the theme of modernist art. In this last chapter, Alfred exposed the intimate relation between art and the activation of temporal consciousness which is grounded in the momentary and point-like, if spatial, collapse of past-present and future. This nonlinear, non-narrative framing of remembering, described as 'active mode of awakening' in Aleida Assmann's (1993) work on memory, was of course of fundamental importance to the modernist project as it enabled it to turn its back to the notion of creativity and innovation inherent in the 'tradition' of Western art since the age of Alberti. The turn away from eschatological modes of remembering, with its play on 'passive' awakening that was popularized in the nineteenth century in the form of 'dreamscapes' of hysteria and nostalgia, meant also a turn away from the fear of the present which was hitherto seen as a phase to be overcome (cf. Assmann 1993: 33; Roth 1994). Freed from its linear and narrative trappings, the present becomes the generative (prospective and retrospective) principle of temporal consciousness.

This celebration of the present as a state of consciousness, which both requires art and 'is' an art, is for me the most important insight of 'Art and Agency'. It is both deeply moving and profoundly thought-provoking – opening the re-examination of the complex interplay between temporality and intentionality in ways that will shed new light on old issues such as attention which proves that thought conducts itself in art.

Notes

1. Schiller (1967). For a detailed discussion of the positions on the conception of art prefigured in the aesthetics of Kant and Schiller see M. Podro (1989: 9–16).
2. Godfried Semper (1803–79) formulated Schiller's theoretical account into a project on the systematic ordering of architectural style. He explored the way visual artists, in particular architects, took structural features such as the plaited twigs of buildings in Palau, an island in the Pacific where he resided for a number of years in the 1840s, or woven thread of textiles, and exploited their potential for pattern making, transferring motifs to different materials and in this way generating architectural metaphors.
3. see Bateson on 'abduction' (1979: 157–9); the prominence of Yates's rediscovery of memoria, the conscious recollection of forgotten experience for the humanities, has led to a virtual suppression of mnemic recollection.
4. I am indebted to Strohecker's dissertation (n.d.) at MIT for the discovery of Papert's writings.
5. My understanding of knot theory is almost entirely governed by C. Adams's (1994) extremely enlightening book.

References

Adams, C. 1994. *The Knot Book: An Elementary Introduction to the Mathematical Theory of Knots*. New York: W.H. Freeman and Company.

Assmann, A. (ed.) 1993. *Mnemosyne: Formen und Funktionen der kulturellen Erinnerung*. Frankfurt am Main: Fischer Taschenbuch Verlag.

Babadzan, A. 1993. *Les Dépouilles des Dieux: Essai sur le Religion Tahitienne à L'époque de la Découverte*. Paris: Editions de la Maison des Sciences de L'homme.

Banchoff T. 1990. *Beyond the Third Dimension*. New York: Freeman.

Barrow, J. 1992. *Pie in the Sky: Counting, Thinking and Being.* Oxford University Press.

Bateson, G. 1979. *Mind and Nature: A Necessary Unity.* London: Wildwood House Ltd.

Baxandall, M. 1976. *Painting and Experience in Fifteenth Century Italy*. Princeton University Press.

Bill, M. 1949. 'The Mathematical Way of Thinking in the Visual Arts of our Time' reprinted in M. Emmer (ed.) *The Visual Mind*. 1995. MIT Press.

Brisson, D. (ed.) 1978. *Hypergraphics: Visualizing Complex Relationships in Art, Science and Technology*. Boulder: Colo.: Westview Press.

Cipra, B. 1994. 'What is Happening in Mathematical Sciences'. *Journal of Mathematics* Vol. 9.

Davis, W. 1986. 'The Origin of Image-making', *Current Anthropology* 27: 193–215.

Denari, N. 1996. *Interrupted Projections: Another Global Surface or Territorial Re-codings on the World Sheet*. Japan: Atsushi Sato.

Eastrop, D. n.d. 'Exploring String-Figures'. MA project, University College London.

Emmer, M. (ed.) 1993. *The Visual Mind: Art and Mathematics*. Cambridge, Mass.: The MIT Press.

Francis, G. With B. Collins 1995. 'On Knot-spanning Surfaces: An Illustrated Essay on Topological Art', in M. Emmer (ed.) *The Visual Mind: Art and Mathematics*. Cambridge, Mass.: The MIT Press.

Gell, A. 1986. 'Umeda Dance Styles', in P. Spencer (ed.) *The Anthropology of Dance*. Cambridge: University of Cambridge Press.

—— 1996. 'Traps as Artworks, Artworks as Traps'. Journal of Material Culture Vol. 1(1): 15–38.

—— 1998 *Art and Agency: An Anthropological Theory*. Oxford: Oxford University Press.

Ginzburg, C. 1991. Repräsentation: das Wort, die Vorstellung, der Gegenstand. *Freibeuter* 22: 3–23.

Hauser-Schaublin, B. 1996. 'The Thrill of the Line, the String, and the Frond or why the Abelam are a Non-cloth Culture'. *Oceania* Vol. 67(2): 81–106.

—— 1987. *Leben in Linie, Form und Farbe*. Basel: Schweizerisches Museum für Volkerkunde.

Kantorowitcz, E.H. 1957. *The King's Two Bodies: A Study in Mediaeval Political Theology*. Princeton, N.J: Princeton University Press.

Küchler, S. 1997. 'Sacrificial Economy and Its Objects'. *Journal of Material Culture* 2(1): 39–60.

Levinson, S. 1991. 'Primer for the Field Investigation of Spatial Description and Conception'. *Pragmatics* 2(1): 5–47.

MacDonald, R. 1987. *The Burial Places of Memory: the Theme of the Underworld in Epic Poetry from Homer to Milton*. Amherst: University of Massachusetts Press.

Mackenzie, M. 1991. *Androgynous Objects: Stringbags and Gender in the Pacific*. Harwood Press.

Meehan, A. 1995. *The Knotwork: The Secret Method of Scribes*. London: Thames and Hudson.

Papert, S. 1980. *Mindstorms: Children, Computers, and Powerful Ideas*. New York: Basic Books, Inc.

Podro, M. 1989. *The Critical Historians of Art*. Harvard: Yale University Press.

Rosenfield, I. 1992. *The Strange, the Familiar and the Forgotten*. New York: Knopf.

Roth, M. 1991. 'Dying of the Past: Medical Studies of Nostalgia in Nineteenth-Century France'. *History and Memory* 3(1): 5–29.

Saunders, P.T. 1997. 'Nonlinearity'. *Architectural Design Profile* No. 129: 52–7.

Schiller. 1967. *Letters on the Aesthetic Education of Man.* ed. and tr. E.M. Wilkinson and L.A. Willoughby, Oxford.

Semper, G. 1878. *Der Stil in den Technischen und Tektonischen Kunsten.* 2 vols. 2nd edn. Munich.

Stafford, B. 1991. *Body Criticism: Imaging the Unseen in Enlightenment Art and Medicine.* Chapter 1. Cambridge, Mass.: MIT Press.

Strohecker, C. n.d. *Why Knot?* PhD Dissertation. Epistemology and Learning Group. Media Arts and Sciences. Massachusetts Institute of Technology.

Thompson, D'Arcy (1961). *On Growth and Form* Cambridge: Cambridge University Press [1902].

Valeri, V. 1985. *Kingship and Sacrifice in Hawaii.* Chicago: Chicago University Press.

Wassmann, J. 1994. 'The Yupno as Post-Newtonian Scientists: The Question of what is "Natural" in Spatial Descriptions'. *Man* (N.S.), 29(3): 645–67.

Yates, F. 1966. *The Art of Memory.* London: Penguin Books.

$-4-$

Captivation, Representation, and the Limits of Cognition: Interpreting Metaphor and Metonymy in Tahitian *Tamau*

Anne D'Alleva

In *Art and Agency*, Alfred Gell argues that works of art and human beings occupy effectively equivalent positions in the networks of human social agency. The artwork is a Peircean index, one perceived as 'the outcome, and/or the instrument of, social agency' (Gell 1998: 15). In this formulation, art works are 'secondary agents', for they do not initiate events through acts of will, as primary (human) social agents do. Rather, works of art are objective embodiments of the power or capacity to will their use: social agency manifests and realizes itself via the proliferation of fragments of 'primary' intentional agents in their secondary, artefactual form (Gell 1998: 21).[1]

Gell discusses two primary ways that a work of art exercises its agency. The first is the captivation exerted by artistic virtuosity. Developing an argument that he first articulated in 'The Technology of Enchantment and the Enchantment of Technology' (Gell 1992), Gell argues that an artwork acts as an agent when the artist's skill is so great that the viewer simply cannot comprehend it and is therefore captivated by the image. Taking as an example Trobriand canoe prows, he contends that the spectacle of the artist's virtuosity gives rise to a blockage in cognition at the point when the spectator cannot follow the sequence of steps in the artist's 'performance', which is congealed in the finished work (Gell 1998: 71). In the case of the canoe prows, this spectacle demoralizes the viewer and induces him to trade his shell valuables for much less than their equivalent. Gell extends this argument in a discussion of the psychological functionality of decorative patterning in a variety of artworks (1998: 74–95).

According to Gell, a work of art also exerts its agency via representation. The indexical work of art engages in a double session of representation, for it both portrays and stands in for its prototype (Gell 1998: 98).[2] Focusing his discussion on images of gods ('idols'), Gell notes that the idol *is* the god, but in artefactual form. He develops this argument through an analysis of Society Islands figures called *to'o*, which represent the god 'Oro. Although 'Oro was the most powerful of the gods before the establishment of Christianity, priests and titleholders were able to manage his intervention in human affairs through their control over the index, the image of the god. When titleholders and priests ritually bound the *to'o*, the power of 'Oro diffused into the feather and fibre bindings. These feathers then became the currency of political control, circulated among titleholders and priests (Gell 1998: 109–14).

In his discussion of representation, Gell makes two provocative assertions about the relationship between index and prototype, assertions that form the starting point for this discussion. He declares that the artefactual body of the god, the idol, need not be either realistic (mimetic) or metonymic in order to represent the prototype. The idol is not a portrait rooted in actual physical resemblance to the god but 'a "faithful" rendition of the features of the accepted image of the body of the god, triggering "recognition" of the god among his worshippers' (Gell 1998: 99). Furthermore, the index is a detached fragment of the prototype: the image is part of what it represents. For Gell this means that it does not stand metonymically for the prototype, just as exuviae are not metonyms for the victim of volt sorcery, but detached fragments of the victim's 'distributed personhood' (Gell 1998: 104).

Gell excludes metaphor and metonym from his theoretical model as part of his insistence that the visual and material specificity of the work of art should determine the modes of interpretation. He pointedly rejects both the search for symbolic meaning in art, exemplified by Panofsky's iconographic approach, and also the adaptation of linguistic modes of interpretation, exemplified by a semiotics that approaches art as a form of 'language' or 'communication' (Gell 1998: 6, 14–15). For Gell, both of these approaches fail to take into account the 'presented object'.[3] He offers as an alternative an 'action'-centred approach that emphasizes agency, intention, causation, result and transformation in ways intrinsic to the visual arts (Gell 1998: 6). This argument rests in part on an assumption, explicitly articulated in 'The Technology of Enchantment and the Enchantment of Technology', that the symbolic aspects of the work are extraneous to the technology used to produce it, that is, to its material and visual characteristics (Gell 1992: 43).[4]

Taken simply within the framework of this theoretical project, Gell's rejection of metaphor and metonym might not be particularly troubling. But this is a theory built in large part on the analysis of Polynesian art, and in this context, the role of metaphor and metonym in representation becomes an important issue, for they are central to Polynesian modes of visual representation. Perhaps the best account of this is Adrienne Kaeppler's discussion of metaphoric practices of representation in Hawaii and other Polynesian cultures (Kaeppler 1982). She argues, for example, that *kaona*, veiled meaning or symbolism, is an essential aspect of Hawaiian poetry, music, dance, and sculpture. According to Kaeppler, *kaona* allowed the metaphoric visual representation of religious and social concepts, such as *mana*, genealogy, respect and disrespect, aspects of nature, and sorcery (1982: 83).

For Tahiti and the Society Islands, my own area of expertise and a particular focus in *Art and Agency*, the use of metaphor and metonym is most extensively documented in language, although, as I hope to show, it was also characteristic of visual representation. Cook wrote in the official account of his third voyage that the Tahitian language 'abounds with beautiful and figurative expressions, which, were it perfectly known, would, I have no doubt, put it upon a level with many of the languages that are most in esteem for their warm and bold images' (Cook and King 1784: II: 151–2). For example, the paddles for a titleholder's canoe were called metonymically *mehine-i-te-ata*, moon-in-the-clouds, because paddlers looked up into the sky when using them (Henry 1928: 189). Similarly, *marae* attendants were called *'opu-nui*, which Henry politely translates as 'august stomachs'. When on duty, the *'opu-nui*, were privileged to cook their food using wood of the *marae* grounds and to eat food offered to the gods (Henry 1928: 151). A warrior's chant, recited in answer to a challenge, is replete with metaphors. Although Henry does not cite a source, her grandfather, the missionary J.M. Orsmond, probably collected this chant in the first half of the nineteenth century:

Pa'ipa'i i te rima ia huha	Clap the hands upon the thighs,
A fava ei pua'a tote!	Rush head first as a hog enraged!
Auaa i ape au nei i te rao!	I do not flinch at a fly [his antagonist]
E puahiohio te riri, e Te-aho-roa,	A whirlwind is anger, O Te-aho-roa,
Ei vavahi papa te riri,	A rock breaker is anger,
Ei oropua puai te riri,	A strong north wind is anger,
E ia pupu nonoha	That blows away *nonoha* (grass)
I taai hia te ata.	sheaths are clouds underrating the enemy.
Homai i te toa o auta'ata	Give me the undaunted warrior
O te riri e te fatiai.	With rage and endurance
Ovau teie, O Huriaau toa hau a'e	This is I, Huriaau. My father was
tau metua i ta 'oe.	a greater warrior than yours.
E 'ore tau 'omore e mae ae ia 'oe.	You cannot lift my spear.

This chapter will reconsider the role of metaphor and metonym in visual representation by conjoining Gell's two primary modes of agency. In essence, I will take up Gell's invitation to explore modes of captivation other than the stylistic (Gell 1998: 72), and argue that the metonymic and metaphoric indexing of a prototype is a form of captivation quite characteristic of Tahitian visual representation in the late eighteenth and early nineteenth centuries. My point is not to use metaphor and metonym to reintroduce the search for meaning or literary modes of interpretation – although I will return to these issues in the end – but to explore further the mechanics of representation, the nature of the relationship between the indexical artwork and its prototype, in a Polynesian context. As they enable the index to represent the prototype in effective ways, metaphor and metonymy can be located not only in iconography and the construction of meaning, but also in materials and techniques in ways that are specific to Tahitian visual arts.[5] This project faces certain challenges, given that the sources for discussing this material are relatively few and do not address in any direct way the kinds of question I ask. Although my conclusions will be somewhat speculative, I hope that the process of interpretation will push me to ask new questions about a frequently overlooked art tradition, even as it enables me to engage more fully with Gell's theoretical argument.

In doing so, I will employ a cognitive model of metaphor and metonymy that does not situate them exclusively within language, but recognizes that they are basic to a much broader range of perceptual and conceptual processes (see for example Gibbs 1994; Lakoff 1993; Lakoff and Johnson 1980; Mio and Katz 1996; Sacks 1979).[6] Metaphors and metonyms can be textual, visual, gestural, and more – and they are apprehended (seen, read, heard) accordingly. In fact, historians and philosophers of art have engaged productively with the concept of visual metaphor, if not metonymy, in relatively recent years (Carroll 1994; Danto 1981; Goodman 1976; Summers 1988). It is important to note that in this cognitive model, metaphors and metonyms are not denotative: they are not simply ornamental, expressing more pleasantly that which can be expressed otherwise. Rather, they act as an additive instrument of knowledge (Eco 1984: 89; Gibbs 1994: 5). Metaphor and metonymy stimulate the mind, provoking the imagination and creating understanding in sometimes new and unexpected ways.

It might be best to take a moment here to define both metaphor and metonymy. Eco has noted the difficulties of articulating a simple definition for metaphor, for to speak of metaphor is to speak of rhetorical activity in all of its complexity (Eco 1984: 87). However, in the context of this discussion, we can understand metaphor as a process of figuration operating fundamentally according to the principle of substitution based on similarity, as in 'flame' for 'passion'. A metonym, on the other hand, operates according to the principle of contiguity (Jakobson 1956). It takes an attribute, adjunct, or part and substitutes it for the thing meant, as in 'crown' for 'king'. Metonymy in general, and synecdoche in particular, is frequently produced by deleting one or more items from a combination generally perceived as natural (Lodge 1977: 76).

This discussion will focus on a remarkable Tahitian art form, the skeins of finely braided human hair called *tamau* (Figure 4.1). *Tamau* present a challenge to interpretation within this framework, for there is little direct exegesis of these artworks in Tahitian or early-voyage sources. Moreover, their current incarnation as museum specimens makes it difficult to imagine *tamau* as exercising any captivation whatsoever. Rarely on exhibit, they sit in drawers and boxes, brittle skeins of braided hair without sheen or lustre. Yet despite their unprepossessing

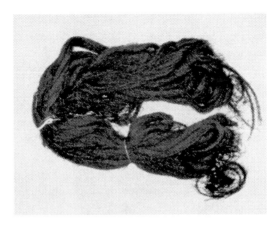

Figure 4.1 *Tamau* Tahiti, Society Islands. Braided human hair. Collected on Vancouver's Voyage, 1792. Courtesy Trustees of the British Museum.

appearance today, the textual record does suggest that *tamau* were highly prized objects in eighteenth-century Tahiti. On Cook's first voyage, Joseph Banks observes that *tamau* were the ornament 'they value more than any thing they have' (Beaglehole 1962: I: 324). In his third-voyage account, Cook himself notes that the standard punishments for thieves were rarely strictly enforced unless 'the articles that are stolen be reckoned very valuable; such as breastplates and plaited hair' (Cook and King 1784: II: 172).

Though *tamau* may appear strange, perhaps even repellent, in the context of contemporary museum practice and scholarship that prefer to focus on Tahiti's spectacular mourning dresses and figural sculpture, these hair ornaments are no anomaly. Many cultures have realized the symbolic potential of human hair in artefactual form, and there are several related artistic traditions in Polynesia. Perhaps most similar is the Hawaiian *lei niho palaoa*, a necklace composed of bundles of finely-braided human hair strung with a bone or tooth pendant. Special headdresses in Samoa and the Cook Islands incorporate locks of human hair, and human hair ornaments decorate a variety of important Marquesan objects, including shell trumpets. Although many of these art forms have received rather limited scholarly attention recently, Jeanette Mageo's provocative analysis of hair symbolism in Samoa suggests that young women's hair styles, as well as the headdresses they wear, have been historically and continue to be richly symbolic of sexuality and fecundity and often directly affect the interests of the lineage (Mageo 1994).[7]

As in other Polynesian cultures, Tahitian men and women wore *tamau* on special occasions. Perhaps the most spectacular – and frequent – use for *tamau* was as the headdress for high-ranking young women who performed a dance called *hura.*

No headdress survives intact today, but several Cook-voyage images convey a good sense of their appearance (Figure 4.2). Reinhold Forster includes a detailed description in his journal:

> . . . on their heads they had a high twist or turbant of plaited hair; on the crown in the circle between ye plaited hair all was filled with Cape Jasmin flowers & the front of the bunch of plaited hair was ornamented with 3 or 4 rows of the white flowers of the *Morinda citrifolia*, which looked so pretty as if the head had been set of by pearls. (Hoare 1982: II: 360)

The *Bounty* mutineer James Morrison notes that men wore girdles of braided hair when attending *marae* rituals:[8]

> . . . all who enter of the Morai [*marae*] Must be Naked to the Waist, but when they attend any Ceremony off the Morai they have their Shoulders covered and their Head annointed with Oil, a kind of Turban bound on with Secred leaves a Breastplate (called *tawmee*) [*taumi*] on their Breast and their Clothes bound on with a Sash or Girdle of Braided hair or Coconut Fibers neatly plaited of a Great length, and Made up in Bights or doubles, with a Tasell at each end. (1935: 183–4)

Figure 4.2 John Webber. *A Dance at Otaheite*. 1777. Pen, wash, and watercolour on paper (43.2 × 54.6 cm) British Library, London

Men wore *tamau* in two other forms. Short lengths of *tamau* were sometimes used to bind the dog hair tassels that ornamented the *taumi* breastplates to which Morrison refers (D'Alleva 1997: 376–80). High-ranking men wore these breast-plates not only for *marae* rituals but also in battle (Cook in Beaglehole 1961: 385; Davies et al. 1807–1808: f. 19). The Oxford mourning dress, worn by a male chief mourner during funerary rituals for a high-ranking titleholder, incorporates whole skeins of *tamau* in its headpiece.

A closer look at the surviving *tamau* reveals their extraordinary physical properties. Each skein consists of a very fine three-ply braid, with each ply typically composed of anywhere from fifteen to thirty-five strands of hair. The hair itself is uniformly brown and straight, and perhaps it was sorted for colour and texture, for there are never grey or curling hairs in evidence. While the fineness and evenness of the braiding is remarkable, what is most impressive about *tamau* is their great length, seemingly many yards, and the fact that the braids are absolutely seamless. It is impossible to distinguish where hair has been added to create such long, smooth braids. Although the surviving skeins of *tamau* are far too fragile to unwind and measure today, the records of the Cook voyages provide some useful information in this respect. With typical exuberance, Joseph Banks unwound a dancer's headdress made of *tamau* to find that 'a common head dress contains at least 2 Leagues and I have measur'd a peice made upon an end without a knot above an English mile and three quarters in leng[t]h . . .' (Beaglehole 1962: II: 332).

Although the evidence is fragmentary, it seems fairly certain that women made the *tamau* of their own and living female relatives' hair. When Purea gave skeins of plaited hair to Wallis and the officers of the *Dolphin* in 1767, she indicated by word and gesture that she herself had made them of her own hair (Wallis n.d.).[9] In a short description of curiosities acquired during Cook's second voyage, the naturalist Reinhold Forster describes *tamau* as 'des fils qu'on a fait des cheveux de leurs femmes' (Hoare 1982: IV: 780–1). J.M. Orsmond also briefly notes that Society Islands women made *tamau* of their own and relatives' hair (n.d.). Only high-ranking women and men are documented as possessing or wearing *tamau*, and they were almost certainly artefacts associated with elite status.

That *tamau* were made at least largely, if not exclusively, from the hair of the living is important, for they cannot truly be classed as relics.[10] Relics, including hair, fingernails and skulls, were frequently preserved in Tahiti. Bligh mentions that an uncle of Tupaia, the priest who left Tahiti with Cook's first voyage and died abroad, asked him for Tupaia's hair as a memento (1961: 120). Bligh also notes that preserving hair 'perhaps is the greatest satisfaction these people can have after the death of a Freind, and is kept as a most sacred relic . . . after a certain time that the body has been carried to the Toopa-how [*tupapa'u* or funerary bier], the hair is cut off and hung up in their house made into the form of a false curl' (1937: II: 47). Thus hair relics were distinct from *tamau* both physically, in the way that they were fashioned and preserved, and in the contexts in which they circulated.

Given that Tahitians valued *tamau* so highly, it is not surprising that eighteenth-century voyagers collected at least fourteen of them between 1769 and 1792, during Cook's three voyages, Bligh's second breadfruit voyage, and Vancouver's voyage (D'Alleva 1997: 540–4, 636–7).[11] Those with specific provenances belonged to prominent members of these expeditions: Reinhold and George Forster, naturalists on Cook's second voyage; John Webber, artist on Cook's third voyage; and Francis Godolphin Bond, a lieutenant on Bligh's second breadfruit voyage. In addition to the *tamau* themselves, a number of surviving eighteenth-century artefacts incorporate lengths of *tamau*, including the Oxford mourning dress mentioned above and several *taumi* breastplates.[12]

The historical records indicate that voyagers received *tamau* as gifts in the exchanges that accompanied the formation of *taio* friendships. *Taio* friendship was a special institution in Tahiti, one that signified the establishment of a familial relationship that often carried significant economic, political, and spiritual obligations (Oliver 1974: II: 842–50; D'Alleva 1997: 247–56). In addition to *tamau*, *taio* friends received gifts of decorated barkcloth, large rolls of undecorated barkcloth, and massive amounts of food, and they also exchanged names during the gift-giving ceremony. The institution of *taio* friendship became an integral part of relations between European voyagers and Tahitians. During the first European voyage to Tahiti, in 1767, the high-ranking woman Purea gave *tamau* to Captain Samuel Wallis and his officers; although Wallis does not use the word *taio* to describe the bond established by this ritual, he notes that it was one of peace and friendship (Wallis n.d.). In 1792, 'Itia, the wife of Pomare I, the pre-eminent titleholder on Tahiti, bestowed on her *taio* George Tobin 'a present of plaited human hair, about the thickness of a double thread' (Tobin in Oliver 1988: 170). A few years later, in 1797, Pomare I's consort Vaiareti gave her *taio*, William Wilson of the missionary ship *Duff*, 'a quantity of human hair made into fine sinnet' when he visited her house in Papara (Wilson 1966: 209).

The giving of *tamau* in the context of *taio* friendship, which established familial relationships carrying extensive obligations, suggests their importance as artefacts and their value to the lineage. *Tamau* seem to be the kind of object that Annette Weiner describes as an inalienable possession, something imbued with the intrinsic identity of its owner that is not easily or casually given away (Weiner 1992: 6). As Weiner points out, families or descent groups ideally keep such things from one generation to the next, although the need to create and perpetuate social relationships often compels them to bestow these precious objects on others. *Tamau* were perhaps so strongly associated with the lineage that they could not, in a certain sense, be given away – *tamau* instead made the recipient part of the lineage. The *taio* received not only that lineage's wealth, in the form of barkcloth and food, and the identity of one of its members, in the exchange of personal names, but also its very substance, in the form of braided hair. The hair of the head may have been particularly resonant in this context, for the head was the seat of an individual's spiritual power (sometimes glossed as *mana*), an inherited life force that enabled that person to achieve in many arenas and to contribute to the power and renown of the lineage.

The physical characteristics of *tamau*, plus the contexts in which they appeared, suggest that these skeins of braided hair indexed the lineage of the artist and the wearer through visual metaphors and metonyms. The hair in *tamau* came from the lineage, was worn by relatives, and given to relatives (both *taio* and blood). Human hair has unusual properties: it is extremely strong, and grows throughout life (and even after death), and is thus intimately tied to the life cycle. Hair grown on the head had special significance for eighteenth-century Tahitians, for whom the head was the repository of the individual's spiritual force (Oliver 1974: I: 66–7). That it was the hair of the living, and not of the dead, that went into *tamau* may have served as a reminder that the lineage was not only of the past, but a living thing, something that extended into the present. The contexts in which high-ranking Tahitians wore *tamau* – *hura*, *marae* and funerary rituals, battle – were ones in which lineage and genealogy were important factors (D'Alleva 1997).

Tamau is not literal; it does not painstakingly depict a series of ancestors to index the lineage as prototype. Instead, *tamau* works metaphorically by bringing together two terms – braided human hair and genealogy – and inviting the viewer to find the similarities between them. The form of the hair braid, especially its extraordinary length, is similar to the uninterrupted flow of the lineage, its ever-increasing length, and its strength. In its technique, the knotless addition of hair to the braids and the combination of many strands of hair into one tight braid evoke ancestral continuity, the seamless joining of the current generation to those of the past.

Like the stylistic virtuosity discussed by Gell, the captivating metaphorical virtuosity of *tamau* hinges on a challenge to understanding. Metaphoric representation relies on a play of similarity and distance, or likeness and difference between index and prototype – in this case, braided human hair and the lineage. The metaphor and its referent must belong to different spheres, despite their likeness on some level, in order for the metaphor to be effective (Lodge 1977: 75). Danto describes this distance between the metaphor and its referent somewhat differently. He draws on Aristotle's explanation of a metaphor as finding a middle term *t* (a similar idea or image) so that if *a* is metaphorically *b*, there must be some *t* such that *a* is to *t* what *t* is to *b*. The mind is moved to action as the viewer is prompted to find that middle term, to fill the gap (Danto 1981: 171). For Ricoeur, too, the reader (or viewer) is also active, assimilating the metaphor by bringing imagination into play, by '*making* similar, that is, semantically proximate, the terms that the metaphorical utterance brings together' (Ricoeur 1979: 146).

The *tamau* works metonymically to represent the lineage because each body, each person, was both the summation and the dissemination of the lineage in Tahitian society. In this perspective, the individual's personhood is fractal, for he or she is not a unit standing in relation to an aggregate, or vice versa, but always an entity with relationship integrally implied (Wagner 1991: 163). Because the hair of any one person is also part of the hair of (and so the persons of) all others in the lineage, living or dead, *tamau* can index on a metonymic principle of contiguity the lineage and all its members. Gell, too, draws on this notion of fractal personhood to explain the ways that Polynesian sculptures incorporating subsidiary figures, like the Rurutuan figure of A'a and the Rarotongan staff god, visually express genealogical principles (1998: 139–40).[13]

Like metaphor, metonymy exercises the imagination in that it asks the viewer to follow the artist's creative process of selection. The viewer understands that the metonymic expression is not literally truthful, and engages in a process of sense creation to make it comprehensible – that is, to connect the index with the prototype (Gibbs 1994: 336–7). Metonymy often works in two ways: first, by personalizing a complicated issue and, second, by encouraging the viewer to make generalizations from the specific (Chantrill and Mio 1996: 173–4, Eco 1984: 117). Through this metonymy, *tamau* enables the viewer to connect to and make concrete several complicated and abstract ideas: the existence of a vast and ancient lineage and its continuing relevance and presence in this world. *Tamau*'s status as regalia, the ways that it was worn on the body, reinforces this indexical process.

Tamau is not an isolated art form in making use of metaphoric and metonymic representation in this way. A number of very important Tahitian artworks index the lineage by similar means, through the combination of material from the body, remarkable length, and a technique of accretion. Perhaps the most significant of these was a small number of feather-girdles, no longer extant, that could be claimed only by the highest ranking titleholders.[14] Anywhere from ten to twenty feet long, the girdles were composed of small squares of red and yellow feathers set on a barkcloth foundation (Figure 4.3).[15] Henry describes how a lappet was added to a feather girdle upon the accession of a new titleholder (1928: 189). Thus, in ways similar to *tamau*, the girdle's remarkable length and its additive principle of construction both metaphorically indexed the ever-growing lineage. The materials of the feather girdle are also metonymic in ways similar to the human hair of *tamau*. Titleholders were descendants of the gods, who were often conceptualized as having feather-covered bodies (Henry 1928: 339, see also Gell 1998: 112–13), so that the feathers of a girdle were the exuviae of the lineage, just like the hair that compose *tamau*.

As the viewer experiences these complex processes of figuration in *tamau* or feather girdles, there is a tension between secrecy and revelation – between understanding and incomprehension – because of the gap created by bringing two

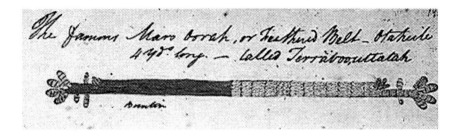

Figure 4.3 William Bligh. *The famous Maro Oorah, or Feathered Belt – Otaheite/4 Yds long – called Terràboo, uttatah.* 1792. Watercolour on paper (31.4 × 19.7 cm.). State Library of New South Wales, Sydney

spheres together metaphorically, or by moving from the part to the whole metonymically. Even as it stimulates new ideas and new understandings, the metaphor or metonym may not be easily comprehensible, and purposefully so. Far from being a simple, straightforward representation of the 'facts' of the prototype, an index that incorporates metaphor or metonymy is necessarily rich with imagination and feeling, as Ricoeur has observed (1979).[16] Or, to put it another way, a metaphor or metonym is at once a source of clarity and an enigma in that it has the capacity to generate unlimited semiosis (Eco 1984: 102, 123–4). This is one source of the captivation of the artwork, for it attracts and sustains the interest of the viewer through the continual presentation of new possibilities, new ways of understanding the metaphoric and metonymic connections between index and prototype.

The extent to which the viewer can follow the artist's virtuoso handling of visual metaphor and metonymy depends not only on the viewer's powers of imagination, but also on the viewer's contextual knowledge, what Eco calls the 'sociocultural format of the interpreting subjects' encyclopaedia' (1984: 127). The indexical potential of *tamau*, for example, was probably understood differently by artists, *taio* friends, or *hura* dancers based on their general cultural knowledge, position in the lineage, and role in the making or wearing of *tamau*, all of which were determined at least partly by factors such as age and gender. Metaphor and metonymy make clear the contextual and interpretative nature of even such a fundamental process as identifying the prototype represented by the indexical artwork.[17] Interpretation and signification cannot be separated out – especially in a Peircean formulation, for the interpretant is the essential third element in any sign.[18] That Gell, in his discussion of idols, can only identify the *to'o* as 'Oro on the basis of information that lies outside the object itself is an indication of the difficulty of engaging in a purely non-interpretative identification of the index, whatever the theoretical desirability of doing so (1998: 109–10).[19]

I want to return briefly here to two key elements of Gell's theoretical project, his rejection of linguistic modes of interpretation and the search for meaning, since my emphasis on the centrality of interpretation in signification could be seen as reintroducing both of these approaches. The interpretation of metaphoric and metonymic representation certainly does not require the kind of Saussurian linguistic semiotics to which Gell objects, in which works of art are simply vehicles of meaning that viewers decipher according to a pre-established code. Interpretation is a multivalent process, not a mere matter of recognizing a stable equivalence (Eco 1984: 42–3). This is, of course, why Gell himself turns to the process of abduction to explain the ways that viewers infer the social agency in the sign (1998: 14–16). In the end, metaphoric and metonymic representations suggest that the interpretation of the indexical artwork is not a reductive search for meaning. Grounded in the artwork's specific visual and material qualities, interpretation is a fundamental aspect of its action and its agency, both in its originating context and in the context of art history or anthropology.

The contextual nature of interpretation, that indispensable third part of the sign, is also why metaphors and metonyms can go not only stale but dead (Danto 1981: 174; Eco 1984: 100–1, 127–8). As cultures change, viewers may lose access to essential elements needed to make the conceptual leaps and connections demanded by metaphoric and metonymic representations. The limits to cognition come not only in the form of the virtuosity of the artist, whose creative use of metaphor and metonymy challenges the viewer's ability to comprehend the work, but also in the form of lost history that makes understanding all but impossible.

This has certainly been the case with eighteenth-century *tamau*. Any attempt to understand these objects faces the challenge of their transfer from Tahiti to European museums, their storage over two centuries, and the many changes that occurred in Tahitian culture in the meantime, including evangelization and colonization. We contemporary observers have lost the ability to be captivated by *tamau*, not just because they became tangled and brittle with age, but because the metaphoric and metonymic connections between index and prototype were ruptured. Once we can begin to feel and imagine again the metaphor and metonymy of *tamau*, we create our own susceptibility to their captivation.

Notes

1. Gell's argument accords with recent theoretical developments within the discipline of art history critiquing the idea that artworks are passive, that they simply exist *in* a previously constituted social context (Bryson 1994). Art history

has also engaged productively with Peircean semiotics in recent years (see, for example, Bal and Bryson 1991, Moxey 1994).

2. Gayatri Spivak makes this same distinction toward different ends in 'Can the Subaltern Speak?' (Spivak 1988: 275–7). Engaged in a critique of Deleuze and Foucault's concept of the intellectual, Spivak derives from Marx's 'Eighteenth Brumaire' the distinction between *darstellen* and *vertreten*, to represent tropologically and to represent politically. For Spivak, these modes of representation are always complicit yet cannot be elided (see also Spivak 1990: 6, 108–9, Landry and MacLean 1993: 6).

3. Elsewhere Gell does acknowledge the insights to be gained from iconographic analysis (1992: 42–3).

4. Gell takes up the question of style and meaning later on in *Art and Agency*, when he elaborates the idea of 'axes of coherence' that connect artistic style with other systematic properties of culture (1998: 155–68).

5. Along these lines, Danto has pointed out that while both textual and visual metaphors represent subjects, properties of the mode of representation itself must be a constituent in understanding them (1981: 189). A visual metaphor of this type is Picasso's use of a toy car to represent a baboon head in his sculpture *Baboon and Young* (1950), which Gell cites as an example of an artist's technical virtuosity in non-illusionistic mode (Gell 1992: 52–3). Picasso's toy car is a visual metaphor for a baboon head, for its effectiveness depends on the principle of substitution on the basis of similarity – in this case, an amusing formal similarity. We can understand it as such without pursuing a search for meaning or applying linguistic models of representation.

6. This is, of course, a very ancient understanding of metaphor, one that traces its origins to Aristotle, who asserted in the *Poetics* that creating metaphors 'is a sign of a natural disposition of the mind' (cited in Eco 1984: 101).

7. In fact, as Mageo points out, the symbolic value of human hair has been a subject of some concern in cultural anthropology (1994: 408–10, see also Hiltebeitel and Miller 1998). She notes two basic concerns in this literature, which theorizes both the comparability of body symbols between cultures and also the communicative value of hair intraculturally, as a public symbol that individuals adopt to conceptualize and express private complexes.

8. According to Roger Rose, these hair girdles were made of thicker braids than the *tamau*, with up to eighty strands of hair per ply (Rose 1971: 260).

9. When Purea gave *tamau* to Wallis and his officers, she placed the bundles around their necks. While this was not a customary way to wear *tamau*, Purea's gesture seems to affirm that they were meant to be worn and were not simply relics to be stored away with other treasures. Of course, given that Wallis's voyage was the first encounter between Tahitians and Europeans, Purea could have been improvising to a certain extent in this situation. It would have been at the very

least highly unusual, if not completely unprecedented, to engage in formal *taio* friendship with more than one person in a particular situation. However, given Purea's political ambitions for herself and her young son, and the many radical innovations she undertook in trying to achieve them, it would be characteristic for her to attempt to monopolize these foreigners (see Oliver 1974: III: 1217–25).

10. William Wilson, of the missionary ship *Duff*, does assert that *tamau* were worn only by women dancers and were made of the hair of the deceased (Wilson 1966: 338). Wilson is certainly mistaken on the first count, as *tamau* are documented in a variety of contexts. He is probably also mistaken on the second count, for he is the only source to make this assertion.

11. As described below, Samuel Wallis and his officers received *tamau* during the *Dolphin*'s 1767 visit to Tahiti, but none of these seem to have survived.

12. Two very fine nets of braided human hair cord, similar to the cord that makes up *tamau*, were also collected on Cook's and Vancouver's voyages; a netting needle threaded with human hair in the Australian Museum, Sydney is also associated with the Cook voyages (D'Alleva 1997: 540–4, 636–7).

13. The subsidiary figure also appears in Society Islands art, most notably in the columns of stacked figures displayed on *marae* and smaller versions used on canoes. Several bone fly-whisk handles and stone *ti'i* depict a larger figure holding a smaller figure over the stomach.

14. After the widespread establishment of Christianity in the early nineteenth century, most titleholders buried the girdles in their *marae* (Henry 1928: 195). Feather girdles sent to the London Missionary Society at that time by Tamatoa of Ra'iatea and by John Williams have since been lost (Henry 1928: 189, n. 46; Montgomery 1832: II: 125).

15. In his third-voyage journal, Cook describes in detail the girdle later depicted by Bligh:

> ... it was about five yards long and fifteen inches broad, and composed of red and yellow feathers but mostly of the latter; the one end was bordered with eight pieces, each about the size and shape of [a] horse shoe, with their edges fringed with black pigeon feathers; the other end was forked and the ends not of the same length. The feathers were in square compartments ranged in two rows and otherways so desposed as to have a good effect being first paisted or fixed to thier Country cloth and then the whole sewed to the upper end of the English Pendant, Captain Wallis desplayed, and left flying a shore the first time he landed at Matavai . . . About six or eight inches square of the Maro was not compleat, that is there were no feathers upon it except a few that were sent by Waheatua [Vehiatua] as before mentioned (Cook in Beaglehole 1967: I: 203).

16. Ricoeur asserts that his concept of imagination and feeling is akin to Jakobson's poetic function, the valorization of the message for its own sake (Ricoeur

1979: 142). It is worth noting here that Jakobson sees poetic function as belonging not only to language, but also to the whole theory of signs, including, specifically, the visual arts and film (Jakobson 1960: 350–1).

17. Panofsky makes a similar point in his division of iconology into three stages, a programme that is rather similar in some respects to semiotic forms of enquiry. The first of Panofsky's stages is the pre-iconographic identification of formal motifs. The second is the iconographic identification of conventional subject matter, which connects motifs with themes or concepts. The final stage is iconographic analysis, which searches for intrinsic meaning or content, interpreting motifs and their related concepts to reveal the underlying principles or beliefs of the nation, class, religion, etc. (Panofsky 1972: 5–7, 14–15). Panofsky notes that these first two stages, while focusing on the work of art as such, are nonetheless always dependent not only on perceptual information but also on the viewer's understanding of the work's historical conditions, the social and cultural context in which it was produced (Panofsky 1972: 11). For an analysis of the relationship between Panofsky's iconography and semiotics, see Hasenmueller 1978.

18. For Peirce, the interpretant is an essential component of semiosis, which he defines as 'an action, or influence, which is, or involves, an operation of *three* subjects, such as a sign, its object, and its interpretant, this tri-relative influence not being in any way resolvable into an action between pairs' (*Collected Papers*, cited in Eco 1984: 1). Briefly defined, the interpretant is the sign or sequence of signs generated in response to a sign; the interpretant both translates the content of the sign and increases our understanding of it.

19. Whether Tahitians would have experienced the same difficulty is an interesting question, since *to'o* figures can represent different gods and even the use of red feathers is not exclusively associated with 'Oro. As with *tamau*, the viewer's ability to interpret the relationship between index and prototype would probably have varied according to age, gender, social class, and ritual status.

References

Bal, M. and N. Bryson. 1991. 'Semiotics and Art History'. *The Art Bulletin* 73(2): 174–208.

Beaglehole, J.C. (ed.) 1961. *The Journals of Captain James Cook on his Voyages of Discovery: The Voyage of the Resolution and Adventure 1772–1775.* Cambridge: Cambridge University Press.

—— 1962. *The Endeavour Journal of Joseph Banks 1768–1771.* 2 vols. Sydney: Public Library of New South Wales.

—— 1967. *The Journals of Captain James Cook on his Voyages of Discovery: The Voyage of the Resolution and the Discovery 1776–1780.* 2 vols. Cambridge: Cambridge University Press.

Bligh, W. 1937. *The Log of the Bounty, being Lieutenant William Bligh's log of the proceedings of His Majesty's armed vessel Bounty in a voyage to the South Seas*. 2 vols. London: Golden Cockerel Press.

—— 1961 [1789]. *A Voyage to the South Sea, Undertaken by Command of His Majesty, for the Purpose of Conveying the Breadfruit Tree to the West Indies, in His Majesty's Ship the Bounty, Including an Account of the Mutiny on Board the Said Ship*. New York: New American Library.

Bryson, N. 1994. 'Art in Context', in M. Bal and I.E. Boer (eds), *The Point of Theory: Practices of Cultural Analysis*, 66–78. New York: Continuum.

Carroll, N. 1994. 'Visual Metaphor', in J. Hintikka (ed.), *Aspects of Metaphor*, 189–218. Dordrecht: Kluwer Academic Publishers.

Chantrill, P.A. and J.S. Mio. 1996. 'Metonymy in Politics', in J.S. Mio and A.N. Katz (eds), *Metaphor: Implications and Applications*, 171–84. Mahwah, NJ: Lawrence Erlbaum Associates, Publishers.

Cook, J. and J. King. 1784. *A Voyage to the Pacific Ocean Undertaken by the Command of His Majesty, for Making Discoveries in the Northern Hemisphere . . . Performed under the Direction of Captains Cook, Clerke and Gore, in His Majesty's Ships the Resolution and Discovery, in the Years 1776, 1777, 1778, 1779 and 1780*. London: G. Nichol and T. Cadell.

D'Alleva, A. 1997. Shaping the Body Politic: Gender, Status, and Power in the Art of Eighteenth-century Tahiti and the Society Islands. Unpublished PhD thesis. Columbia University.

Danto, A.C. 1981. *The Transfiguration of the Commonplace: A Philosophy of Art*. Cambridge, Mass.: Harvard University Press.

Davies, J. et al. 1807–1808. [Journal of the Proceedings of the London Missionary Society on Tahiti, August 26, 1807–November 22, 1808.] Unpublished manuscript (South Seas Journals, Box 3, Folder 31). London Missionary Society Archives, School of Oriental and African Studies, London.

Eco, U. 1984. *Semiotics and Philosophy of Language*. Bloomington: Indiana University Press.

Gell, A. 1992. 'The Technology of Enchantment and the Enchantment of Technology', in J. Coote and A. Shelton (eds), *Anthropology, Art, and Aesthetics*, 40–63. Oxford: Oxford University Press.

—— 1998. *Art and Agency: An Anthropological Theory*. Oxford: Clarendon Press.

Gibbs, R.W. 1994. *The Poetics of Mind: Figurative Thought, Language, and Understanding*. Cambridge: Cambridge University Press.

Goodman, N. 1976. *Languages of Art: An Approach to a Theory of Symbols*. Indianapolis: Hackett Publishing Company, Inc.

Hasenmueller, C. 1978. 'Panofsky, Iconography, and Semiotics'. *The Journal of Aesthetics and Art Criticism* 36 (Spring): 289–301.

Henry, T. 1928. *Ancient Tahitian Society*. Honolulu: Bishop Museum Press.

Hiltebeitel, A. and B.D. Miller (eds). 1998. *Hair: Its Power and Meaning in Asian Cultures*. Albany: State University of New York Press.

Hoare, M.E. (ed.). 1982. *The Resolution Journal of Johann Reinhold Forster 1772–1775*. 4 vols. London: The Hakluyt Society.

Jakobson, R. 1956. 'Two Aspects of Language and Two Types of Aphasic Disturbances', in R. Jakobson and M. Halle (eds), *Fundamentals of Language*, 55–82. The Hague: Mouton and Company.

—— 1960. 'Closing Statement: Linguistics and poetics', in T. Sebeok (ed.), *Style in Language*, 350–77. Cambridge, Mass.: The Technology Press of MIT.

Kaeppler, A.L. 1982. 'Genealogy and Disrespect: A Study of Symbolism in Hawaiian Images'. *RES* 3: 82–107.

Lakoff, G. 1993. 'The Contemporary Theory of Metaphor', in A. Ortony (ed.), *Metaphor and Thought*, 202–51. Cambridge: Cambridge University Press.

Lakoff, G. and M. Johnson. 1980. *Metaphors We Live By*. Chicago: University of Chicago Press.

Landry, D. and G. MacLean. 1993. *Materialist Feminisms*. Oxford: Blackwell.

Lodge, D. 1977. *The Modes of Modern Writing: Metaphor, Metonymy, and the Typology of Modern Literature*. London: Edward Arnold.

Mageo, J. 1994. Hair Dos and Don'ts: Hair Symbolism and Sexual History in Samoa. *Man* 29 (June): 407–32.

Mio, J.S. and A.N. Katz (eds). 1996. *Metaphor: Implications and Applications*. Mahwah, NJ: Lawrence Erlbaum Associates, Publishers.

Montgomery, J. 1832. *Journal of Voyages and Travels by the Rev. Daniel Tyerman and George Bennet, Esq., Deputed from the London Missionary Society, to Visit Their Various Stations in the South Sea Islands, China, India, etc., between the Years 1821 and 1829*. 3 vols. Boston: Crocker and Brewster.

Morrison, J. 1935. *The Journal of James Morrison, Boatswain's Mate of the Bounty, describing the Mutiny & Subsequent Misfortunes of the Mutineers, together with an account of the Island of Tahiti*. London: The Golden Cockerel Press.

Moxey, K. 1994. *The Practice of Theory: Poststructuralism, Cultural Politics, and Art History*. Ithaca: Cornell University Press.

Oliver, D. 1974. *Ancient Tahitian Society*. 3 vols. Honolulu: University of Hawaii Press.

—— 1988. *Return to Tahiti: Bligh's Second Breadfruit Voyage*. Melbourne: Melbourne University Press.

Orsmond, J.M. (John Muggridge). n.d. [Notes on Tahiti.] Unpublished manuscript. Mitchell Library, State Library of New South Wales, Sydney.

Panofsky, E. 1972 [1939]. *Studies in Iconology: Humanistic Themes in the Art of the Renaissance*. New York: Harper and Row.

Ricoeur, P. 1979. 'The Metaphorical Process as Cognition, Imagination, and Feeling', in S. Sacks (ed.), *On Metaphor*, 141–57. Chicago: University of Chicago Press.

Rose, R.G. 1971. The Material Culture of Ancient Tahiti. Unpublished PhD thesis. Harvard University.

Sacks, S. (ed.). 1979. *On Metaphor*. Chicago: University of Chicago Press.

Spivak, G.C. 1988. 'Can the Subaltern Speak?' in C. Nelson and L. Grossberg (eds), *Marxism and the Interpretation of Culture*, 271–313. Urbana: University of Illinois Press.

—— 1990. *The Post-Colonial Critic: Interviews, Strategies, Dialogues*. New York: Routledge.

Summers, D. 1988. 'Real Metaphor: Towards a Redefinition of the 'Conceptual' Image', in N. Bryson, M.A. Holly, K. Moxey (eds), *Visual Theory: Painting and Interpretation*, 231–59. Cambridge: Polity Press.

Wagner, R. 1991. 'The Fractal Person', in M. Strathern and M. Godelier (eds), *Big Men and Great Men: Personifications of Power in Melanesia*, 159–73. Cambridge: Cambridge University Press, 1998.

Wallis, S. n.d. His Majesty's Ship Dolphin's Log Book. Unpublished manuscript (Adm 55/35). Public Records Office, London.

Weiner, A.B. 1992. *Inalienable Possessions: The Paradox of Keeping-While-Giving*. Berkeley: University of California Press.

Wilson, J. 1966 [1799]. *A Missionary Voyage to the Southern Pacific Ocean, 1796–1798*. Graz: Akademische Druck und Verlagsanstalt.

What Makes *Singo* Different: North Vanuatu Textiles and the Theory of Captivation

Lissant Bolton

On the island of Ambae, in the western Pacific nation of Vanuatu, women make plaited pandanus textiles.[1] These textiles, which are always dyed red, are pervasive in Ambaean life. Laid out in great heaps on a hamlet plaza during an exchange of valuables, wrapped around the bodies of dancers, textiles act as a visual marker of special occasions. They are also a feature of everyday life in a hamlet. People spread older textiles on the ground to sit on, and there is nearly always evidence of textiles in production. Women prepare pandanus and plait in the hamlet, spreading leaves to dry on a convenient surface (a thatched roof, the top of a concrete water tank), sitting in the shade to transform a mass of spiky pandanus threads into the smooth surface of a woven textile. Hidden in the houses (into which visitors never trespass) great baskets hang suspended from the rafters. In them a woman stores her textile wealth, prepared for the exchanges which form the basis of all significant social occasions. Also stored carefully in the house are the special textiles which mark an individual's achievements in the status-alteration systems which have been, and to some extent still are, the ritual focus of Ambaean life. Such special textiles, which operate somewhat like the hood on an academic gown, are nowadays only worn on important occasions, and are often lent from one person to another. In the past, everyone made the payments necessary to acquire one, and then the further payments necessary to earn the right to wear it.

Ambaeans do not perceive textiles as a unitary category: they classify them separately. These things are, to an Ambaean, as self-evidently distinct from each other as carpets and shawls are to a European. There is no language term in North East Ambaean which refers to all the textiles women make from pandanus: no word meaning 'textile'. Rather they fall into four groups: *maraha, qana,* clothing textiles, and *singo. Maraha* are high-value exchange items and are used to wrap the dead. *Qana* are used when new as exchange valuables of lesser importance, and when they are taken out of the exchange system are used as domestic furnishings – to sit upon and sleep under. Some *qana* also have specific roles in ritual contexts. A third category, textiles worn as clothing, has fallen into disuse with the introduction of European cloth. Textiles in this category still exist, but the distinctions between them and textiles in other categories are becoming blurred. If there is an overall name for this category, I have never learnt it. Finally, there are the *singo* – textiles that are used to symbolize and confer status or rank.

The differences between the objects in these categories are not, to the ignorant eye, immediately evident in their material form. In appearance they are rather similar, consisting generally of two longitudinal panels, joined side by side with a seam, often decorated with tassels at the ends, and fringes along the sides. They do vary in length from a metre to about 100 metres, but in width from .4m to 1.5m only. Many consist of plain weave (one over one), but some have designs plaited into them using float weaves (where one thread passes over two or more opposing threads). After they are plaited they are dyed red, either in a single wash of colour or with largely geometric designs imposed on them using stencils.

If there are differences between these four categories, there is one category which is more different than others, and that is the category *singo*. *Singo* are far more different to the other categories than those categories are to each other. This is because *singo* are fundamentally dangerous objects, especially when they are being made. They should be handled with care, being able to inflict a number of illnesses upon mishandlers. No one, broadly speaking, should own or use a *singo* who has not paid for the right to do so, and, by the same token, those who have paid for those rights obtain a kind of status which is both conferred and expressed by using them. One of the enduring questions of my research on Ambae has been the question: what makes *singo* different? Why, when the range of visible difference between *singo* and other textile categories is roughly the same as the range of visible difference between each of the other categories, do *singo* have this powerful character?

Within his anthropological theory of art, Alfred Gell proposes that some art objects have a particular form of agency which he calls captivation. Gell's formulation of captivation offers insights which address my question about what makes *singo* different. My discussion in this chapter is thus both a consideration of Gell's concept of captivation, and an application of it to the question of *singo*.

Captivation

In *Art and Agency*, Gell sets out to devise a specifically anthropological theory of art – that is, one which addresses the role of art objects in the social process. He focuses on the way in which objects exercise agency, mediating and entering into social relations between and with persons. The problem with which most theories of art struggle is the problem of how to securely identify certain objects from among all others as art. Aesthetic judgement, semiotic efficacy and institutional inclusivity (what is in art museums) have all been variously proposed as ways to identify art objects. Gell's theory sweeps all these identifiers away. Since in this theory an object can be considered as art on the basis of the relationships it mediates, 'art' is no longer an intrinsic status. An object is art on the basis of what it does, not what it is. As a result, 'anything whatsoever could, conceivably, be an art object from an anthropological point of view'. Gell is able to discuss cars and anti-personnel mines as having social agency, and thus as falling into 'the "slot" provided for art objects' in his theory (1998: 7). Thus his theory is not so much a theory of art-objects (conventionally identified) as a theory about all objects.

This approach removes some of the enduring issues inherent in previous anthropological approaches to art. Gell's theory applies to objects from every context, from Marquesan tattoo designs, to a painting by Joshua Reynolds, to a Hindu girl worshipped as the goddess Durga: the problematic distinction between Western and non-Western art has no relevance. Although Gell himself does not discuss this, his theory also obviates the oft-made distinction between objects identified as art and those identified as almost-but-not-art – as craft. There are very few kinds of object that do not mediate social agency, and thus very few objects that cannot be treated as art within the terms of this theory – even a chipped stone found on the beach, can, as Gell himself demonstrates, be found to qualify as a location for the investigation of the social relationships which it mediates or indexes (1998: 16). Throughout, Gell uses the term 'index' to refer to objects which have agency in relationships.

Gell's theory thus addresses that other anthropological category, material culture, quite as much as it does art, and in doing so addresses a proposition that has been debated for some time by those concerned with this category. This is the argument that, since what is significant about an object is the social relationships which surround it, the object itself is not important. As Marilyn Strathern observes, in such analyses objects become 'merely illustration'. Strathern elaborates her point by arguing that 'if one sets up social context as the frame of reference in relation to which meanings are to be elucidated, then explicating that frame of reference obviates or renders the illustrations superfluous' (1990: 38). In attributing social agency to objects, albeit a 'kind of second class agency' (1998: 17) Gell provides a way to interlink object and context. More to the point, Gell proffers an analytical model by which the agency of objects can be investigated. And, to reiterate the point, his approach allows not just for what people do through objects, but what the objects themselves do, which makes them far from merely illustrative.

However, while acknowledging that 'theoretically, there is no limit to the kind of agency which can be mediated by indexes' Gell avers that 'it would be disingenuous on my part to suggest that I do not attach more priority to certain types of agency than to others' (1998: 68). If his theory makes it possible to attribute agency to a chipped stone found on the beach, he is nevertheless principally concerned with objects that are 'recognisably works of art' – that is, objects whose making is 'a particularly salient feature of their agency' (1998: 68). At this point, he develops what can perhaps be understood as the theory within the theory. If agency can be attributed to most objects, it is the particular kind of agency which Gell calls captivation that interests him most. He defines captivation as 'the demoralisation produced by the spectacle of unimaginable virtuosity', as the effect created by being unable to comprehend the origination of the object (1998: 71).

Captivation is a special case of agency. In creating this special case, Gell is producing, at a different level, a distinction which looks very much like the distinction between material culture and art. He observes 'where indexes are very recognizably works of art, made with technical expertise and imagination of a very high order, which exploit the intrinsic mechanisms of visual cognition with subtle psychological insight, then we are dealing with a canonical form of artistic agency which deserves specific discussion' (1998: 68). In contrast 'many indexes are crude and uninteresting artefacts, whose importance rests solely on their medi-atory function in a particular social context – for instance the figurines used in African divination' (1998: 68). This seems to be a case of having one's cake and eating it. The idea that some objects are more art-like than others is the root and foundation of the whole problem of the anthropology of art which Gell is attempting to overturn – the idea of the intrinsically 'art-like' character of art. However, although more 'art-like' objects can be explained through the idea of captivation, art-likeness is not the key to this concept. Rather, captivation is a theory which attempts to address a specific kind of agency which, while it can be applied to aesthetically powerful objects, is not exclusive to them.

Although Gell discusses captivation through the concept of aesthetic impact, explicating the term, for example, in a discussion of Vermeer's painting *The Lacemaker*, his formulation of captivation is not solely about aesthetic impact. He discusses the agency of Trobriand canoe prow-boards as captivation. And while the prow-boards are beautifully carved, their efficacy is understood and operated by the Trobrianders as magic. The *dis*connection between captivation and aesthetic impact is made clearer in his chapter six, where Gell discusses decorative art. In decorative art, and specifically in complex decorative figures or designs, Gell finds the same indecipherability, the same unimaginable virtuosity, in the difficulty of holding together in one's mind the 'wholes and parts, continuity and discontinuity, synchrony and succession' of complex designs (1998: 95). The very complexity of the design makes it difficult to comprehend its origination. Captivation occurs where there is 'a certain cognitive indecipherability' (1998: 95) in the object, or indeed, in a performance (of music, of dance).

Gell also reflects on the concept of captivation by discussing some material from Vanuatu. Drawing on Bernard Deacon's ethnography of the island of Malakula, he considers the complex designs known as sand-drawings, commenting that Malakulans 'practiced pattern-construction as an art form, and as part of the typical Vanuatuan male competition to demonstrate knowledge and mastery' (1998: 90).

Observing that 'Melanesian aesthetics is about efficacy, the capacity to accomplish tasks, not "beauty"' (1998: 94), Gell argues that it is the performance of the sand-drawing which is important, the demonstration of mastery of memory and skill. This is 'the demoralisation produced by the spectacle of unimaginable virtuosity' where 'the index embodies agency which is essentially indecipherable' (1998: 71). Captivation is a special kind of agency effected through performance, and embodying indecipherability. As with sand-drawings, so with *singo*, pattern construction lies at the heart of how both operate. The idea of captivation provides an analytical tool to investigate the distinctiveness of *singo*.

Some background

The island of Ambae is in the centre of the northern part of the archipelago on which Vanuatu is based.[2] Oval in shape, and about forty kilometres long, the island is dominated by a dormant volcano at its centre. The central dome of the island, usually shrouded in cloud, is uninhabited, and is considered by Ambaeans to be the place of the dead. The living keep to the lower slopes and ridges of the volcano, and to the shoreline, living in locally defined districts which are distinguishable on the basis of minor linguistic and cultural differences.

East Ambaean social relationships are understood and organized through dispersed exogamous matrimoieties. The two most salient smaller social groups are the immediate group of people connected by descent through mother, daughter, grand-daughter – a group known as *garo*, meaning rope or line – and the collection of people living in a hamlet. This second group most usually consists of a man, his sons and their families, living together on land to which the group holds use rights. Hamlets are considered private space: people do not visit each other's hamlets unless connected by close kin ties, or to attend a formal occasion of some kind (a marriage, a meeting). All formal social occasions apart from meetings, church services and traditional court hearings involve exchanges between members of the two moieties: marriages, funerary ceremonies, adoptions, and so on always involve the exchange of goods.

Although pigs and food are also sometimes exchanged, these occasions are dominated by pandanus textiles, and at important occasions such as marriages many hundreds of textiles are exchanged. Although men do exchange *maraha* (the most valuable exchange items), women are the principal exchangers of textiles. Indeed a woman without a textile to contribute would be ashamed to attend such an occasion. The production of the textiles is labour-intensive, involving harvesting, drying and softening the pandanus, plaiting the threads together one by one, and subsequently dyeing the completed fabric. The most valuable textiles can be up to one hundred metres long, and most last only about three years: textile production is a very significant component of women's work. In laying their textiles on the hamlet plaza women are presenting, and demonstrating, their very considerable labour.

In the east Ambae district of Longana (the area from which I am drawing the account here), there are twenty-five named textile types, each of which falls into one of the four categories I outlined earlier. These twenty-five types are distinguished from each other on the basis of the woven form – most frequently on the basis of discriminations between different kinds of selvage edges or fringes on the long sides of the textile. Within each category, each named textile type has a distinctive set of uses. They are distinguishable in the same way, for example, as different models of car made by the same manufacturer. As different car models have different purposes and different values (as a Toyota Land-Cruiser is different to a Toyota Corolla) so the different textile types within each category have different purposes and values. There are thus about eight different kinds of *maraha* (the high-value exchange valuables), each separately named and identified. People understand and operate with these categories and types with a fine and calculated discrimination about which textile to give and when. A person only distantly connected to the one of the parties in a marriage, for example, will participate in the occasion by contributing a *qana*, those more closely connected will give some *qana* and one or more of the low-value *maraha*. A woman whose brother is to be married will spend up to a year before the ceremony feverishly plaiting exchange textiles of all types so that she can walk onto the hamlet plaza with a large basket of all of them on her head. In all these contexts it is not the individual textile which matters, but the kind of textile that it is. It is not a case, as it is in other parts of the Pacific, where individual textiles are named and have known histories of ownership and transmission.

Although both *maraha* and *qana* are dyed, they are not dyed in the same way. *Maraha* are dyed by being dipped in a dyebath, resulting in a pink wash over the surface of the fabric. *Qana* however are dyed with stencils, using a technique – log-wrap stencil dyeing – which is unique to north Vanuatu. Two types of stencils are used on Ambae. *Qana* are always dyed with *bwagavi* stencils, which are cut in a prepared section of banana spathe. The *qana* is wrapped around a special log of wood, (so that it looks rather like a Christmas cracker), and the stencil is tied carefully over the textile, using a rope which is permeable to the dye. The whole is then placed in a dye bath and boiled. The stencil is destroyed by this process, so that new stencils have to be cut for every *qana*. While theoretically this offers the opportunity to cut new designs in every stencil, in fact only a limited number of stencil designs can be applied to each *qana* type. Thus for example the *vule* or moon design can only be used on *qana vivi*, while the *matanaho* or rising sun design can only be used on *qana vuvulu*.

Today, *qana* designs have no especial significance. I was never able to elicit either stories or meanings for them beyond the simple identification of the design name. They seemed to act rather as a floral design does on a length of cotton cloth – being pleasing but without significance. I suspect (partly on the basis of examination of museum collections) that in the past these designs had a significance which has now disappeared, but there is no prescription, where *qana* are used in exchange, about which design should be used on which occasion. A *qana vuvulu* with *matanaho* would do as well as one with the *kavtingqe* (red-spotted crab) design on it at a wedding or a funeral.

The only instance in which designs have significance today is in the case of a special *qana* type known as *qana hunhuni*. When a girl is married the ritual pays considerable attention to her actual transfer from her natal hamlet to that of her husband. She is leaving one place, and going to become part of another. As the moment of her departure from her own hamlet approaches, she is dressed in new clothes, oiled and decorated by her mother and mother's sisters, and given a last meal to celebrate the nurturing she has received in her home and to which she will no longer have access in the same way. Then she is led out and sat down on a stool on the hamlet plaza, and her classificatory fathers and fathers' sisters bring textiles of the special type known as *qana hunhuni* – umbrella *qana* (see Figure 5.1). They place these *qana* on her head and she holds them there as she makes the transition first to her new hamlet, and then across the central plaza of that hamlet, and into her new family. In placing the *qana* on her head her fathers are acting to protect her (and especially her head, the most sacred part of her body) from danger. My understanding of that danger is that it lies in the vulnerable space of transition, the moments of belonging nowhere. There are other contexts in which, in moments of ritual danger, people hold textiles over their heads to protect themselves. Usually, it is the group of textiles known as short *maraha* that are used to provide this protection. *Qana hunhuni*, however, are always used to cover the bride's head, and they are only used protectively in this context.

The women making *qana hunhuni* always do so for a specific girl. For Gell this would be a case where the prototype determines the artist's production of the index, which then has protective agency over the recipient, the girl. In fact, many more relationships are indexed in this use of this textile, not least the protective care of the girl's father's moiety and specifically his *garo*, his line, for her. *Qana hunhuni* are very similar in appearance to two other kinds of *qana* (*qana maho* and *qana vivi*), and are decorated with the stencil designs appropriate for those two *qana* types. However, the stenciled design on a *qana hunhuni* is carefully chosen for each bride: each design has a known meaning in this context, which acts as a message to her new family. This is an interpretative phrase, which is read from the design. It might comment on the girl's own merit, or, for example, on the fact that the groom must now settle down and cleave to his wife. In the past, the design on at least one of the *qana hunhuni* given alluded to the tattoo designs embellishing the girl's own body, and in particular to the secret design tattooed on

Figure 5.1 Susanne Woivire sitting on the hamlet plaza at Saraisese, holding a *qana hunhuni* on her head, prior to leaving for her new husband's hamlet. Longana, east Ambae, 22 May 1992. Photo L. Bolton

her inner thighs. A girl preserves her *qana hunhuni* to wrap her first-born child: the textiles she holds over her head as she arrives in her new home allude to her fertility. Indeed, there is a great richness of metaphor and allusion in the way in which this textile is used which goes beyond the design and message it conveys.

The other case where design is significant is actually the significance of absence: that is, in the use of undyed *qana vuvulu*. Generally textiles in all categories are not considered to be complete, finished, until they have been dyed. However, in some specific contexts the type *qana vuvulu*, which I mentioned earlier, is used undyed, in which case it is known as *qana mavute*, meaning white *qana*. One important use of *qana mavute* is in contexts where knowledge is being imparted.[3] The person learning sits on a white *qana vuvulu*, a *qana mavute*, which assists in his or her ability to absorb knowledge. The night after they are married a couple sit on a *qana mavute* while their fathers' sisters speak to them about married life. This is a kind of sacred or restricted talk, and they must sit on the textile to hear and absorb it. Similarly, a woman who wishes to learn how to make a *singo* brings a *qana mavute* with her and sits down on it to be taught, returning with the same textile each lesson, and giving it to her teacher in payment when she has learnt the skill. If she does not sit on the textile she will not be able to absorb what she is learning. The textile enables the learning process. Here again, in Gell's terminology, the prototype determines the artist's production of the index, which then has agency over the person sitting on it.

Neither the agency of *qana mavute*, nor that of *qana hunhuni*, is what Gell means by captivation. In both cases there is a specific agency attached to the textile, but in neither case is this agency a matter of 'the spectacle of unimaginable virtuosity' (1998: 68) in the object. Perhaps, although the analogy is less than flattering to the skills involved in making them, *qana* are more like the figurines used in African divination, which Gell rejects as 'works of art' (p. 68). Of course, *qana hunhuni* should be beautifully made: tightly plaited, neatly shaped, with a clear and evenly dyed stencilled design. I imagine that there might be criticism if a bride arrived in her new hamlet with a badly made *qana hunhuni* on her head, though I never heard any myself. Even so, the making of this textile is not 'a particularly salient feature' of its agency. It could protect the bride even if it was badly made. Likewise *qana mavute* do not have to be well made to have agency in assisting the absorption of knowledge, it is their undyed (absorptive) state that is significant. Acknowledged virtuosity – the virtuosity of the design – is, however, a factor in the operation of *singo*.

Singo

Despite the importance of exchanges, the major life preoccupation for most people in east Ambae, as in all of north Vanuatu, has been and to a lesser extent still is, a lifelong cycle of status-alteration rituals. By performing these rituals, individuals achieve greater and greater social, economic, spiritual and political power and authority. These rituals are commonly described in the anthropological literature as 'graded societies', and are generally treated as the preoccupation of men.

However, although women's status-alteration rituals were less dramatic and hence less visible, they were and are important throughout the region. On Ambae there are two principal status-alteration systems, the *huqe* and the *huhuru*. *Singo* are important to both rituals, but there are two kinds of *singo*, *singo tuvegi* and *singo maraha*, and one is connected to the *huqe* while the other is key to the *huhuru*. *Singo tuvegi* are worn by grade-takers in the *huqe*, while the *huhuru* turns upon *singo maraha*.

The *huqe* is the men's status-alteration system, based on pig exchange and pig-killing, which involves a sequence of ten specified grades or steps. It takes a man his entire lifetime to progress through these grades, and only some men reach the last. Until the last decade or so, the *huqe* was the principal focus of men's lives in east Ambae. At the achievement of each grade a man earns certain rights which represent his new status. These include a new name, new privileges in the community of men, rights to eat certain food, and the right to new items of attire. One of the most important of all of these is a textile which he wears suspended from his belt at the front. This is the particular kind of *singo* known as *singo tuvegi*.

Finely plaited and highly decorative, *singo tuvegi* are about a metre long and forty centimetres wide. The textile is presented to the grade-taker by his classificatory father with a branch of decorative leaves immediately before he kills the pig (see Figure 5.2). The grade-taker dons the textile, sticking the leaves in his belt at the back, and steps forward to kill the pig. Thereafter he has the right to wear the textile, and the leaf type – a right implemented today mainly on occasions when people dance local dances. *Singo tuvegi* operate, as I mentioned earlier, on the same principle as the hood on an academic gown. There are a number of different *singo tuvegi* types, which mark the different grades of the *huqe*. Significantly, whereas *qana* and *maraha* types are distinguished from each other largely on the basis of the fringes and selvages used on each type (the in-weave and stencil designs being treated as incidental), *singo* are distinguished from each other by the designs they embody. There is not a different textile for each of the ten *huqe* grades, rather the design of the highest *singo tuvegi* is also worked into the shell belt and armbands which are earned at subsequent grade-takings. The relationship of textile to grade varies from district to district.

In Longana, three *singo tuvegi* are now known, of which two are commonly made. The three are *vovaho*, *matai talai*, and *buto vudolue*. The designs are all based on motifs of repeated diamonds and zigzagging lines, the zigzags surrounding and echoing the form of one diamond and gradually resolving so as to create the next. Although to the untrained eye the diamonds appear to be the key to these patterns, for Ambaeans it is the lines which are important – the diamonds are merely the basis around which they are formed. The word for these diamonds is *butogi*, meaning navel. The navel is understood to be seen from above, an aerial

Figure 5.2 *Singo tavalu mataitalai* folded in half over an associated leaf type, waiting to be presented to a grade-taker. Losaraisese, Longana, east Ambae, 21 May 1992. Photo L. Bolton

view. The lines are called *rangagi*, meaning branch. The ways in which the lines zigzag distinguish the different named designs, and these differences are very subtle; I myself took years to learn to distinguish them. Once learnt, however, they are easy to identify.

The distinction between *vovaho* and *matai talai* lies in the way in which the lines pass around the points at the apexes of a series of diamonds. In *matai talai* the lines follow the shape of the diamond as repeating 'V' shapes – like the profile of the clamshell adze blade which gives the design its name. In *vovaho* (the name is untranslatable) the lines surrounding the diamond are squared at the apexes, and the further out from the diamond they get, the longer these squared lines become. The number of diamonds, the number of lines, the way one diamond is resolved into the next, all these issues are subsidiary to the crucial issue of whether the lines are pointed or straight as they pass the apexes of the diamond. *Buto vudolue*, however, literally means 'one hundred *butogi*', 'one hundred navels', and in this case there are many diamonds in the design, the lines zigzagging and resolving from one to the next with considerable visual complexity. *Buto vudolue* is the highest grade *singo tuvegi*. All these designs are visually complex, involving some figure-ground reversals. Especially with designs such as *buto vudolue*, *singo* designs are difficult to comprehend as a whole, in that following one part of the pattern necessarily involves neglecting another.

Unmarried girls take the preliminary junior grades of the *huqe*; each girl takes her last *huqe* grade the day before she is married. On the morning after her marriage, she is introduced to the *huhuru*, the women's status-alteration system. This system is based not on pigs but on the production, display and exchange of pandanus textiles. The *hurhuru* rituals focus on the other kind of *singo*, which is called *singo maraha*. This is not a textile to be worn by a woman, but, somewhat confusingly, it is a textile which is so to speak 'worn' by the highest grade of exchange valuable: by the four most valuable types of *maraha*. It is 'worn' by them in the sense that the *singo maraha* is joined to one end of the *maraha*, and is a necessary completion of it. Some of the designs on the *singo maraha* are identical to the designs on the *singo tuvegi* which the men wear in the *huqe*, although they are called by different names. The question of which design, which *singo maraha*, is added to which *maraha*, is dependent not on the identity of the *maraha* itself, but on the status and rights of the women who make it or commission its making.

Singo maraha are also finely plaited, long and narrow, usually about one and a half metres long, and thirty to sixty centimetres wide. The eight textile types in the *maraha* category are ranked against each other. The four highest-ranking *maraha*, the most valuable textiles only exchanged at very significant occasions such as marriages and funerals, all have *singo* attached to them. These high-value *maraha* are referred to casually as 'long *maraha*', for the very obvious reason that they are very long. All long *maraha* must have a *singo maraha* joined to one end in order to be complete. I once attended a wedding at which a long *maraha* without a *singo maraha* was presented. (It was raining, so the textiles were not unfolded to be presented as normally happens, allowing this absence to go undetected.) When this deceit was discovered the textile was immediately returned with a demand that it be replaced forthwith. Although a long *maraha* without a *singo* is not complete, it is not the case that the two are treated as being one thing. They are distinct entities. This is not least because any woman can plait a long *maraha* but only certain women have the right to produce the *singo*. A woman who makes a long *maraha* must commission and pay a *singo* specialist to make a *singo* for it.

There are four *singo maraha* designs now known and made in Longana. These are *singo tau marino* (*singo* from Malo), *gingini* ('to pinch with the fingers'), *bebe* (moth/butterfly), and *bugu* (several triggerfish species, family *Balistidae*). Although the key to distinguishing these designs is also the shape of the lines, the number and disposition of the diamonds is more significant. *Singo tau marino* is the same pattern as *vovaho*, that is, it is based on squared lines around a diamond. *Gingini*, likewise, is the same pattern as *matai talai*, that is, pointed lines around a diamond. In *gingini* there should be two or three diamonds, navels, side by side. *Bebe* is the same as *gingini* in the disposition of the lines, but is distinct because there is only one diamond at the centre of each panel, not several side by side.

Lastly, *bugu* is distinctive because the lines around the navel are not continuous, but appear rather as blocks of parallel lines which take as their reference point the sides of the diamond.

I have never been given an explanation for the way in which the same designs have different names when they appear on *singo tuvegi* and *singo maraha*, especially given the fact that the same women make both. The explanation may lie with proprietary rights. In the past, some *singo tuvegi* designs were exclusively made only in part of Ambae, and men who needed them for their status-alteration ceremonies would be obliged to trade to that place to obtain them. The very acquisition of the correct *singo* was thus part of the achievement and the challenge of taking a *huqe* grade. *Matai talai*, for example, was only made in the west Ambae district of Nduindui, until at least as late as the Second World War. However, since women did not travel to trade, and since the maker had to be present to dye the *singo maraha* in the *huhuru* ritual, *singo maraha* would always have been produced locally: the design can only have been exclusive when applied to *singo tuvegi*.

Both the *huqe* and the *huhuru* express Ambaean preoccupations with order and ranking, with the creation and control of difference. Everything of importance is ranked on Ambae. Men, women, pigs and textiles are all ranked in separate but inter-related systems. Although these ranks are at times seen to be equivalent to one another, and although they may symbolize one another, they cannot be substituted for each other. The different ranks are separate and distinguishable hierarchies. Pigs are ranked with reference to the growth of the pig's tusk, textiles by their plaited form. Men are ranked on the basis of their achievements in the *huqe*, married women by the number of times they have performed the *huhuru*. There is no ranking of the different hierarchies against each other. The different kinds of pig and the different types of textile constitute different orders of value. Women's ranks are not subordinate to men's ranks but are distinct from them. A man may even stand a little in awe of his wife's achievements in the *huhuru*. Likewise, there is no point of reference between *singo tuvegi* and *singo maraha*: they cannot be ranked against each other.

Both kinds of *singo* are distinguished by the use of a distinctive plaiting technique in their production. This is a technique in which the pandanus threads are floated, wrapped and transposed so as to create a raised effect, not unlike bas-relief, which can be called overweave (see Figure 5.3).[4] This technique is itself somewhat mazelike – it is very difficult, when looking closely at a *singo*, to trace the route of an individual pandanus ribbon, as it loops, bends backwards, and reappears at a distance, all in a diagonal progression across the fabric. *Singo* are also dyed using a distinctive stencil type, known as *gigilugi*. Unlike the *bwagavi*, the banana-spathe stencil, which is cut as a whole, the *gigilugi* stencil is built up using lengths of cut leaf stem, and small pieces of banana spathe. The stencil is cut to fit the in-weave design, so that the raised surface is highlighted with colour.

Figure 5.3 Margaret Solomon plaiting a *singo*, creating the raised design surface. Longana, east Ambae, November 1991. Photo: L Bolton

Singo is the only textile type in which the patterns stencilled onto the fabric are connected to the designs plaited into it, and it is the only textile type where these designs are significant to the textile-type template. And as only some women have the right to make *singo*, so also only those women have the right to make *gigilugi* stencils.

The crucial characteristic of all *singo* is that they are considered to be inherently dangerous, capable of inflicting various kinds of harm on those who handle them incorrectly, including their makers. All *singo* are subject to restrictions on their production, handling and use. A woman who is making, or has even merely touched, a *singo* should wash her hands before she touches food or holds a child. To fail to do so would result in damage to the eyes, and in boils and sores transmitted to herself and others through food, or directly to the child. A *singo* is dangerous from the moment a woman begins to make it, and is in fact most dangerous during production. All the debris from its making, the bits and pieces of left-over pandanus and the rubbish from the stencilling process, must be carefully gathered together and buried at the foot of a fruit-bearing tree. The fruit of the tree can thereafter only be eaten by a person who has paid for the right to eat the restricted food associated with that *singo* type, something which is obtained during the *huhuru* ceremony. The power of *singo* is such that a person should not even step over a long *maraha* which has a *singo* attached to it, for fear of the harm it could inflict on them.

The women's status-alteration ceremony, *huhuru*, involves the dyeing of a suite of at least eleven *maraha* (of several prescribed types), the preparation of food specific to the ritual, and an exchange of textiles between the woman and her husband and his family. The focus of the occasion is the dyeing of the *singo* for the long *maraha* – *huhuru* actually means 'to make red'. In the Longana district the different *huhuru* ceremonies are distinguished solely by the identity of the *singo* which is dyed in it, and the restricted food associated with that *singo* design. It is on the production and celebration of that *singo*, and specifically of its design, that the ceremony turns, even though the ceremony celebrates the woman's productivity in preparing the textiles she needs to mount it.

A woman who wants to take a grade in the *huhuru* must produce the necessary textiles herself (usually with assistance from close female kin), and must commission a *singo*-maker to produce the *singo* to be joined to the long *maraha* she has made, and, on the day, to dye the *singo* and prepare the food associated with it. At the conclusion of the ceremony, the woman presents the textiles she has produced for the ceremony to her husband (and hence his family), as a return for the textiles he and his family gave for her at her marriage. Indeed, women speak of making *huhuru* for their husbands, rather than of making it for themselves, although the status a woman achieves by making *huhuru* for her husband is something that belongs to her alone. In order to take a grade in the pig-killing rituals a man needs the textiles his wife gives him through the *huhuru*, so that a man's grade-taking is dependent to some extent on that of his wife.

A *huhuru* ceremony which I observed was that of a woman from Longana called Lena Jasper. She made the ceremony for two *singo* at one time (which required her to prepare at least twenty *maraha* – a very substantial achievement in itself). Two *singo* specialists came on the day bringing the undyed *singo*. While they carefully worked on the cutting and placing of the stencils, other women helped Lena to dye the *maraha*. The *singo* specialists dyed the *singo*, and then prepared the restricted food. (*Singo* are only joined to long *maraha* after both are dyed.) Then the woman, and those members of her family who were paying for the right to eat the restricted food associated with that *singo*, came holding textiles over their heads, to look at the food. The *singo* specialists talked to them about each *singo* design, its history and its rank.[5] The culminating moment for Lena was when the *singo* were removed from the dye bath. They became her responsbility at this point, and with shy, but palpable pride, she removed the dyeing rope which held the stencil to the textile and both to the dyeing log, and revealed the completed *singo*. This was the moment at which, perceptibly, the honour of the rank passed from the *singo* to the woman. She became a person of greater substance, worthy of respect.

A person taking a grade in the *huqe* does not obtain status directly from the *singo*: the culminating moment is the point at which he kills the pig. However, the *singo tuvegi* is an expression of that grade, it is a visible embodiment of the grade-taker's new status. In the *huqe*, as in the *huhuru*, it is the design itself which is crucial in expressing and embodying rank. In the past a man planning to take a *huqe* grade would commission the making of a *singo*. The rituals associated with this required the man to visit the *singo*-maker to observe the production process, and to listen to the *singo*-maker talking to him about the *singo*.[6] The commissioning process also, it appears, involved the preparation of restricted food specific to the *singo*, just as restricted food is still prepared for the *singo maraha*, but this is now largely forgotten.

The Distinctiveness of *Singo*

Only very rarely have I heard an Ambaean admire a textile in terms of its appearance, its aesthetic appeal. People derive considerable pleasure from seeing piles of new *maraha* and *qana* laid out on a hamlet plaza during a marriage exchange, and in a myth about the origin of the north Ambae textile known as *vola walurigi* it is admired as being very beautiful. However, I do not recall ever hearing anyone admire a *qana* or a *maraha*. Exchanges, especially at marriage, now involve literally hundreds of textiles, the sheer quantity militates against the admiration of any individual object.

The appearance of *singo* operates a little differently. Nowadays women admire carefully preserved older *singo* for their skilful and fine plaiting, and the precision of the stencilling. In general, however, people do not admire *singo* in aesthetic terms. The focus of Ambaean interest in *singo* is both implicitly and explicitly on the designs, and, in particular, it concerns the idea of their power, power to confer and embody rank, and power to harm. This is not the power of Trobriand canoe prow-boards – there is no explicit magic associated with the making of *singo*. Nor is it the purposeful power of Asmat shields, intended to produce terror in the enemy (Gell 1998: 6). A *singo* has a power which inheres in it from the moment that the maker puts the first two ribbons of pandanus together to begin plaiting it, and this is a power to harm, not enemies, or others, but the maker herself and anyone else around her who might touch the textile. This power is concentrated during the period of its manufacture. A *singo* is most potent while it is being produced, until it is paid for and the restricted food is made for it.

It is this power which puzzles me about *singo*. My question is in fact not so much what makes *singo* different as what makes them powerful. I have never succeeded in eliciting an Ambaean exegesis of the source of this power, beyond the slightly surprised response that (self-evidently) the power comes from the *singo*. There are no spirits or other external powers invoked in discussion either of the making of *singo* or in the related rituals. Equally, the power of the *singo* is not linked to any narratives. Although there are some stories about the origin and distribution of *singo* designs, these do not occur consistently. The *singo tuvegi* design *vovaho*, for example, has no known meaning at all. Neither I, nor the linguist Catriona Hyslop, was able to obtain a translation or explanation of the name (Hyslop personal communication 1999). Stories about *singo*, where I was able to obtain them, are more about how certain men introduced a new *singo tuvegi* design into their own *huqe* in a bold act of innovative flair than they are about a story which the design might represent. The design thus operates in a different field of significance: it has a visual import rather than a narrative meaning.

It could be hypothesized that the power of *singo* is a function of the technically complex overweave technique, knowledge of which is formally restricted to just a few women. However, there is some evidence to suggest that in the past in Longana, and in the present in other districts, there were or are *singo* the designs of which are not worked using the overweave technique. Moreover, when talking about the power of *singo*, women do not nominate the overweave technique itself as powerful, and in fact not all women even know a name for it. It seems that it is the design which the textile embodies which is important. The designs represent and embody rank, it is the designs for which the restricted food is prepared, and it is the designs about which the makers speak to the person commissioning the *singo*. However, if it is the designs that are important, this is not an importance related to meaning or narrative.

The idea of cognitive indecipherability is contextually dependent: a design may seem dazzling in one visual context and not in another. Set against other decorative patterns and mazes in chapter six of *Art and Agency*, *singo* designs may not appear to exhibit too unimaginable a virtuosity. However, on Ambae, nothing else offers the same kind of untraceable visual complexity. Even sand-drawings are comprehensible as a line followed. If one investigated closely the indecipherability of *singo* designs and their origination, it might be easy to argue that the designs are not so very complex, and the technical skills which produce them not so very hard to acquire. But the skills are protected by many restrictions, which allow only certain women to produce them, and the complexity of the plaiting, and of the designs themselves, are dazzling, it seems to me, and all the more so in contrast to other Ambaean textiles.

Gell's suggestion that cognitive indecipherability is linked to performance also resonates with this material. It is significant that so much is made of the act of making the textiles. Makers used to actually perform the plaiting of *singo tuvegi* (and possibly also of *singo maraha*) requiring the person commissioning the textile to sit down with them and watch the textile being made. Moreover, the whole women's status-alteration ritual, the *huhuru*, turns upon and celebrates the dyeing of a specific *singo* design. Indeed *singo maraha* are most powerful while they are being made; after the rituals are over their power is more subdued. I do not think that these occasions are concerned specifically with admiring the technique of manufacture: I suggest that they represent a celebration of the performance of the design.

The idea that it is in the performance of *singo* designs that the power of these objects is located resonates with the role of designs throughout north Vanuatu. This is not only to do with the performance of sand-drawings in ritual and religious contexts, for elsewhere in the region patterns are produced in association with membership of secret societies, and other kinds of arcane knowledge. It is significant, however, that, for *singo* at least, these designs have no articulate meanings.

Gell's exposition of captivation allows for a visually complex design to have a significance which is to do with its visual form, and specifically its form as it is performed. *Singo* have agency, agency to harm and agency to confer and embody rank. The relationship between the power and status of the *singo* and the power and the status of the person is complex. However, what the theory of captivation does is to allow us to take the idea of the power of the *singo* seriously and to recognize that some or all of that power lies *visually* in the design itself, rather than in intellectually comprehended meanings or histories attached to it. The virtuosity, the complexity, and thus especially the performance of the design is formulated, on Ambae, as a dangerous power. The Western imagination allows that some objects do have a power to affect, which is, loosely, referred to as aesthetic power. But once that power is linked to the idea of art – is understood as a property of objects in the category 'art' – then the idea of visual power is restricted to only those objects which are (by whatever definitional frame) identified as belonging to that category. Gell's discussion of the agency of objects, and of the agency of certain objects through qualities of their material form, provides a way to reflect on other ideas about the power of objects. The concept of captivation makes it possible to attend to Ambaean ideas about the distinctiveness of *singo*, without becoming tangled in questions as to whether these objects are, or are not, art.

Notes

1. I was based in the Longana hamlet of Loqirutaro in east Ambae during my doctoral research in 1991–92, returning briefly in 1995 and 1999. Through my ongoing work at the Vanuatu Cultural Centre, and especially through the annual Women Fieldworker Workshops with which I assist, I have also had

ongoing annual discussions with Ambaean women about their knowledge and practice, and especially about textile production and use. In particular I have a significant continuing exchange with Jean Tarisesei, an east Ambaean working as the Women's Culture Project Co-ordinator at the Cultural Centre. I am indebted to Jean for many of the ethnographic insights in this chapter.

2. Vanuatu was formerly the New Hebrides, and was administered by a Anglo-French Condominium Government. It achieved Independence in 1980. The nation's citizens are referred to as ni-Vanuatu.

3. *Qana mavute* are also given with a bride at marriage, and are dyed the morning after the marriage, in a ritual which explicitly prefigures her future participation in the women's status-alteration, *huhuru*.

4. The east Ambaean term for overweave appears to be *walivetu*, although it was hard to establish this term. It appeared to me that women did not generally think of this as a distinctive form of plaiting requiring a separate name.

5. I am constrained in providing details here, as in most parts of east Ambae this is still a highly restricted ritual, details of which should not be divulged. This is very frustrating, as these details would substantially assist me in making the argument of this chapter.

6. This is not (in my experience) a contemporary practice, possibly falling out of use only in recent decades as the importance of the *huqe* has declined. Although the production of *singo maraha* has if anything increased in recent years, due to the increased importance of textiles in exchanges, the production of *singo tuvegi* has declined, and people often now borrow them for grade-takings, rather than commissioning new ones.

References

Gell, A. 1998. *Art and Agency: An Anthropological Theory.* Oxford: Oxford University Press.

Strathern, M. 1990. 'Artefacts of History: Events and the Interpretation of Images', in J. Siikala (ed.), *Culture and History in the Pacific.* Transactions of the Finnish Anthropological Society No. 27. Helsinki: The Finnish Anthropological Society.

−6−

The Captivating Agency of Art: Many Ways of Seeing

Shirley Campbell

It is not by chance that art captivates. It is by design. Just what the captivating agency of art is and how it, still a largely ill-defined genre, succeeds in mesmerizing its audience continues to present philosophical quandaries that have occupied the minds of those who care to look beyond art and ask the questions. Because human beings, as a collective species, seem to have a desire to embellish objects, themselves, and the environment, as well as to create sounds, word and movement patterns which allure select audiences, anthropologists too have become drawn to the captivating effects of art.

Alfred Gell's enduring interest in art as a meaningful yet elusive human activity is well known to all who knew him. In his latest work, and sadly the swansong of his 'oeuvre', he has constructed a significant treatise on art, or as he more boldly declares, on the 'anthropology of art'. In the context of constructing an 'anthropology of art', he has argued for the revival of old tenets distinguishing anthropological theory from other lines of enquiry which delve into human activity. In so doing, few among those who knew him could fail to see the impish grin and bedevilled glimmer in his eyes as his words would, he well knew, taunt those who have written on the subject of art within an anthropological context. He knew that many of his arguments would raise the proverbial 'hackles'. I suspect one of his lingering regrets was that he would not be with us to watch the hotly contested debate he so knowingly would engender.

In *Art and Agency*, Alfred sets out to define what an 'anthropology of art' would look like. In constructing an anthropological theory of art, Alfred's argument steadfastly takes as its point of departure the tenet that 'Anthropology . . . is a social science discipline, not a humanity' (1998: 2–3), albeit, as he admits, an 'elusive' distinction but none the less the sine qua non of an 'anthropology of art'. That is, the focus of any such sub-discipline of anthropology would of necessity be on the 'social context of art production, circulation, and reception . . .' (1998: 3). An 'anthropology of art' then is 'the theoretical study of "social relations in the vicinity of objects mediating social agency" . . .' (1998: 7). This definition does not immediately seem a radical departure from most anthropological analyses of art systems, particularly those analyses developed in the last thirty years of the twentieth century. What is a striking, and to me an exciting genesis of Alfred's thinking about art and its relationship to people within a social context, is Alfred's thesis that the art object (or one presumes 'art experience' if we include non-material artistic expression) becomes a social actor, merging with and standing for human agents and/or other supernatural 'agency' given anthropomorphic vitality by significant human actors. In this sense, Alfred treats art as more than a static object or act, eliciting some kind of response from a public and encoded by what-ever means with information pregnant with often obscure inferences. As a genre, art becomes for the anthropologist an 'actor' positioned within a sea of social activity; at times the passive recipient of activities impressed upon it by human agents with specific ends in mind, while at other times the embodiment of a far more aggressive agency 'acting' upon a passive audience.

In working towards this position, Alfred considered previous intellectual territory anthropologists writing about art have visited. Apart from the early forays into other people's 'art' by anthropologists, which overwhelmingly provided detailed descriptions of material culture, more recent enquires have taken two directions; 'cross-cultural aesthetics' and 'semiotic' approaches (1998: 5–6, 9). Both these approaches Alfred takes exception to on the basis that the theoretical foundations of both have been formulated outside the discipline of anthropology. Therefore these two approaches cannot form the raw material from which an 'anthropology of art' can be struck. 'The aim of anthropological theory is to make sense of behaviour in the context of social relations. Correspondingly, the objective of the anthropological theory of art is to account for the production and circulation of art objects as a function of this relational context' (1998: 11). Alfred's intent is to jettison any approach to the 'anthropology of art' that takes as its starting point anything other than the 'social processes surrounding the deployment of candidate 'art objects' in specific social settings' (1998: 5). Could this prescription for an 'anthropology of art' be too restrictive?

It is doubtful that anyone would contest the fact that art has meaning only within a social environment. Artistic production occurs within a social group, following specific patterns of form and style, encoding intelligible meanings, and judged to be doing so by a rehearsed group of consumers. To restrict any anthropological study of art to a simple description of the craft, to the evaluative processes that may be applied to an art object or act, to the system of signs and symbols that seem invariably to be 'attached' to works of art, or to discussions of the social relationships identified, defined, sustained or mediated by art objects or perform-ances is, if any one approach is preferred over another, to only view part of the whole. More appropriately, it is the 'building up of context' (Kroeber, 1953: 362) utilizing a variety of methodological enquiry that provides the fertile grounds from which art and the people who are captivated by such productions are understood.

Art operates in different ways and at different levels within a single context. Its role within the wider social context extends the complexity of its captivation, and requires a flexible approach that enables various lines of enquiry to be followed. Even the ways in which individuals view, interpret, and are moved by art objects or actions provide few insights into the complexity at which art functions within a sea of social relationships. The levels of efficacy to which we instinctively 'know' art operates can only be revealed by a variety of approaches seeking to understand not only the levels themselves, but also the manner of their efficacy. The means by which anthropologists arrive at any level of understanding of the place of art within a social context requires a variety of programmes for interrogating the material. Cross-cultural aesthetic investigations and semiotic analyses are but two of these programmes. Although Alfred does not entirely relegate these to the rubbish bin, he dismisses them as inappropriate points of departure in any anthropological investigation of art.

The incorporation of a people's evaluative processes, for example, within anthropological discussions of art is not, for Alfred, grounded sufficiently in social interaction, which to his mind, is the stuff of anthropology. '. . . I do not think that the elucidation of *non-western aesthetic systems* constitutes an 'anthropology of art . . . such a programme is exclusively cultural, rather than social' (1998: 2). Alfred argues that any anthropological theory of art must fit within the guidelines that inform anthropological enquiry. 'Distinctively "anthropological" theories have certain defining characteristics, which these accounts of evaluative schemes would lack. Evaluative schemes, of whatever kind, are only of anthropological interest in so far as they play a part within social processes of interaction, through which they are generated and sustained' (1998: 3). But Alfred doubts that, to date, discussions of indigenous aesthetics have been successful in locating indigenous systems of evaluation in the processes of social interaction. In *Art and Agency* Alfred unveils his most cherished of principles, that anthropology is fundamentally about social relationships, resolutely planting the British flag, boldly emblazoned with 'social anthropology' upon the contested ground of what would constitute an 'anthropology of art'.

To Alfred's mind any discussion of aesthetics, be it Western or non-Western, is more appropriately left to other disciplines, who traditionally have laid claim to such intellectual territory. Indeed, Alfred wonders whether the attribution of a non-Western system of aesthetics reflects more upon our own 'quasi-religious veneration of art objects as aesthetic talismans' (1998: 3). He puts the boot in by accusing any such desire to incorporate 'indigenous aesthetics' as misguided attempts to make indigenous art 'meaningful' to Western sensibilities. Certainly there continues to be a demanding public in the West who are ravenous for 'ethnic' or 'primitive' art. Perhaps there is some justification in the accusation that some of what has been written about non-Western art, not always I hurry to add from the pen of anthropologists, has been directed at the contextualization of non-Western art so that Western connoisseurs can 'appreciate', and see 'beauty' in an object, for example, where the intended response by the artist may be something quite different. Western consumers of others' art need the 'stories' behind the works so that they too can 'feel' its captivating effect. This is not, however, why I, and I dare say others are interested in the ways in which other people's art captivates the audiences for which the pieces are constructed or performed. I would argue that the emergent 'anthropology of art', generated by those who have contributed in various ways to descriptions of artistic production, developed systematic and sophisticated analyses of form and style, engaged in the discourse of meaning and context, analysed the social interplay of actors and agency, as well as attempted to elucidate indigenous aesthetics, is not merely directed to a Western audience caught up in its own veneration of art. Those anthropologists who have contributed to discussions of art in non-Western societies, particularly in the last thirty years of the twentieth century, have, I would argue, done so because art is recognizably a part of a people's lives; part of the social and cultural fabric that anthropologists in particular find fascinating. The various ways in which anthropologists have submitted art systems to analysis have provided a variety of means for understanding human society within an anthropological framework.

While I have some sympathy for Alfred's position, there are examples of anthropological analyses of art that successfully utilize aesthetic and semiotic investigations, massaging them along the way to more appropriately and accurately reflect what is happening in an anthropological context. By way of example let us look at some of the analyses of cross-cultural aesthetics or 'evaluative schemes' that have emerged over the last few decades.

Indigenous Aesthetics as a Programme of Enquiry

Generally speaking, the sentiments expressed in discourse connected to Western aesthetics are concerned with 'beauty'. As was the case with early endeavours to write about economic systems in tribal societies from the analytical basis of Western economic theory, the early forays into non-Western aesthetic evaluations grappled with indigenous notions of 'beauty'. Perhaps we should loosen the stays somewhat and break free from the culturally bound context of aesthetics as defined within a Western framework. Much as the Substantivists reformulated economic theory to more accurately describe non-Western economic behaviour, discussions of non-Western aesthetic sensibility have found ways of better reflecting the essence of cross-cultural aesthetic responses. For example, '. . . African aesthetics opens onto African sensibility. Aesthetic criticism suggests the relation of art to emotional ideals. These ideals, in turn, reveal the hidden unities which impose meaningful design upon the face of a culture' (Thompson, 1973: 19).

Robert Thompson, in his analysis of Yoruba sculpture, takes a plunge into Yoruba 'feelings' and 'sensibility' by means of focusing his discussion with Yoruba carvers and consumers on the formal lines carved into Yoruba sculpture (1973). The clarity of line, the depth of incision, the path the line takes on the sculptured surfaces all elicit responses from a discerning Yoruba public which are more than expressions of awe at the technical feat mastered by the best of the Yoruba carvers. This does not negate the extremely seductive thesis Alfred develops for the 'technology of enchantment' (1992). This too, I would suggest, operates at a different level for Yoruba viewers. Simultaneously, however, in Yorubaland the line is also the focus of Yoruba critical assessment. As well as the formal analysis of line in Yoruba sculpture, Thompson delineates a complex terminology to describe various kinds of lines and the feelings they invoke. It emerges that the Yoruba are interested in marking all manner of surfaces with lines. In pursuing the value of linear accomplishment in a carving genre, Thompson is able to successfully demonstrate the pervasive use of the line in Yoruba design and thinking, finally extending Yoruba intellectual conceptions which connect lines to the existence of civilization. Could Thompson have arrived at this level of comprehending the significance of lineal markings in Yoruba philosophy had he not pursued the evaluations applied to Yoruba sculpture? Taking as he did the 'aesthetic' responses of his Yoruba guides and plotting through the system by which art is assessed beyond its technological proficiency and its social context, Thompson may have unveiled a level at which the sculptured art of Yorubaland has significance within the Yoruba social *and* cultural contexts not immediately achievable by any other method of enquiry.

Evaluative schema, in other societies, is likewise well articulated. Thompson's analysis of Yoruba artistic criticism comprehensively documents the contexts in which it occurs, the kinds of evaluations made in relation to Yoruba sculptures, and the meanings derived from these evaluative contexts. Strathern and Strathern described the aesthetic criteria applied to body decoration among Hageners of highland Papua New Guinea (1971), demonstrating for the first time that completely different concepts of quality are applied to colour, for example, than that which is generally held by those used to Western colour aesthetics. Their findings heralded a new line of enquiry into how people evaluate their world, opening up perspectives once locked within Western boundaries delineating possible ways for 'seeing'. O'Hanlon too analyses the evaluative discourse used to assess Wahgi body adornment as the most significant means of understanding the ways in which this art communicates and encodes meaning (1989). Vakutan aesthetics likewise boasts an evaluative scheme by which negative and positive criticism considers the 'face' of a carving. Categories of criticism define the quality of a line, the relationship between lines, the balance of specific features according to internal organization, the balance of colour, and the overall 'strength' of colour are all associated with Vakutan artistic criticism (Campbell 1983; see also Beier 1974; Beran 1996). But consideration of evaluative schemes in relation to specific works of art provides only one line of enquiry and can lead us away from consideration of other relevant aesthetic responses which evoke cultural constructions of idealized values; idealizations of 'good' and 'bad', 'order' and 'disorder', perfection and human shortcomings.

> ... that to study an art form is to explore a sensibility, that such a sensibility is essentially a collective formation, and that the foundations of such a formation are as wide as social existence and as deep, leads away not only from the view that aesthetic power is a grandiloquence for the pleasures of craft. It leads away also from the so-called functionalist view that has most often been opposed to it: that is that works of art are elaborate mechanisms for defining social relationships, sustaining social rules, and strengthening social values (Geertz 1983: 99).

Enquiry into a people's aesthetics cannot be banished to the 'back benches' as these may be defined by anthropological analyses of art which choose as their 'front bench' line of enquiry the social relationships mediated by and through art. In the production of art, people are not merely mastering the technology, nor incorporating motifs, designs, movement and/or speech patterns at whim. Those regarded as artists in any given society are working to supply an audience of consumers who are well 'educated' in the process of assessing works, determining whether they meet the requirements, as these are defined by 'tradition'. These assessments may be based upon ideas of 'beauty', but this quality may be more related to the depth and clarity of lineal incisions, flow of body parts in precise movement patterns, or even a reasonable expectation that the correct magical treatment has been incorporated into the work. Alfred's objection to the 'indigenous aesthetics' programme' (1998: 4) is its tendency to reify that part of art which is associated with culture and its use as a vehicle for cultural transmission which plays down the structural role of art within a social context. While this may be so, and *Art and Agency* goes a long way to rectify any perceived reification of the 'cultural' over that which is deemed 'social', I suggest that there is a danger in throwing out the baby with the bathwater. Could both approaches be equally revealing?

Anthony Forge, to my mind a significant figure in the anthropology of art (not to mention a supervisor and mentor to Alfred himself), argued that the value of art lay primarily in its ability to communicate that which was not communicable in any other way (1966, 1967, 1970, and 1973). Art communicates not only through elaborate symbolic systems but also through emotive stimuli. Although that which is communicated is not too difficult to discover, given exhaustive and detailed discussions with both artist and audience, it is the emotive stimuli that are more elusive in an analysis of art. Hence descriptions of form and style analysis are pervasive in the literature.

Although aesthetics is partly about how people 'feel', or 'appreciate' art, its value to an 'anthropology of art' is how these 'feelings' reflect wider sentiments which reflect patterns for behaviour. At this point I feel the scorn radiating from Alfred's argument, questioning the value of patterns *for* behaviour to anthropology when what is really relevant are the patterns *of* behaviour. But the ideals set within a cultural context for social interaction remain, to my mind, fertile escarpments from which to view the ways in which people strive to meet those ideals. Surely what lies between ideals and the actualization of these provides information that can deepen our understanding of social and cultural processes. An analysis of aesthetic sentiments in any given society extends our understanding of 'feelings' lineally along a path leading to culturally significant philosophies reflecting social values which ultimately propel the enquirer towards social behaviour and the social processes which circumscribe that behaviour. Art is not merely 'enjoyed', or displayed in non-Western societies. This phenomenon is partly why Alfred seeks an 'anthropology of art' grounded in social significance. Art has a role within a defined social and cultural context. A people's 'appreciation' of an artwork, whatever form that may take, is inherent in its ability to perform that role adequately as well as to connect people to their ways of thinking about the world. Can an 'anthropology of art', developed within a scheme promoting investigation at the level of social interaction as its *primary* line of enquiry provide us with enough of the picture to assist us in placing the captivating agency of art within its social *and* cultural context?

Among Vakutans aesthetic value is based upon the way in which a carving, a skirt, a dance, a voice, or a person's face achieves its defined role, its 'work' as it is expressed by Vakutans. The 'feelings' evoked are related to being able to draw attention to a skirt, for example, so that people are mesmerized by its magnificence. But its magnificence has more to do with other social values than merely its 'beauty'. As Alfred eloquently argued in the construction of his model for 'the technology of enchantment', a significant captivating engagement which art extracts from its audience is based upon the mere knowledge that the object or act has been conceived in magic or that there is some supernatural power which is the font of its existence (1992). Alfred makes extensive use of the Vakutan material to demonstrate his point that the act of transforming a natural substance, for example, into an embellished object emanating formal properties designed to capture the attention of others is the 'technology of enchantment'. If magic is then layered into the transformative process, in some contexts becoming the active agent in its transformation, an 'enchantment of technology' casts a spell over those who would 'see the real world in an enchanted form' (1992: 44). The technological expertise required in the construction of Vakutan skirts provides a certain 'halo' of enchantment. But it is the knowledge that the woman who has made the skirt was able to achieve such magnificence through magical inculcation of substances and utterances that imbues the skirt with another level of enchanted power, from which the viewer is unable to escape. While the exact technical and training processes may be known only to a select group of Vakutans, the effect of the skirts to enchant does not require any further knowledge other than that magic is involved and its aim is to render the viewer incapable of escaping its powers of attraction.

Although there are many contexts in which Vakutans embellish their world with art through design, song, dance or construction, in this chapter I will turn to the production of art for the purposes of undertaking Kula expeditions by Vakutans, who live on a small island of the Trobriand Islands within the Milne Bay Province of Papua New Guinea.[1] Leaving aside the formal analysis of form, I will present the data as an example of the intellectual processes underpinning the choice of elements within the Vakutan environment and argue that the representations are more than a desire to imitate characteristics of that which is represented (see Figure 6.1).

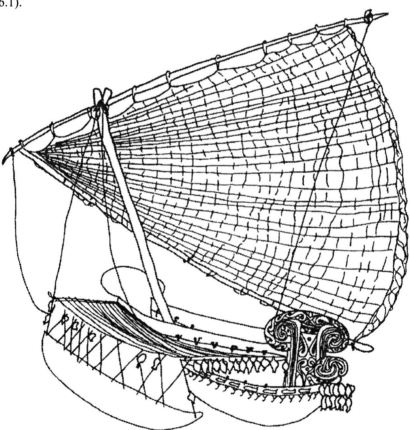

Figure 6.1 Vakutan *Masawa*. This drawing depicts the full sail and outrigger together with the two end boards; the prowboard and the splashboard

A Vakutan System of Aesthetics

Vakutans participate in a system of art production which is not only esoteric in its training of 'artists', but is also highly selective. Particular aspects of the Vakutan environment are chosen to be represented according to perceived qualities. Only certain men are endowed with the skills that qualify them as master carvers (Campbell 1978, 1983) while particular women are given the magic to promote their skills in the construction and design of skirts. These skills are not only based upon the technical knowledge and ability to transform the wood of trees, for example, into culturally rich icons, permeated with magical substances and incised with lines that represent particularly 'knowledgable' animals. The carvers and skirt makers have also undergone stages of magical transformation so that valuable qualities of 'wisdom', 'knowledge', and 'precision' become part of their very essence.

Vakutans have chosen to represent certain elements of their environment based upon perceptions that these elements embody particular qualities which Vakutans idealize. By representing these elements on carvings destined for specific ends, they are not only appropriating those qualities for their own purposes (that is, there is a functional purpose in their representation), but they are, in essence, assimilating those qualities to personify the ideal Vakutan. It is the emotive stimuli of these icons on the sensibility of Vakutan personhood that people respond to at a conscious and unconscious level. My intent is not merely to make the art produced by a select group of Vakutan carvers more meaningful to non-Vakutan consumers, to assist them to 'see' through Vakutan eyes, but to pursue a better understanding of Vakutan emotive responses to their art work. By so doing, an opportunity emerges for us to come closer to an understanding of the captivating spell Vakutan carvings have for Vakutans and how this operates within an informed social context.

As stated above, the designs carved on the canoe prow and splash boards of Kula outrigger canoes are part of a system which incorporates particular elements of the Vakutan environment, real or imagined, which embody key features associated with ideal qualities of Vakutan personhood. Identifying the relationship between form and meaning is, for my current purposes, a separate task. In attempting to demonstrate that an analysis of Vakutan aesthetics is not only appropriate to any anthropological investigation of their art, but inseparable from it, I will gloss over the formal elements of Vakutan carving for Kula, although certain formal elements will creep into the discussion from time to time.

The human body is divided into spatially distinct areas which are further associated with and responsible for different aspects of human sensibility, feelings, and behaviours. These associations are transposed onto the boards, endowing them with perceived anthropomorphic qualities, which are further enhanced by those elements of the environment which are chosen for representation (see Figures 6.2

and 6.3). I propose to generate a parallel discussion of Vakutan semiotics together with concepts that underpin Vakutan values. My purpose is to bring forth those aspects of their art which activate Vakutan responses and thereby captivate within a Vakutan cultural context. The value of this line of enquiry to the social context of Vakutan life will partly emerge from this.

The repertoire of Vakutan design is made up of a variety of visual components (form and colour) and ordered in accordance with structural principles dictating design organization; the depth and angle of carved line, delineated planes, repetitions and orientations. The corpus of form is limited by prescribed Vakutan principles for generating designs which must ultimately comply with a Vakutan style. The forms have associated meanings which are generally derived from the physical environment. The range of potential, representational elements within the environment is extensive. The nature of the relationship between form and representation is not, in the Vakutan context, necessarily based upon likeness. Rather, there are specific qualities thought to be represented by particular 'animals' in the Vakutan environment which receives formal representation in the carved lines and embellished surfaces of the board assemblages. Form and colour provide the visual iconography to which body parts and 'animal' representations are attached.

The foremost part of the board assembly to present itself to an audience of potential enemies (Kula partners) and to potential rivals (other Vakutans) is Section 1 of the prowboard (see Figure 6.2). The animal represented here is the osprey, and all forms in this Section are related to the head, neck and beak of this bird of prey. The representation of this particular bird in this Section is no coincidence to Vakutans. This fish-eating raptor personifies highly valued qualities. It embodies an innate 'knowledge' of the skills necessary to be successful: its fishing ability exemplifies precision and with it, perpetual victory. The osprey is perceived by Vakutans to sit at the tops of trees (also associated with value in relation to success) waiting for just the right moment to make its direct strike at a seemingly incon-spicuous spot on the water's surface. It enters the water without fuss, only to re-emerge with its prize securely displayed. Vakutans believe that the osprey's sagacious behaviour is sustained by his embodied knowledge and experience. The osprey is, to Vakutans, beyond failure because it embodies the magic of perpetual victory. This quality is the ultimate goal of Vakutan men in their pursuit of Kula specifically, but also in their goals to achieve status vis-à-vis other Vakutan men, and renown beyond their lifetime.

The central focus in Sections 1 and 2 of the prowboard is the head and contains within it all that this body part represents in Vakutan thinking. The head is thought to be that part of the body which generates wisdom, knowledge and intelligence. The animal associated with designs in Section 2 of the prowboard is the *doka*. Although spoken of in the same manner as all the other 'animal' representations

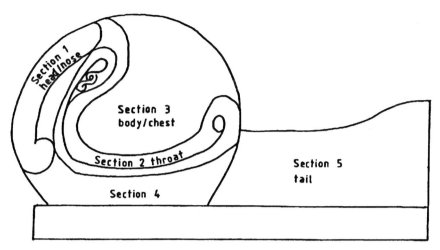

Figure 6.2 Delineated sections of the prowboard, with body-part associations

in the repertoire, the *doka* is not an animal of the real world. Instead it represents human fallibility. Unlike that of the osprey, the *doka* head represents achievable human intelligence and human rational knowledge. Whereas the osprey's wisdom is sustained by internalized magic, human intelligence is achieved by an active and creative mind. There is a distinction between wisdom and intelligence in Vakutan thinking; on the one hand, wisdom is innate, while on the other, intelligence is achieved.

Although the wisdom of the osprey is conceived as unachievable by humans, there is hope in the more attainable qualities represented by *doka*. The word itself is morphologically similar to the verb -*doki*, to think. This relationship was pointed out to me by a Vakutan man who, during the course of our discussion, went on to deliver a Vakutan philosophy on the nature of human intelligence. Men, it was argued, can think and assimilate, through experience, knowledge which can be put to future use. A man can think out the ways by which he can attract a woman, make a successful garden, or persuade a Kula partner to give up a shell valuable; all significant achievements in a Vakutan social context. A man can rationally calculate the effect of specific behaviours and modify these accordingly so as to achieve a desired outcome. Whereas man, as he is represented by the *doka*, must think and thereby employ all the knowledge gleaned through experience before he acts to achieve specific goals, the ideal, as represented by the osprey, need not think but simply acts as a response to internalized knowledge and wisdom.

Section 3 contains within its boundaries the Vakutan representation of a bat. While Sections 1 and 2 focus attention on the head, it is the head, wings, and tail that are given schematic representation in Section 3. The specific quality addressed in Vakutan sentiment is the exceptional 'wisdom' displayed by these animals in their effortless nocturnal flight. Other animals can fly, but they are aided by the light of day. They can *see* where they are going, while the bat is said to *know* its direction. As well as the positive nature of this animal, there is a darker side which invokes fear both on land and sea.

Colour attributes have qualities that provide further recourse into Vakutan evaluative schemes. The space which the bat occupies on the prowboard affords a relatively large surface area for the black paint representing the bat. Whereas the osprey symbolically, as well as in fact, carries magic associated with success (magical bundles are placed under the 'nose' of the prowboard, directly under the osprey), the black of the bat represents malevolent magic. Black is associated with human ageing, and some older men are thought to utilize the magic of sorcery. The activities of sorcerers, as well as those of witches, are carried out under the protection of night. Bats too are creatures of the night. The magic of sorcery and the activities of witches pose the greatest threat to men on Kula expeditions. For Vakutan men, success in Kula has a substantial effect on success within the Vakutan social milieu. The activities of sorcerers and witches threaten a man's success in the garden, in matters of the heart, as well as posing threats to one's physical and emotional health. The white and red displayed in conjunction with the black are said to provide 'relief', both visually and conceptually, from the black of Section 3, counterpoised in a relationship between victory and failure.

Section 4 of the prowboard, while incorporating various arrangements of form associated with other sections of the board assemblage, is the area where the artist is given greater freedom to demonstrate his creative abilities. While symbolic associations are generally tied to various forms delineated in the other sections, in the context of Section 4 these become disassociated so that the carver is relatively free to arrange the forms in his own way.

Although there are several identifiably separate forms displayed in Section 5 of the prowboard, the entire complex is perceived by Vakutans to be one unit. The animal associated with the design complex is the *weku*, an unidentifiable animal. It is most often described as a small black bird. Several Vakutans claimed that this animal truly existed and that they had heard it calling to them in the bush. It always succeeds in disappearing, however, providing a perpetual frustration. Its song is heard in the forest into which people venture with the sole purpose of catching a glimpse of this alluring animal. It is significant that its 'voice' not only is 'heard', but also entices its listener to seek it out.

A voice, if valuable according to Vakutan standards, is associated with eroticism and the enticement of one of the opposite sex. Malinowski records, 'As the natives put it: "The throat is a long passage like the *wila* (cunnus) and the two attract each other. A man who has a beautiful voice will like women very much and they will like him"' (1935: 478). When asked what was important about *weku*, nearly all informants were ambiguous about its habitat, 'work', and colour, yet all spoke of the attraction its voice had on people.

There are five delineated planes on the splashboard which similarly contain recurring forms associated with specific 'animals' and drawing upon particular sentiments reflecting Vakutan values (see Figure 6.3). Section 1 outlines the upper form of the splashboard. The important representations in this Section are the egret/ *doka* and *tokwalu*, or human figure(s). These two forms are the visual focus of the entire board.

Although the *doka* is represented alone on the prowboard, its place on the splashboard is associated with the egret. According to Vakutan conceptualization of animal behaviour, the egret is a master of fishing technology. But unlike the osprey, who is the embodiment of its own wisdom and technological achievement, the egret, like a man, has to turn to the bush when its fishing techniques fail, resorting to the agencies of magic to rejuvenate its ability. Men also have to perform magic to succeed in their work. A master carver has to resort to 'refresher' magic if, when carving, he finds it hard for the design to 'flow' from his mind through his hands. When it is at its best, the egret is seen to stand perfectly still in the shallows, waiting for the right moment and, knowing when to strike, it snaps up its prey with speed and precision.

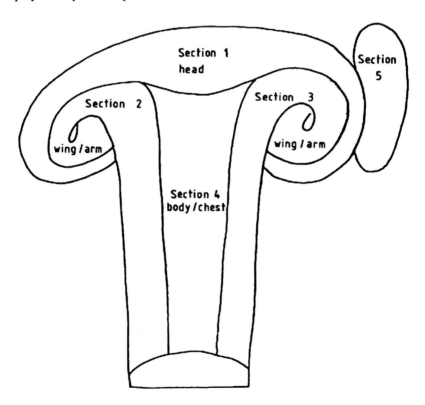

Figure 6.3 Delineated sections of the splashboard, with body-part associations

The *tokwalu* figure is said to represent humanity and is always placed in the centre of section 1 between the two major egret/*doka* designs. While all of the other 'animals' are given abstract or limited graphic representation, the human figure receives complete figurative treatment. There is no second-guessing the prototype of this design.

The conceptual likeness between the egret and mankind is given symbolic persuasion by their close proximity on the splashboard and their spatial relationship with *doka*. The central theme of Section 1 recalls the human mind and the process of thinking which, not being infallible, must be reinforced by magic. Mankind, as described in various mythological events, lost many of his previous powers: powers such as rejuvenation (Malinowski 1922: 307–11 and 322–6) and the knowledge of the magic to make a canoe fly (Malinowski 1922: 311–21). Through experience, humans remain vulnerable, devoid of the heroics of the mythological past. Alfred makes much of this contrast in his argument identifying the 'halo-effect of resistance' enhancing the value of an object or an action (1992: 48). Similarly, although from a different perspective, Malinowski develops his theory on the use of magic as an indicator of situations where there are perceived dangers and difficulties or when an outcome is uncertain (1925).

Sections 2 and 3 contain the design elements associated with the egret/doka. The designs of all three sections are associated with the head, invoking important body parts such as the eye, beak/mouth, neck/throat, mind and its associated intelligence. This region of the body is, for Vakutans, the locus of human power on the one hand, and human frailty on the other. It is the face which is the visual focus of beauty and the key to a person's potential for success. Others cannot refuse a beautiful face, offering up whatever is desired. It is thought that beauty stuns the beholder and in this state the hapless victim unwittingly gives over his or her wealth, magic, and knowledge thus securing status, fame, and with this the greatest prize, immortality (Campbell 1983). Although spirits are reincarnated, individuals die. Through fame Vakutan men can achieve immortality beyond their biological death (see also Weiner 1976). The eyes, too, are a means of enchantment and are the orifices through which desire is channelled. The mouth is the gate through which magical substances are taken and magical chants are spoken. Before a man dies he instructs his relatives to gag his mouth so as to impede the passage of magic from his body. The head is the receptacle of all acquired knowledge and the locus of desired wisdom.

Section 4 is unlike all other delineated planes on the board assemblages. There are no fixed design representations nor any conventions governing design patterning. There is a palette from which master carvers choose design form and representation, but this area is by and large a carver's space within which to identify his own prowess in design utilization and innovation. While Sections 1, 2 and 3 are said to 'steal' the eye of the beholder, more discerning eyes may roam to Section

4 where the identity of the individual master carver and his 'school' of carving are apparent.

Although the head and its attendant body parts are the focus of Sections 1, 2 and 3, the chest is associated with Section 4. The chest is an important part of the body in that it is where the emotional centre of consciousness is located. The chest is where pain, love, sorrow and loss are felt. These feelings result from accumulated experiences that represent the ageing process, a process which moves people from white (infancy) to red (youth) and to black (elderly). As with Section 3 on the prowboard where the bat appears in the assembly of 'animals', the association of Section 4 on the splashboard with the chest has a darker side. There are relatively large areas where black is given more visibility. As already noted, black is conceptually linked to the ageing of humans. Those who have lost the beauty of youth, particularly visible in the head, develop strengths in other ways, through accumulated knowledge, magic and sorcery. Not only does Section 4 provide a surface upon which master carvers, imbued with lots of magic and generally not carving in the prime of life, display their individual talents, but there is also reference to the life cycle of men and the inevitable process of ageing following upon the inevitable loss of youthful beauty.

Section 5 may or may not be included on the splashboards. When it is incorporated it is in the form representing either a reptile or a butterfly.[2] Reptiles possess the ability of shedding their skins, enabling rejuvenation from 'old', non-glossy and unattractive surface beauty to 'young' glossy and attractive images. So too the butterfly whose metamorphosis from a caterpillar, unmistakably attached to land, into a beautiful butterfly enables a new, acquired ability to become detached from land and fly.

The preceding analysis suggests a relationship of tension between the 'animals' embodied within the boards. Those with inherent 'wisdom' who, because of their perceived qualities, represent the quintessential success desired by other 'animals', are juxtaposed with those who must resort to magic to enable even a sniff at the successes they seek. Also sharing space on the boards are elements which impede success, representing the precarious nature of human endeavours (see Table 6.1). These tensions men experience in their efforts to achieve the significant successes in life deemed essential to a satisfaction with life as well as with the afterlife. Ultimately, success in gardening, fishing, attracting the opposite sex and Kula partners, as well as rebirth, remain elusive in the face of the competition with others and the vagaries of nature.

Conclusion

In considering the Vakutan evaluative scheme through which the value of certain 'animals' informs us of a Vakutan blueprint for behavioural stratagies in practical

Table 6.1 Aesthetic qualities associated with the board assemblage

'Animal'	Qualities	Evaluative Characteristics
Prowboard		
osprey	innate wisdom	innate magic
		idealized skill
		successful
doka	achieved knowledge	achieved magic
		intelligence
		fallible
bat	innate wisdom	innate magic
		idealized skill
		successful
		dangerous
		threatens success
weku	innate wisdom	innate magic
		idealized skill
		successful
		elusive
		alluring
		frustrates success
Splashboard		
egret	achieved knowledge	achieved magic
		intelligence
		fallible
		dangerous
tokwalu	achieved knowledge	achieved magic
		intelligence
		fallible
		dangerous

affairs, the enquiry demonstrates the application of indigenous aesthetics as a system of evaluation which, at one level, underpins processes of Vakutan social interaction. I did not approach this analysis taking as my starting point the relationship of the carved Kula canoe boards to the Vakutan (and their Kula partners') social context, although I could have. Rather, the point of departure was the system of symbolic representation associated with the formal characteristics circumscribing Vakutan carving traditions. From there my methodology focused on the evaluations made by Vakutans of the 'animals' represented so as to reach an understanding of why certain 'animals' are chosen over others in a process of aesthetic reasoning. This line of enquiry led me to a Vakutan preoccupation with success and failure. From here it is apparent that Vakutan aesthetics is intimately related to fields of behaviour within the social context of Vakutan life. It identifies ideals to be pursued and patterns for behaviour which inform Vakutan social interaction.

In building up the contexts associated with Vakutan Kula carving we can achieve a greater understanding of the role art has in the social and cultural fabric of Vakutan life. The relationship between the formal elements utilized by carvers to represent a select set of natural elements is iconographic. The process by which specific animals in the Vakutan environment are perceived as embodying particular characteristics deemed to possess ideal qualities is mimetic. The system by which form and meaning converge is symbolic, and the means by which the images invoke in their audience feelings that are laden with cultural significance is aesthetic. Vakutan aesthetics is ultimately about the search for success, and by that means, immortality.[3] The range of qualities associated with certain animals and represented on the carved assemblages of Kula outrigger canoes have meaning within the Vakutan construction of ideals. These in turn stimulate emotive responses among those who can 'read' the messages. Not everyone is likely to know the full range of meanings encoded on the carvings, but every child knows that the egret is a very intelligent bird and that, when its fishing is a bit off the mark, it has recourse to powerful magic to improve its success. Likewise, every child knows that the osprey is the personification of wisdom and that it can achieve its goals without fail. As a master carver points to an image on the prowboard and says, 'That animal, that's the osprey. That animal is very wise', the sum total of the knowledge his listener has of the osprey is invoked, and an emotive response brings forth feelings recalling that, like the osprey, Vakutans desire effortless success.

A question arises when considering Alfred's proposed programme for an 'anthropology of art' as to whether I can discover anything more than what I could have discovered had I subjected the material to an analysis of the boards as social agents, participating in a scheme reflecting Vakutan social interaction. Alternatively, by following an analysis which first elicits the semiotics of the design complex, and working towards the relationship between that which is symbolized and Vakutan's more general evaluation of the symbolized, am I able to probe a Vakutan social context in a way that is different from that directed towards the social embeddedness of the art? It seems to me that such a course does provide another, complementary view from which to pose other questions. On the other hand, what would an analysis of the system reveal if pursued from the perspective suggested by Alfred? Looked at as part of a system of social interaction, the Kula boards may well reveal layers of social efficacy hitherto undiscovered. My inclination, however, is to interrogate the material in a variety of ways.

Clearly, Alfred's cautioning hand justifiably warns against any attempts to 'see' through the eyes of another, to 'feel' in a way that replicates another's experience, or to 'understand' from the same perspective as someone else. The pursuit of these is fraught with difficulties. The ability for us to adequately remove our cultural lens so that we can view the world through another's is, admittedly, problematic, and just grounds for us to scurry for the known terrain that already encompasses 'sound' anthropology. Attempting to venture into territory which may lead us to embark upon further paths of enquiry and furrow deeper levels of understanding is, I submit, a worthy endeavour. To turn away is to shut the door and limit the possibilities. Anthropology is arguably the most eclectic of the social sciences, taking up the insights offered by other disciplines and shaping them to better enable us to address the questions posed by the complexities found in human societies.

While I doubt that many would disagree with Alfred's thesis that art is produced within a social context by social actors with social ends in mind, I suspect that some are likely to resist his tantalizing suggestion that it is only through an investigation of the social interplay between art and human actors that an 'anthropology of art' can emerge. It may well be that this line of enquiry provides the springboard for anthropological investigation, but I wonder if it offers the only point of departure. Indeed, while the development of Alfred's argument in *Art and Agency* springs from a brilliant argument outlining the social interplay between artist, art object, and audience as agent, index, and recipient respectively, proceeding to an elaborate analysis of the various intentions and permutations of potential interplay between these, he later develops an analysis of specific artistic systems as layers melding a rich tapestry constructed of interwoven lines of investigation, incorporating varying levels of function, interpretation, evaluation, and meaning. He too cannot escape the lure of multiple lines of enquiry.

Notes

1. Field research was undertaken on Vakuta Island between August 1976 and February 1978. I gratefully acknowledge the Australian National University's support of this research, and in particular, that of the Department of Prehistory and Anthropology.
2. The structural elements circumscribing Sections 2 and 3 of the splashboard can also be referred to as 'butterfly wings'.
3. The focus of this chapter has not allowed for an extensive discussion of the range and breadth of meanings associated with the art developed to enhance Kula activities. It is hoped that this will ultimately be discussed in future publications (see Campbell 1983).

References

Beier, U. 1974. 'Aesthetic Concepts in the Trobriand Islands'. *Gigibori* 1(1): 36–9.

Beran, H. 1996. *Mutuaga: A Nineteenth Century New Guinea Master Carver*. Wollongong: University of Wollongong Press.

Campbell, S. 1978. 'Restricted Access to Knowledge in Vakuta'. *Canberra Anthropologist* 1(3): 1–11.

—— 1983. *The Art of Kula*. Unpublished PhD thesis. Australian National University.

Forge, A. 1966. 'Art and Environment in the Sepik'. *Proceedings of the Royal Anthropological Institute for 1965*: 23–31.

—— 1967. 'The Abelam Artist', in P. Mayer (ed.), *Social Organisation: Essays Presented to Raymond Firth*, 65–84. London: Tavistock Publications.

—— 1970. 'Learning to See in New Guinea', in P. Mayer (ed.), *Social Organisation: Essays presented to Raymond Firth*, 269–91. London: Tavistock Publications.

—— (ed.) 1973. *Primitive Art and Society*. London: Oxford University Press.

Geertz, C. 1983. *Local Knowledge: Further Essays in Interpretive Anthropology*. New York: Basic Books.

Gell, A. 1992. 'The Technology of Enchantment and the Enchantment of Technology', in J. Coote and A. Shelton (eds), *Anthropology Art and Aesthetics*, 40–63. Oxford: Clarendon Press.

—— 1998. *Art and Agency: An Anthropological Theory*. Oxford: Oxford University Press.

Kroeber, A.L. 1953. *Anthropology Today: An Encyclopedic Inventory*. Chicago: University of Chicago Press.

Malinowski, B. 1922. *Argonauts of the Western Pacific*. London: Routledge & Kegan Paul Ltd.

—— 1925. 'Magic, Science, and Religion', in J. Needham (ed.), *Science, Religion and Reality*. London: The Sheldon Press.

—— 1935. *Coral Gardens and their Magic*. London: George Allen & Unwin Ltd.

O'Hanlon, M. 1989. *Reading the Skin: Adornment, Display and Society among the Wahgi*. London: British Museum Publications.

Strathern, A. and M. Strathern. 1971. *Self-Decoration in Mount Hagen*. London: Gerald Duckworth & Co. Ltd.

Thompson, R.F. 1973. 'Yoruba Artistic Criticism', in W.L. d'Azevedo (ed.), *The Traditional Artist in African Societies*, 19–61. Bloomington: Indiana University Press.

Weiner, A. 1976. *Women of Value, Men of Renown: New Perspectives in Trobriand Exchange*. St. Lucia: University of Queensland Press.

–7–

The Fame of Trinis: Websites as Traps
Daniel Miller

Introduction: A Tribute to Alfred Gell

The power of significant new ideas is never restricted to merely the materials that first generated them or exemplified them.[1] In this chapter I want to argue that Gell has provided us with a superb instrument for understanding a phenomenon quite apart from any that he himself studied: that is, the contemporary website. More specifically I will argue that in his posthumous book *Art and Agency* (Gell 1998) constructs an approach which may be applied with astonishing ease to the study of websites and the development of the internet. As such this chapter is intended as a tribute to Gell. It aims to demonstrate through the direct application of his ideas that Gell has left to the study of material culture a tremendous legacy, in the form of some of the most significant and innovative insights and perspectives ever constructed for understanding the fundamental relationship between society and things. The other intended reference point evoked by my title is to the book *The Fame of Gawa* by Munn (1986). Both I myself in previous work and Gell within *Art and Agency* build on a concept of objectification exemplified by the Kula ring, and in particular the way this was analysed by Munn. Once again I want to argue that the Kula provides an ideal reference point for understanding the nature and significance of the internet.

Based on a study of 60 commercial and 60 personal websites created by Trinidadians, in the form they appeared during January–March 1999, I want to argue that these websites are best understood, following Gell, as attempts to create aesthetic traps that express the social efficacy of the creators and attempt to draw others into social or commercial exchange with those who have objectified themselves through the internet. In parallel with the Kula ring these websites attempt to expand their creators through casting themselves out into a larger world of exchange with distant places. The creation of cyberspace is clearly a direct expansion of the space-time within which can be expressed the agency of the creators of websites. The ideal is that they thereby will influence the mind of potential exchange-partners to transact with them as against others. As in the case of the Kula this is most often not simply an expression of particular individuals so much as a collective construction which attempts to expand individuals largely by expanding the fame of the entity they most fully identify with, in this case the nation-state of Trinidad and Tobago. As such they use the internet above all to create the conditions for expanding the fame of Trinis, through enlarging the culture of exchange within which Trinis are able to operate and gain an international reputation. The fundamental principles that account for the existence of the Kula and for the current exploitation of the internet are therefore closely aligned. The similarity between them is made evident when Gell's analysis of artworks is extended to that of websites as aesthetic traps.

Genres of Personal Website

It is very hard to gauge how many Trinidadian personal websites exist: I have come across (February 1999) around 500 but there may be many at American university sites not yet seen. Some are attached to the local servers in Trinidad, but more take advantage of free sites such as geocities and tripod. One such site with 120 entries allows only single pages, but many others are far more elaborate. Not surprisingly the personal website is not an entirely homogeneous category, and three sub-genres will be considered here, those of schoolchildren, students and unofficial national home-pages. The latter two categories probably include as many Diaspora Trinis as home-based but this reflects my own survey data which showed that the majority of Trinidadians now have members of their nuclear family based in the Diaspora (Miller 1994: 21).

The most striking characteristic of post-teenage sites is the way personal identity is subsumed within the sense of being Trinidadian, irrespective of whether the individual actually lives in Trinidad. The assumption is that to understand the individual the viewer must first understand what it means to be Trinidadian. At its simplest this means the home-page is replete with various core symbols of that country, such as its flag, crest, a map and some basic statistics, while links lead to photographs and further information. This may even include the playing of the national anthem automated by someone landing on the page. Core symbols include those evocative of carnival, calypso and soca music, the local beer, or key Trinidadian personalities. But in some cases the process goes much further than this rather bland presentation of the nation-state. In such cases specifically Trinidadian idioms are used for the process by which the stranger is drawn into acquaintance with the world of Trinis.

An example is a site called Weslynne's Big Lime. The Lime (see Eriksen 1990) is the crux of Trinidadian sociality as an ideally spontaneous gathering of friends to spend some time together such as at street-corners or drinking. As well as being used here for the website, the word is often applied to describe a group of friends listed under 'links', the main ICQ (I seek you) forum for Trinidadians is also called

De Trini Lime, and the Yahoo chat line is called the Rumshop Lime. On this site it is critical to the author that the visitor learns what is meant by the term 'lime'. The site starts with a picture of the creator currently in Sweden looking wistfully out of her window at a large apartment block opposite, with a tissue in her hand. Underneath it says 'First and foremost I am from The Republic of Trinidad and Tobago, affectionately known as Trinbago. I don't normally speak the Queen's English or American, and I'd like to give you some insight into my language, those words appearing in boldface are (you guessed it!) Trinbagonian.'

As well as liming with the creator, the visitor is in effect going to invade the 'private' space of an individual and come to find out quite a bit about her. In Trinidad a particularly nosy stranger (e.g. an anthropologist) is likely to be known as a Maco or be called Macotious. If they try to find out too much too quickly they are accused of being farce (or fast). These terms imply there is a normal and comfortable speed at which people should get to know about each other and this should not be transgressed. A website cannot be controlled in the same way as other social intercourse, and so the creator uses these terms to try to give a local inflection to the process. At one point she introduces links to her friends' websites by saying 'So now that you've found out more about me, yuh macoed good maybe you'd like to maco some of my friends'. While the visitor is looking at some photos she says 'Well I find yuh getting real farce, you want to know everything about me. How about a look at my high school . . .' At another point in her site she has a longer section on what a lime means, the varieties of limes and their descriptions.

Some sites use the home-page to present the creator, but it is more common to use the home-page as a site of aesthetic and technical brilliance with much to catch the eye and to include there a link called 'about me' and sometimes also to a formal 'résumé'. These include information on family, education, friends, and sometimes current occupation, often with photographic illustrations. Other links may provide evidence of creative work such as poetry, drawings or clever webpage constructions with music and moving images. On this site the author not only gives her history, but talks of herself as a 'big mout 'oman'. Her poetry says something about her general politics, outlook on life and most of all her nostalgic longing for her home island of Tobago. Almost all these sites soon move from the individual to their social contexts. Diaspora students will usually have separate links to their college and to their college friends. They may also implicate webgroupings of what they see as those with similar attitudes such as 'power chicks'. In other cases one has the sense of an extended family, with particular emphasis on siblings and others with their own sites and some intra-family banter included within the texts. Trinidadians of Chinese origin, for example, seem particularly inter-linked. A few men appeared defensive about appearing as loners, or geeks, while women, by contrast, seemed to put more stress on the empowering properties of the net. There may also be an explicit concern with the kind of contact that has been made, as in another site which states 'I'm very glad that you made it this far . . . and I hope that you'll stick around long enough to get to know just a little bit more about me and my life. After all, these days, acquaintances that begin in cyberspace are often the most real, vivid, and long-lasting – and maybe that will be true of us'.[2]

The most important contextualizing is, however, within national identity. Even the personal pages will include exemplary Trinidad and Tobago settings, such as a particularly picturesque beach, or a scene from Carnival. Indeed this creates a certain paradox in that individuals who are not in Trinidad can nevertheless identify themselves as sites in virtual Trinidad. They may start with 'Well, for those of you who have no idea where you are', and follow with a map of Trinidad's location. Most sites have a separate page on links, which will tend to include Trini-based ICQ, chat and information sites about Trinidad. A more evocative page starts with:

> Whoa! That was a big wave! Glad you surfed on in here . . . never mind the dents you put in the coral reef! Hi I'm Sharon, and I am thrilled to welcome you to my little piece of Paradise! I live on a tiny island (not much more than a blob covered with grass and trees, surrounded by water) called Trinidad, which is in the Caribbean.

Similarly for many individuals there is a presupposition that the individual's encounter with the outer world is simply a microcosm of the Trini encounter. As one website tells us:

> The citizens of Trinidad & Tobago have only recently been introduced to the great halls of cyberspace but we are catching on fast. I've been into computers all my life so the net seems like the next logical step for me. Since I've been on the net I've been all over the world (virtually) without leaving my house and have seen a lot of cool things and met a lot of interesting people.

The degree of Trinidadian content is often commented upon in its own right as with the statement 'Welcome to yet another proud Trinidadian's homepage. Plenty Trini *ting* here. Browse around and enjoy it'. As well as links to statistics and photographs, key personalities are represented. It says something for the 'event-centred' nature of Trinidadian identity described elsewhere in terms of the values of 'transience' (Miller 1994), that Brian Lara the cricketer who dominated Trinidadian nationalism up to a year or two before, is barely present, replaced by the figures of Ato Boldon the world champion sprinter and above all Wendy Fitzwilliam the 1998 Miss Universe. Both of these are often included with their photos and sometimes links to their home-pages. In one case personalities are split between those described as gntts (gifted and talented Trinis) and the list of kats (kool ass Trinis). Even when sites only consist of a single page, the same subsumption often exists in a more attenuated version. A sub-genre is that of those who focus upon website technology sharing their own experience and giving hints to others about website construction. This in turn reflects back on the representation of Trinidad, through the use of sophisticated multi-media such as the sounds of waves crashing as one opens onto a local beach, or the borders of each webpage done in the colours of the national flag.

While there is then a clear normative model for the personal website – a pattern including the link to 'about me', another to 'my friends', 'cool links', etc., not every site conforms to this, and there are idiosyncratic sites. Given the centrality of religion to many Trinidadians this is surprisingly absent, though one website on ruched purple satin wallpaper (background) has many Christian links and a fairly chaste link to her boyfriend – two sides of a heart that come together as one watches. Far more common is a focus upon music which may come to dominate, as in a site which introduces itself as follows 'Probably You Never Heard of We . . . Well, give thanx and praises to da most high . . . Yeah, Yeah, Yeah, starring, da Wickedest SLAM, come fi brighten up your world. Featuring sound clash, soca monarchs, dee jays, reggae bound, and reggae links. So get ready for a 2012 Bashment'. A whole series of links follow to various music sites, both Trinidadian soca and Jamaican music. Less stylish but illustrating the same point, is a site titled Welcome to DarenD's Joke Page with smiley faces on either side of the title, over sky wallpaper. It starts with 'its good to know other people have nothing to do with their time like me. So go ahead, enjoy the joke of the week'. There follows about a hundred, mainly one-line, but some longer jokes. There is also a link to a further page of Trini jokes along the lines of 'you know you are a Trini when . . .' A subsidiary point is that this particular form of Trini joke follows a pattern which can be found throughout the Trini personal websites. It permits a whole swathe of jokes about 'How to recognize a true true Trini'. These typically present a list of characteristic traits of being Trinidadian from the way people lime to the way they clink ice in glasses to well-known brands or persons in Trinidad. So even the joke becomes a focus upon the specificity of being Trinidadian. (For an analysis of this particular variety of joke see Miller 1993.)

Almost all sites are intended to act not as end-points of a search but as conduits directing the surfer along further links, which are constituted by the society and interests of the author. Family websites may be prominent, but so can websites of those who share a dominant interest in a particular sport or hobby. Encouragement is given to the surfer to join the relevant newsgroups or host sites. The 'lime' is important here as a network of links to those personal friends that also have websites, so that in meeting one person you also have access to the people they hang out with in cyberspace and in a sense also of the way they are defined by the type of people they choose to associate with. Students may relate back to common high-school graduation. One such lime has its own name, and mission statement: '"Zero Tee" is a group of friends from Fatima College, whose only goal is to promote idleness (See About Me section) in Trinidad and Tobago'. At this point there is a clear continuity with the dominant characteristics of teenage websites.

The sites that have been described so far are still recognizably personal websites. There has, however, already emerged a further genre of sites that take the dominant trend much further. These are individuals who have taken upon themselves the role of producing national home-pages and have completely subsumed their own presence within the larger concern to present the nation. In the most extreme cases the site will have a name such as the Unofficial Trinidad Home Pages, and the only way of registering the individual concerned is at the base of the home-page where it states this site is maintained by (whoever). Some sites have a more individual style to the way this is done. For example a site called 'A Workbook on Trinidad and Tobago' presents itself in the form of a traditional Carnival figure. It is headed by the crest of this figure – a crowing cock – under which is the national crest. It introduces itself in the following style: 'For I am Chanticleer, cock-of-the-rock, master of this barnyard: your Tourguide. I am the herald of the new and the old. My diversity, magnificent in the rising sun as I announce the new day, gives rise to the multitude of opportunities the day offers. My majestic silhouette as I put the day to rest, exemplifies the serenity of a job well done: I invite you now to follow my tracks. Click on the "Welcome" balloons for an enjoyable Virtual Tour of Trinidad & Tobago. To see and hear how we celebrate Christmas, go to "Visit our Christmas Page" where there are recipes for preparing foods and drinks enjoyed in Trinidad & Tobago during the Christmas season.' This site thereby employs the classic banter of the traditional Carnival figure (Pearse 1956).

In addition to a plethora of national symbols, these sites often include a list of local recipes, a small dictionary of favourite Creole terms, and in some cases instructions on how to compute the value of the Trinidadian dollar. There are two main concerns that dominate such sites. Some impress by the sheer number and scale of their (sometimes over a hundred) links to other Trinidadian sites, leading to every server, many useful commercial sites, as well as news, weather, media and other information. They thereby make themselves into key on-line gateways to virtual Trinidad as constituted on the net. Alternatively such sites make an attempt to become virtual guide books, with pages of photographs and accompanying texts, which cover well-known tourist sites. Some examples stress the natural resources of Trinidad and Tobago with particular emphasis on ornithology.

If these two types of site – the virtual guide book, and the link to virtual Trinidad, represent the core to the genre then others shade off into other classes of website. For example one website concentrates on all the Carnival-related sites of Trinidad but also serves as a guide to Carnival world-wide; for example, its link to 'London' leads to a dozen sites dealing with the Notting Hill Gate Carnival. One or two of the 'classic' unofficial home pages are in fact commercial sites who want people to subscribe to their services. Others lean back towards the more personal sites:

for example, one that has many photos of beaches in Trinidad, but with a strong tendency to include the author herself posed at the beach in question.

None of the commercial websites, even those which have clearly had large sums of money invested in creating attractive effects, come even close to the sheer explosive creativity and aplomb of teenage sites created by individuals aged 12 to 17. These tend to be produced by circles of secondary school friends who are aiming to compete over how much of an 'experience' the visit to the site can be.[3] Indeed it soon becomes clear that the key to the site as a whole is the visitors' guest book comprising comments by previous visitors and now open for anyone to see. This is where the site is judged and comments will be of a clearly personal nature as banter between school friends, and will also often be explicit about the reciprocity expected of each making comments on the other's sites as well as the rivalry between them. For example one site includes twenty-seven comments such as 'this site dread but ya need to get some good mp3's (music links) the ones you have is shit . . .' or 'yeah saga boy, yuh homepage is changed i noticed dat!! but spit on it for not including my name'; another site includes 'Roses are red Violets are blue What the hell I'm bored too. Go to my page please, I had to suffer through yours', and playground nonsense such as 'I have come to haunt you, Fraggles still live and we will haunt you till you die. MWAHAHAHAHA !!!!' Still others will incorporate gossip about who fancies whom at school.

The experience starts by often characterizing the site as a place either by name – such as Sheena's Palace, or the Jimmy experience – or graphically, such as a brick wall with visitors having to click on the key to get through the front door. In one case the following is strung out through three messages 'you feel a deep malicious chill piercing through your veins. As the colours dim you see a glowing green lizard welcoming you to a completely different world. Not to worry it is just your computer is amazed at the coolness of this page and he also says that this site has moved'. Eight messages later one finally comes to the smoking green dragon that starts the site. Once inside the ideal is to be lively, with a whole series of characters moving around, of which the most popular seem to be animated fish and cartoon characters from the television show *South Park*. Lights flash, strings of bulbs go on with alternate colours, names revolve, fonts are wonderfully elaborated and music plays as one enters into a particular page.

In effect such pages conform well to Trinidadians' concern with style and 'gallerying'. Sites appear as a kind of dressing-up in which the individual selects the particular elements of popular culture he or she wishes to be 'seen with'. Sometimes these are direct references to clothing such as links to Calvin Klein or Nike, more common are the music links, especially mp3s that the visitor can download directly from the site. The choice of music is particularly important and teenagers may be defensive or apologetic about what they haven't included or achieved. By comparison teenage Trinidadians have far less concern with sports and particular teams and almost no reference to the computer games and game play that I suspect dominates other national teenage sites. Music is in a sense the key adornment that the Trinidadian teenage website wears to look good in cyberspace.

The other essential feature is that a site's links should be hot or cool (synonymous terms). These links may include the websites of particular TV programmes they follow, as well as music and brands or simply links to sites they approve as interestingly (to use another common teenage expression) 'weird'. Quite often they will allow their websites to be dominated by a particular icon, in one case that of *South Park*, while another makes the site a homage to the rock-band Metallica – it opens with skull and crossbones dripping blood and the whole site is effectively an exercise in the style of the modern Goth.

Some sites express what have become internationally seen as stereotypical teenage forms of angst. In particular there is a site called 'Maria's So Called Life', with the address 'sullengirl'. This dwells on the delights of annoying other people, has words like 'pathetic' and 'wasting away' that come and go within a frame. Instead of a simple 'about me' link this site states 'Stuff on me, WARNING! – Before you proceed to waste your time by reading this page I should warn you . . . it SUCKS!!! I don't know why I'm doing this really, guess it's because I have a lot of time on my hands'. It comes as no surprise that all the representations of the creator are in the form of an alien, or that the 'heart of gold' side of this teenager comes across with the extremely positive way she describes her best friends, of whom three have their own website links. Several other teenage sites talk of themselves in terms such as 'stupidgirl', or say how pathetic they are, and how they really shouldn't be working on this site one week before taking their examinations but . . .

However fast website technology develops, the capacity for irony of teenagers is far quicker and these sites already parody what are becoming the conventions of websites. One site mainly constructed by a 14-year-old girl scorns the obviousness by which people give their names although it is already evident in the page name ('my name is ,,, DUH!!'). Many websites repeat their links at the bottom of the home-page as well as in a column on the left hand side. She introduces those at the base with the note that its for those visitors who were too stupid to see the list of links on the left. In many such pages what comes over most clearly is the desire for friendship and approbation balanced by derisory scorn for anything too uncool or obvious. These anxieties and imperatives seem as clear from websites as they would be in any school playground.

The focus of these sites seems almost always geared to their popular reception and the sites are highly socialized. There is some emphasis on families, but less than found in student sites. Most important are peers with up to 60 named friends, quite often organized into limes that they hang around with. Visitors are exhorted sometimes several times to sign the guest book, and the e-mail and website addresses of friends and relatives are liberally provided. There is at least as much cooperation as competition and a constant call for comments or help to make their sites more interesting. There is much to these younger sites that speaks to the general ideal of 'making friends'. That one should not just visit but come into more regular communication, and become part of a connected web that bring links between the circuits of friendships that each has already established.

Commercial Websites

Compared to the teenage or even the student sites, most commercial websites look relatively conservative in their construction. It is hard to assess the total number. One directory lists 401 individual companies with links to their websites and my guess would be a figure of 500 websites at this stage. In general this initial phase quickly betrays its reliance upon precedents outside of website construction, in advertising, using other media. For example most food manufacturing sites seem to emulate the traditional 'flyer' with a single page, some simple graphics or photographs of the food in packages and a list of the products in terms of quantities and forms available. A similar format would be found for wholesalers of toilet tissues and such like. By contrast, clothing retailers tend to more or less incorporate their traditional catalogues. Each page shows photographs of models wearing outfits from their range of clothes, and there are links to pages of accessories or to the biographies of the designers, where they were trained and prestigious places where the goods have been sold. Some may also have a section on the ethos or alternative spirituality that lies behind the concept. Many more focus on a genre of what might be called 'tropical nationalism' with motifs and sentiments full of images of coconut palms, hibiscus flowers, humming-birds, carnival figures and steelband.

By contrast to this influence of precedents, it is evident that within a very short time one can already discern the characteristics of the 'classic' website, partly the influence of the software packages that are used to create websites. These are based around two kinds of convention, one created by the constraints of technology, the other stylistic.

An example of the former is the blue hyperlink, which thereby efficiently informs the viewer that some text is also a link, and the way the cursor turns into a hand at this point. Stylistically there is the classic 'wallpaper' which is based on a faded out version of the company logo repeated as a motif in the background of every page, thereby stylistically unifying the whole website. There is also the convention of a distinct left hand column where links are listed vertically, and the repetition of these along with credits for the site in small fonts at the base of the home-page. A local 'classic' form established by a government organization promoting commercial websites, consists of two columns in green and yellow, one with categories of information and the other with the responses appropriate to that particular company, making a 'minimal' website.

Not surprisingly, larger companies tend to more elaborate websites, but these vary according to their intended audience. A transnational conglomerate such as Neal and Massy (Miller 1997) has links to the 21 of its 70 companies that have their own websites. It also includes an intranet, guestbooks and a clear pride in the sophistication of the site as a whole, as well as specialist sections such as a discussion group devoted to security issues. A company such as KC Confectionery is more directly attuned to its customer base. Their site is full of child-friendly effects with plenty of 'neon' colours, and words that cut across the screen or flash. Such movement is, of course, much more elaborated in television adverts but what a website offers to both the advertiser and the visitor is the potential for interaction, so that there is much for the child surfer to do as a visitor with exhortations such as 'burst this bubble to find out how we can make life sweeter' and links decorated as sweets or special effects. Within the same site a visitor also learns about the distribution network of their 60 products to 19 countries and a list of helpful 'facts' for parents such as 'Sugar doesn't make kids hyperactive', 'Chocolate does not cause acne' and even how 'candy doesn't make your tooth decay', with texts citing supportive scientific journal articles. The Republic Bank's extensive network has a much more sober cast, mainly devoted to information about the location of branches and automatic tellers and the increasing possibilities for on-line dissemination of, for example, certain standard forms. The use of links gives unusual clarity to the structure of ownership as one is led upwards to major shareholding companies or downwards to partly owned subsidiaries. Even here a little fun is incorporated as the home-page allows the visitor to click on two of the current jingles used in the bank's advertising. Most such sites also include 'mission statements' and a history of the company.

In general commercial websites are resolutely commercial. Information about persons may be included where, as in the case of an artist selling their craftworks, the nature of the person is part of what is being sold through their products. But some sites also adopt a more proselytizing and educational aura. In particular the several sites devoted to the sale of steelband instruments have very extensive 'virtual exhibitions' about their manufacture or extensive technical guides to the musical potentials of the instruments concerned. These are amongst a whole swathe of sites, including those for hotels and tourist facilities and the arts and craft sites that sell their particular products partly through selling 'Trinidad' itself as a place to be visited or as the site of particular creativity and style. The link between commerce and the nation is also very evident in the organization and hierarchy of commercial sites. Many of these are most easily found through what have become virtual trade fairs. One set up by the government organization TIDCO and another directed at companies based in the South of the country. These include photos of trade stalls and the kind of directions for finding one's way around the site that would be found in a typical trade fair. Since Trinidad is effectively linked to the world through six competing locally based servers such as wow.net and carib-link, these too can become alternative gateways to both commercial and to the personal sites that are registered with them. Less developed but emerging are links to smaller localities – such as the Mousepad computer firm in the small central town of Couva that with its photos of local parades and the offering of a local community webpage (one entry so far!) – which represent attempts to become gateways for their particular locality.

Without comparative studies it is hard to be clear about the degree to which any of these genres are specific to the area. I imagine the teenage sites, for example, could be easily matched elsewhere. But even when the contents appear to be the same, the significance of such sites may differ considerably, because the context of Trinidadians expanding their space-time through their presence on the net, and the implications that has for their sense of the place of Trinidad in the world, may be quite different from that of US citizens.

The Website as a Trap

The term aesthetic refers here not to some criterion of beauty but to the visual properties of sites as forms of social efficacy. As such it is instructive to not start with the most striking but the least striking of all the sites that were inspected, which were those commercial sites that seemed to be based on the precedent of flyers. What is noteworthy about these sites is that as a genre they seem almost wilful in refusing to adopt what might be termed the 'production values' that might have been predicted for a brand new medium such as the web. The quality of the photos is generally poor, and there is little concern with overall design. There is no reason to assume that such companies could not have produced better looking sites; the suggestion is instead that the aesthetics of the sites should be understood within the larger context of the sites. One of the problems of the web is the lack of control the producer of the website has over the audience. Anyone may choose to look at such sites. One purpose of the sites appearance, then, is to instantly tell the audience whether or not the producer regards them as appropriate. My expectation would be that the ordinary surfer or even shopper would dismiss such sites with a flick of the mouse. But these sites would be regarded as failures if they drew the attention of such an audience to the company. After all, in most respects wholesale companies don't particularly want shoppers to know about wholesale prices, nor does a company selling processed meats necessarily want shoppers to know that they also manufacture mosquito coils. One reason these are marketed as separate brands is that this draws the shoppers' attention away from what might be seen as a lack of commitment to the qualities of particular kinds of manufactured goods.

The audience that such websites are seeking are commercial firms such as retailers or exporters who are looking among wholesalers for cheap sources of the products they wish to sell. The low production values suggest a firm that has not spent money on the mere appearance of the firm but kept costs to a minimum providing retailers or exporters with the opportunity to make the profits for themselves. This is, of course, the reason the flyers that acted as precedents for these websites were themselves so 'cheap'-looking. A glossy website that had kept my attention or that of other individual purchasers and who then contacted the firm would simply be an annoyance for that firm. So what might be seen as a lack of aesthetics may be just as effective an aesthetic strategy as the more obvious innovatory and striking forms.

Similarly the entire site of the law firm of Fitzwilliams, Stone, Furness, Smith and Morgan is comprised of simple-font black text on a white background, and the emphasis throughout is on the precise and the concise. The home-page provides basic information that the firm was established in 1919. The only colour is the hyperlinks to standard information which includes a list of areas in which the firm practices, and short terse paragraphs about each of their fourteen lawyers, giving information on their training and specializations. The site is so prim that no-one could suggest its 'descent' into web advertising was in any respect demeaning. This makes the web as other artworks conform to Gell's notion of a trap as 'both a model of its creator, the hunter, and a model of its victim, the prey animal. But more than this the trap embodies a scenario, which is the dramatic nexus that binds these two protagonists together, and which aligns them in time and space' (1996: 27). The flyer and the prim legal office are aesthetic forms that help orientate the web as trap to their specific victims – those who would be drawn to such services. The aesthetic represents an attempt to align web creator and potential surfer in time and space, so that each can, as it were, dock alongside the other in cyberspace.

Once this point is established for the least striking sites, its application is quite obvious to the often highly impressive websites found in other genres. The teenagers themselves are seeking to become (if you'll forgive the pun) Kula and cooler at once. What they desire most is to create a circuit of sociality in which they can grow their fame as the fame of their individual website among a group of peers. This requires not only the work on the aesthetic of the site itself to make it a trap that will draw in any passing surfer but also work to elaborate the circuit of peer teenagers within which this fame can circulate. This may be done by having guest comments grow at the base of their site, so that their fame can be seen clearly to grow in length rather like the beard of a respected elder in other societies, but also they expand through linking their circle of friends with those of others who are seduced by the aesthetics of one's site.

By the time the website constructors are of student age the mini-Kula of school groups becomes the full imperative to develop the fame of Trinis. As was noted, the tremendous emphasis on representing the individual as Trinidadian and the visit to the site as the inculcation of Trinidadian culture was true for those in the Diaspora such as Students and others at American Universities, but was also true for those that remained within Trinidad. The website links entirely disregard this distinction. These sites also use the mechanism of the web to draw the visitor into channels which keep them within Trinidadian circuits of relationships. It is not just that their links include other Trinidadians as part of their lime, but there is a constant encouragement also for surfers to visit these others sites. For example one site notes 'This is a link to my friend Giselle. A very cool page so go to it, you know you want to see it' and also 'The home of the Cyber Trini. See it to believe it'. Sites will also offer to create mutual links to any other Trinidadian with a website who is interested in doing so, such that the circuit is defined above all through common nationality. This is also made concrete through the development of a Trini-Web-ring, which allows visitors to go either systematically or randomly around the 61 connected sites which include a mixture of commercial and personal websites of people from Trinidad. In all such cases there is a pooling of resources to make each of them a contribution to an overall sense of the fame or web-brilliance of Trinidad per se. This is even clearer when one includes the personal websites that have become guides to virtual Trinidad or themselves virtual guide-books as informal Trinidad home-pages.

The term 'trap' as coined for aesthetic forms by Gell, combined with the terms 'web' and 'net' as coined for the internet provides an appropriately evocative sense of the experience of surfing. There seems minimal semantic work involved in moving from Gell's (1996) analysis of Vogel's net to the inter-net as traps. Even as a researcher I found that almost on a daily basis I would start with the intention of following one particular route of investigation and then find myself seduced by the aesthetics of one of the websites visited and moved by the simplicity of clicking to follow a link proffered by that site. A few more clicks would send me hurtling down some channels carved out of cyberspace by the sculptured links of these website creators, often to such a degree that it was hard to retrieve the original place from which this diversion had begun, but often grateful that my lack of determination had in fact led to me to view some unexpected vistas and delight in some other creations than those I would otherwise have encountered. For there are traps in cyberspace that seem almost wilfully designed to snare the unwary anthropologist, with their promise of insights into the intimacy of other people's sociality and revelations of the contradictions of the self.

Website Time-Space

Gell was unusual in that he gave equal weight to the transformation of temporality involved in such an expansion of space-time as to the more obvious metaphor of expanded space. Although most of the art-works he described are from genres and styles based on relatively stable contexts and although anthropology does not usually work with phenomena quite as dynamic as the internet, Gell, one of whose previous books had been on the topic of time (1992), was much concerned with the temporal context of the art-work. This is evident if the Maori meeting house of the final paragraph of his book *Art and Agency* (1998) is transposed for the current topic:

> The *web* (in its totalized form) is an object which we are able to trace as a movement of thought, a movement of memory reaching down into the past and a movement of aspiration, probing towards an unrealized, and perhaps unrealizable futurity. Through the study of these artifacts, we are able to grasp 'mind' as an external (and eternal) disposition of public acts of objectification, and simultaneously as the evolving consciousness of a collectivity, transcending the individual cogito and the coordinates of any particular here and now' (1998: 258).

The only way we can comprehend such material is, as Gell suggests, as a moment in a trajectory. On the one hand it points backwards to its own and various precedents, forms such as résumés, catalogues and flyers, from which it borrows through sometimes clear and sometimes convoluted intertextuality. Yet at the same times it is obvious that what has been described within this chapter will later on be seen as the blueprint for some future development which we cannot at this time predict or envisage even though we are dealing with its origins. For example, the major constraint at present is not what people can do in creating websites but the technology that makes downloading so slow. If as seems likely this is removed as the bottleneck in the next few years then we can expect an explosion of creativity in web construction. As Gell says, 'An artifact or event is never either traditional or innovatory in any absolute sense' (1998: 256). Only in its relationship to others of the trajectory of which it is a part. This is true also of writings about the web. Even those discussions that have recently been published tend to focus more on *text-based* communication simply, in my view, because the *visual* forms I have concentrated on have become this common only within the last two years (e.g. see Shields 1996; Jones 1997).

Perhaps even more than other forms of advertising, commercial websites are burdened by their own heightened temporality. Basically there are few things as stale-looking when surfing the web as a website that has clearly not been updated for quite some time. This is pertinent since websites give so many hostages to fortune with respect to their temporal immediacy. For commercial websites the fact that they often give dated information on events in Trinidad such as Carnival, or an offer of a Christmas sale which is being looked at several months after Christmas, makes the site stale. The problem for teenage sites is that for them, as for so much of the web, status is based around the concept of 'cool' where cool is the place to be at any particular time. This tallies well with a Trinidadian sense of events more generally, where people hang around for hours outside a fête or party until they are sure this is really the place to be that night, and a lime can easily be said to be 'out of juice' if it is not really a 'happening' event. Cool as a semantic term does not easily divulge its networks of connotations and evocations, but clearly it is a place where one has to keep on running to stay still on the site of cool. Websites that do not update, either evidently because of some dated character or because they look the same as they did when the surfer last inspected them, at a time when change is so normal risk becoming quite uncool rather swiftly. Just as outer space is becoming littered with old parts of redundant satellites and so forth, so even more is cyberspace strewn with debris and relics of sites that were going to become cool personal pages, key conduits that would channel the surfer's interest. But with their faded signs of 'site still under construction' or data which ends in 1996, they have become instead the dead-ends a surfer wades through on the route to something genuinely cool.

Websites as Objectifications

In *Art and Agency* (1998), Gell applies his ideas equally to the traditional subjects of the anthropology of art and to the oeuvre of modern artists such as Duchamp. The foundation of his approach is a theory of objectification. I would readily acknowledge that this represents many advances upon the approach to object-ification I developed in Miller (1987). Such theories are intended to overcome the basic dualism of subjects and objects. Gell contends that objects should in many circumstances be regarded as in and of themselves social agents with social efficacy, not merely the sign of some other agency. As a sub-set of this theory he argues that works of art, in particular, act as 'traps' – forms that are intended or are able to entrap and capture the mind and purpose of others. Complex and convoluted patterns trap the mind of the observer and aesthetic forms captivate the attention and will of others.

Works of art, suggests Gell, should be regarded as external extensions or objectifications of mind, just as personhood extends inwards in various layers. The idea is elaborated by reference to Ibsen's *Peer Gynt* peeling away the layers of an onion (as a metaphor of the self) to find nothing but layers within. So also the self can extend outwards in further layers where the self is externalized. This may be through the stylistic oeuvre of the individual artist such as Picasso. But for Gell an equal case may be made for collective ritual works, such as Malanggan (see Küchler 1988) wooden funerary memorials which as artworks extend the capacity of the dead person to retain his or her collected social efficacy, for example land rights, until these can be formally distributed, and the corpse thus emptied of its social relations.

In understanding culture as a form of extension both Gell and I were drawn to the arguments of Munn (1986) applied to the classic anthropological case-study of the Kula ring. I wish to argue now that these attempts to engage with Munn's analysis of the Kula are enormously enhanced thanks to the development of the internet. Not only are websites works of art in Gell's sense that they are attempts to develop social efficacy that will entrap the will of others, but also as in the Kula they employ aesthetic forms to go out into the world – whose infrastructure they constitute – in order to grow the collective fame of those who create them and who move around this virtual circuit through them.

Indeed the parallel is so close that there are several places where Gell's words can be slightly modified (see my italics) from the case of the Kula to that of the internet and still be used as profound insights. For example: 'when we come to consider the expanded, transactable, "persons" and personhood on which the *web* is founded, we are brought to recognise that "mind" can exist objectively as well as subjectively; that is as a pattern of transactable objects' indexes of personhood in this instance, . . . *the web* is a form of cognition that takes place outside the body, which is diffused in space and time and which is carried on through the medium of *virtual* indexes and transactions involving them' (1998: 232). 'A *web* operator is clearly a "spatio-temporally extended person"' (1998: 229). 'How does one, in practice, become a great *web* operator, a person able to "move minds" at great distances and dominate an expanded region of social space and time? How does one become so enchantingly attractive, so irresistibly persuasive, that the paths of *international* exchange converge ineluctably in the desired direction?' (1998: 231).

If I were to draw back, with respect to one issue from Gell's approach to objectification, to that I developed in Miller (1987) it would be in terms of my greater stress on the dialectical – that is, the way the objectification changes and develops the subject. As Keane (1997) has so clearly demonstrated, we ignore at our peril the consequences of the particular materiality within which objectification often takes place. Gell constantly reminds us that art forms are not mere reflections of some other agency, they need to be understood also as social agents. Websites have considerable autonomy from their initial creators in their capacity within cyberspace to 'do stuff'. As such these outer layers of the self re-engage and transform those who created them, both selves and companies, who may find themselves caught up in the enthusiasms, consequences and sheer speed of web involvement. The creator of the site tempted to make one more link and one more page mirrors the surfer caught by some 'sticky' visual effect, and led on to some other channel. We become entrapped by our own creations, drawn into the intricacies of their aesthetics. In the extreme case there is the nerd or geek, trapped in his or her technological involvement, but for many others the sheer fascination of the web draws one into its labyrinthine networks. Once we set a trap we too can become ensnared by its complexity and aesthetic brilliance.

Conclusion

There are several factors that make this approach to websites as traps particularly appropriate. First, it helps us appreciate the precise aesthetics of the websites, and consider how as traps they have to model not only the forms of their creators but also those of their intended victims. Secondly, this approach helps us break down the internet from some reified icon of the Zeitgeist encountered in much of the contemporary literature on this subject to something that is highly recognizable in terms of that most classic of anthropological case-studies – the Kula. Thirdly, the approach allows us to break down the phenomenon of the internet into a whole series of sub-genres that reflect the considerable diversity of the communities that use the net.

Following Gell, the argument has been made that, as aesthetic forms, websites may be considered artworks whose purpose is to entrap or captivate other wills so that they will come into relationship with them, exchanging either in economic or social intercourse. They are not mere idiosyncratic or individual extensions, since even after a very short time they take on genred and conventional forms as a collective oeuvre of artworks that enable us to recognize and respond to what is presented, and constrain the individual or company into the techniques and strategies of the web. With respect at least to Trinidadian websites the intention as in *The Fame of Gawa* (Munn 1986) seems to be to expand Trinidadian persons and companies in cyberspace by capturing the attention and custom of others to come back in that form of social efficacy that may be called Fame, which includes wealth, power and reputation. The web is hardly unique in this: I am very aware that I write so soon after the sad death of Gell, whose mind is objectified in his own book. I have been willingly entrapped by the exhilarating beauty of his creation and my sense that his ideas seem so easily extended beyond the application he had envisaged. It is as though the internet was almost invented to illustrate his theoretical propositions with particular clarity and thus Malanggan-like to extend his distributed social efficacy beyond his death.

Notes

1. This chapter is written on the basis of a visual inspection of the websites only, examining them as art forms. This was carried out prior to the main ethnographic study of the internet in Trinidad, which was undertaken with Don Slater (Dept. of Sociology, Goldsmiths College). The results of the ethnography have since been published (Miller and Slater (2001)). For that book we created our own

website which includes illustrations of a wide range of Trinidadian websites including many of those discussed in this chapter. These may be viewed at ethnonet.gold.ac.uk. In some cases the appearance of the sites changed between the time they were analysed for this article and the collation of an archive of these sites for the book, so there are a few discrepancies between the descriptions given here and what can be observed there. In addition the book includes further research that was carried out in Trinidad on the production of websites and on the consumption of websites. This research supported the conclusions that emerge from this chapter and I have therefore not attempted to re-write the chapter in the light of the ethnography, but the ethnography provides considerably more contextual information and other theoretical and substantive conclusions than can be supplied in this limited forum. This chapter was written while I was a British Academy Research Reader.

The island of Trinidad is part of the nation of Trinidad and Tobago; my experience is largely confined to Trinidad itself and along with many of the people of that island I will use the shorthand of Trinidadian or Trinis for nationals.

2. During the ethnography we came across a remarkable number of cases of Trinidadians who had established sustained relationships with people from other countries they had encountered on chat lines, later on met in person, and in some cases subsequently married.

3. The extensive use of the internet in some secondary schools is discussed further in Miller and Slater (2001). In one case we were told chat had become so ubiquitous that a class of schoolchildren have come to call each other by their ICQ nicks (on-line chat names) rather than their real names!

References

Eriksen, T. 1990. 'Liming in Trinidad: The Art of Doing Nothing'. *Folk* 32: 23–43.

Gell, A. 1992 *The Anthropology of Time*. Oxford: Berg

—— 1996. 'Vogel's Net: Traps as Artworks and Artworks as Traps'. *Journal of Material Culture* 1: 15–38.

—— 1998. *Art and Agency: An Anthropological Theory*. Oxford: Oxford University Press.

Jones, G. 1997. *Virtual Culture*. London: Sage.

Keane, W. 1997. *Signs of Recognition*. Berkeley: University of California Press.

Küchler, S. 1988. 'Malanggan: Art and Memory in a Melanesian Society'. *Man* 22: 238–55.

Miller, D. 1987. *Material Culture and Mass Consumption*. Oxford: Blackwell.

—— 1993. 'Spot the Trini'. *Ethnos*: 3–4: 317–34.

—— 1994. *Modernity: An Ethnographic Approach*. Oxford: Berg.

—— 1997. *Capitalism: An Ethnographic Approach*. Oxford: Berg.

Miller, D. and Slater, D. (2001) *The Internet: An Ethnographic Approach*. Oxford: Berg. Illustrations published at ethnonet.gold.ac.uk

Munn, 1986. *The Fame of Gawa*. Cambridge: Cambridge University Press.

Pearse, A. (ed.). 1956. *Trinidad Carnival*. Port of Spain: Paria Publishing.

Shields, R. (ed.). 1996. *Cultures of the Internet*. London: Sage.

8

Piercing the Skin of the Idol
Christopher Pinney

Religion is the oldest of archives in our subcontinent. All the principal moments of the ancient relationship of dominance and subordination are recorded in it as codes of authority, collaboration and resistance.

(Guha 1985:1)

The 'anthropological' theory of art proposed in *Art and Agency* 'merges seamlessly with the social anthropology of persons and their bodies' (Gell 1998: 7). Building on David Freedberg, among others, Alfred Gell does a brilliant job of persuading us that anthropologists should concern themselves with the performative dimension of artefacts. In the first part of the book, at least, he rejects a linguistic approach, dwelling instead on the agency of images.

The analysis of image-worshipping practices in a central Indian village which I shall present in this chapter confirms Gell's stress on the agency of images, but my concern is also to try to resolve an earlier question of Alfred's about the nature of aesthetics, and to transpose some of the discussion onto an avowedly political ground. In his 1992 article on the technology of enchantment, Alfred drew a parallel with Peter Burger's suggestion that analysts of religion should adopt a standpoint of 'methodological atheism'. Anthropologists of art required an analogous 'methodological philistinism' which would involve 'an attitude of resolute indifference towards the aesthetic value of works of art' (Gell 1992: 42).

Rather than a resolute indifference, I will propose a sideways step away from 'aesthetics' to 'corpothetics' as one way of comprehending the praxis through which enchantment manifests itself. I will present this argument in relation to the history and contemporary village consumption of mass-produced religious chromolithographs. The first part of my discussion considers a shift from what Michael Fried (1980) terms 'absorptive' to 'theatrical' images from the late nineteenth century onwards, and the second part draws on Susan Buck-Morss's work (1992) to articulate a practice of 'corpothetics'. In my concluding comments I question whether, when seen as part of practice rather than of formal analysis, what appear to be related art practices can be said to form a 'macroscopic whole' (Gell 1998: 221) rather than – in some contexts – divided and mutually antagonistic forms.

Space permits me only to briefly skate over the impact of Government Art Schools in creating a new form of 'strategic mimcry' in nineteenth-century India. The convention of single-point perspective was seen as the key which would unravel an Indian resistance to the 'powers of observation'. In an elusive manner Panofsky (1991) hinted that single-point perspective co-opted a religious expectation into a technical procedure, and there are grounds for suggesting that the value of perspectival representation to its colonial proponents lay in its capacity to translate value from content to form. Just as gold had migrated from the surface of the picture to the frame, perspective facilitated the displacement of fetishistic representation into the very structure of representation itself. Advocates of Art Schools, such as Richard Temple, positioned perspective as part of a larger scientistic project which they imagined would lead to the supercession of 'traditional' paradigms by 'modern, rational' ones.

We can also understand the representational changes encouraged by the Art Schools in terms of Michael Fried's distinction between 'theatricality' and 'absorption'. The European art whose shadow was cast over India had passed through engagements with vanishing points that incarnated corporeal viewers to a practice that in Norman Bryson's words implied a 'transcendent point of vision that has discarded the body' (1983: 106–7). Bryson's arguments parallel those of Michael Fried who observes the rise of what he calls the 'supreme fiction' of an absent beholder in late eighteenth-century French painting. This disembodied 'absorption' was exported to India and can be seen as an attempt – in tandem with the Art School's stress on 'naturalism' – to deny the magical origin of images. The move towards absorption is clear in the output of the Calcutta Art Studio. Formed in 1878 by graduates of the Calcutta School of Art, many of its chromo-lithographic images were structured by an internalized gaze. Nala looked at Damayanti, not the viewer of the picture; likewise Shiv turned his vision towards the 'Oriental cupid', not to the devotee gazing at the image. Pre-existing ritual images, and later (post-1920s) 'magical realist' paintings by contrast, assumed an embodied 'corpothetics'. By corpothetics I mean the sensory embrace of images, the bodily engagement that most people (except Kantians and modernists) have with artworks.

In Michael Fried's work the driving forces of change in European art – from French eighteenth-century history painting through to modernism – are strategies that deny the presence of the beholder through strategies of 'absorption'. Drawing in detail on Diderot's critical commentaries, Fried describes an increasing disparagement of paintings that acknowledge the presence of the beholder. These acknowledgements usually involved direct eye-contact between the picture's subject and the beholder, a relationship Diderot disdained:

> Lairesse claims that the artist is permitted to have the beholder enter the scene of his painting. I do not believe it, and there are so few exceptions that I would gladly make a

general rule of the opposite. That would seem to me in as poor taste as the performance of an actor who would address himself to the audience. The canvas encloses all the space and there is no one beyond it. When Susannah exposes her naked body to my eyes, protecting herself against the elders' gaze with all the veils that enveloped her, Susannah is chaste and so is the painter. Neither the one nor the other knew I was there (cited in Fried 1980: 96).

In addition to its more obvious explanation, this voyeurism can also be thought as a circumlocution that constructed a 'privileged' art as the antithesis of ritual art, i.e. that art whose sole raison d'être is to act as a conduit between beholder and deity. We can also treat this as part of an archaeology of the aesthetic mystification of art which is critiqued in Alfred's earlier work and the first sections of *Art and Agency*.

Fried thus emerges as the antithesis of Gell for Fried deprecates anything that reminds us of art's primary function.[1] 'Good' art for Fried is art which negates the presence of the beholder. Making a link between his study of eighteenth-century French art and 1960s modernism he concludes that mediocre work has a 'theatrical' relation to the beholder, whereas the 'very best recent work' is 'in essence *anti-theatrical*' (1980: 5). The emergence of modern art, Mitchell writes in his valuable gloss,

is precisely to be understood in terms of the negation or renunciation of direct signs of desire. The process of pictorial seduction Fried admires is successful precisely in proportion to its indirectness, its seeming indifference to the beholder, its antitheatrical 'absorption' in its own internal drama (1996: 79).

Fried's privileging of indirectness might be condemned in a Bourdieuan idiom as Kantian reification, but it might also be seen as a strategy to numb the human sensorium, taking the image away from the direct presence of the beholder and from the realm of 'corpothetics' to what Susan Buck-Morss (1992) terms 'anaesthetics'. The internalized absorption of the paintings becomes a means of transferring the beholder's own encounter into the subject of the image in what might be termed the fetish that dare not speak its name. Absorption, indirectness and history painting, were part of the package exported by the colonial state into its Government Art Schools in the nineteenth century. The 'supreme fiction' of the absent beholder becomes – in colonial India – a mark of Western 'distinction' and a marker of distance from Hindu idols. Here, in Hans Belting's words is the epochal divide between an 'era of art' and an 'era before art' (Belting 1994).

However, whereas in Fried's account 'absorption' marked an irreversible shift towards a desirable indirection, in popular Indian art its tenuous hold was quickly lost as consumers started to demand images stripped of this 'supreme fiction', images that fundamentally addressed their presence and invoked a new corpothetics.

The difference here reflects not so much a cleavage between France/Europe and India, as a difference between an elite and a public aesthetic, for there are many centrally important aspects of 'Western' visual culture (for instance pornography, or the iconography of sport) that reject indirection and value corpothetics just as there are numerous Old Masters in Western galleries which function as ritually sanctified persons.[2]

The hold of absorption and history painting was tenuous and reached its apogee in the work of Ravi Varma, the Indian painter who is most amenable to the Western genre of art historical evaluation. Partly this is the result of his own self-mystification in Vasarian mode but it is, more importantly, the result of his adoption of a painterly style that strove for the 'supreme fiction'. His most canonized works are those that look past the beholder. Ravi Varma's characters behave as if they had heard and ingested Diderot's command: 'think no more of the beholder than if he did not exist. Imagine at the edge of the stage, a high wall that separates you from the orchestra. Act as if the curtain never rose' (cited by Fried 1980: 95). It is this which his imperial patrons so admired. Conversely it is this (dominant) element of Ravi Varma's work which is so utterly invisible in the archive of Indian popular visual culture. The fragments that do survive of his work are those sensory images which unequivocally acknowledge the beholder's presence. In these images the beholder is a worshipper, drinking the eyes of the deity that gazes directly back at him.

We can conceptualize this historical transition as that between 'absorptive' and 'theatrical' images (to invoke Fried), but we can also think about them in terms of the difference between what Susan Buck-Morss describes as 'anaesthetics' and 'aesethetics'.[3] In rethinking Benjamin's 'work of art' essay she has argued that the original field of aesthetics encoded in the Greek *aisthitikos* connoted a broad domain of sensory reality. The 'modern science of aesthetics', however, 'understood as detached contemplation rather than instinctual cognition, functions as a form of anaethetization, a way for numbing the human sensorium, overwhelmed by the shock of war or the shock of industrialization' (Efimova 1997: 75). In a wonderful application of these ideas Alla Efimova shows how Soviet Social Realism mobilizes an aesthetics in its original sensory meaning. 'From this perspective, the aesthetics of Soviet everyday life no longer appears to be a paradox. As a powerful stimulation of the senses, by means of pain, fear, or exaltation, life did not need to be beautiful or pleasing to be "aesthetic"' (ibid.). The aesthetics of Socialist Realism, therefore, are not of the anaesthetizing variety. They 'touch on the raw', and de-anaesthetize.

Buck-Morss's[4] archaeology of aesthetics is peculiarly useful for our understanding of mass-picture production in India for here we encounter images produced within and mediated by the anaesthetizing discourses, and those produced within and mediated by sensory practices. If we envisage this as a continuum, rather than a dichotomy, we can place images produced in Calcutta in the late nineteenth century nearer the 'anaesthetized' end, and the popular twentieth-century 'magical realist' images can be placed at the other. It is the numbing of the human sensorium which makes the colonial mimicry of earlier images so compatible with conventional art historical exegesis. It is the sensory immediacy of the later images which makes them so intractable to conventional analysis and regard, one important reason being the absence of 'aesthetic' exegesis by those that consume them. The central Indian villagers whose picture-buying and worshipping practices I now want to briefly consider do not surround them with reified discourses. Rather, they speak of a depicted deity's efficacy, and link the origination of the image to their own biographies (for example it may have been purchased at a pilgrimage site). For an Anthropology driven by the need to accumulate linguistic testimony, this is a severe problem. Buck-Morss's ideas, however, lead us to an understanding of a different dimension of significance in which it is not the efflorescence of words around an object that gives it meaning but a bodily praxis, a poetry of the body, that helps give images what they want.

In India, the reawakening of the human sensorium went hand in hand with the insertion of mass-produced images into spaces of Hindu worship. This relocation had a twofold characteristic, involving movements towards, on the one hand, sacralized spaces and, on the other, domestic spaces. Thus there was a movement from mundane spaces such as the Art Schools into temples where images had a different work to perform. The need to demonstrate appreciation through explanation was replaced by bodily gestures and the look of the devotee. The other parallel movement involved the displacement of pictures from the drawing rooms of colonial India's elite to the crowded shelf of the domestic puja-room. This entailed new forms of physical intimacy with images and an increasing irrelevance of formal 'anaesthetized' discourse. Something of this trajectory can be seen in the way in which technologies of reproduction – first chromolithography and then photography – have allowed Pushtimarg devotees an increasing bodily intimacy with Shri Nathji, the Nathdvara *svarup*. Today the photographic studios outside the temple contain painted simulacra of the deity in front of which devotees pose and physical proximity can be recorded.

A recurrent refrain in the analysis of popular art traditions concerns the ways in which consumers of images are either unable or unwilling to speak about their form. This hesitancy to produce reified discourse about art objects is, indeed, sometimes taken as an excuse to maintain the distance between such unarticulable practices and the great industry of art historical exegesis (a divide which *Art and Agency* will do much to erode). True, Pierre Bourdieu (1984) has chosen to eulogize what he sees as a popular elision of life and art as an alluring opposition to the idiocies of the bourgeois enchantment with form, but generally the absence of such discourse is taken simply as proof of a disabling lack.

Shifting the level of analysis from aesthetics (i.e. anaesthetics in Buck-Morss's terms) to corpothetics discloses not a lack but a rich and complex praxis through which villages articulate their eyes and bodies in relation to pictures. The 'meaning' of the images lies in their 'needs' – the necessity of worshipping them, in 'corpothetics' rather than 'anaesthetics'.

The village of Bhatisuda,[5] located on the Malwa plateau in Madhya Pradesh, is inhabited by many eager consumers of the images whose history has been fleetingly touched on earlier. Chromolithographs are popular across all castes and religious groups. Jains and Muslims own images as well as Hindus, and Scheduled Caste Chamars and (warrior) Rajputs or (priestly) Brahmans own similar numbers of images. (Across the village as whole there is an average of 6.9 images per household.)

Bhatisuda's population is spread through 21 castes, and although village income is still overwhelmingly derived from agriculture (the main crops being maize, sorghum and wheat), the presence of the largest viscose rayon factory in Asia a mere six kilometres away in the town of Nagda has had an enormous impact on the economic fortunes of landless labourers, and has structured local discourses on history and the nature of progress. The village cosmology reflects the nature of popular Hinduism in this area and there are temples and shrines to the main gods: Ram, Hanuman, Krishna, Shiv, Ganesh, Shitala; and also to local deities: Tejaji, Ramdevji, Jhujhar Maharaj, Bihari Mata, Lal Mata, Rogiya Devi, Nag Maharaj, and many more.

The horizontal and vertical topography of the village encodes a symbolic separation and hierarchization of the diverse *jati* groupings that make up Bhatisuda. Higher-caste households are predominantly built on higher ground in the centre of the village and most Scheduled Castes live in untouchable *jati mohallas* on the south side of the village. Chamars live nearest the village in compact groups of small huts, and Bagdis inhabit a more dispersed *mohalla* which forms a spur, spreading from the village down towards the River Chambal.

Villagers encounter religious 'objects mediating social agency' in various different forms. Here I will briefly consider consecrated temple images, the presence of deities in the human bodies which they 'thrash' (i.e. 'possesss')[6] and (at more length) chromolithographs. The first two of these manifestations are fully and illuminatingly discussed in *Art and Agency* and a chromolithograph by B.G. Sharma of Santoshi Ma features as an illustration.

Although a small number of temple images are *svarups* – that is, 'self-made' images – most are of the two sorts described in *Art and Agency*: reincarnations of existing ones (as in the Puri *navakalevara* [Gell 1998: 144–5]), or (more commonly) the 'more abstract' Brahmanic consecration through *mantras*. Both of these equally depend on an indexical contiguity, for in these contexts Brahmans are simply conduits for a pre-existing power which is summoned in the material form of *mantras*.[7]

I asked Pukhraj Bohra, a Jain landlord living in the central square of Bhatisuda, which images in the locality were *chamatkari* (miraculous, wonderous):

Nageshvar Pareshavar near Alod is a very *chamatkari* image. It came out from the inside automatically. It was in the earth. It's possible that someone made it and buried it but I don't think so. When I first went there 15 years ago I made a wish (*man*). I asked that my business should go well, that the crops should prosper and then I came back. But there was some psychic (*mansik*) effect from this, some allurement (*akarshan*) born in the *murti*. When I was away I felt that I had to go back and see the image, had to see it again and again.

This sense of *akarshan* – the spell that the image produces on those who get its *darshan* – was articulated even more forcibly by Hemant Mehra, the Bombay resident son of Har Narayan the famous chromolithograph publisher in Jodhpur, Rajasthan:

I first went [with my mother] to the Chamunda Devi temple in Jodhpur Fort 20 years ago. Then 6 years ago I woke up in the middle of the night and couldn't get back to sleep. It was 5 am and I just couldn't get the temple and the fort out of my mind. At 6 am I took my scooter up to the temple[8] which was closed. I felt that the temple was mine. The priest opened the temple and I meditated for 5–10 minutes. Before that I never used to meditate and suddenly I just felt like I was floating in the sky, upside down, like jumping from a parachute (sic) . . . sitting but couldn't feel the ground. I felt I belonged to this place. I don't know what happened but I looked into the eyes of the statue and something happened eye to eye. I started crying . . . pure tears were coming out and I thought what is happening? The pandit told me that Chamunda Devi had called me. I had been twice to Vaishnoo Devi[9] but nothing like this ever happened. I walked away and I felt like I was under some shadow of protection . . . [then for a long time] I had to keep going back to Jodhpur and spending more and more time there. It was like a magnetic power.[10]

What emerges strongly in these accounts is the erasure of the recipients' agency as they are propelled towards actions over which they have no control. In Bhatisuda a parallel sense (of the index as patient) emerges as the chief criterion for adjudicating the genuineness of possession.[11] Alfred considers Michael Allen's ethnography of Newar *kumaripuja*, the worship of the living embodiments of Durga, and concludes that *kumaris* are consecrated in the same ways as manufactured artefacts: 'there is an insensible transition between "works of art" in artefact form and human beings . . . they may be regarded as almost entirely equivalent'. I will argue at the end of this chapter that while those who 'thrash' are clearly similar in some way to artefacts such as temple images, there are also fundamental differences and they often find themselves in conflict.

Our understanding of the role of chromolithographs for many people in Bhatisuda must start from a recognition of the prohibitions that still prevent most Scheduled Caste members from entering village temples. Although many Scheduled Castes have their own caste-specific shrines (*autla, sthanak*) they are generally unable to enter village temples to the main gods. Whereas 'clean' castes may enter temple precincts, Scheduled Castes are required to squat outside, at some distance. Channu and Lila Mehta – the village Bhangis[12] – are quite explicit that it is this denial which necessitates their domestic engagement with the Gods through chromolithographs. Confirming that her family were still unable to enter most of the village temples, Lila remarked, 'for this reason we have made a temple inside our house'.

Channu and Lila Mehta live in a low mud house on the eastern periphery of Bhatisuda overlooking a steep gulley which drops down to a Chamar *mohalla*. The most striking feature inside the house is a small black and white television, a gift from one of Channu's Nagda resident brothers. To the right of this, two-thirds of the way up the wall is a display of fifteen assorted images, together with a few clay *murtis* (three-dimensional images). In the sort of arrangement which is common in the village, a line of images are displayed above and below wooden shelves bearing an assortment of three dimensional images, colourful decorations and steel cups. Among Channu and Lila's display there are large laminated prints depicting Laksmi and Ganesh, Arjun, Ram Sita and Lakshman, a large black Shivling, and various images of Lakshmi showering wealth from the palms of her hands. There are also two framed prints of the Rajasthani renouncer king Ramdevji, and the Krishnalila, a large glittered image of Satyanarayan in a wooden shrine-like structure, and a mirrored glass panel depicting the local Krishna incarnation Samvaliyaji. Add to this a couple of postcards of Shiv and the Buddha, a couple of paper prints of Durga and Shiv, plaster images of Ganesh and Shiv, two women with their hands folded in a welcoming namaste, a couple of mirrors, some peacocks, tinsel and sundry other plastic decorations together with a flock of frenzied green parrots and the ensemble is complete.

Apart from the glass mirrored image these were all purchased in Nagda – the nearby town – where there are two shops, and one stall specializing in 'framing prints', which prior to the festival of Dipali are supplemented by about a dozen small stalls and itinerant tradespersons selling religious images. Most of Channu and Lila's images were purchased in successive years just before Dipali, and this is reflected in the predominance of images of the goddess Laksmi who is worshipped during this festival which marks the start of the financial year.

The glass mirrored image depicts Samvaliyaji, Avari Mata and Bhadva Mata who are the subject of a recently flourishing cult in Mandsaur District. Channu and Lila had visited the Samvaliyaji temple, as also the nearby Bhadva Mata shrine several years ago and had purchased the image from a stall there. At Samvaliyaji, and also Pavargadh in Gujarat which they had recently visited, Channu and Lila's *madhyam* (low)[13] *jati* and *uttam* (high) *jatis* are indistinguishable for here there is no *chhuachhut* (untouchability) or *bhed bhav* (hierarchy).

Lila's testimony also clearly marks out pilgrimage as an egalitarian activity, not only because many *tirth* (i.e. pilgrimage) sites operate in liminal caste-free spaces, but also because the dislocations of travel and the anonymity of the crowd nullifies any attempt at the sort of *jati* identity which is so entrenched and enforceable in a stable village community. Beyond this parallelism between the dissemination of the divine permitted by lithography, and the comparative openness of the spaces in which pilgrimage happens, we might also point to a simple logistical entanglement – a substantial minority (18 per cent) of all the images in the survey households were purchased at pilgrimage sites and depict deities associated with those.

Hans Belting opens his awesome study of the first millennium of Christian religious images with a series of observations about the relationship between images

Figure 8.1 Glass mirrored image of Samvaliyaji

and theologians in the European tradition. He presents a history of a 'war' between popular images and religious hierarchies, and between the figural and the linguistic. The growing popularity of images was seen as a direct threat to the power of the Church since they might 'act directly in God's name'. Images spoke to a deep level of experience and desire which was profoundly subversive of the linguistic imprisonment of the divine that institutional religious structures projected. Theologians assumed a reactive position towards images seeking to 'explain' them and 'rather than introducing images, theologians were all too ready to ban them' (Belting 1994: 1).

The contrast between the practices Belting describes and those in India is powerful and unavoidable. It is true that there were occasional iconoclastic movements in modern India (for instance the early Arya Samaj and many currents within the 'Bengal Renaissance') but overwhelmingly images have had a great freedom to act on their own, untrammelled by the concerns of theologians. Indeed theology has frequently concerned itself with the eulogization of images.

This suggests a profound orientation within societies to either discursive closure (e.g. through the endless debate about the intentionality of sacred texts) or figurality in which significance is part of an ongoing visual and performative project. Attention is directed not towards a precise interpretive closure, but towards an ongoing performative productivity. One is put in mind of Lyotard's remark that there is always something happening in the arts that 'incandesces the embers of society'. This differential accentuation of the discursive and figural moulds different models of causality. In the one it is language which constrains the image, and in the other it is the image which appropriates language. In Western historiography images are habitually over-determined linguistically (and, as Carlo Ginzburg [1989] notes, this tradition then creates the visual as a puzzling anomaly).

In this light the battle between Bryson's semiotic, linguistically driven approach to art and W.J.T. Mitchell's stress on the 'pictorial turn's' figurality is something of a false contest inasmuch as it concerns itself with a general theory of visuality, rather than with specific theories for diverse traditions. Something of this is also apparent in *Art and Agency* for though it commences with a muscular Mitchellism, disavowing Panofskian and other varieties of linguistic iconography, the structuralist 'formal analysis' that increasingly invades it is ineluctably determined semiotically (though not, Alfred insists, linguistically: cf. Gell 1998: 165–6).

In Bhatisuda the mere possession of visual forms gives access to the ongoing project of divine energy. Although it is undoubtedly true that in certain key respects popular Hinduism mobilizes a recuperative idiom within a decaying universe, it is fundamentally constructed by what the playwright Brian Friel (in a very different context) once described as a 'syntax opulent with tomorrows' (1981: 42). Mass-reproduction gives formerly excluded classes access to all the high gods whom they can approach directly without the intercession of priests.

The 'syntax opulent with tomorrows' which emerges in Bhatisuda practice is one that springs from a corpothetic practice in which it is the devotee's visual and bodily performances which contribute crucially to the potential power – one might say completion – of the image.

Some sense of the mechanism here can be gleaned from the following fragment of a taped interview with Lila. (I should note at this point that I interviewed members of 117 households in the village, and Lila's is consistent with all but one of these others.)

[CP] when the picture is on the trolley in the market is there any energy (*shakti*) in the picture?]

[Lila] It's just paper (*kagaz*). That's all? Yes, paper. It's just paper, it hasn't been seated. You see those pictures that are seated? (Lila pointed to the images on the wall.) Those are paper but by placing them before our eyes (*ankh rakna* = to love, to entertain friendship, to admire), *shakti* has come into them [. . .] We take (the pictures) inside and do *puja*. We place incense sticks (*agarbatti*) against his name, against the God's name. Yes, its a paper photo but we recite, we recite while the *agarbatti* burns. OK, so its a paper photo but [that makes no difference]. We entreat the God and the god comes out because the god is saluted. That's how it is.

The other sense in which Bhatisuda images are opulent with tomorrows lies in the stress on their capacity to give *barkat* – plenitude. Samvaliyaji is an example par excellence of a deity who gives *barkat*. Whereas orthodox deities such as Shiv are considered essential to *alaukik labh* ('disinterested profit'), i.e., transcendental concerns, Samvaliyaji can produce *bhautik labh*, that is material or physical profit. Under the general label of *bhautik* are subsumed uncertainties relating to wealth, bodily health and illness, matters relating to employment and agricultural productivity. Like the vast majority of villagers Pannalal Nai (a retired factory worker) lights incense sticks in front of his images at sunrise and dusk. I ask him what he 'says':

Not much . . . give wisdom, give comfort (*gyan rakhna, aram se rakhna*) I just say that. And then in the evening at say 7.30 or 8 o'clock I say the same things that I said in the morning. God, ensure our protection, give *barkat*, food, water, children, small children, protect all this.

The consumption of images by Bhatisuda villagers needs to be understood in terms of these processes of bodily empowerment which transform pieces of paper into powerful deities through the devotee's gaze, the proximity of his/her heart and a whole repertoire of bodily performances in front of the image (breaking coconuts, lighting incense sticks, folding hands, shaking small bells, the utterance of *mantras*).[14] However, many of these images also bear traces of these activities in their form, and in some cases prescribe the process of viewing itself.

The most fundamental mark of the images' sensory quality – their predisposition to this corpothetic regime – is their non-absorptive directness. The vast majority of images behold their owners directly, engaging and returning their vision. As Diane Eck observes, the primacy of sight as the idiom of articulation between deity and devotee is lexically marked so that devotees will usually stress that they are going to the temple for darshan, to see and be seen by the deity: it is this 'exchange of vision [which] lies at the heart of Hindu worship' (Eck 1981: 5).

There are vivid examples of this process to be seen in popular Hindi films. In *Amar Akbar Anthony* (1977), for instance, the process of *darshan* is literally vision-enhancing: an elderly blind woman pursued into a Sai Baba temple regains her sight through her physical proximity to the *murti* of Sai Baba. Sai Baba's *darshan* is depicted as a pair of lights which physically transfer to the devotee's eyes, restoring her sight.[15]

Most villagers 'seat' their pictures without the assistance of Brahmans. Pannalal Nai, however, calls a Brahman to install newly purchased images. On these occasions the priest will swing the image in front of a mirror and perform a *sthapana* (installation) of the deity.

The desire to see and be seen by deities is also evidenced in the prevalence of mirrored images within the village. These images are usually associated with pilgrimage. *Darshan* can be thought of as a physical relationship of visual intermingling. The value of images is related to the visual access they give to the

Figure 8.2 Chromolithograph of Ramdev pasted behind mirrored glass

deity. As *Art and Agency* documents, mirrored images allow the devotee to (literally) see himself looking at the deity (in this case there is a double corpothetics – of the devotee's movement through space on pilgrimage where he bought the image, and of the devotee's visual elision with the deity when he places himself in front of the image).[16]

Other modes of image customization – such as the application of glitter, or *zari* (brocade) or the adhesion of paper surrounds or plastic flowers – are also corpothetic extensions that move the image closer to the devotee, transforming the ostensible representation or window into a surface deeply inscribed by the presence of the deity.

Parallel to this we might note the manner in which other objects of value are occasionally introduced onto this surface. There were several examples in the village of the placing of auspicious banknotes against the glass of framed images. Sitabai is the wife of a contracted worker in the nearby factory, and once came across a two-rupee note in the mud road to the next village. 'Found' notes are considered auspicious and should not be re-entered into the cycle of exchange from which they have recently departed. Sitabai chose to stick her note on an S.S. Brijbasi chromolithograph of the Ram Durbar. This practice is not confined to Hindus, for there are two prints owned by a Muslim family against which are pasted two Rs.2 notes which bear a serial number containing sequences (the numbers '786') which Muslims hold to be auspicious.[17] The dressing of images takes the place of words. Instead of exegesis, instead of an outpouring of language – there is a poetics of materiality and corporeality around the images.

Arati is a procedure in image worship in which a flame is moved in a circle around an image. In Bhatisuda, villagers then cup their hands over the flame and wash the blessing from the deity onto their face. *Ramdevji ki arati* painted by B.G. Sharma in the mid-1950s (and still in print) exists in several copies in the village and in this artist's characteristically semiotically dense manner inserts the narrative of the deity Ramdev into the very act of worship. The process of *darshan* and the transmission of the 'content' of the picture onto the devotee's face becomes itself the subject, and dictates the form of the picture.

Finally we may note that the whole process of the progressive empowerment of images through daily worship involves a continual burdening of the surface with traces of this devotion. Although some households replace all their images every year at Divali, most have a number of old images which continue to accrue potency as they become accreted with the marks of repeated devotion – vermillion tilaks placed on the foreheads of deities, the ash from incense sticks, smoke stains from burning camphor.

Even at the end of its life, a picture's trajectory is determined by corpothetic requirements, in this case the necessity of ensuring that the image never comes into contact with human feet. Again a fragment from a conversation with Lila:

Figure 8.3 Banknote containing the sequence '786' pasted onto a chromolithograph of Burak-ul-nabi

(The images) are paper and when they have gone bad (*kharab*) we take them from the house and put them in the river. That way we don't get any *pap* (sin). [CP You don't throw them away?] No. no, we don't throw them away. You take them out of the house and put them in the river or in a well, and place them under the water. This way they won't come under anyone's feet. You mustn't throw them away or they will get lost. That's the proper way (*tamizdar*; decorous) to do it – in the river or well. In our jat we say *thanda kardo* – make cold. That way they won't come under [anyone's] feet.

I asked Pannalal whether he threw his old pictures away:

No no, no. It's become just like a small temple (*madhi*). We put them in water, we break a coconut and give them *paraba*[18] – in the water. If you throw them in the street they will come under someone's feet.

In Hindi the phrase *pair ankh se lagana* literally means to look at the feet, and idiomatically 'to respect, venerate' and to touch someone's feet is to physically express one's obeisance. Certain images in Bhatisuda encode this hierarchical relationship in which the devotee submits his or her body – through his or her eyes – to the feet of the deity.[19] It is fundamentally important to Bhatisuda villagers that the bodies of the deities which they have so carefully brought to life should not suffer the dangerous indignity of having this relationship reversed.

Sometimes in Bhatisuda I succumb to the regrettable temptation to brag to villagers about my meetings with the producers of the images which adorn their walls. However, my allusions to artists such as B.G. Sharma or Yogendra Rastogi or others of my acquaintance are always greeted with a supreme indifference that suggests that villagers recognize that they themselves are the true artists who have brought the images to their full fruition.

The images purchased and worshipped by Bhatisudans are very different from Vermeer's *Lacemaker* and Trobriand canoe prow-boards. They produce no sense of 'captivation' (Gell 1998: 68–72) and there is no interest in or recognition of these images as the product of particular artists. Villagers have no conception and no emotional investment in the 'materials artists manipulate', since without the devotee's creative imput the image's do not function properly. Like the *'Slashed' Rokeby Venus* by Mary Richardson (Gell 1998: 63–4), villagers produce infinitely more powerful images than the original artists ever managed.

Villagers' indifference to the base materials from which they fashion their 'seated' images is not reciprocated by the artists, however, for many see themselves as victims of the ritually driven demands of the rural market. Many contemporary artists bemoaned the constraints of commercial picture publication. Their predicament is to be 'artists' in a world that has little need for them. Whereas they construct the most valued parts of their self in terms of a personal style, the industry on which they depend requires only repetition and finesse. This is the reflection of the demands of a mass-market that lives, to quote Hans Belting's phrase, in an 'era before art'. A large part of these frustrated artists' predicament can thus be seen as an outcome of this simple division: the producers live in an era of art, but their consumers do not. This dilemma was forcefully expressed by the Meerut-based painter Yogendra Rastogi:

> There are so many restrictions. Suppose we are preparing a scene with figures, we can't have any weeping, any anger, anything like this. The images a person wants for his puja room cannot depict anything cruel. Calendar pictures are not concerned with art. They are concerned only with images that can be worshipped . . . Gods or Goddesses giving their *ashirvad*, their blessings, with a smile.
>
> Suppose (he continued) I am painting a picture of a boy studying. He should be looking down at his book, but we have to paint him so that he is looking at the person looking at the picture. But if he is studying, how can he look at you?

Freedom Fighter (Figure 8.4), a popular print of a Rastogi painting showing a patriotic boy with a history of the Indian freedom movement, was a compromise that retained some signs of its author's intransigence: the boy's eyes look not at the viewer, but obliquely to the left. Rastogi's complaints suggest that the struggle between absorption and theatricality is a real one for many commercial artists with pretentions: the fact that, as Fried once wrote, 'one primitive condition of the art of painting [is] that its objects necessarily imply the presence before them of a beholder' (1980: 4) is of more than purely theoretical concern to them.

In addition to the disjunctions created by most Bhatisuda villagers' refusal to inhabit the era of art, we must briefly map a much more profound conflict that informs the relationship between mass-produced images, temple *murtis* and those that 'thrash'.

At one level there is much in popular Hinduism to support the general argument of *Art and Agency*. A common response by villagers when questions of differences between deities is discussed is to throw up their hands and say '*ek hi maya hai*' – it is all (just) one illusion, one 'play'. They mean by this that 'ultimately' all the

Figure 8.4 Yogendra Rastogi's 'Freedom Fighter'. Courtesy of Yogendra Rastogi

differences are resolvable into a single central imaginary form. In this sense villagers affirm that the gods can be thought of as a network of stoppages. One might also see in images of Hanuman – composed of an endless repetition of the name of his master (Ram)[20] and of the *trimurti* of Ramakrishna, The Mother, and Kali (in which the three faces coalesce in a common physiognomy) – further evidence of a concentric/fractal idiom.

But rather in the same way as I have suggested above that we need to theorize a bodily praxis in order to understand the reception of Hindu chromolithographs, we need also to position the formal discourses and representational conventions described in the paragraph above in the context of the chaotic physical enactments of being Hindu in Bhatisuda village. Once we do this, the formal articulations and synoptic overviews start to assume the same marginal position that 'aesthetics' has in relation to everyday 'corpothetics'.

During Nauratri – two periods of nine nights each year associated with goddesses – some Scheduled Caste households remove their domestic chromolithographs and place them in the Jhujhar Mata *autla* (shrine) which is maintained by Badrilal, a Bagdi (Scheduled Caste) *pujari*. The (usually framed) prints spend nine lunar days nestled against the red stones and paraphernalia that form the centre of the shrine and accumulate an additional power from the excess energy of the conse-crated shrine during this period. Domestic images are also installed in the Bihari Mata shrine which also lies in the Bagdi *mohalla*. Bihari Mata lives under a *nim* tree on the southern fringe of the village and large laminated prints of Durga and Kali are nailed to the trunk of the tree and an old framed image of Durga is propped behind several red tridents that sprout from the base. This framed image is taken in the parade around the village at the conclusion of the nine nights along with the bowls of wheat shoots (*javara*) which will be cooled at the end of the procession. However, the relationship between chromolithographs and consecrated images, and that between those that thrash and consecrated images, is not always so tranquil.

Nauratri is a very dangerous period: it is 'hot' (*tamsik*) and vast numbers of *bhut pret* (ghosts and spirits) thicken the air. They live 'with a free hand' (*khuli chhut rehte*) and 'play' without restraint. The unpredictability of events is intensified by the numbers of villagers who thrash. Several *bhopas* or *ojhas* (mediums) will without fail thrash, and a further dozen or so villagers (some predictable, some not) will also thrash with sundry goddesses, spirits of ancestors who met violent deaths and *jhujhars* and *sagats* (warriors who died from either a single blow to the neck, or several blows, respectively).

In Bhatisuda, Nauratri is often eventful. During the Kvar Nauratri in 1995, Kushal Singh – the village psychopath – strode up to Kannaji, a Chamar *ojha* who, thrashing with Shitala (the goddess of smallpox), was making his twice-yearly circuit of the village. Dressed in a sari, Kannaji is led backwards around the village and those seeking protection for the coming year sit in his path, waiting

Figure 8.5 Hemraj with his framed Durga image, two days prior to the Nauratri procession

to be stepped over. Kushal Singh faced Shitala/Kannaji and then punched him ferociously in the mouth. The following year Kushal Singh – sober and contrite – prostrated himself in front of Shitala/Kannaji inscribing his inferiority so that the whole village could see.

But it is events in 1993 which have a special relevance for the argument I want to make here. An extract from fieldnotes:

The predominantly Bagdi procession which had set out from the Bihari Mata shrine was outside Mohan Nai's house near the central *chauk*. Bihari Mata had entered the body of Hemraj and she was wearing a green veil and holding a lime-tipped sword. She danced wildly around Lal Mata who was in the body of Badrilal – the *pujari* of the Jhujhar Maharaj *autla* – in an orange sari and mixed in this melee was a *sagat* in the body of the Rajput Balwant Singh. Two girls carried pots of *javara* (wheat sprouts) and between them a Bagdi boy carried Hemraj's framed Durga picture which had until then been displayed in the Bihari Mata shine. As this swirling mass of people made its way down anticlockwise through the village, women and children, and Rup Singh knelt down to have their afflictions cast out. This involved a curative fanning (*jhadna*) effected with the bedraggled peacock whisks held by the two goddesses. Every so often Badrilal would appear to choke and then, with cheeks bulging, a lime would appear from his mouth.

What happened next showed the extent to which this frenzied outpouring of ecstatic energy fractured the normally hierarchical ordered space of the village. Outside the house of Kalu Singh the Rajput *sarpanch*, Badrilal swirled in a particularly agressive manner as the goddess succumbed to some intense rage and it seemed as though everyone would invade the premises. Then the procession veered suddenly away toward the nearby Krishna temple where the ferociously angry goddess ordered that the *javara* and the image of Durga be taken inside. The *javara* were then placed on the platform at the front of the temple and at this stage Jagdish Sharma the Brahman *purohit* who lives just to the left of the temple shot across the front of his verandah and started to plead with the Goddess in Badrilal. Badrilal was frenzied, shouting and spluttering, his cheeks bulging as though his throat would at any moment disgorge limes.

This was an extraordinary and dangerous moment. Jagdish was clearly terrified. For about ten seconds it seemed completely probable that Badrilal might try to chop off Jagdish's head with his sword but in the event he retreated. Marigold and rose petals were scattered over the front of the temple and the procession moved on through the Bagdi *mola* southwest towards the Lal Mata *autla* and the Chambal river.

Later, discussing this incident, Mohan Singh and Pukhraj Bohra (both of whom are non-drinking vegetarians), opined that Jagdish Sharma had imposed his *rok-tok* (restriction/obstruction) because Badrilal was drunk and if he had polluted the purity of the temple space that protected the Krishna *murti* there would have been *nuqsan* (destruction). The 'skin' that surrounded the *murti* was imperilled, and it was to protect this that Jagdish had risked his life. Badrilal produced a corpothetic engagement with the Krishna *murti* that was incommensurable with the dominant order. The ecstatic dimension to thrashing brought Badrilal very close to piercing the skin of the Krishna idol.

Art and Agency does consider the 'relationships that exist between [artworks] as individuals, and other members of the same category of artworks, and the relationships that exist between this category and other categories of artworks' (1998: 153). However these questions are only ever framed stylistically and formally, never politically. The three different categories of divine embodiment

Figure 8.6 Lal Mata, in the body of Badrilal, approaches the Krishna temple

that I have discussed in this chapter do not support a 'fractal' view of artworks or of 'concentric idols'. The wonderful description that Alfred provides of the multiple skins of the Jagannath temple in Puri elides a Brahmanic fantasy about how the cosmos should be ordered with the messy reality of contemporary India. That contemporary reality – with which a different sort of anthropology of art might engage – is not a place of tranquil homunculi. It is, rather, structured by disadvantagous flows and the conflict that this gives rise to. In these conflicts – as I have tried to document ethnographically – the skins of some idols may be pierced by others. Alfred Gell does a brilliant job of focusing on the ways in which objects mediate social relations: the task now is to analyse the different and conflictual social relations that make objects work for them.

Notes

1. Despite this Fried's concepts retain a conceptual utility if read against the grain.
2. Paralleling the argument in *Art and Agency*, W.J.T. Mitchel writes: 'Pictures are things that have been marked with all the stigmata of personhood: they

exhibit both physical and virtual bodies; they speak to us, sometimes literally, sometimes figuratively. They present not just a surface, but a *face* that faces the beholder' (1996: 72).

3. My intention here is not to simplistically conflate these various dichotomies, for they are clearly not assimilable in this way. Rather, I am interested in the way in which the resonances between these (in many ways very different) conceptual pairs can illuminate the material at hand.

4. There are continuities between Buck-Morss's argument and David Freedberg who suggests that 'Much of our sophisticated talk about art is simply an evasion. We take refuge in such talk . . . because we are afraid to come to terms with our responses' (Freedberg 1989: 429–30).

5. The 1991 Census recorded the village population as 1,366.

6. *dhunana* = to beat, to thrash, and also to card cotton. Villagers will say *mataji dhun rahi hai* (the goddess is thrashing), *jhujhar dhun raha hai* (jhujhar is thrashing) and so on.

7. In this context I would qualify Gell's stress on the internality of images. Within this wider genre Indian versions of the 'vierge ouvrante' are relatively rare and the eyes of Hindu deities are less commonly 'holes' ('giving access to the hidden interior within which "mind" resides') than surface organs from which emanates a physical *extrusive* form of vision (as Gell makes clear elsewhere in his discussion of Kramrisch [1998: 116–17]. See also [Babb 1981]).

8. This early morning allurement which pulls the devotee to the temple is also a trope in Hindi movies (e.g. Yash Chopra's *Deewar*).

9. An enormously popular Goddess living in Kashmir.

10. This conversation was in English.

11. Bapu Singh possessed by the pastoral deity Tejaji has become an almost weary sight in Bhatisuda. At every Satya Narayan puja (held in the Tejaji shrine) he starts to 'thrash', much to the amusement of village children. But most adults are not impressed: Mohan Singh said 'he acts as if he owns it but it can't be his slave (*ghulam*) . . . *shakti* is not tame/submissive for anyone (*shakti kissikoi ka dabbu nahi*)'.

12. Sweepers, and removers of what is usually euphemistically referred to as 'nightsoil' (human excrement).

13. Literally 'middle', metaphorically 'low'.

14. On these grounds one might wish to qualify the claim made in *Art and Agency* (1998: 118) that imagistic devotion is achieved 'entirely by looking'. The notion of corpothetics is intended to draw attention to the much wider sensory field within which agency is manifest.

15. I once asked Pukhraj Bohra whether blind people could take *darshan*: 'Yes. You get *darshan* through *divyajyotish* ['celestial astrology' implying luminence, and related to *divyadrishti*, celestial vision]. If your desire is truthful then an

internal eye comes into being. It's like some natural state of rest [*prakratik nind*] in which the *murti* is just there in front of the soul [*man*].'

16. This corpothetics is often reinscribed as the owner traces the journey either with his eyes or his fingers as he or she recalls the journey. Bhavaralal Ravidas pointed out various parts of his Pavagadh image, 'there is a temple here that you can't visit because there's a tiger living near the path'.

17. At the village level, Muslim image practices are hard to distinguish from Hindu and Jain ones. Nane Khan, who noted that he owned 7 *dharmik tasviron* (religious pictures) said: 'They're from Macca-Medina [You've been there?] No . . . They're from Ajmer . . . they have lots of *shakti*. After bathing we wave an *agarbatti* (incense stick), clasp our hands, *bas*. We offer flowers, garlands . . . we get *prasad*. If you have a completely truthful heart you'll get what you want. There's a Ramayan isn't there? Well, it's like that but better (*aur zyada*) . . .'

18. Malwi. Hindi = *visarjan*.

19. For instance in photographic images of a Surat-based guru, Shri Paramhansji, and some Jain images of the (literal) footprints of *acharyas*.

20. In Devanagri script, conceptualized as a *mantra*.

References

Babb, L.A. 1981. 'Glancing: Visual Interaction in Hinduism'. *Journal of Anthropological Research* 37: 387–401.

Belting, H. 1994. *Likeness and Presence: A History of the Image before the Era of Art,* translated by E. Jephcott. Chicago: University of Chicago Press.

Bourdieu, P. 1984. *Distinction: A Social Critique of the Judgement of Taste*, translated by R. Nice. London: Routledge.

Bryson, N. 1983. *Vision and Painting: The Logic of the Gaze*, Cambridge: Cambridge University Press.

Buck-Morss, S. 1992. 'Aesthetics and Anaesthetics: Walter Benjamin's Artwork Essay Reconsidered'. *October* 62: 3–41.

Eck, D.L. 1981. *Darsan: Seeing the Divine Image in India*. Chambersburg: Anima Books.

Efimova, A. 1997. '"To Touch on the Raw" The Aesthetic Affections of Socialist Realism'. *Art Journal* Spring: 72–80.

Freedberg, D. 1989. *The Power of Images: Studies in the History and Theory of Response*. Chicago: University of Chicago Press.

Fried, M. 1980. *Absorption and Theatricality: Painting and Beholder in the Age of Diderot*. Berkeley: University of California Press.

Friel, B. 1981. *Translations*. London: Faber.

Gell, A. 1992. 'The Technology of Enchantment and the Enchantment of Technology'. in J. Coote and A. Shelton (eds), *Anthropology, Art and Aesthetics*. Oxford:Clarendon Press, pp. 40–63.

—— 1998. *Art and Agency: an Anthropological Theory*. Oxford: Oxford University Press.

Ginzburg, C. 1989. 'From Aby Warburg to E.H. Gombrich: A problem of method', in *Clues, Myths, and the Historical Method*, translated by J. and A. Tedeschi. Baltimore: Johns Hopkins University Press, pp. 17–59.

Guha, R. 1985. 'The Career of an Anti-God in Heaven and on Earth', in Ashok Mitra (ed.), *The Truth Unites: Essays in Tribute to Samar Sen*, Calcutta: Subarnarekha.

Mitchell, W.J.T. 1996. 'What Do Pictures *Really* Want?' *October* 77, Summer.

Panofsky, E. 1991. *Perspective as Symbolic Form*. New York: Zone Books.

9

The Politics and Personhood of Tibetan Buddhist Icons

Clare Harris

In this chapter I argue that though religious images currently in circulation among Tibetan Buddhists retain some of the features which Gell describes as 'distributed personhood', other factors in their production and use are of greater significance for Tibetan viewers than his 'general theory of idolatry' would suggest. In the seventh chapter of *Art and Agency* Gell demonstrates with characteristic subtlety and lucidity how objects become person-like and god-like within social networks to the extent that artefacts and human beings occupy 'equivalent positions'. I share his desire to locate images, sometimes described as art, within a field of agency and distributed efficacy as this approach is particularly effective when examining the functionality of images in a ritual context. However, in the period following the Chinese take-over (beginning in 1950) Tibetan society can be characterized by an all-embracing sense of rupture. All pre-existing activities whether of a religious, social or cultural nature had to be reinvented either by refugees in the alien conditions of host nations or by Tibetans who remained 'at home' in a country which had been renamed as the Tibet Autonomous Region (TAR) of the People's Republic of China (PRC).The experience of exile or of becoming members of a *minzu* (national minority) of a colonizing Communist state has led to the politicization of all aspects of Tibetan lives. Hence when Gell points to a deficiency in his approach, noting that it may lead to a denial of artistic and aesthetic agency I could concur, but a more pressing omission is the absence of reference to the capacity for 'icons' to be 'sources of' and 'targets for' political agency. In the nexus in which Tibetan images circulate, political factors are undeniable and their production is enmeshed in discursive regimes in which both elite individuals and the larger community negotiate. Even the icon of the highest-ranking religious figure in Tibetan Buddhism, the Dalai Lama, is not immune from the mutability of politicized 'ways of seeing' which have beset Tibetan images since the rupture of invasion.

In 1988 an unsuspecting Westerner was arrested in Lhasa, the capital of the Tibet Autonomous Region. The story of this 'innocent abroad' made international news, but her crime was neither incitation to riot nor theft of official secrets, nor even of straying into delimited territory. The offence: sporting a Phil Silvers T-shirt without due care and attention. Though questions might be raised over the sartorial merits of such a get-up, few would suspect that this item of clothing could be viewed as a provocative political statement, but the felon had failed to notice the striking resemblance between the image of Phil Silvers, an American comic of the 1950s, and the Dalai Lama, incarnation of Avalokitesvara, bodhisattva of compassion, Nobel Peace Prize winner and exiled spiritual and political leader of the Tibetans (Figure 9.1). Nor did she realize that a ban on displaying his image

Figure 9.1 Photo-icon of the fourteenth Dali Lama in the home of a Tibetan refugee. Ladakh, India, 1992.

was in force at the time of her visit to the TAR. Since they are viewed as emblems of Tibetan neo-nationalism and independence, depictions of the Dalai Lama have been repeatedly banned by the Chinese authorities. However, despite Draconian attempts at cultural control in the TAR, the image of the Dalai Lama remains the figurehead for a cultural currency which has yet to be devalued. Within the TAR and among refugees this coinage moves across borders, continues to have purchase and has been reinvented by contemporary artists to the extent that the 'personhood' of the Dalai Lama embodied in his image has become decreasingly god-like and increasingly art-like. By this I do not mean to deny the continuing significance of the Dalai Lama icon as a religious signifier, but I suggest instead that he is no longer simply the recipient of the admiring gaze of devotees. To display or view his form is a political act and hence his 'personhood' has been re-envisaged through the agency of artists and their audiences.

Images of Exilic Tibet

The frontispiece illustration (Figure 9.2) to a refugee painter's manual[1] places Tibet at the centre of the world suggesting the impact of the sense of loss and displacement that accompanies what De Vos (1981: 32) calls the 'virtual social identity' of refugees, an identity whose core element is 'the root of their troubles – they leave home because of who they are'. Thinking about the Tibet they have been forced to abandon unifies exiles and asserts the sense of vacated place as a key image in exilic identity formation. Gega Lama's drawing depicts the situation perfectly. The form of the historic Tibetan homeland is demarcated as it appears in publications, T-shirts, maps and books of the neo-nation in exile. The shape of the land 'Tibet' has taken on an iconic status, instantly recognizable to Tibetans and their supporters worldwide, as confirmation that an independent Tibet existed and covered a section of the globe as large as Western Europe. It is essential that the exiles remember and depict the 'Tibet' which was taken over by the Chinese beginning in 1950 and fully effected by 1959 and continue, despite the ravages of Chinese colonialism, to imagine it in a state of unity and boundedness.[2] This is the nation which they hope to reclaim but in the meantime are forced to reinvent in other locations.

Creating exilic Tibet was initially a matter of dealing with the brute facts of physical survival in host countries, particularly India, which is given due prominence in Gega Lama's mapping of the Tibetan local-to-global nexus. The so-called 'capital-in-exile', at Dharamsala in Himachal Pradesh (India), which contains the exile government, monastic institutions and the home of the Fourteenth Dalai Lama, Tenzin Gyatso, has been the primary location in and from which the self-conscious reconstruction of pre-1959 'traditions' has been executed. An exilic elite of religious figures and artists, writers, performers, musicians have been at the

Figure 9.2 The frontispiece illustration to a refugee's painter's manual. India 1983.

forefront of the promotion of an 'invented tradition' of what it means to be Tibetan after 1959; an invention defined in terms of the imagined communities of Tibetan Buddhism and neo-nationalism. Within and without the elite, Tibetan exiles refer to themselves as *nangpa* or Buddhist 'insiders', a term which emphasizes their membership of a community of Tibetan Buddhists and in which pre-exilic regional and sectarian identities have been subsumed for the sake of social and political survival. The *nangpa* sense of Tibetanness is reflected in cultural style and the dream of redrawing Tibetan nationhood is therefore depicted by Gega Lama in the hand of an artist gripping a Tibetan-style brush whose point touches on the hem of the seated Sakyamuni Buddha as he makes the earth(globe)-touching gesture. The preservation-in-practice ethos of the Dalai Lama and the exile government has emphasized that the connection between the Tibetan homeland and the global community into which the refugees have been displaced must be mediated through the Buddha and Buddhist image-makers; that is, a religio-cultural definition of what it is to be Tibetan has been privileged. Hence *thangka* (religious paintings) produced by *lha bris* (makers of gods) according to pre-exilic methods remain empowering within Tibetan Buddhist practice and as markers of important life-events. They continue to have a role when commissioned for the commemoration of the dead, to aid good rebirth, to tell tales of the Buddha and bodhisattvas, to gain merit and to assist in meditation and visualization and so on as they did in pre-1959 Tibet. As objects animated by 'external' methods such as the *rap nes* ceremony in which the 'vision' of the god is inserted thereby activating the 'personhood' of Buddhist deities, *thangka* fulfil Gell's criteria for idols. These images are most commonly displayed in the institutional environment of exile, such as monasteries and *lha khang* (image chambers). Here they function within the Tibetan 'presentation' of the culture of a neo-nation which is consumed by an internal (*nangpa*) audience and an external group which consists of tourists and an intermediate category of non-Tibetan Buddhist practitioners. Though it is the intention of the exilic elite that the social contexts for such idolatry should remain static, in practice such 'traditionalist' icons are often beyond the economic means of ordinary refugees. Hence, beyond the elite and public image nexus it is the Dalai Lama photo-icon which is most visible, present and active in *nangpa* lives rather than the consecrated Buddha index. This is due in large part to the combination of facets of the personality of the Fourteenth Dalai Lama who is both god-like (he being the incarnation of the Buddha of Compassion, *Chenrezig*) and an individual (Tenzin Gyatso) whose thoughts, actions and biography are received as a narrative of a nation in exile.

Images of *nangpa* Solidarity: the Dalai Lama Icon

The Dalai Lama carries a heavy burden of representation. For Tibetans the hope of engaging with his personhood is the defining aspiration of their lives. Every new arrival in Dharamsala makes the experience of *darshan* with the Dalai Lama his or her first act after the arduous journey into exile, a rite of passage which the newly arrived undertake as he had done in 1959. Kalachakra ceremonies and other religious teachings given by him in Dharamsala and elsewhere are communal ritual occasions when the *nangpa* sense of identity is asserted in his presence. But due to the dispersal of Tibetan bodies in various locations around the globe, an arte-factual diaspora has also been generated. Since the first decade of exile (1960 +)

photographic reproductions of the Dalai Lama have been deployed to consecrate domestic shrines in which he may stand alone or among a selection of photographed 'root gurus' and other reincarnate Tibetan Buddhist teachers.[3] When exchanged among *nangpa* the Dalai Lama photo-icon accrues merit for the donor and recipient so long as the object is displayed respectfully in a prominent place. In more public contexts the Dalai Lama icon is installed in thrones awaiting his actual physical presence. The construction of a shrine or chamber for the Dalai Lama was a practice of the Geluk order prior to 1959, but one which is now continued by all *nangpa* (i.e. irrespective of affiliations to other orders of Tibetan Buddhism) in refugee communities all over India. Religious festivals and ceremonies such as the March 10th Commemoration (of the Lhasa Uprising in 1959) and New Year which bind the refugees, wherever they may be in the diaspora, are only conducted when at least the two-dimensional Dalai Lama is present. In India his image protects the service vehicles of the exile community as Tibetans insert their icon into a local symbolic structure replacing Hindu deities at the windscreens of autorickshaws and Tata trucks. But the Dalai Lama icon does not merely emulate the apotropaic function of the Hindu gods, nor even their role as signifiers of religious affiliation, but marks a bald political fact: the Dalai Lama is abroad in the world, literally and pictorially, due to his ejection from Tibet. For *nangpa* this is a bitter memory which dominates the quotidian experience of life in exile; hence the display of the Dalai Lama icon is part of a strategy of cultural solidarity in the face of loss.

Aesthetics meets Politics

As was apparent in Gega Lama's mapping, a sharp demarcation between Tibet and China is a key component of the ideology of exile. For exiles and their image-makers, drawing the lines of difference is not only a geo-political task but a matter of emphasizing Tibetan style as a statement of resilience and resistance. Hence in one notable instance the Dharamsala audience rejected a depiction of the Three Kings of Tibetan Buddhism which had been commissioned for the assembly hall of the Dalai Lama's monastery on the grounds that it was too 'realistic' and therefore un-Tibetan. In point of fact their objection did not arise from a general discomfort with mimesis but with a style of representation which they viewed as abhorrent: Socialist Realism. Even though the painting was executed by a Tibetan who had been trained in Lhasa (a fact which generally attracts an aura of legitimacy and authenticity to a maker's work), was a friend of the Dalai Lama and by no means a Communist, it was found to be offensively similar in style to the Socialist Realist portraits of Mao, People's Liberation Army generals and other propa-gandistic mythologies which had been forcibly inserted into the lives of Tibetans back home in the TAR. Consciousness of the brutal colonization of Tibet inevitably runs deep among exiles and the narrative of events which unfolded after 1959 impinges on them through the oral and published accounts of later refugees. Following the murder and starvation of hundreds of thousands in the homeland, the destruction of monasteries and all Buddhist imagery (which was particularly rigorously implemented during the Cultural Revolutionary period of 1966–1976) inflicted another searing wound across the body of Tibet. As Norbu (1997) reports, 'Before the sacred mantra "Om Mani Padme Hum" were carved on rocks; the Red Guards now inscribed quotations from Mao's red book. In short, Mao replaced the Buddha in every respect during the Cultural Revolution'. The Tibetan reaction to the destruction of the distributed personhood of the Buddha was to replace his form with that of the Dalai Lama. In conditions of cultural obliteration and Maoist 'organised forgetting' (Connerton 1989) it was he who could provide the agency to fight back. During the 1960s and 1970s guerrilla fighters from the Eastern region of Tibet (Khampa) attempted to do battle with the People's Liberation Army. Alongside guns and knives they wore *gau* containing photographs of the Dalai Lama. Prior to the Chinese take-over Buddha amulets had been worn in battle as the icon was believed to deflect arrows and bullets, just as the Buddha himself had diverted the weapons of his enemy Mara, but in the battle to reclaim the land he had been forced to abandon, the Dalai Lama was enlisted for service. As a boddhisattva the Dalai Lama exhibits a dual personality: he is both god of compassion (*Chenrezig*) and fierce protector of Buddhism (*tam drin*). Khampa guerrillas sought to embody the agency of a *tam drin* and transport the compassionate personhood of the Dalai Lama back to his rightful home, transforming the photo-icon into an ensign of the battle for the independence of Tibet. Accordingly thereafter the possession and display of Dalai Lama icons has been repeatedly banned by the Chinese authorities in the Tibetan Autonomous Region of the People's Republic, though TAR Tibetans continue to risk arrest and even death by secreting the icon of their absent leader about their person. For them his personhood is intimately incorporated into their sense of self, as I witnessed when a group of monks from the monastery of Ganden insisted on revealing Dalai Lama badges concealed under their robes.[4] Their identity as Tibetans and practising Buddhists cannot be expressed without the Dalai Lama – if their sense of self were imagined as a body, the absence of the Dalai Lama would leave it headless. But this identity must generally be secreted and only revealed to those who understand the literally undercover nature of Tibetanness in the TAR. For exiles, who are fully aware of the repression of the TAR, the Dalai Lama icon must be defiantly exteriorized and visible. It Tibetanizes spaces and bodies at a simple, cheap and democratic level, in contrast to the more public architectural statements of Tibetanness constructed by the monastic institutions and the government-in-exile. The ownership and display of such an image is therefore a key component in *nangpa* strategies for solidarity and self-preservation in exile. Alongside the politicization of the Dalai Lama icon after 1950 there has also been a movement which transfers it from the domain of sanctity (in which it might conform with Gell's 'general theory of idolatry') into an increasingly aestheticized sphere, a migration that has been assisted by a shift in the status of key individuals (religious and artistic).

Before the Chinese invasion Dalai Lamas were portrayed by *lha bris* (makers of gods) in a style similar to that devised for the Buddha. (A sixteenth-century *thangka* from Guge, Western Tibet, for example, depicts the Third Dalai Lama seated on a lotus throne and surrounded by scenes from his life.) They were iconized in the style of a deity with few distinguishing marks of an individual physiognomy but always with eyes open to receive and release the 'glancing' (Babb 1981) of the icon–devotee relationship. Since 1950, an exceptional phase in Tibetan history has generated conditions in which the visage of the Fourteenth Dalai Lama has become highly recognizable to his followers and the power of the photographic index of the Dalai Lama could not be ignored by the 'makers of gods'. Hence when Sherap Palden Beru, a *thangka* painter trained in Tibet, attempted to make the first exilic depiction of the Dalai Lama he both incorporated a photograph and copied the resulting photo-icon for mass circulation in exile. In it the photographed Dalai Lama appears framed by Tibetan monastic architecture, with two dragon-entwined pillars and multiple-layered pagoda-style roof. A subsidiary frame of flat blue colour is then used to house the man himself, who is surrounded by four deities, Amitayus, White Tara, Avalokitesvara and Namgyalma, goddess of longevity. This is a rather ungainly composition. The (painted) bent hand and arm of His Holiness exposes the artist's problem: how to represent a reincarnate bodhisattva who lives among you in the refugee community of Dharamsala and whose features are intimately known to people through his appearances and teachings or through photography. Palden's solution, employing a hybrid photo-painterly technique, constitutes a surprising departure for a Tibetan artist when we consider the strict regulations which in pre-1950 Tibet had been placed on the mastery of iconometric systems for the depiction of divine as well as not-so-divine figures. Deviation from these rules was a risky business for both producer and viewer. Any involvement with an ill-formed *thangka* could 'lead one to hell' as the painter Pema Namdol Thaye comments in his *Concise Tibetan Art Book*: 'The image must be accurate. An erroneous image cannot be blessed and consecrated. Such images should be in remote and deserted places as they are more harm than benefit to Human society' (1987: 23).

When specifying exactly how human beings should be drawn Thaye states that 'The general human measurement, according to the ancient artists is eight thos. similar to the divine forms' and he adds that 'the religious heads and personal Root-Gurus who show the sentient beings the Vajrayana ways should be represented according to the measurements of Lord Buddha' (1987: 183). Despite this, Thaye's own book includes an illustration of his personal 'root' guru (the head of the Nying-mapa school of Tibetan Buddhism, Mindroling Trichen Rinpoche) in a photo-icon style similar to that of Sherap Palden. Iconometric codes are not adhered to, an omission which in pre-1959 Tibet would have precluded the image from entering into use and from becoming a fitting receptacle for a god or a guru. In the photo-icons of exile the camera has been allowed to take on the responsibility of correctness previously ascribed to iconometry. That is, the device through which an object previously gained sanctity has been abandoned.

The explanation for this departure derives in part from the assimilation of the 'modern' into the lives and work of Tibetan image-makers as they began to adopt influences from the host environment of India. Photography had played a part in Indian visual culture since the mid-nineteenth century and the camera had become increasingly accessible as a tool for studio portraiture by the mid-twentieth century when the exile community was established. An argument can be made that there were no grounds for a Tibetan objection to this particular technology of modernity. If not mechanically produced, identical copies of religious objects, from stamped clay *tsa tsa* (pilgrimage votives) to wood block-printed prayer flags, had been in common use in pre-1959 Tibet. In fact the *gtsagpar* (stencil copy) technique in which popular *thangka* designs were mass-replicated with a pin-prick stencil (while also ensuring iconometric correctness) shares an etymological connection with the neologism *par gyap*, meaning 'to take a photograph'. *Par* refers to a mould for making lettering or three-dimensional forms as well as that which was produced from it, such as a print. The verb *gyap* can mean a number of things from 'build', 'shoot' to 'mark' or even 'bite'. So (to use Gell's example) where a Greek involved in sorcery writes 'I bind, I bind', a Tibetan photographer thinks 'I bite, I bite'. This comparison is suggestive, as it is Gell's contention that the 'action of making a representational image' means that the image of the prototype is 'bound to, or fixed and imprisoned within, the index'. From the linguistic evidence at the very least, the modern Tibetan act of representation may be described as more akin to a fleeting, ephemeral bite from, or shot at, the prototype rather than the immobilizing bondage of Gell's index of personhood. Tibetan artistic agency is perhaps more Baudelairean, emphasizing the ephemeral, the fugitive, the contingent over the other half of art which is eternal and immutable. Most importantly, in the icon I focus on here, the subject (or prototype) is an individual whose identity is eminently mutable – as we have seen, the current Dalai Lama metamorphoses between his roles of god and man in the view of his followers. Moreover, his human form is but a temporary, ephemeral body for an immutable reincarnatory 'spirit', Avalokitesvara. I might also note that since he is political leader of the Tibetans and embodiment of the imagined homeland of Tibet, his followers increasingly express some disquiet about the fact that Tenzin Gyatso is subject to the laws of human mortality. There is a sense amongst Tibetans that the demise of this Dalai Lama may lead to the collapse of the dream of returning to Tibet. We shall return to this a little later. In the meantime it should be noted that it was Tenzin Gyatso's pioneering predecessor, the Thirteenth Dalai Lama, who created a precedent for the novel photo-icons of exile and challenged the traditional Tibetan notion of the sanctity of the reincarnate body.

The Thirteenth Dalai Lama

According to Tibetan Buddhist principles, the personhood of any individual is only temporarily housed within a particular body. The Dalai Lama is at the pinnacle of a reincarnatory hierarchy in which Tibetan bodies are seen as receptacles for the fleeting presence of *rinpoche* (precious) transmigrated souls. The current Dalai Lama (the fourteenth) was 'discovered' inhabiting the body of Tenzin Gyatso in Amdo in 1940, but here I need to speak of his previous incarnation. In 1910 the Thirteenth Dalai Lama had taken refuge in Darjeeling after the Chinese sent four hundred troops to Lhasa, an act he and his government interpreted as the beginnings of a mission to kidnap him. While in temporary exile in British-run India he established a relationship with Sir Charles Bell, British Representative to Tibet, Bhutan and Sikkim. Under Bell's guidance the Thirteenth was the first Tibetan to encounter some of the more sophisticated technologies of Empire, including photography. He even asked Bell to make an indexical record of his form. For a Christian European, recording the impression of a living body was an acceptable part of the process by which an image functioned in the 'cult of remembrance of loved ones, absent or dead' (Benjamin 1992) hence he perhaps unwittingly (but at the Thirteenth's instigation) overturned a Tibetan tabu. In pre-1959 Tibet, portraits of religious figures were made only after their death. So that:

> When So-nam Gya-tso, the Dalai Lama who introduced Tibetan Buddhism among the Mongols, died, 'In memory of his body his portrait was painted on cloth, in memory of his speech one copy of the Kan-gyur was printed in gold letters, and in memory of his mind a silver tomb thirteen cubits in length was built by the people' (Bell 1928: 294).[5]

A picture of the deceased was also used by Tibetan families during *bardo* ceremonies over the 49-day period when the spirit of the corpse was encouraged to move to its next incarnation. Hence Tibetans had good reason to express concern about the production of an index: 'In November, 1933, the Dalai Lama summoned one of the Nepalese photographers in Lhasa to take his photograph. This alarmed the people of Lhasa, who took it as a sign that he intended to die soon.' (Bell 1946: 383). Unfortunately their collective premonition proved true. By mid-December the Thirteenth was dead. However, he had been having his picture taken since 1910 and Bell describes how his first portrait was quickly converted into an object of veneration by Tibetans:

This was, I believe the first photograph of him seated in the Tibetan style. I gave him a large number of copies, and these proved useful to him; he used to give them to monasteries and to deserving people. These all used the photograph instead of an image, rendering to it the worship they gave to images of Buddhas and deities (1946: 114).

Bell comments that thereafter he saw thousands of these icons in circulation throughout the Tibetan communities of the Himalayas. But how had the tabu been overcome, allowing a photographic portrait of the living Dalai Lama to become an object of sanctity? This index was the collaborative work of three agents: the Thirteenth Dalai Lama, Sir Charles Bell and an anonymous Tibetan painter.

From Presence to Likeness

Bell's account of his relationship with the Thirteenth (appropriately entitled *Portrait of the Dalai Lama*) includes a copy of the photograph he had taken but with accretions. His picture was re-presented to him with both the seal and signature of the Thirteenth, emphasizing the sense of direct – indexical – contact with its subject and had been tinted by a member of the Thirteenth's retinue in Darjeeling. Bell notes that the artist had used 'the appropriate colours for his hat, his robes, his throne, the religious implements . . . and the silk pictures of Buddha which formed the suitable background of it all'. That is, the areas surrounding the Thirteenth had been Tibetanized through the agency of a Tibetan artist. However, Bell fails to mention that the undressed parts of the Thirteenth's body, his head, arm and hands remained in unt(a)inted monochrome. That is, the primary features which expose an individual identity were left undisturbed by pigment. The Tibetan painter, still wary of proscriptions against portraiture, allowed the camera to produce the simulacra of a religious body, just as according to Tibetan accounts the living Buddha could only be depicted from a reflection in water or an imprint in cloth. Looking closely into the eyes of the divine therefore remains an occupational hazard which Tibetan artists, like Sri Lankan Buddhists, must avoid at all costs. In this sense the Dalai Lama icon complies with Gell's analysis of idols but the indexical power of the camera has also been used to capture the 'aura' of an exceptional individual. The Thirteenth Dalai Lama seems to have deliberately encouraged an 'ideology of the charismatic individual' (Cardinal 1992: 6), and selected Bell to be his Felix Nadar. For him the photo-icon provided the possibility of making Barthesian 'certificates of presence', attesting that what is seen has existed, and that his very particular body had housed the incarnate godliness of a boddhisattva. For artists, the tinted zone surrounding the photographic 'certificate' became an area in which their agency could be asserted. Exiled artists have taken this model (the source of a lineage of images, as Gell would have it) and expanded its referential possibilities to acknowledge the social and political facts of relocation.

Incorporating the Dalai Lama index into a wider field, they began to use photography within an aesthetic dialogue which, contra Barthes, could restore what has been abolished (by time, by distance).

In 1930 Bell took further photographs of the Thirteenth and the Ninth Panchen Lama which he published in 1946. Copies of these pictures evidently found their way across the Himalayas and became the subject of photo-icons, as is evident in one displayed in the Ladakhi monastery of Likir (Figure 9.3) Again, as in the 'certificate' of the Thirteenth, the body of a divine individual is replicated in monochrome but the painter has ventured further than mere tinting. The Ninth Panchen Lama is seated alongside a table set with offerings in a landscape painted in the manner of *thangka* paintings, with heavily stylized mountains, rivers and lakes. Peaceful and wrathful deities at top and bottom respectively are also painted and positioned as they are in *thangka*. However, the attempt to place the Panchen in a readable (there is even a degree of perspectivalism in the treatment of the offering table), if idealized, space is extremely novel – almost comparable to the representational shift which Belting identifies in Bellini's *Madonna del Prato* (*c*.1505). By placing the Madonna in a north Italian landscape, Belting suggests, the Bellini image demonstrates a move from ritual icons to a 'new kind of painted poetry'. Not only was the image made 'subject to the general laws of nature' but viewers would be flattered by their ability to recognize painterly references to Virgil's poetic evocation of rural life. I am by no means suggesting that Tibetan images became 'subject to the general laws of nature' but Belting's observations are potent in any discussion of the move from what he calls 'presence' towards 'likeness'. Presence refers to icons in the 'era before art' when 'the image had been assigned a special reality and taken literally as a visible manifestation of the sacred person'. In the move towards art the image became 'a simulated window in which either a saint or a family member would appear in a portrait. In addition, the new image was handed over to artists, who were expected to create from their own fantasy' (Belting 1994: 471). Tibetan exilic artists are not yet at liberty to create worlds of pure fantasy, particularly when they reference a religious prototype. There remains a degree to which (as in the era of iconometry and the use of stencils) human agency must be underplayed in the representation of a divine body, but since the actions of the Thirteenth, the technology of camera enacts this principle. It allows the artist to 'bite' at the subject without entering into the dangerous process of copying from life. However, while the indexicality of the camera creates a simulated reality, the landscape of recent Tibetan paintings has increasingly become the domain of artistic agency which references a poetics of place. Placed alongside the 'presence' of photographic elements (which deny human agency), the 'likeness' of the imaginal land is highlighted. Where Bellini's viewers saw Virgil in the naturalistic portrayal of contemporary Venetian vistas, the landscapes of Tibetan exilic images reference a dream of the past and a place no longer tangible or visible to their viewers in India and elsewhere. For exiles the landscape of Tibet can only be an artistic creation, a 'fantasy' in which the agency of the maker is asserted. Due to the political and psychological realities of the condition of exile it is the 'artness' of these images which enable a Benjaminian 'cult of remembrance' of a 'loved one' (such as the Dalai Lama) but especially of a 'beloved place absented' (Tibet).

Figure 9.3 Photo-icon of the ninth Panchen Lama in the monastery of Likir. Ladakh, India, 1992

However, Tibetan exilic identity should not only be defined in terms of nostalgia. The 'likeness' of other images reflects adaptation to the reinvented social and political boundaries of *nangpa* life. When representing the environment of the host country India, landscape appears to fall into the domain of photographic indexicality. In a 1990s photo-icon the Fourteenth Dalai Lama is shown to occupy the same time and space as his followers. (Figure 9.4). Like them he can stand in Indian locations such as Bodh Gaya (a favoured exile pilgrimage site and scene of Kalachakra initiations given by him), though his status as a sacred person is demonstrated by the image-maker in lines of irradiating light (emitted from his body as they had from the Buddha-body). Proportion, which presents the Dalai Lama as larger than the photographed life around him, also suggests that he eclipses the architectonic embodiments of the Buddha and those who perform *pradakshina* around the base of the Bodhi stupa. Here the Dalai Lama's status as boddhisattva of compassion (rather than *tam drin* or protector) and representative of pan-Asian Buddhism is privileged, acknowledging that he and his followers take solace in the fact that their 'home from home' locates them in a wider community of Buddhists. In contrast to the imagined space of Tibet, this 'home' is observable and subject to different systems of viewing and representing: the camera shoots India, while the brush bites Tibet.

Figure 9.4 Photo-icon of the fourteenth Dalai Lama at India's most important Buddhist pilgrimage site, Bodh Gaya. India, 1990's

Fundamentally the possession and viewing of such images also relates to a condition of aspiration and expectation that both the Dalai Lama and the independent nation of Tibet will be reincarnated. This principle has been activated by monks at Likir where the Thirteenth Dalai Lama photo-icon hangs in the *du khang* (assembly hall) as an object of veneration but also as a record of history and future expectations. They reference the reincarnatory lineage of Dalai Lamas by attaching two images of Tenzin Gyatso outside the Potala and surrounded by a crowd displaying the Tibetan flag to that of his predecessor. The Thirteenth had designed this, the first ensign of the Tibetan nation, and predicted the calamitous events that would occur in the lifetime of the Fourteenth, though he did not foresee that both flag and icon of the Fourteenth would be banned on Tibetan soil. For Tibetans the vulnerability and ephemerality of images and bodies is counteracted by the indestructible (eternal?) concept of transmigration of 'souls'.

The politicized conception of reincarnation is also powerful within the TAR, and in recent years photo-icons have been utilized in a restorative process in which absent persons are returned to their rightful places. Young reincarnates, discovered in exile, are imagined at their monastery in the 'homeland'. The Dalai Lama revisits his seat of power, the Potala Palace, accompanied by an iconic representation of *Chenrezig* and the tenth Panchen Lama and the Potala is located in a landscapeless blue void – the tourist facilities, parades of shops, karaoke bars and other monuments to Deng-style consumerism which currently surround it are obliterated. This image was available in Lhasa in 1993 during a period when the prohibition against the production and sale of images was 'relaxed'. In the summer of that year the Barkhor, the ancient trading centre of the Tibetan capital and also a circumambulation zone around the most important temple in Tibet, the Jokhang, was filled with stalls selling photo-icons. Such images were bought by pilgrims, many of whom were en route to Tashilunpo, the Panchen's monastery thirty miles south-east of Lhasa, where his remains were to be placed in a commemorative stupa. As the second-highest ranking figure in Tibetan Buddhism, the Panchen Lama had not followed the Dalai Lama into exile but stayed on during the Chinese take-over to attempt to negotiate with PRC leaders. For his pains he spent much of his life in prison, hence it was undoubtedly politic that his death (which some suspected was not from natural causes) should not lead to unrest. It should also be noted that the point of sale for his image, the Barkhor, had also been the primary zone for expressions of dissent during the 1989 riots in which monks and nuns were shot and killed by Chinese police. Hence for a brief period in the TAR Tibetans were allowed to remember their dead and perhaps to dream of a different future in which the impact of China has been erased. Given the history of battles fought over images in Chinese-occupied Tibet it appears rather surprising that this activity was condoned by the Chinese authorities in Lhasa. I would suggest that this was possible due to contrasting systems of viewing between Chinese and Tibetans.

PRC officials apparently saw no danger in Panchen photo-icons because for them they were mere memorials to the dead: certificates of presence without ongoing personhood, whereas for Tibetans such icons imply a lineage of individuals and a larger communal identity. Another Barkhor photo-icon of the same year (Figure 9.5) illustrates this point. It depicts three figures who no longer had physical presence in the TAR: the Dalai Lama (absent), the Panchen Lama (deceased) and the Buddha (long deceased). Here all three are re-presented photographically: the two monks by portraits taken in different locations (India and Tibet) and the Buddha by a photographed *thangka*. The image condenses large expanses of time and geography in order for all three to appear in the same space which they occupy in the minds of Tibetans – that is, as part of a lineage of Buddhist teachers whose physical forms may alter but whose spirit transmigrates to an imagined place which currently does not exist: an independent Tibetan Buddhist nation. Only 'likeness' can distribute such a concept.

It is arguably in the TAR that the 'likeness' of images has had its most liberating effects. In 1985 a group of Tibetan painters set up the first Tibetan artists' association which they named 'The Sweet Tea House Group' after the huts around Lhasa University where they met and later exhibited their works. The tea houses had been the sites of political debate among students and young Tibetan workers for

Figure 9.5 Photo-icon of the Buddha, fourteenth Dali Lama and tenth Panchem, Lhasa, Tibet, 1993.

some time, but in the 1980s dissident voices were raised to a high pitch. Artists trained in the university art school participated in the discussion and began to openly question the Sinicization of the institution, its staff and the styles in which they had been instructed. Their work began to reflect a desire to reclaim the cultural and political space that Chinese artists had colonized. They began to produce abstract evocations of the Tibetan landscape in which sites of historic and religious significance to Tibetans were rediscovered. A modernist formal vocabulary (i.e. non-realist) was deployed to make these images unreadable to the Chinese administration. When printed in a Chinese publication, one landscape proved literally undecipherable to the Han editor who did not (or could not) read the Tibetan inscription. The artist defined it as '*Lhamo Latso*', the name of the sacred lake whose spirit (*lhamo*) was consulted to find Dalai Lama incarnations. In Chinese this image was labelled 'Extreme Land', a tag by which majority China defines the home of 'minority' Tibetans. The Sweet Tea artists also attempted to subvert the ban against images which asserted Tibetan Buddhist identity (especially of the Dalai Lama) by reconfiguring the form of the Buddha. In the mid-1980s Gongkar Gyatso, a founder member of the group, painted 'Buddha and the White Lotus' (Figure 9.6) in which the Buddha-body appears as a nebulous silhouette while in others the Buddha is decapitated and dismembered. The artist described these works as representations of the abuse which Buddhist culture had undergone in Tibet but also as a tactic for evading the hostile reception which a more explicit

Figure 9.6 *Buddha and the White Lotus,* by Gongkar Gyatso, Lhasa, Tibet, 1989.

pro-Dalai Lama imagery would elicit. For a short time the Sweet Tea painters enjoyed the freedom of exhibiting to their fellow Tibetans but after two years the authorities forced them to disband.

Between 1987 and 1990 Gongkar Gyatso was among the residents of Lhasa who witnessed Tibetan protests against the Chinese regime and the brutal suppression of the monks and nuns who led the campaigns. Like thousands of others before him, he decided to leave Lhasa and the hollow mausoleum of the Potala Palace to go in search of its rightful incumbent on the refugee pilgrimage to Dharamsala. In 1992 he began a new life in the 'capital-in-exile' in India. Initially the move was a source of inspiration. He found the Dalai Lama, a library and a group of people who made him feel 'at home', but as an artist who had formulated a new style in the TAR, he soon realized that no one knew where he was coming from. In Dharamsala, the values of the guardians of Tibetan cultural identity impacted upon him in a graphic sense, as his products enter a world of antagonistic codes of interpretation. Both fresh-faced foreigners on the Dharma tour and his fellow exiled Tibetans complained about the lack of iconometric measurement and the split Buddha in 'Buddha and the White Lotus'. To the Dharamsala artworld this was sacrilege or 'artness' gone too far. Gyatso now finds himself in the ironic position that outside of his country of birth (Tibet) he feels more 'at home' in political and spiritual terms, but his involvement in the recent history of image-making in the TAR means that he is still culturally displaced. His search for a Tibetan identity, both as an individual and an artist, has led him across borders of many kinds: national, political and stylistic, but the journey has left him caught in a no-man's-land between the imaginative territories which currently constitute 'Tibet'.

Notes

1. Cf. Gega Lama 1983: Gega Lama was born in Rinchen Ling in eastern Tibet in 1931.
2. Goldstein (1994) following Richardson and Bell analyses the categories of 'ethnographic' and 'political' Tibet, in use since 1959, in which the political heartland of the Tibetan Autonomous Region (TAR) of the People's Republic of China (PRC) is contrasted with the larger category of ethnic Tibetans who are located in the nearby Chinese provinces of Qinghai, Sichuan, Gansu, Yunnan and Xinjiang, and parts of neighbouring states such as India, Nepal and Bhutan. Gega Lama's map shows 'political' Tibet.

3. Klieger (1989:318) noted that Dalai Lama photographs were also 'the object most in demand for the consecration of recently reconstructed private and monastic chapels and altars' in the period of relaxation of religious prohibitions in the TAR in the early 1980s.
4. The portablility and accessability of photographic images of key 'nangpa' figures provide what Pinney (1997) has called 'proximal empowerment' both in exile and within the Tibet Autonomous Region.
5. The quotation is taken from *The Biography of the Reverend Omniscient Sonam Gya-tso, like a Chariot in the Ocean.*

References

Babb, L. 1981. 'Glancing: Visual Interaction in Hinduism'. *Journal of Anthropological Research* 37: 387–401.

Barthes, R. 1993[1980]. *Camera Lucida*. London: Vintage

Bell, C. 1928. *The People of Tibet*. London: Collins.

—— 1946. *Portrait of the Dalai Lama*. London: Collins.

Belting, H. 1994. *Likeness and Presence: A History of the Image before the Era of Art*. Chicago: University of Chicago Press.

Benjamin, W. 1992 [1955]. 'The Work of Art in the Age of Mechanical Reproduction', in H. Arendt (ed.), *Illuminations*. 211–44. London: Fontana.

Cardinal, R. 1992. 'Nadar and the Photographic Portrait in Nineteenth Century France', in G. Clarke (ed.), *The Portrait in Photography*. London: Reaktion.

Connerton, P. 1989. *How Societies Remember* Cambridge: Cambridge University Press.

De Vos, D.M. 1981. 'The Refugee Problem and Tibetan Refugees'. *The Tibet Journal*, 6(3), 22–42.

Gega Lama. 1983. *The Principles of Tibetan Art*. Darjeeling: Gega Lama.

Gell, A. 1998. *Art and Agency: An Anthropological Theory*. Oxford: Oxford University Press.

Goldstein, M. 1994. 'Change, Conflict and Continuity among a Community of Nomadic Pastoralists: A Case Study from Western Tibet, 1950–1990', in R. Barnett and S. Akiner (eds), *Resistance and Reform in Tibet*. London: Hurst.

Klieger, P.C. 1989. Accomplishing Tibetan Identity: The Constitution of a National Consciousness. Unpublished Doctoral Thesis, University of Hawaii.

Norbu, J. 1993. *The Works of Gongkar Gyatso*. Exhibition catalogue, Dharamsala, Amnye Machen Institute.

Pinney, C. 1997. *Camera Indica: The Social Life of Indian Photographs*. London: Reaktion.

Thaye, P. 1987. *Concise Tibetan Art Book*. Kalimpong, West Bengal: Pema Namdol Thaye.

–10–

Aboriginal Cultural Production into Art: The Complexity of Redress

Francesca Merlan

An Anthropology of Art

Attempting to lay the groundwork for an 'anthropology of art', Gell (1998: 1) argued:

> There is no sense in developing one 'theory of art' for our own art, and another, distinctively different theory, for the art of those cultures who happened, once upon a time, to fall under the sway of colonialism.

I would argue, to the contrary, that a theory which would make sense of the notion of 'art' in the colonial and post-colonial interface, must be able to specify the power of Western art traditions to make themselves relevant to those who 'happened' to fall under the sway of colonialism. This chapter is a story about some of the conditions under which that relevance, or partial relevance, has been achieved in Australia in the processes of creation and contestation of an 'Aboriginal art'.

Though he is convinced that the anthropological theorization of art can and must be universalist in its scope, Gell is also persuaded that a project of elucidating non-Western aesthetic systems has been mistaken for an 'anthropology' of art. The theorization of aesthetic systems treats matters that are social as cultural, according to Gell; and in his view, anthropology is a social science discipline which focuses on social relations (1998: 4). He sets about re-defining the art object, not in aesthetic terms, but as a participant in social relations, with its own forms of agency. For Gell (1998: 16), 'agents' can be persons, or things, that are seen as initiating 'causal sequences' of particular types (which differ from mere 'happenings', or physical concatenations of events). So defined, art objects (or maybe we should say, 'art agents') are indices (1998: 37–8) of forms of power, or potency. Gell (1998: 6) summarizes his concern as an 'action-centred' approach to art, pre-occupied with the 'practical mediatory role of art objects in the social process'.

Elaborating his objection to aesthetic treatments as an inappropriate content for an anthropology of art, Gell (1998: 3) writes:

> The project of 'indigenous aesthetics' is essentially geared to refining and expanding the aesthetic sensitivities of the Western art public by providing a cultural context within which non-Western art objects can be assimilated to the categories of Western aesthetic art appreciation. This is not a bad thing in itself, but it still falls far short of being an anthropological theory of art production and circulation.

In this chapter, I do not plan to treat Gell's attempts to exemplify an anthropology of art in the style he imagines it. Rather, I want to show how widely dispersed across social locations is the impetus for the revaluation of non-Western objects in terms of Western appreciation; not only within the academy, and not only or even fundamentally on aesthetic grounds. I will explore how the social materials of interrelationship between indigenous and non-indigenous Australians intersect with the activities of the 'art world' to make the appreciation of non-Western art objects within the categories of Western art appreciation initially seem a 'natural' function of the objects themselves, thus apparently treating them as having kinds of indexicality which would be consistent with Gell's notion of 'agency'. However, I also argue that, in the complex interface between what emerge as 'indigenous' and 'non-indigenous' social spaces, the capacity of the objects is recast as part of a wider public reorientation toward their meaningfulness as largely indexical of the indigenous/non-indigenous relationship, rather than as discrete or autonomous. As Aboriginal art has gained in centrality over recent years within the field of Australian and international art, its forms of indexicality range from pointing to the distinctiveness and values of Aboriginal cultural traditions, to the dynamics of struggle between indigenous and non-indigenous domains in the way characteristic of much 'urban' Aboriginal art. Thus, it seems to me that Gell's notion of art objects as 'agents' requires particular treatment in colonial and post-colonial contexts, and the conditions of their indexicality need to be treated as equal in complexity to the social interface in which their significance is re-shaped.

Closely tied to my theme of the changing indexicality of indigenous objects is another concern with how the revaluation of Australian Aboriginal cultural production *as* 'art' has been an aspect of a larger, and essentially socio-political, project of redressing the devaluation of this formerly colonized indigenous people. Given this as one fundamental source of dynamism behind the changing, more central position of Aboriginal art within the wider art scene, some of the selectivity of that revaluation has been revealed in just some of those social contexts – recently, particularly in relation to highly prestigious art exhibitions – in which their celebration as 'art' was placed in focus and seemingly recognized in a consummate way. The tensions thus revealed between the apparently aesthetic bases for the recognition of cultural production as 'art', and the post-colonial socio-political grounds for its recognition as art, point in at least two directions. First, they make us more explicitly aware of the biases within a contemporary Western social formation for the evaluation of art as a superior mode of human activity, and of some of the assumptions concerning creativity, and its association with social transcendence, that underlie this. We gain a clearer appreciation of why the revaluation of others' cultural production as art can suggest itself as a form of redress of their situation – crudely put, it shows that they are capable of transcending it. But secondly, the tensions make us consider why those assumptions concerning art, with their in-built historical drive to distinguish a domain as aesthetic from the residually social, only contribute selectively to the revaluation of an indigenous people whose subjection has mainly been naturalized and grounded in the terms of combined racial-and-cultural, rather than more limitedly cultural distinctions. The tendency to assert the equivalent worth of 'their' cultural objects with 'ours' is underlain by a pervasive and much broader systematization of social inequality which constantly re-emerges to interact with the liberal project of revaluation. This interaction produces new forms of complexity, which may also provide potential for 'Aboriginal art' to alter some of the forms of valuation and practice characteristic of the field of Western art. However, the persistence of systematic inequality fuels questions concerning the equivalence of the objects to Western art, revealing some of the social grounds underlying aesthetic judgement. In addition, this persistence serves to police the borders between art as theirs and ours, blurring of which problematizes the liberal project of revaluation in its most categorical, and publicly most available form: the according of equivalence to that which is presumed to be 'different' in a clear-cut way. But as indigenous cultural production becomes increasingly valued as art, it also comes to participate in the movements of the wider art world, and may free itself of some of the constraints of categorization. Though constantly subject to pressures to remain recognizable as 'Aboriginal art', it also bursts the bounds of such constraints in some ways, both in its material forms and in the changing self-positionings of its practitioners.

'Higher in the Human Scale'

James Clifford (1991: 241) has written that identification as fine art is 'one of the most effective current ways to give cross-cultural value (moral and commercial) to a cultural production'. There are numerous instances of scholars and members of the public, in Australia and elsewhere, having claimed for fine art a valued status for a very long time. For example, Australianist anthropologist and Sydney University professor A.P. Elkin, active from the 1940s into the 1960s in the effort to shape an assimilationist government Aboriginal policy as a progressive alternative to the previous exclusion of Aborigines from Australian society (Wise 1985), wrote in the introduction to Fred McCarthy's *Australian Aboriginal Decorative Art* (1961) that '[A] people possessing an art is much higher in the human scale than had previously been thought' (cited in McLean 1998: 91). More recently, other commentators have alleged the significance of the Australian Aboriginal 'art boom' of the last several decades in creating respect for Aboriginal people and culture. The journalist Jane Cadzow (1987: 15) quoted Clyde Holding, then Minister for Aboriginal Affairs, expressing a version of this valuation:

> Many Australians have been taught that Aboriginal people have no traditions, no culture . . . When they come to understand the depth of tradition and skill that's involved in this area [art], it's a very significant factor in changing attitudes.

Myers (1991: 34–5) has suggested that the presentation of Aboriginal culture in terms of its art (his discussion focuses on the acrylic paintings of Central Australia) has involved the construction of a '*permissible* Aboriginal culture, that is, a representation that meets the approval of the dominant white society's notions of "common humanity"'. This, he further suggests, involves assertions or presumptions at two levels: that Aborigines have 'art', and value it, and that the tradition is very old; and that this 'art' contributes something of importance to the wider world of art. The often synechdochic representations of Aboriginal culture as 'art' which come to circulate in locations of the wider society are closely linked to the political discourse of 'nationalism', and the spiritual and aesthetic discourses of 'modernism' (1997: 39; see Nicoll 1996, Benjamin 1998).

Myers's perspectives remain focused on the issue adumbrated by Clifford, of production regarded as fine art conferring 'cross-cultural value'. But they also begin to suggest some of the ways in which such valuation can be problematic, and generate some of the grounds of its own contestation. Let us briefly consider the two 'discourses' with which Myers sees Aboriginal art having become thoroughly entwined in Australia.

Aboriginal visual art has played a very prominent role in the constitution of national- and international-level representations of Australia since at least the 1970s, a period in which Aboriginal art began to attract significant government support (Myers 1996) as part of a general concern for the revaluation of indigeneity. This followed a long period of continuing but less organized support for what McLean (1998) calls 'Aboriginalism' in literature and art, the effort of mainly literati and artists who would have found in Aboriginal cultural sources the means for producing a distinctive Australian identity. A 'nationalist' concomitant of the relatively recent state support for indigenous cultural production (coming as it has during a period of heightened international emphasis on indigeneity, ethnicity and other forms of difference politics), and the promotion of some forms of it into acclaimed 'art', has been an unusual degree of investment by the Australian nation-state in 'indigeneity' as a mode of its own being, or essential part of itself (Hamilton 1990). Through this identification, the nation-state works to constitute for itself a continuity of identity which some commentators have alleged is otherwise lacking but others have claimed allows for the constitution of continuity in more primordial and gripping ways than the underlying 'Benthamite' variant of (Anglo)-Australian political culture otherwise provides for (see e.g. Collins 1985 for an analysis of Anglo-Australian continuity in these terms). In short, the Australian nation-state has, over the last few decades of the twentieth century, experimented with self-representation in a way that 'elicits' indigeneity to an unusual extent (perhaps rivalled among the successor states of English colonization only by New Zealand). In an effort to suggest some of the political-economic underpinnings of this nexus between art and the state, Nicoll (1996: 714) has written of the Aboriginal art 'industry' as a 'Utopian vision of reconciliation produced by the state imagination at a moment of economic rationalism'. Myers (1996) also discusses the connections between the revaluation of Aboriginal cultural production, and economic rationalism.

Benjamin (1998) has explored some of the modes and implications of the linking of Aboriginal 'art' with the spiritual and aesthetic discourses of modernism. Benjamin has suggested that the acceptance of Aboriginal cultural production as fine art (he argues from an examination of the work of Central Australian painter Emily Kngwarreye) has depended upon the interpretation of artwork in terms of some of the conventions of artistic modernism. While such readings enable the work to be seen in the art world as having cross-cultural value, and support their valuation as something beyond objects of mere ethnographic interest, such shifts in the processes by which Aboriginal production is received and appreciated also entail some movement away from ethnographic understanding of the work, in other social, cultural and historical terms, and are connected with some changes that can be detected in the nature of cultural production itself. With respect to the latter, Benjamin shows, for example, how Kngwarreye's later work moved away from imagery that is explicitly seen in Australia as evoking Aboriginal tradition(s) towards the 'all-over' style of modernism, and changed in its colour schemes.

With some differences in emphasis from both Nicoll and Myers, who to date have placed considerable weight upon the promotion of art as an aspect of government policy, Morphy (1995) and Morphy and Elliott (1997) argue for a more explicitly interactive and overall more agentive view of the relation of Aboriginal producers to the globalizing art market. Morphy (1995; see also McLean 1998) traces a history of promotion of Aboriginal cultural production from 'ethnographic object' to 'primitive fine art,' to 'fine' and 'contemporary' art, an associated shift in the kinds of spaces in which indigenous art tends to be displayed, and the extent to which it is now 'collected by the same institutions, exhibited within the same gallery structure, written about in the same journals as other Australian art' (Morphy 1995: 233). He also discusses the increasing breadth of Aboriginal art exhibitions which have sought to alter previous art-historical practices by being more inclusive, particularly of so-called 'urban' or 'Koori' art which had not been represented in equal measure in earlier exhibitions of 'Aboriginal art'. This greater breadth paralleled the growing inclusiveness of the category 'Aboriginal' in the late twentieth century, and the demand from many social locations for the abandonment of invidious practices of 'blood-quantum counting'.

Recognition that the promotion of indigenous cultural production into fine art is not unproblematic also requires that we consider the historical background against which issues arise in the processes of the social implementation of this shift. 'Aboriginal art' was constantly in the Australian news during the remarkable year 1997, and mostly as a subject of contention, a circumstance that stimulated my thinking about the matters treated in this chapter. Those concerned with the relations between Australia's indigenous people and the nation-state were forced to take notice. What was going on? What were said to be the issues surrounding Aboriginal art in these media representations? Was their high media profile, cast in ways I will shortly describe, just a temporary aberration, or was it an indicator of social processes and tensions that are neither minor nor impermanent?

From my comparative perspective as an American who earlier worked in North American indigenous contexts, but by now has become a long-term observer and participant on the Australian scene, I have concluded that Aboriginal issues, in general, have had a remarkably high profile in the Australian media for at least the last several decades of the twentieth century. Art is only one of these issues; others have included land rights; debates (and often conflict) over development, heritage and sites matters; national indigenous health and welfare status; all examples of the extent to which 'Aboriginal affairs' are daily made part of Australian consciousness. The art episodes of 1997 were consistent with this general salience, and thus, I suggest, were (further) indicators of continuing social processes and tensions. The way these episodes developed was also consistent with a general tendency for Aboriginal affairs to receive heightened media attention as 'problems'; or, perhaps more fully and accurately, for Aboriginal affairs to be represented to the nation as either problematic or halcyon, laden from the outset with a value weighting that marks them as non-normative and out-of-the-ordinary. Thus, while for some the recent prominence of Aboriginal art has been one way of demonstrating the worth of Aboriginal culture to wider Australia, there are many others who, as the following episodes will illustrate, seem ready to diminish its value as Aboriginal production or, one suspects, as an area of distinction and appreciation cultivated mainly by educated, cosmopolitan elites. Myers (1996) put the socioeonomic and class implications of the emergence of Aboriginal production as fine art in terms compatible with such a view:

... I discern [that Aboriginal fine art] emerges in relation to a particular form of 'modernization' in Australia – transformation of the managed Australian economy, a postcolonial shifting of cultural identifications, and the ascendancy of a new technocratic-managerial class at the heart of this 'enterprise'.

Hage (1998: 201), building on Bourdieu's appreciation of the class-linked nature of cosmopolitan 'symbolic capital', designates relevant class-race protagonists as bearers of 'cosmo-multiculturalism', referring principally to government promulgation of tolerance for cultural diversity in the period following the Second World War under the rubric of multiculturalism. His account is like Myers's in identifying specific sectoral or class-linked types in the dominant social formation as crucial bearers of change. But overall, he does not assign all agency to this kind of protagonist, or to self-conscious action. His view is that change proceeds at the level of the ordinary and the everyday in ways that policy-makers and 'cosmo-multiculturalists' fail to recognize, and over which they are able to exercise little actual control.

While both Myers and Hage locate sources of change in these sectorally specific ways, Morphy (1995: 219–220) expresses the set of enabling conditions around the growing centrality of Aboriginal art in broad terms:

The essentialist argument would be that the richness of Aboriginal art became visible at last, whereas previously the evolutionary eye had been blind to it ... However ... [I]n part the increased interest resulted from a combination of Aboriginal political action and Australian political circumstance. Aborigines used art as an instrument in asserting their rights both to land and to cultural recognition. As Australian governments in the 1960s and 1970s became more sensitive to issues of Aboriginal rights they saw support of art as one of the least divisive ways of furthering Aboriginal interests. Political action also increased the visibility of Aborigines in Australian society ... Aboriginal art also benefited from the movement of Australian nationalism away from its European roots, and from the opportunities presented by the Bicentennial celebrations in 1988 to dramatise issues of national identity.

In what follows, I want to examine two recent episodes of what I will call allegations of inauthenticity in the area of Aboriginal art. Artists who had been presumed to be engaged in cultural production as Aborigines, upon their receiving some very notable form of recognition, were alleged in one case to be collaborating with 'non-Aborigines' in ways that led to high-profile media 'scandal' and the questioning of the authenticity of the works; and in the other, were revealed not to be Aboriginal at all, in any commonly accepted sense. The two cases I will examine involved visual art; but it is to be noted that parallel instances have occurred in other 'high culture' forms (especially literature).[1]

This scrutiny came in the wake of two and more decades of regional and federal support for activity by Aboriginal producers. This support and the promotion of production had enabled presumed 'Aboriginal' works such as these to enter into institutional circuits (e.g., of 'art awards') and to cross into an aesthetic register where they were notionally displayed and assessed as 'art'. The assumption had already been widely made, and widely accepted, at least by certain liberal elites, that Aboriginal art had something of universal value to offer to the wider art scene. But dispute revolved around whether the works in question were the works of Aborigines. Their attributability to persons recognizable as Aborigines was a central, and crucial justification for the inclusion of works in the particular institutional venues. However, once the authenticity of the paintings was questioned in terms of the Aboriginality or otherwise of the artists, it began to emerge from the ex post facto nature of the dispute among experts that the form and presumed content of the works could not be taken as certain guides to their social provenance, as might be presupposed by a constraining view of the kind of 'difference' Aboriginal art can make. Efforts were made in each case to adduce some material or materially-linked aspects of form – technique, imagery and its presumed content – as a guide to the work's Aboriginality (or otherwise), and its stylistic traditionality; but in each case the results were casuistic. Given the circumstances of these cases, the looseness or openness to participation of culture and art practices, and the consequences for social valuation and identification of the products, obviously required clearer discussion.

But the media debate also demonstrated that it was extremely difficult for this kind of question to be formulated, much less adequately or widely discussed. I speculate that this was so in large part because, at the broadest public level, the promotion of Aboriginal production into wider, cross-cultural circuits of value as art had been strongly formulated and understood as a recuperative strategy. Accordingly, at that level, indigenous forms of cultural production had had certain major expectations held of them: first, that they be part of the building (or rebuilding) of a culturally appropriate indigenous economy; second, that they be and remain distinctively and recognizably Aboriginal; third, that they contribute to a national heritage (and economy) in an integrative rather than divisive way; and fourth, that they be exemplary of the contribution that Aboriginality can make to national identity and heritage. Though there was considerable public support for these goals, this paradoxically has made it difficult for Aboriginal 'art' to rise above the strong and continuing tendencies towards naturalist identifications of cultural production with categories of person in terms of discourses and relations of bodiliness – in short, in terms of what has often been called the identification of culture with race. Even within an art-appreciating sector of the public, more aware of the diversity within 'Aboriginal art' and among kinds of producers, there is constant discussion and contestation around the categories of 'Aboriginal art' and 'Aboriginal artists'.

Annus horribilis: 1997

Over the last several years, Australia has been shocked several times over by Aboriginal 'art exposés'. The year 1997 was particularly notorious in this respect, and it does not seem fortuitous that it was otherwise marked by a seeming retreat from an attitude of tolerance which had characterized government policy on immigration and related matters for some years. There was a great deal of commentary around two particular allegations of 'inauthenticity', characterized by a media vocabulary of scandal and moral outrage. 'Black Art Scandal', bannered the *Australian* of 15 November, concerning events surrounding Central Australian Aboriginal female artist Kathleen Petyarre, winner of the Telstra art award, a prize then in its eleventh year. Kathleen's de facto partner, Jim Beamish, a man of Welsh origin who had lived with her in the remote Central Australian community of Utopia for some years, was alleged to have contributed more than an acceptable share of work to the award-winning canvas. He spoke of his relief in 'coming clean' about his role in the award-winning, and other, now famous, canvases. An additional headline in the same issue of the *Australian* also employed the same vocabulary of moral stain and subsequent cleansing. An article headlined, 'Chance to start again with a clean canvas', opined that Petyarre could begin again in her own right as the leading painter she was acknowledged to be; and Beamish, too, could start a new career, as an 'artist in his own right'.

When you came right down to it, the number of media commentators and public spokespeople casting news stories in this way appeared to be few but their outlets very public and influential. The presence and partiality of particular art dealers and collectors in the underlying events and subsequent shaping of the stories was evident, even if all the details of their interests were not clear to the general public. Despite the seemingly small number of such active participants, noteworthy nevertheless was the noise they could make, the receptivity of the media to 'scandal' of this kind, and the extent to which the media publicists claimed to position themselves as watchdogs of 'authenticity' on behalf of the wider public.

Kathleen Petyarre had begun to produce works of art for sale during the energetic period of government sponsorship of Aboriginal arts and crafts which began in the 1970s (see Altman et al. 1989; Anderson and Dussart 1988; Bardon 1979; Baume 1989; Johnson 1994). At first working in batik (as did a number of other women at Utopia who formed a core of producers), she later turned to producing acrylic paintings, which (after a period of limited acceptance) from the 1980s (see Anderson 1995) have shown the potential to be accepted on the art market as 'fine art' rather than merely craft. In 1996, she won the Telstra National Aboriginal and Torres Strait Islander Award, worth $18,000, for a painting 'Storm in Atnangkere Country II' (Figure 10.1). She was subsequently invited to submit paintings to other exhibitions, her public recognition as an Aboriginal artist having been given significant impetus by the conferring of the award. Her home base had continued to be the cattle station (ranch) community of Utopia (which had been converted to Aboriginal tenure under a federal statute enacted in 1976). Jim Beamish lived with her at Utopia for some years. Among the art producers at Utopia was Emily Kngwarreye, who by the time of her death in 1998 was suggested to be Australia's foremost Aboriginal artist (see Neale 1998). Coming from a remote-area background in which art and craft production had been fostered by government within local communities, and with limited command of (standard)

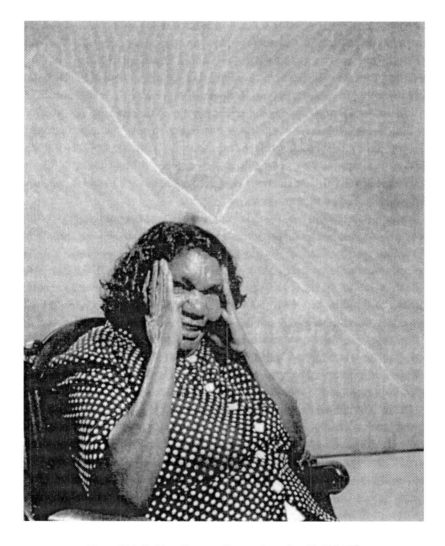

Figure 10.1 Kathleen Petyarre. Source: *Australian* 15–16/11/97

English, these producers were reliant on a small number of art advisors and dealers for conceptions about the wider contexts into which their products might enter.

Seemingly against the background of some conflict among art dealers, Susan McCulloch, an arts writer of the *Australian* newspaper, made some inquiries into the painting of 'Storm', and came up with some of the following conclusions (which others, as we will see, contested). Beamish's participation in the execution of the painting was considerable, and he might be said not only to have done a large portion of the canvas, but even to have authored it conceptually in certain ways. He had also participated in the execution (and maybe the conceptualization) of other paintings that had been sold as Petyarres. All these things were seen to raise questions about the identification of this work, and maybe others, as Petyarre's work and as Aboriginal art.

The media debate along some of these lines became heated. One of the notable outcomes was the formation of a professional body of the country's Aboriginal art dealers. They were reported in the *Australian* of 2 March 1998 to have decided to band together to tackle issues of 'ethical standards, accountability, authenticity and grievance management'. They also are said to have voted to adopt a code of silence, choosing to speak officially to the media only through a designated spokesperson.

The reported media debate involving the two principals, Petyarre and Beamish, did not clarify conceptually what might be relevant questions concerning these allegations, or their applicability (in large part, because the media reporting was exposé-oriented). Their reported remarks did suggest different perspectives on issues, never formulated with any great clarity, of the relation between execution and authorship, and the identification of content and rights to it. For his part, Beamish seems to have been willing to accept the credit for the Telstra award-winning work as attributed to him by McCulloch's statements, claiming to have painted 90 per cent of its two square metres. He also averred that the idea for the painting arose from an experience he had had when lost in the desert, and had nothing to do with Petyarre's Dreaming stories, which he said she regularly painted. He said that the story of his having been lost in the desert was well known to Utopia elders, but it remained unclear whether they had a view on the authorship and content of the painting. It is worth noting that the caption on the painting described its subject as a sacred women's Dreaming associated with the Green Pea (*Australian*, 21 November 1997).

There has long been recognition among collectors and dealers that a great deal of Aboriginal art, including painting for sale, is the result of collaborative work. It is also recognized that in many contexts of Aboriginal production, there is no simple relationship between the execution of a work, and attributed authorship/ ownership. Family members and associated people may all work on a canvas that is understood to embody a set of relations between people and landscape or

Dreaming. Attributions of paintings may be be based on a number of different, socio-culturally relevant dimensions of those relationships, the scope of which may vary, and rights to produce paintings may be sourced to more than one. There are related incomparabilities between sources of value in Aboriginal contexts and ones associated with the Western art tradition. The latter places great value upon creativity and notions of individual artistry as manifested in objects which are seen as the artist's creation; whereas by many Aborigines, including some of the producers at Utopia, great, even hieratic value is placed upon designs and images as manifesting a transcendent order to which people also belong, rather than upon the creativity of the maker. (See Morphy 1991, Chapter 4, for discussion in a context of these different kinds of right in paintings and designs, including the right to produce certain paintings, the right to divulge meanings, and the right to authorize or restrict the production and use of paintings.) Although no claim is sustainable that personal agency is unimportant, it is nevertheless apt to say that local identification and attribution of agency and prerogative to socially constituted persons has a complexity in many indigenous contexts that goes beyond any simple equation of an individual as 'artist' with a cultural product. This complexity clearly continues to present problems for the art market, and for its valuation and pricing mechanisms. Frequently compared in this context are hallowed Western conventions of collaborative work (for example, the studio practices of acknowledged classical masters). But these, too, are problematic for the art world. These practices have problematized the attribution of many works (and there is an industry of related investigation and authentication). Indigenous art practices may come to be juxtaposed with these practices of joint work, as well as with more avant-garde Western collaborative practices, to pose some challenge to Western art conventions.

Given the range of possible different, relevant considerations that can play a part in the attribution of works to Aboriginal people, there remains a question of exactly what Kathleen Petyarre may have thought of newspaper allegations that the work in question was not 'hers'. There seems to have been some focus on questions of execution (whether he or she 'did more') and of conceptual content (was the content his or hers, and how would one know?), but it is not clear what she may have made of these issues either. Presumably, Petyarre had long experience and considerable sophistication as an art producer, but she cannot be assumed to have seen all issues against the same kind of background assumptions evident in the writing by media commentators. Difficulties of analysis also exist because, in the media, she was constantly 'voiced over' by others who put the issues rather differently than she can reasonably be assumed to have done. Through her lawyers, Phillips Fox, she was quoted as saying:

> I was particularly concerned that rumours have been circulated by my former husband, that he is the author of some of my works . . . this unfortunate situation is also being

manipulated by other art interests who have unsuccessfully sought the right to sell my paintings. There have been occasions on which he assisted me with the preparation of canvases under direction and supervision. In recent years he has assisted me in marking out larger canvases, particularly where accurately locating the middle of the canvas is required (*Australian*, 22 November 1997).

Television footage of Petyarre leaves no doubt that she does not speak this kind of English, and suggests that she would have found it difficult, if not impossible, to understand a statement formulated in this style. About the question of execution, she was quoted somewhat more directly as saying: 'Ray started with the white cross and did all the white dots, I just followed with the yellow dots . . . He started this type of "round" painting [so called because of the work's radiating circles] but not the others I do'. By McCulloch, this seems to have been taken as an admission that the work was, in some significant sense, more his than hers. But it is not clear to me that this is what she thought she was conveying, by giving these descriptions.

Other statements from Petyarre, however she may have intended them, were cast so as to seemingly constitute an admission of Beamish's priority in the work on certain canvases. About the stylistic 'radiating' device, mentioned above, she is reported to have said that she was uncertain whether she could do this since having split up with Beamish. 'When I come back from holidays in a few weeks I'll try', she is reported as having said; 'I can do them but they come out different. I tried to do one a few weeks ago and it got all mixed up' (*Australian*, 23 December 1997).

Elsewhere, Petyarre is reported to have said that Beamish 'been pinch'im' (had stolen) her dreaming in the award-winning canvas (a perspective that seems to attribute the work to him in some significant way). But as we have seen, Beamish alleged the idea for the painting had come from an experience of his own in the desert, and that he would never 'pinch' any of her Dreaming.

While these two were reported to have answered questions on the matter of who did what on this canvas, and its subject, much of the media argument seemed to presuppose that one way out of the apparent difficulties was for Beamish to be seen as an artist in his own right. If he did the canvas, or could be thought of as having done a great deal of it, the reckoning seemed to run, the simplest thing is to identify him as the artist. But what of the undoubted stylistic similarities between the contested canvas and other works of Petyarre and Utopia artists? Would there be any serious sense in which Beamish could be seen as the conceptual source of the contested canvases, according to the pairing of inspiration and execution normally attributed to the artist-producer in the Western tradition? There seems little doubt that Beamish gained his relevant artistic experience through working in this Aboriginal community and art milieu. 'At first I used to see Kathleen do the paintings and just be sitting there talking to her. One day I just picked up a stick and started helping her with them' (*Australian*, 24 December 1997). If the question about what might and might not be attributed to Beamish had been debated systematically, an area of inquiry would have emerged concerning the openness to wider participation and influence of what are clearly historical art traditions developed by Aboriginal people, and also the terms of identification and evaluation of the objects produced under such conditions of intercultural influence and participation. But most of the issues raised in the press seemed rather more pragmatically oriented. Fred Torres, an art dealer with family connections to Utopia, opined (*Australian*, 19 November 1997) that the art industry and the nature of its controls should be scrutinized, but also that Beamish should be given appropriate recognition. Torres' view was that 'Any works done by Beamish should be attributed to him as non-Aboriginal art with influences from the culture. The works should be newly titled to suit their creative strength'.

One is struck by the oddity of the oppositions being posed. Many people might think they have a practical feel for what is meant by a category of 'Aboriginal art'; or at least, would feel able to identify a core of stylistic conventions (no doubt regionally differentiated) that this term evokes for them. But Torres's suggestion is that Beamish's productions should be recognized as 'non-Aboriginal art'. Such a negatively defined category does not evoke anything, except by opposition. In this context, it seems to mean art which is reminiscent of recognized Aboriginal styles, but is done by somebody who is clearly not an Aborigine. I have already expressed doubt whether, under the circumstances, it would have been adequate to merely acknowledge Aboriginal cultural 'influences' upon his work. Such a solution is only a very limited one, and approaches matters from the point of view of art marketing.

Janet Holmes à Court, a wealthy collector and connoisseur, was reported as saying that for some years, she had had 'a gut feeling of unease that some of the works that are purporting to have been painted by Aboriginal artists may not have been' (*Australian*, 17 January 1998). Her unease, note, is about the value of the paintings as Aboriginal art, something that is strongly tied to their commercial value. It is not about the aesthetic values of the painting, which presumably do not arise as problematic where the art objects appear to conform to expected stylistic conventions. Her primary concern as stated is about whether paintings marketed as 'Aboriginal art' can unproblematically be classed and traded as such, and thus about the issue of authenticity of the producer rather than 'aesthetic values'. To meet such concerns, Torres's proposed labelling of Beamish's paintings as 'non-Aboriginal art' would be meaningful. But this would not remove the underlying anomaly that many of the media reports appear to accept without explicit comment: from the combined perspectives of many art dealers, collectors and art exhibitors, it is less problematic for the art objects which Beamish produced or helped to produce, in styles that he has learned at Utopia, and that obviously relate to a collective historical tradition, to be identified for marketing and exhibition purposes as *his* work, the result of *his* artistry, than it is for those objects to be identified as Petyarre's work, or as 'Aboriginal art'. Such judgement accords a centrality to the negatively-defined category of 'non-Aborigines' as those who can appreciate, absorb and encompass art which, stylistically, is seen as linked to recognized Aboriginal traditions. There is a presupposition, again strongly tied to commercial concerns (though probably less evident in some other areas of art-related activity), that art needs to be identified as 'Aboriginal' (in the sense of being done by an Aborigine), or as 'non-Aboriginal', and that a work cannot be both. By the time of this controversy Petyarre already had gained recognition as an 'Aboriginal artist', working within certain externally imposed conventions of authenticity and marketing; while Beamish's recognition as an 'artist' was both merely potential and unconstrained by a requirement of Aboriginality – despite the fact that he only existed as a producer on the fringe of an Aboriginal social context. The question about Beamish raised most explicitly in the media debate was the hypothetical one of whether he had artistic potential in his own right; while for Petyarre, the question taken to be of public interest was how his participation affected the value of her work as an already recognized 'Aboriginal artist'. Her category, in short, can be sullied and disrupted; his cannot, because there is no hermetically sealed notion of 'non-Aboriginal art', even though this categorization has a specific meaningfulness (as above) in the context of the recognized 'Aboriginal art market'. Beamish can adapt and receive from Aboriginal culture, and those adaptations can be favourably seen as part of his (potential) artistry (which might nevertheless exist as some kind of variant of recognized 'Aboriginal art'). In contrast, the identification of Petyarre's work as 'Aboriginal' can be disrupted by his contribution, if it is deemed to be too great, and the recognized value of her work thereby severely diminished.[2]

Another possibility would have been for the award-winning work to continue to be recognized in these debates, in some significant way, as hers, but with 'influences' from Beamish. Some other dealers and collectors – perhaps aware of some of the tangled thickets one might enter in either probing closely the identification of any 'art' in essentializing and bounding terms of established tradition, or allowing the 'Aboriginality' of a work to be a matter of degree rather than categorical – seemed to be persuaded of the simplicity of the approach taken by Christopher Chapman of the Art Gallery of South Australia. He attached Beamish's name to Mountain Devil Lizard Dreaming (Figure 10.2), on advice from Petyarre that this was mainly his work. 'We see Aboriginal art in the context of contemporary art so correct labelling may be all that is necessary', he suggested. This, however, would not seem to meet the 'unease' of Janet Holmes à Court, which arises from questions about authenticity and, ultimately, the possibility of

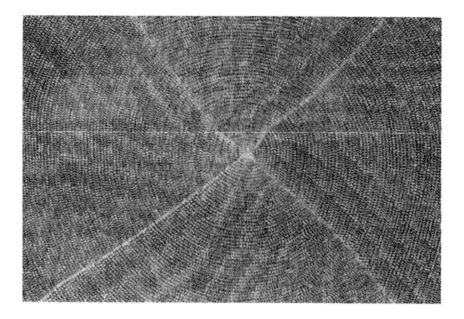

Figure 10.2 Mountain Devil Lizard Dreaming. Source: *Bulletin* 3/12/97

maintaining a clear market category of 'Aboriginal art'. Simple re-labelling does not recognize questions of hybridity as relevant; It also – in the contemporary context where cultural and social interinfluence is possible and even common, and Aboriginal art has heightened public value – fails to recognize as a relevant issue the indeterminacy of appearance and material form for the identification of objects which have such extended potential for circulation.

It seemed as if some practical or technical differences in the quality of Petyarre's and Beamish's work demanded to be identified, given the strength of suggestions that the award-winning and other related works were, in some significant way, not hers. There was some commentary along these lines from art connoisseurs and dealers. The art writer Susan McCulloch approached the problem by suggesting that Petyarre and Beamish were, or might be, both 'artists' (*Australian*, 3 December 1997) whose work differed stylistically. Petyarre, she averred, painted in meandering layered dots such as had characterized the style of her works appearing in the National Gallery of Victoria's McCaughey Prize. Beamish, on the other hand, painted in a style identical to that of the Storm picture. The clear inference was that the main authorship of the Storm picture was thus to be attributed to him.

For while Petyarre was undoubtedly painting works in a way similar to the award-winning work – characterised by diagonal lines leading to a central point – from the late 1980s on, there is a precise, almost mechanical quality and geometric construct in the award-winning and similar works that, as a number of art-aware people have said repeatedly, stands out.

Fred Torres put the matter similarly:

> While it may come as a surprise to some, paintings in the style of the National Aboriginal and Torres Strait Islander Art Award winner Storm in Atnangkere Country II are far from the average traditional artwork and have outside influences that stand out. Why haven't experts, critics and collectors picked up on it? The radiating lines require intense concentration to evenly place and calculate the right amount of dots in every dip of the stick. This is far different from the style of a traditional Aboriginal artist (*Australian*, 19 November 1997).

But all such technical judgements lacked circumstantial independence. Though the allegations of Beamish's collaboration were seen to mar the identification of the Storm painting as worthy of a prize as Aboriginal art, initially the canvas was not recognized as anything other than that. Underlying these comments about stylistic differences between the two painters also lurked the suggestion that the style of an Aboriginal artist does not change, if that work is to remain within the canon of the 'average traditional artwork'. And further, even if Petyarre's work were to show 'outside influences', is the necessary conclusion that the work is no longer 'hers', or 'Aboriginal', from the relevant perspectives of the art market and art exhibitors? What if, as I have suggested might have occurred, the contested canvas had been identified as hers, with acknowledged 'outside influences'?

After months of reportage, an article appeared declaring, 'Petyarre's Storm Clouds Clear'. It reported a decision by the board of the Museum and Art Gallery of the Northern Territory confirming her authorship of the 1996 Telstra award-winning painting, and her right to the associated prize of $18,000. 'There's no more trouble. I'm just happy inside my heart', Petyarre was quoted as saying. The board found 'that the allegations by Mr Beamish regarding authorship were not proved. That leaves the decision of the judges to award the Telstra Prize to Ms Petyarre intact'. The Board also found 'Ms Petyarre's position to accord with widely accepted Australian indigenous attitudes to artistic practice and ownership, which freely acknowledges the concept of assistance in the production of artworks'. According to later report, Beamish was said to have phoned his brother-in-law at Utopia, and to have begged for forgiveness over the phone, also expressing a wish to reunite with Petyarre.

Even if all ended well, from Petyarre's point of view, one cannot assume that the problems brought to view have been worked through, practically or conceptually. The main conclusion that some commentators seem to have drawn from this episode, given their institutional interests, was that the collaborative nature of much

Aboriginal work should be recognized (but implicitly, this has tended to mean, collaboration among people recognizable as Aborigines); and that the conditions and authorship of work should be clear and transparent, and properly documented by museums and exhibitions. But although clear documentation is no doubt desirable, the attitude that fosters it is often closely linked to prescriptivism. And 'clear documentation' is a practical but insufficiently theorized position in relation to the questions of contemporary identifications of a category of 'Aboriginal art', and of particular products and objects in these terms. Under present circumstances, conditions of production and inter-cultural influence, perception and reception are likely to become more complex rather than 'clearer'. What will this imply in terms of public recognition and valuation? of marketing? of stylistic change? of the social relations among people as producers? of the legitimacy of the kind of public discourse about 'authenticity' that we see having pervaded this case? Though seemingly progressive, the protective demand for 'clear documentation' does not address the issues in a sufficiently bold and future-oriented way.

Profound puzzlement and, again, outrage from many quarters accompanied the revelation from Robert Smith (1997), art critic and acquaintance of the elderly white painter Elizabeth Durack, that she was actually the producer of canvases which had been displayed and sold under the fictitious Aboriginal name, Eddie Burrup. Until the revelation, 'Eddie' had been assumed to be a black man of the Kimberley region in Australia's north-west. Particular tension arose from 'Eddie's' having been invited to contribute to the 1996 Native Title Now exhibition at the Aboriginal cultural institute, Tandanya, in Adelaide, given the political and liberatory theme. The work was also subsequently included in a nationwide tour – all on the understanding that it was by an Aboriginal person. A Burrup had been submitted for the Telstra award of 1996, but had not won.

Elizabeth Durack is the scion of a renowned family whose association with the Kimberley goes back to earliest occupation of the area by pastoralists in the 1870s. Her sister Mary is the author of Australian classics about early Kimberley settlement, *Sons of the Saddle* and *Kings in Grass Castles*. Why, everyone asked in amazement, would the other sister take it into her head to paint as an Aborigine?

Elizabeth Durack's own account is a complex one, of Eddie as 'a synthesis of several Aboriginal men I have known', and of her own re-subjectification as a result of her long-term association with Aboriginal people. She said that 'since working in direct union with Eddie', she had 'experienced a feeling of tremendous happiness and a sense of deep fulfilment'. What was found especially objectionable in Durack's actions was her allowing the public to think of the painter as an Aboriginal man – there seemed to be elements of hoax and deception. This was no Carlos Castañeda, stating clearly that he was Indian*ized* but not an Indian; Durack allowed the public to think the painter Aboriginal, knowing (whatever psychic complexities she experienced) the conventions of artistic attribution.

When Elizabeth Durack was accused, not only of deception, but also of having engaged in cultural appropriation, she replied with some feeling, 'I don't see how you can appropriate something that is within you' (ABC Television, *7:30 Report*, 16 September 1997). She was expansive about the extent to which her association with Aborigines over many years had led her to certain ways of seeing and feeling. It seems, then, she would count as a person whose practice has been deeply influenced by her contact with Aborigines. Her style would not, however, be readily identified with the major recognized Aboriginal visual traditions (see Figure 10.3, Burrup). And it seems that her comment about the impossibility of appropriating what has been internalized may be taken as asserting the subjectification that is a recognized ideological dimension of the Western artistic tradition: what the experiencing self takes in, becomes part of it and available for expressive externalization.

Figure 10.3 Eddie Burrup. 'Mulunga, the book'. Source: Rosalin Sadler, 'Is There No One to Untie Us? An Australian Tale of Totemic Tumult', *Modern Painters,* Summer 1999, pp. 44–9

Figure 10.4 Elizabeth Durack. Source: *The Art of Elizabeth Durack*, Angus and Robertson 1982, p.64

A different view of what is available to one, and the limitations of one's own agency in expression, were articulated by Paddy Nyawarra, an elderly Aboriginal man from the Kimberley, regarded as knowledgeable and a 'lawman'.[3] He observed that, even if nobody had previously heard of Eddie Burrup, he 'must be sitting on her [Durack's] shoulder, she's been in that country long time'. He saw the situation as one in which Elizabeth had become infused with the Eddie Burrup being, which he took to be the ghost of a deceased person. Without knowing the disputed canvases, or making any judgement on the basis of their appearance, he was prepared to think it quite plausible that Elizabeth could paint, in some sense, as an Aborigine. His further thought was that perhaps she should be smoked in order to rid her of this presence (that is, the cleansing smoke of a fire should be made to waft over her). For he assumed that one normally wishes to distance such spirit familiars. While Elizabeth's own statements about her relation to the Eddie Burrup figure put aside questions of appropriation by appealing to understandings of the complexly shaped, boundary-crossing but ultimately free-standing creativity of the artistic subject, Nyawarra initially did not resort to any accusation of appropriation, on a different basis. He appealed to understandings of another kind, having to do with the presumption of continuing influence between the living and the dead, which may also easily cross the everyday boundaries between black and white, and differences in forms of life, of people who live in the Kimberley.

Later in 1997, though, Paddy and other men of his age group and community wrote a letter to Bank West in Perth, protesting the display of a Wanjina[4] painting done by Durack under the name Burrup. 'We want to teach you that this wanjina can only be used if it is your birthright', they wrote. They added that it is only people from the three tribes, Ngarinyin, Worrora and Wunambal who can tell the stories about the Wanjinas.

However, a group of Nyoongar men from Perth supported Durack, and issued a statement saying: 'We the Metropolitan Nyoongar Circle of Elders accept that Mrs. Elizabeth Durack is the "Human Body", that her alter ego possesses spiritually to work his art . . . so essentially her art is a spiritual form of expression of a present living spirit of an Aboriginal person' (*The West Australian*, 10 December 1997). As we have seen, this was the sort of acount Paddy Nyawarra had initially advanced, but had articulated differently. He had spoken in terms of an experiential dimension of Durack becoming subject to the country: she had been in the Kimberley 'long time' and thus had become open to it. At that time, Nyawarra evidently had little familiarity with, and made no comment upon, the appearance of her paintings. Later, though, he was affronted to be made aware of Wanjina forms displayed under the Burrup name. With respect to these, he evidently found it implausible that any Aboriginal familiar could be 'sitting on her shoulder', as the Wanjina are originary creator forces. The Nyoongar statement is articulated in terms of painting as an 'expression' of an Aboriginal spirit, a view less explicit than Nyawarra's about the country's influence upon Durack, and perhaps more oriented to the vocabulary of creative representationalism.

Visual Imagery, Content and Authenticity: Shifting Frames of Significance

With respect to these two 'cases', the rough judgement might be made that the Storm painting showed clearer stylistic commonalities with an existing (though changing) Aboriginal art tradition as practised around Utopia; while most of Durack's works, which treat Aboriginal people and country as subjects from a specular viewpoint, obviously have less in common with any known Aboriginal art tradition (and a great deal in common with Durack's previous artwork). Yet this observation, while perhaps supportable despite its obvious subjectivity, does not yet come to the heart of the commonalities between these two episodes as public events. Despite great differences between them in many respects, at the crudest level the media interest in these two cases depended upon the prurient stimulation of questions about authenticity of the works, and specifically whether their Aboriginal authorship, as had been first established by experts operating in their specialist areas of judgement, was fraudulent. The media salience of the cases seems to rest on presumptions that the public will be interested in issues which show that the boundaries of an 'Aboriginal art' are not practically well-defined or recognizable, and in fact are being breached; and perhaps also, that the judgements of so-called 'experts' (such as the judges involved in the exhibitions) cannot be depended upon to be reliably discerning. Media releases appear to me to sometimes have claimed to present alternative sources of expertise and expert opinion, but more fundamentally, to have assumed a moralistic, 'watchdog' stance against alleged possibilities of the public being defrauded. It may not be far-fetched to suggest that underlying the issue about the clarity and boundedness of Aboriginal art lies a sense of some public disposition to question its distinctiveness and its value as contributing to a national legacy; while regarding the second issue, the media presumption that it is possible to elicit skepticism about the knowledgeability of experts seems quite up front (and Bourdieu's 1993 discussion of the class-linked bases of disposition and taste quite relevant). There is here a sounding chamber for the ideological resonance of an excluded 'common person', the *hoi polloi*. The claims of a minority of connoisseurs and experts to have distinguished themselves through an expertise of judgement and taste about Aboriginal art is confounded by the apparent demonstration that, from the particular institutional contexts established over the last twenty years or so of the twentieth century, emerges art of questionable authenticity.

To understand why such resonances can be elicited and played upon in a self-consciously matured and multicultural, indigenously-aware Australia, apparently more accepting than before of cultural diversity, it is necessary to remind ourselves of the position that such cultural production had been recently cultivated to occupy – or at least one of the most widely-available public discourses about its position – in liberal recuperative terms. As earlier observed, Aboriginal art had been broadly promoted in terms of a number of formulations (art as economic venture for Aboriginal communities, art as Aboriginal renewal and culture, Aboriginal art as distinctive, enriching contribution to a national legacy; see Myers 1996). Drawing the common strand from these perspectives, we can say that Aboriginal art was to be a medium not only of internal reconstitution of Aboriginality, but also of the wider public's reassessment and revaluation of Aboriginality. The comments of Minister for Aboriginal Affairs Clyde Holding, referred to above, regarding common Australian perceptions that Aboriginal people have 'no traditions, no culture', shows that the projected revaluation of Aboriginal people and culture is working against significant odds in the general community (but also *with* some public dispositions towards tolerance, acceptance of plurality, and even empowerment).

As the quotation above from James Clifford exemplifies, a common strategy for revaluation (among others, of previously colonized and now displaced peoples in liberal nation-states) is to make a cultural relativist finding that 'they' have something equivalent to that which is accorded the highest value within (elite sectors of) the dominant society; in this case (as anthropologist A.P. Elkin also anticipated), equivalent to 'art'.

There have been many useful discussions about whether, and under what circumstances, it may be appropriate or useful to characterize cultural production as 'art' (see for example Bourdieu 1993; Errington 1998; Price 1989; Gell 1998). The position I take in this chapter is consistent with a recognition that to characterize cultural production in this way depends upon its location in particular institutional and discursive contexts, and presupposes certain principles of apprehension and judgement of the natural and social world that go along with the construction of properly 'aesthetic' modes of perception. These modes have a presumed generality or universalism (though actually historically constituted and specific) which creates potential difficulty for any attempt to define 'artistry' in relation to a particular category of people, such as Aborigines. At the centre of definitions of people as indigenous (previously colonized), minority or sub-national groupings in popular understandings are supposedly natural (and pre-eminently, from the viewpoints of many, bodily or 'racial') attributes that not only distinguish them from others, but almost always also are at the basis of ways in which they are hierarchized and evaluated with reference to other recognized segments of a public sphere from whom they are distinguished. For many, bodiliness, together with categorical assertions of specific associations between 'race' and 'culture', are the media for constituting a unity of some publicly negotiable kind around the social 'group' in question. In many instances, as Holding's comments show, negative public evaluations which invoke the identification of race and culture are very strong. ('Aboriginal' people are widely devalued as having 'no culture'.)

We all recognize such forms of judgement, which are often realized as discrimination in virtue of putatively different 'racial' membership. What we must also recognize here is that these are the kinds of judgement that, in the view of the sponsoring, liberal governmental establishment, could be at least partly countered by the development of a recognized Aboriginal art. But I would suggest that the view that this could be so is a related piece of liberal ideology. Quite simply, any efforts that are intended to counter such judgements but fail to address the social and historical grounds of their possibility and existence, must leave them largely intact, and are bound to reproduce some of the same forms of social categorization both within and outside the arena of redress, though perhaps in modified form.

While it was principally seen as of ethnographic interest, Aboriginal cultural production had appeared admirable to some, but had remained outside the scope of high achievement. As cultural production becomes recognized as crossing over into an aesthetic register, it also becomes susceptible to scrutiny in terms of a Western art tradition with its notions of (individual) artistry, creativity, and its placing of the focus of artistic creation in the relation between artist and the aesthetic object that she (see Benjamin 1998; also Johnson 1995) produces. (See also Taylor

1991 for discussion of Western notions of authenticity as the realization of the differentiated self.)

The high valuation that is accorded to 'art' in the modern Western aesthetic tradition is predicated upon its constitution as human production which is seen to achieve a certain freedom from social determination. History ceases to have a full weight of social determination and burden of significance; art is made by creative individuals (even if they are recognized to be working within the terms of a collective tradition, in a sense a primary target of revaluation for cultural production emergent as art. Once revaluation at this level is incipient, artists as biographical individuals begin to come into clearer focus. Morphy (1995: 235) suggests that 'Aboriginal art is on the verge of incorporation within the process of individuation that is characteristic of the marketing of European art'). That is also why 'art' is and must remain an ambiguous category, and may be performatively and subject-ively applied to many kinds of objects and endeavours which appear to strive for, or achieve, this kind of transcendent creationism. The epistemological foundations of the order of 'art' (following definitive moves away from the sacral forms of image-production of medieval times) are very different from those which underlie much Aboriginal cultural production, particularly that which is understood to be directly continuous with pre-existing traditions of production. The latter involve the regulated reproduction of parts of a transcendent order, understood to be enacted according to social prerogatives which are organized by and flow from this order.

From the brief discussion of these contrasting perspectives, it becomes more intelligible why according the status of 'art' to the cultural production of a pre-viously devalued people can be widely appreciated within liberal Western societies as a recuperative move. Whereas the devaluation of subaltern peoples was experienced and rationalized as a necessary connection between them and their 'culture' (or lack of it), the revaluation of their cultural production as 'art' proposes that it may be seen in the terms of transcendent creationism. This reassessment, if accepted, provides some of the materials for refuting popular understandings of indigenous 'backwardness' and 'primitiveness', and at least creates exceptions to arguments concerning their failure to 'adjust', 'progress', and 'accommodate' to the world, as popular wisdoms have it, to which they are seen to need to adapt. (It may, however, also deflect attention from the conditions under which art production is being encouraged, and certainly does not dismantle the subaltern category. There is modification of the latter through the identification of exemplary individuals who engage in the activity which is revalued and altered by being institutionally equated with a valued sphere of activity of the wider society.) The worthiness of 'Aboriginal art' to belong within a wider art domain thus arises as something of a philosophical postulate of a liberal humanism making itself of service to a conservatively and culturally- rather than politically- conceived social project of revaluation.[5]

Further, revaluation of cultural production as 'art' is of course mobilized from within particular institutional contexts and understood in varying terms by segments of a wider population. Given its particularities, processes of revaluation become subject to popular scepticisms which already have a considerable social history and class-linked basis (such as of the role of 'experts' in arenas of judgement).

What is striking about the two cases I have described is the extent to which media-led suspicion focused upon the question of authenticity of the art, in the specific sense of whether or not paintings could be securely identified with 'Aboriginal' producers. The public, in short, seems to have made the working presumption that there is a category of Aboriginal art, and that certain works fall within its parameters. Given that valuable art prizes were predicated on artists' meeting the expected criterion of Aboriginality, the public issue revolved around a demand to connect a particular kind of racially-defined agent with a cultural object which had been admitted into that institutional context as the work of that agent, and which had been deemed particularly worthy, according to an expert exercise of judgement. In the case of Kathleen Petyarre, who met all the publicly expected physiognomic requirements of 'full Aboriginal appearance', the question developed around whether or not she, or her de facto, had 'actually' done the canvases, and in what measure. Especially among so-called 'urban' Aboriginal artists, though there are some who do not fulfil public expectations in terms of appearance, their work is seen as 'Aboriginal art'. As Morphy (1995: 223) observes, many were 'trained within the European tradition' and some works are 'indisting-uishable on formal grounds from paintings produced by white Australian artists'. The Aboriginality of such works is partly understood in terms of their explicit reference to the relationship between indigenous and non-indigenous domains, but as well, in the acceptance of the artists as Aboriginal persons. Any public suggestion that such people are somehow 'less Aboriginal' is regarded as provoc-ative and vexatious by many – and as a reversion to the odious 'blood quanta' counts of earlier Aboriginal policy.

There is, as I have noted, a gender issue about whether allegations of 'inauth-enticity' might have been pursued so fiercely in the case of a male Aboriginal artist. It is also hard to know how the public may have reacted to media pictures which made accessible the information that the pair in question were a dark black, middle-aged Aboriginal woman and a slight, white Welshman, also of middle age and unrefined, down-at-heel appearance. To what extent might the anxiety over authenticity have been fed by this pictorial reminder of racial interaction and mixture at fundamental levels? There was, however, no media mention of the 'mixed-race marriage' issue, that I am aware of; in the current context, this might easily be tendentious. The way the debate proceeded did, however, appear to accord something less than full measure to the notion of an 'Aboriginal art', and thus

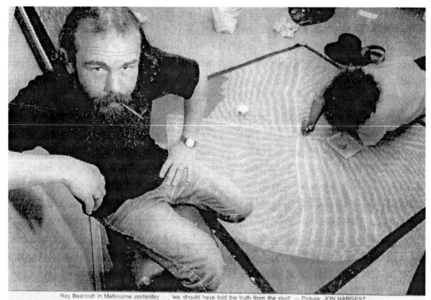

Ray Beamish in Melbourne yesterday ... 'we should have told the truth from the start' — Picture: JON HARGEST

Galleries stamp Beamish name on black art

Figure 10.5 Ray Beamish. Source: *Australian* 24/12/97

perhaps diminished the measure of Aboriginal artistry seen to be involved, in the following ways.

First, the question of collaboration between Petyarre and Beamish was persistently canvassed. As I have observed, any help that he may have given her (and nobody doubts that he did do work on the canvases) was judged by some to be of such nature that it made the works susceptible to suspicion of 'inauthenticity'. Art dealers, in particular, realized the damage that could be done if such suspicions were to proliferate, and some, as quoted above, opined that the problem could be resolved by clear and correct labelling. This had the result, in certain cases, that particular canvases were re-attributed to Beamish. But these reattributed canvases had clear affinities with canvases attributed to Petyarre. How, then, were such affinities to be described and conceptualized?

Clearly, for them to be dealt with expertly, the corpus of works produced at Utopia by Petyarre, Beamish and others, would have needed to be reviewed together, and some perspective gained on stylistic characteristics and changes within it over the years. Whatever else such an assessment might have revealed, the fact remains that Beamish was an outsider who had lately come into this milieu and absorbed many of its practices and conventions, rather than being an already-formed individual artist who introduced many new practices into that community.

Thus the media reports are all the more noteworthy for the readiness of a few art dealers to reattribute canvases to him, and this is all the more surprising in the case of canvases that Petyarre and Beamish are known to have worked on together. For this appears to attribute the 'creativity' involved to him, despite all evidence that he had come latterly to participate in the developments within a community of art producers whose works showed much continuity with stylistic traditions and practices, as well as some material and stylistic innovation. In any case, the more significant investment of art dealers was in the commercial value of Petyarre's works, not Beamish's; and moves to reattribute must be understood in those terms.

Second, the suggestion lurking under such shifts of attribution may be not simply that Beamish may have artistic capacity in his own right (as was proposed), but that this kind of art may be easy to learn and to reproduce. Here Beamish had been around for only a decade or so, and his work was arguably indistinguishable from that of renowned producers. Could anybody, then, learn to do this art? How much skill does it take to do dots and rounds, and follow along doing established patterns in different colours? If his dotting technique appeared more mechanical than Petyarre's, as some critics averred, was this because his work was more disciplined, less rough; or was it really just more machine-like and less inspired? The media discussions did not make explicit what might be involved in such issues as these, much less resolve them. The larger problem underlying such efforts to derive a conclusion about authorship is that of the indeterminacy of form and materiality as independent indices of cultural provenance, on the one hand; and aesthetic worth, on the other. But this problem, that the aesthetic object is never simply given to judgement (an adaptation of Bennett's 1992: 404 argument), was not enunciated. Rather, the comments of connoisseurs, dealers and others proceeded by effectively reducing the terms of debate about attribution and authenticity of the canvases to questions of technique, and avoided broaching questions of the wider artistic parameters within which such techniques were embedded. In the reattribution of canvases to Beamish, his indebtedness to what must be recognized as an extant tradition of cultural production, and how this should be evaluated under the conditions in which he had practised, appears to have been largely ignored.

As the media debate developed around the identification of works with Aboriginal producers, related questions about the relationship of imagery to subject matter or content, and the indeterminacy of visual forms as indices of content, also appeared to be reduced to a minimal level.

A number of analysts have discussed the nature and the implications of the general social premises on which much Aboriginal art is based. The content of art continuous with pre-existing Aboriginal traditions is understood to arise from and be an aspect of human relationships to the land and to the creative forces or 'dreamings' (Sutton 1988) which imbued land with meaning. The products, processes and content of Aboriginal art traditions, when explored closely, can be shown to be rooted in local socio-cultural contexts (Myers 1991: 28) and to have arisen historically from economies of information and knowledge different from dominant Anglo-Australian ones (Michaels 1985). The knowledge encoded in visual art forms which manifest these relationships is, to a considerable extent, intended by Aboriginal artists to remain private. Some specific content, deemed to be decodable from the images by knowledgeable persons, is not available for general dissemination, but restricted to certain contexts and persons authorized to receive it. In these contexts, the activity of cultural production is not conceived as 'representation' but as the ordered reproduction and manifestation of aspects of a transcendent, cosmological order. The development of Aboriginal cultural pro-duction for market has meant that Aboriginal people have had to give some consideration to the implications of wider circulation for the relations, as they conceive them, between visual form and associated levels and kinds of meaning attributed to it under conditions of practice where they have significant control, and the preservation of (some forms of) those relations under the extraordinary conditions of display and marketing that began to prevail. Kimber (1995) reports that when Pintupi began to paint dreamings as acrylic works, intercommunity consultations were held concerning what images might be reproduced, and what was too revelatory or directly indexical of private content to be generally displayed. This seems to have been a large-scale instance of consultation, its high level of organization perhaps partly reflecting the fact that acrylic production was given strong and culturally considerate support by an early set of art advisors in the region, and partly reflecting the strength of indigenous interconnectedness in the region. Travelling dreamings linked people who had ties to broad areas of the desert; decisions about the public circulation of imagery could not be seen to be taken in isolation. Yet there arguably is, and always has been, some productive tension in artists' negotiations of their relations to works as collective and individuated products.

Despite the private character of much of this content and imagery, the conditions of its reproduction and wider display have clearly been loosened over the last thirty years or so of the twentieth century, supported by processes of increasing sophistication and differentiation about what is being made available. From some Aboriginal painters' points of view, innermost private content can be preserved from a wider public that has no access to detailed interpretations and the practices of revelation. Only brief indications of general subject matter need be given as the captions of canvases. As Benjamin (1998, see also 1990) has observed, the wider public is often content with a kind of 'second-level' hermeneutic understanding of Aboriginal works as having spiritual significance, though its specificity remains obscure (and perhaps, in most cases, not of great interest to the general public). The conditions of indexicality between imagery and content are new and different in this wider sphere of circulation. But relatedly, changes in the nature of content are also occurring.

While content may remain relatively unspecified, visual material *is* widely intended and expected by Aboriginal producers to serve as a public declaration of the general nature and strength of Aboriginal culture in a way that can become a public signifier of indigeneity (Nicoll 1996) and a source of pride. This in itself has been a new, broadened frame or level of significance. Benjamin (1998) has suggested that changes over years in the work of increasingly prominent Central Australian artist Emily Kngwarreye exemplify how the acceptance of Aboriginal art into the 'fine art' market is accompanied by reduction of traditional visual imagery suggestive of traditional Aboriginal message content relating people and country in a unifying cosmological order. In Kngwarreye's work, Benjamin finds a move towards stylistic devices consistent with a generalized modernist aesthetics. (There have also been assertions that stylistic shifts were related to the high level of demand on Kngwarreye to produce, and a general reduction in the intricacy of her work; see Cadzow 1995.) In short, Benjamin argues that the entry of her production into new frames of reception and significance as art is correlated with stylistic change. I do not know of any auto-commentaries on the part of people like Kngwarraye on the relation between change in the style of her work, and possible change in associated content. It may be that the more modernist canvases, while evocative of country, are not detailed visual evocations of country in the same way that, for example, many Arnhem bark paintings or many Central Australian paintings are. I infer that, the more removed art production is from local knowledge traditions, the looser (and perhaps more idiosyncratic) becomes the association between style and forms of message content. In some cases, too, art production may become more individuated and specialist, the particular, market-oriented endeavour of a small sub-set of people in any local community such as Utopia.

Clearly, very similar-appearing canvases may be associated with quite different contents, or perhaps subjectively different *kinds* of contents, and ways of associating content with imagery. Though this may always be possible, in the present case we have seen how disparity between understood contents figures as an element of contestation regarding the authenticity of a painting as Aboriginal. Thus, we have the labelling of a painting as a presumed Petyarre in terms of its being a sacred women's Dreaming associated with the Green Pea; and the competing assertion by Beamish that the underlying content of the painting, of which he claims to have been a (if not the) significant producer, arose from his personal experience of having been lost in the desert. Just as painting style is not an unambiguous guide to authorship, so is it not a transparent window on content – but now in a different manner than the traditional mode, in which images are considered to relate in detailed, specifiable ways to country and dreaming, but the codes of interpretation are partly restricted, revelatory, and hieratic.

The Durack case is similar to the Petyarre one in the abstract sense that visual imagery was shown, by itself, to be an ambiguous and unreliable index of the presumptive, general feature of Aboriginality which entitled the Eddie Burrup work to appear in the institutional context of the Aboriginal art exhibition. The visual imagery did, indeed, appear different to what is regarded as 'traditional' imagery of the Kimberley region. But given social and political pressures which underlie *both* the general project of revaluation of indigeneity, and demand for acceptance of greater diversity in the association of Aboriginal personhood (including physical appearance) and culture, narrowing of the field of an Aboriginal art exhibit to the stylistically traditional has become unacceptable. Once the revelation was made by a spokesperson for Durack that she was the painter of the Burrup works, other issues become of explicit relevance and clarity in different ways than in the Petyarre case. Hoax was one: how could she have done what she did, understanding that the public would feel duped? Outright personal and cultural appropriation was another, though perhaps not, as I have shown, immediately for some Aboriginal people of traditional formation such as Paddy Nyawarra, who were inclined to see the matter in other terms. But, sooner or later, the question still remained pertinent: why did she feel justified in impersonating an Aboriginal person (and a man, no less), as an extension and benefit to her career as an artist? When confronted with incredulity, disapprobation and outrage, she perceptively expressed herself in a way that is difficult to dismiss lightly: 'I don't see how you can appropriate something that is within you'. This is fully in keeping with the Western art tradition of individual artistry and creativity, and thus also requires further thought from the perspective of anyone concerned with the changing conditions of production, intercultural influence, and the considerable extent to which Aboriginal cultural production has come to be accepted within the purview of an aesthetic, universalizing register. Having been strongly affected by her particular history of relationship with Aboriginal people (albeit the rest of us would be likely to say, not as one of them), she saw her work as closely linked with an Aboriginal sensibility. She apparently was led to experiment subjectively with painting as an Aborigine. Most would see such impersonation as more illicit than she apparently did, tinged by the psychological experimentalism of 'passing' (Ginsberg 1994), and the moral issue of doing so for some form of personal advancement. But the step is smaller when the gulf of possible achievement separating persons regarded as 'black' and 'white' has been narrowed. Durack, from her position of social privilege and artistic recognition, ventured to step across it.

The difference between Beamish and Durack in how they constituted their personal relations to the works may perhaps be seen as a difference in class-based proclivities, in the situation of relative dominance of a 'white' cultural type to which both, however different, belong. Durack's venture may be linked to her more patrician class position, and the illusion it may offer of one's invisibility and unbounded social access. Her mode of appreciation was to begin to identify herself as artistic persona with 'them'. Beamish, on the other hand, whom we all could roughly evaluate as 'lower-class', identified himself as the (principal) painter of some of the contested objects, leaving Petyarre as different from him but (allegedly) the lesser producer in some cases. His assent to the posing of questions as the most relevant ones about the extent of his authorship of particular objects obscured the question of his complex relationship to the person he was arguably expropriating most directly, as well as to the wider scene of cultural production which had shaped her work (and his).

This exploration should not be taken as a suggestion that the revaluation of Aboriginal cultural production as art, in all its complexity, is to be regretted. Such a suggestion could hardly be entertained, given the value that most of us understand to be associated with art. Nor should it be taken as a suggestion that material objects cannot be analyzed as having social efficacy, or agency, as Gell would have it. I have tried, though, to discuss the limitations and illustrate the complexities of both such revaluations, and to explore some of their unanticipated moral and practical entailments in a situation of long-term, entrenched social inequalities. Promotion of cultural production into art is not simply, as Clifford calls it, an 'effective' way of conferring cross-cultural value, but a move that produces advantage and disadvantage, ambivalences and struggles, as those liberatory values articulate with others across the series of social locations and kinds of persons mobilized as part of this reassessment. These new conditions of indexicality require particular treatment in any anthropology of art.

Acknowledgements

Thanks to those who made comments on versions of this chapter given at Australian National University and Sydney University, and particularly to Ghassan Hage, Neil McLean, Djon Mundine and Tim Rowse. I am grateful to Norman Wilson and Nigel Lendon for providing media reports that might otherwise have escaped my attention; to the Institute of the Arts, Australian National University, for their loan of materials; to Tony Redmond and Paddy Nyawarra for discussion of the events involving Elizabeth Durack; and to Howard Morphy, Alan Rumsey and Jimmy Weiner for their comments on drafts of the chapter.

Notes

1. In a longer work, I consider parallels and differences between these cases in the visual arts and literature, both areas in which 'Aboriginal expression' has

been encouraged in those terms. I also consider recent cases of alleged inauthenticity involving 'ethnic' (or, presumed ethnic) artists, on the basis that race and ethnicity are two flexible and publicly salient dimensions along which belonging in the polity are differentially evaluated and extended.

2. Hage (1998) has made an extended argument regarding the centrality of a 'white' cultural type in Australia. In relation to Hage's central theme of multiculturalism, the centrality of this type is manifested in his (sic) feeling himself empowered to be 'worried' about the presence of (non-white, especially Third-World-looking) 'others' in the nation – a worrying that Hage relates to feelings of loss of control.

3. Paddy Nyawarra is from the west Kimberley, not the immediate area from which Elizabeth Durack comes. My thanks to Anthony Redmond for discussion of Nyawarra's initial comments made to him, and to Nyawarra himself for further discussion on the occasion of a visit he made to Canberra in October 1997.

4. Wandjina, the mouthless, large-eyed figures known from Kimberley rock art, are central to the socio-cultural and aesthetic traditions which Nyawarra relates to as his own, and knows well.

5. It is comparable with anthropologist A.P. Elkin's (1937) redesignation of Aboriginal world-views as a 'philosophy' (or philosophies); and Stanner's (1963) eloquent argument for an Aboriginal 'religion' as reconceptualization of what had heretofore been designated as 'rite', 'totemism', 'magic' and so on.

References

Altman, J., C. McGuigan and P. Yu. 1989. 'The Aboriginal Arts and Crafts Industry: Report of the Review Committee'. Department of Aboriginal Affairs. Canberra: Australian Government Publishing Service.

Anderson, C. (ed.). 1995. *Politics of the Secret*. Oceania Monograph 45. Sydney: University of Sydney.

Anderson, C. and F. Dussart. 1988. 'Dreaming in Acrylic: Western Desert Art', in P. Sutton (ed.), *Dreamings: The Art of Aboriginal Australia*, pp. 89–142 . New York: George Braziller/Asia Society Galleries.

Bardon, G. 1979. *Aboriginal Art of the Western Desert*. Sydney: Rigby.

Baume, N. 1989. 'The Interpretation of Dreamings: The Australian Aboriginal Acrylic Movement'. *Art and Text* 33: 110–20.

Benjamin, R. 1990. 'Aboriginal Art: Exploitation or Empowerment?' *Art in America* 78(7): 73–81.

—— 1998. 'A New Modernist Hero', in M. Neale (ed.), *Emily Kame Kngwarreye: Alhalkere, Paintings from Utopia*, pp. 47–54. Queensland Art Gallery, Macmillan.

Bennett, T. 1992. 'Useful Culture'. *Cultural Studies* 6(3): 395–408.

Bourdieu, P. 1993. *The Field of Cultural Production: Essays on Art and Literature*. Oxford: Polity Press.

Cadzow, J. 1987. 'The Art Boom of Dreamtime'. *The Australian Weekend Magazine*, 14–15 March: 1–2.

—— 1995. 'The Emily Industry'. *Good Weekend*, 5 August, 30–35.

Clifford, J. 1991. 'Four Northwest Coast Museums: Travel Reflections', in I. Karp and S. Lavine (eds), *Exhibiting Cultures* pp. 212–54. Washington and London: Smithsonian Institution.

Collins, H. 1985. 'Political Ideology in Australia: The Distinctiveness of a Benthamite Society'. *Daedalus* 114: 147–69.

Elkin, A.P. 1937. *Australian Aborigines and How to Understand Them*. Sydney: Angus and Robertson.

Errington, S. 1998. *The Death of Authentic Primitive Art and Other Tales of Progress*. Berkeley and Los Angeles: University of California Press.

Gell, A. 1998. *Art and Agency: An Anthropological Theory*. Oxford: Clarendon Press.

Ginsberg, E. 1994. 'Introduction: The Politics of Passing', in *Passing and the Fictions of Identity* pp. 1–18. Durham, N.C.: Duke University Press.

Hage, G. 1998. *White Nation: Fantasies of White Supremacy in a Multicultural Society*. Annandale: Pluto Press.

Hamilton, A. 1990. 'Fear and Desire: Aborigines, Asians and the National Imaginary'. *Australian Cultural History*, July, pp. 14–35.

Johnson, V. 1994. *The Art of Clifford Possum Tjapaltjarri*. Sydney: Craftsman House.

—— 1995. 'Is There a Gender Issue in Aboriginal Art?' *Art and Australia* 32(3): 350–7.

Kimber, D. 1995. 'Politics of the Secret in Contemporary Western Desert Art', in C. Anderson (ed.), pp. 123–42.

McLean, I. 1998. *White Aborigines: Identity Politics in Australian Art*. Cambridge University Press.

Michaels, E. 1985. 'Constraints on Knowledge in an Economy of Oral Information'. *Current Anthropology* 26(4): 505–10.

Morphy, H. 1991. *Ancestral Connections: Art and an Aboriginal System of Knowledge*. Chicago: University of Chicago Press.

—— 1995. 'Aboriginal Art in a Global Context', in D. Miller (ed.), *Worlds Apart: Modernity Through the Prism of the Local* pp. 211–39. London, New York: Routledge.

Morphy, H. and D. Elliott 1997. 'In Place (Out of Time)', in R. Coates (ed.) *In Place (Out of Time): Contemporary Art in Australia* pp. 4–11. Oxford: Museum of Modern Art.

Myers, F.R. 1991. 'Representing Culture: The Production of Discourse(s) for Aboriginal Acrylic Paintings'. *Cultural Anthropology* 6: 26–62.

—— 1996. 'The Wizards of Oz? – The Social Location of Aesthetics and Western Desert Acrylic Painting'. Paper given at 'Reimagining the Pacific: Conference on Art and Anthropology in Honor of Bernard Smith', 4 August 1996, Australian National University.

Neale, M. 1998. *Emily Kame Kngwarraye, Alhalkere, Paintings from Utopia*. Queensland Art Gallery, Macmillan.

Nicoll, F. 1996. 'The Art of Reconciliation: Art, Aboriginality and the State'. *Meanjin* 52(4): 705–17.

Price, S. 1989. *Primitive Art in Civilized Places*. Chicago: University of Chicago Press.

Smith, R. 1997. 'The Incarnations of Eddie Burrup'. *Art Monthly* 97: 4–5.

Stanner, W.E.H. 1963. *On Aboriginal Religion*. Sydney: Oceania Monographs.

Sutton, P. 1988. *Dreamings: The Art of Aboriginal Australia*. New York: George Braziller/Asia Society Galleries.

Taylor, C. 1991. *The Ethics of Authenticity*. Cambridge, Mass.: Harvard University Press.

Wise, T. 1985. *The Self-Made Anthropologist: A Life of A.P. Elkin*. Sydney: George Allen and Unwin.

11

When the (Oven) Gloves Are Off: The Queen's Baton – Doing What to Whom?

Charlotte Townsend-Gault

The graphic design on the cover of BC Hydro's (British Columbia Hydro and Power Authority) Annual Report – in routine corporatist style – shows the Queen's Baton, as if in motion, in action even. The Baton was the defining logo for the 1994 Commonwealth Games held in Victoria; the power utility was a major sponsor of the Games, and thus of the Baton; and the theme of the Games was 'Catch the Spirit'. With action, and perhaps some emanation of spirit, suggested by vapourous swirls, this index – Gell's use of the term – appears to be zooming out of the frame on a diagonal, but not before the defining formlines of Northwest Coast Native art and the silhouette of a soul-catcher can be registered. This object indexes, at minimum, aboriginality. And in this anodyne treatment it appears to have something to do with a relationship between a Crown Corporation and aboriginal people.

Until recently anything like a benign association between the province's electricity provider and First Nations would have been more than implausible. Relations have been strained, acrimonious and litigious. Hydro companies across Canada, endowed as public-service providers with unusual powers and privileges, have habitually taken advantage of the disastrously unresolved state of aboriginal rights in land or sovereignty. Yet another set of power relations that have shaped Canadian history are implicated in the Baton. In what follows it should be remembered that, in Canada, the terms 'the Crown', or even 'the Queen', will mean different things federally and provincially. It appears that they mean a third thing, not foreseen in the Canadian Constitution, i.e. a form of equality between 'sovereigns', in this case the Queen/Crown and each First Nation on Vancouver Island or elsewhere. A long history of unequal relations between these parties has been traversed in order to reach the stage of voluntary agreement between nominal equals encapsulated in, for example, the first contemporary treaty to be negotiated in British Columbia – the Nisga'a Final Agreement of 1998. The idea of the Queen/ Crown as head of a system of oppression and the Queen as equal is not quite covered by the word irony. Yet both are indexed, and their relations enacted, in the ceremonial Baton.

Figure 11.1 Front cover of B.C. Hydro's Annual Report. 1994. Photo: Rob Bos

The Queen's Baton is to the Commonwealth Games what the Torch is to the Olympics, public authenticator of the proceedings and defining logo. As it is passed in relay from one symbolic site to another, it 'enacts', it might be said, historical continuity and some kind of consensus. The Baton's ostensible purpose is to carry the opening speech of the Head of the Commonwealth from Buckingham Palace to the site of the opening ceremonies, and has been an integral part of the proceedings since the 1958 British Empire and Commonwealth Games were held in Cardiff. A new Baton, representing the host country in some way, is created for each Games. For the Games in Victoria, BC Hydro's sponsorship extended to the trans-Canada relay, indicating an understanding that the significance of the Baton extends far beyond the materiality of the thing itself.

What follows is an abbreviated account of this particular entangled object in terms derived from a necessarily simplified, possibly simplistic, reading of Gell's notion of the art nexus. It is a reading which, because it reconfigures their elements, enables a reformatting of local conflicts over authenticity, appropriation, commercialization and sponsorship. Put to use in this way the nexus is a device that is valuable inasmuch as it organizes complexity, rather than offering the means for its reduction. However, the conceptual difficulties resolved in doing so are supplanted by others created by the propensity of the nexus to yield an unweighted mapping of what can only properly be understood as a political terrain. However I would argue that this propensity does not necessarily prevent the terms – prototype, artist, index, patron, retension and protension – being given a workout even in the light of their own critique, a critique widely directed towards much of the legacy of structural-functionalism. That the second part of the book is disjunct from the first may be evidence that Gell himself foresaw the problem. It is possibly compounded, notwithstanding his identification of the art cult, by Gell's discernible belief in the superordinate agency of what David Freedberg (1989) calls 'the creativity of the eye', and from which this writer does not claim immunity.

A couple of years ago, having been invited to write about the contests around aboriginal art where I now live, I described the duty-free shop in the international terminal of Vancouver's refurbished airport – built to approximate some archetypal Northwest Coast 'long-house' – in terms which may serve to introduce the complexities of the social relations in which the Queen's Baton is implicated.

> . . . this duty-free longhouse is subsumed by the functions of the terminal building and yet is dominant enough to stand against them. It overarches the displays of international consumer goods, and the tills, even though it must submit to the ignominy of having its own architectural motifs interspersed with decorations composed, when last seen, of clusters of designer teddy-bears nestling in artificial spruce boughs. Whether the native forms co-opt, or have been co-opted by, some cynical hucksterism on the part of the airport's designers, in a Baudrillardian chaos of signification, is not an argument to settle here. What the structure does is make the argument unavoidable (Townsend-Gault 1997: 149).

In more or less these terms I had been puzzling over the Baton and its relationship to various audiences for some months. *Art and Agency* introduced the possibility of scrutinizing the range of social relations involved in its production and reception without taking sides. Gell does not have much time for chaos and none for signification. The argument over co-opting or being co-opted may be settled by recognizing, and theorizing, both. The art nexus makes it possible to think about the airport long-house as both agent and patient, and the Queen's Baton as both active and passive with relation to BC Hydro.

The aspiration to take on the local heterogeneity itself as a field of enquiry in order to rethink Northwest Coast 'art', or rather, in order to rethink the anthropological study of what is sometimes and in some places, called 'art', can hardly be done without a rereading of its constitutive 'entangled' discourses. A tendency to dismiss, or account for, this kind of shifting muddle as par for the post-colonial course, on the grounds that post-colonial studies tend to lift themselves into a rhetorical a-historical sphere, should not be a deterrent. In preference to the term 'art', and because – following Gell's view of the proper role of an anthropology of art – this is not so much an attempt to define art as to observe how it plays, I make use of the term 'discursive representations', derived from an articulation of John Barrell's:

> The past is available to us only in the form of representations, and it was, equally to the point, available to the past only in the same form. To attempt to reconstruct the precise occasions of history is to attempt to reconstruct them in the only form in which they are or were available to be known, as representations articulated within the different discourses which combine and compete to represent the real (1992).

In an effort to pre-empt the difficulty of 'art' pre-determining its own enquiry, I want to take the art nexus up as a way of thinking about animated social biographies of things, that has the capacity to accommodate the disputed classifications of a contested present, but at the same time some built-in protection against getting bogged down in the polyvalencies of discourse analysis. This I take to have been Gell's intent with his insistence that objects are not reflections/ expressions/symbols of . . . , but social agents.

If it is allowed that Gell's schema can be used to identify local, historical and current shifts, and their nuances, what are the conflicts anyway? This invites the question: what are the inherent ambiguities, created when materials (tangible and intangible) specific to the aboriginal cultures of the Northwest Coast, circulate in the wider society? And who is identifying them? The following count, for this observer, as among the least avoidable in contemporary British Columbia: in one view the designation 'art' is the ultimate accolade, in another it is the supreme act of aesthetic imperialism; the artisanal aspect of contemporary carving either perpetuates its integration in daily life or guarantees its exclusion from the realm of high art – high prices notwithstanding; an account of art as a following of rules, learning a language, opposed to an idea of art as the transgression of rules, as blasphemy; a class of decontextualized objects, masks for example, are still taken as tokens of the mysterious exotic, against strenuous arguments for not doing so; when representations of Northwest Coast crest systems become applied design for oven-gloves, mouse mats and all the rest they are trivialized; alternatively global extension is given to multiple and therefore realistic messages about the societies from which they originate; values inhere in singular auratic objects or values are maintained through the infinite replication of generic object types; objects have a ceremonial potency and inalienable power, a claim which gains its currency, as is intended, against the view that all such power is socially constructed.

There is of course an argument that would maintain that all such polyvalence is nothing but the fragmentation of bourgeois consciousness, and that no sense is to be made of it without an analysis of unequal power relations. And another mode of analysis which would want to focus on the phallocentric power wielded by any Baton. If I understand it correctly, the art nexus distinguishes itself from such analyses by putting itself in a superordinate position as capable of sorting out the various protagonists in ostensibly ambiguous situations where multiple points of view conflict and various analyses are in operation. It bears more than a passing affinity to another brilliantly disputatious account of ambivalence – William Empson's *Seven Types of Ambiguity*, first published in 1930. Empson's work on poetic ambiguity is sometimes acknowledged today as a precursor of postmodern decentring. But there is something resolutely English about the way Empson, like Gell, makes free with ideas but holds them down with a dogged common-sense empiricism.

The strength of such tactics may be tested in their response to conflicts, such as those outlined above, which cannot be accounted for in any simple way as encounters between two distinct cultural value systems, nor can they be confined as disputes within an aesthetic realm. The various formulae proposed in *Art and Agency* for relations between prototype, artist, index and recipient at the very least rearrange the binaries. Gell himself seems to contend with heterogeneity when he asks to what degree each formula, as proposed in his text, is 'to be understood as a schematic description of an "objectively" different situation, as opposed to a different "perspective" on a situation which remains the same.' (1998: 56). He goes on to allow that 'The same basic information is there, but a different syntactical pattern implies a distinctly different "analysis" of the world. Which analysis is the appropriate one is a matter of social or psychological judgement' (1998: 57). This last point leaves a rather large margin but does seem to recognize that ethnographies of the particular cannot be done in an epistemological vacuum.

First then, some 'basic information' is required to establish something of the contested history and heterogeneous contemporary environment in which First Nations people represent themselves and are represented in British Columbia. The province joined the Canadian confederation in 1876, but, with a few exceptions, there were none of the treaties between the aboriginal population and the Crown that marked the settlement of most of what came to be Canada. The mid-eighteenth-century population has been estimated at between 200,000 and 300,000 dropping by as much as 90 per cent to a low of approximately 23,000 in 1929 (Muckle 1998: 37). Today 105,000 status and 75,000 non-status Indians live in British Columbia, about 5 per cent of the province's population (1994 Census), their reservations accounting for less than 0.5 of the province (Muckle 1998: 4–5). After a hundred years of disaffection – under the paternalistic control of the Indian Act (first enacted in 1884, and, with many subsequent amendments, still in force today) work by native labour organizations and political movements, changes in the Canadian constitution recognizing aboriginal rights, and Canada's Multi-Culturalism Act – the BC Treaty Commission was established by the present NDP (New Democratic Party) provincial government to settle the many outstanding claims. Currently fifty-one native groups are engaged at different stages of Treaty negotiations. The first modern Treaty to be derived from the process – involving cash, land and resource management for the Nisga'a – was signed on 4 August 1998. In 1997 the Supreme Court of Canada overturned a BC Court decision, in Delgamuukw v. The Queen, that had been based on a refusal to accept the validity of oral evidence. This, the Delgamuukw decision, at last gives credence to aboriginal people's knowledge about themselves within the systems of the Canadian state. While supported by a majority of the electorate (the most recent poll showed over 90 per cent of respondents were in favour of a speedy resolution of claims, although this does not specify in whose favour), land claims remain a highly contentious aspect of First Nations identity politics.

In spite of its scandalous disregard of aboriginal populations, there is a history in the province of identification with and through relations with them, negative and positive. It can be summarized in a sequence of epithets. Thus it was termed, by Edward Curtis, The Land of the Head Hunters, modified to The Land of the War Canoes, has promoted itself variously as the Land of the Totem Poles, Totemland and now Super Natural British Columbia. Anthropology, broadly defined as the repository of often distorted knowledge about native people, with museums, played a significant if ambiguous role in the sequence, long before the verities of anthropology's field day came up for scrutiny. It appears in local discussions of identity and its representation at land claims hearings, in the courts and in the communications media. The anthropological literature is extensive, well-known, often paradigmatic. In 'The Northwest Coast' it has constructed one of anthropology's classic objects, and in the process contributed substantially to the creation of the eponymous 'Northwest Coast art'.

From the early 1950s and during the 1960s, to simplify drastically, a discourse about art replaced anthropology – 'autonomy' won out over 'context', and 'art' over 'ethnographic art'. The apparent loss of the culture seemed to be a gain for art (Newman 1946, 1947; Lévi-Strauss 1943; Holm 1965, Holm and Reid 1975). The pivotal exhibition at the Vancouver Art Gallery, *Arts of the Raven*, in 1967 (Canada's Centennial Year), sanctioned the idea that items manufactured by local native populations were art. It was proclaimed by Claude Lévi-Strauss and Bill Reid among others, as equal to the greatest anywhere. This encouraged a tendency to study objects and images, old and new, in lieu of the much more problematic, and hard to reach, social relations. In the 1980s the 'high art' apologia began to be challenged publicly by many First Nations as having been responsible for the separation of 'Northwest Coast art' out from the broader cultural revival, if not survival (Crosby 1991; Davidson 1994). The term 'renaissance' is both much used and much out of favour, with contemporary scholarship devoted to relating the particularities of the distinct cultures of the Coast, and demonstrating their continuity rather than decline and death (Dawn 1976; Jonaitis 1993; Bracken 1997). Diversification of cultural forms in native communities, and elsewhere, is both condoned and disapproved – another conflict.

Boasian anthropology has played a large role in the creation of the discourse about the culture, if not of the idea of 'culture' itself. As the culture is re-claimed, along with rights to represent it, anthropology has had to draw back. Kinds of knowledge associated with anthropology came to be seen as having been gained by a form of trespass, a critique similarly directed at other forms of Western knowledge-shaping: the administration of justice, pedagogy, medicine, systems of land tenure and the treatment of natural resources. In part because of its own legacy as an architect of the art, it has seen itself displaced by, or ramified through, art discourse and aesthetic debates (Foster 1995). Ethnography has had to yield to politics, including art politics, where the objects surviving from the past join an array of images inseparable from ideas about a culture's right to self-representation, (Neel 1992; Manuel 1977; Jensen and Brooks 1991; MacDonald 1995). This is in accord with a way of thinking about art where art historians 'interrogate their material with an awareness both of epistemology and of art as part of a wider field of production' (Pointon 1996: 19) that has probed its interdependence on power structures; that reads art as representational strategy, part of a widespread interest in cultural representation and how it should be articulated; that has examined its relationship with the mass media. It has not been easy for some anthropologists to release from their apical protection that type of object referred to, sollipsistically, as 'ethnographic art'. This wide-ranging mode of enquiry is followed in the work of not a few First Nations artists themselves, for example Lawrence Paul Yux-weluptun, Eric Robertson and Jim Logan.

In the current political climate a growing awareness of the legacy of Canada's position as both colonizer and colonized, has situated the struggle over a body of knowledge and over who should represent it, and how, firmly in the public sphere where its extensions include an increasingly heterogeneous array of objects and images, from a growing number of sources reaching different audiences. They range from felled nineteenth-century totem poles, canonized as classical art in a Museum of Anthropology, to new and instantly canonical works, such as the Haida artist Bill Reid's large bronze canoe, *Spirit of Haida Gwaii*, made for Canada's new embassy building in Washington, now also appearing, with a gold border, on postage stamps, to oven gloves and all kinds of domestic and personal items printed with variants of the Northwest Coast designs that anthropologists are likely to have first encountered in the pages of Boas's *Primitive Art*.

Clearly diversification is not a defining characteristic of Vancouver in the sense that it distinguishes it from some other city with an aboriginal population. It could be taken as one more variant of a near-universal phenomenon whereby an aboriginal 'art', formerly local and specific, has been drawn into global marketing and communication systems, often described and variously accounted for, in debates that range across social groups and academic fields. Nor is there an imperative to decide in some absolute sense whether it is art. Arthur Danto notwithstanding, that (some of) it is art for some of the people for some of the time suffices to bring the matter within the purview. However, if the objects/signs/representations have become images, part of a world traffic in images (Marcus and Myers 1995), the corollary is not that they are locally meaningless. In scrutinizing the local social response, the seemingly bathetic trajectory followed by, say, chocolate totem poles in Vancouver airport, can be differentiated from the superficially similar trajectory followed by a toy boomerang on sale in Sydney airport, and related to paintings on canvas by aboriginal artists, or the move in status from carvers to artists, for such particulars come wrapped in a history of ideas that are locally specific.

There are local reasons for extensions and heterogeneity, not least because disjunctures, such as those observed by Myers when Australian aboriginal paintings were shown in a New York gallery (1995), or the processes devised to frame imported exotica in Los Angeles (Kirshenblatt-Gimblett 1995), here occur where they originate – or, in Gell's terms, prototype, artist, index and recipient can be found in the same place. The totem poles are erected here, the barricades go up here, the land claims are heard here, the artists carve, paint, weave here. They exhibit here. The collectors come here, the tourists shop here, the curricula are developed and taught here; promotional copy for native-run museums, shops, businesses, restaurants and guest lodges is written and published here.

The heterogeneous forms of 'art' are coming to be seen as forms of public cultural address. It is a public struggle where these public representations are at the crux. They are used in official, celebratory, and decorative ways. Singular and normative designations and judgements of all kinds can be heard, with the appellation 'Northwest Coast art', one among many: traditional, degradations, kitsch, souvenirs, anomalies, revivals, restorations, innovations, entanglements.

Sometimes, by some standards, they are 'bad' (Michaels 1994). This is a predictable range of opinions – replicated in many other instances and places. In colonialism's culture they do not necessarily follow ethnic divisions. But these descriptives do not say what is going on. For they are not vacuous nor extraneous, nor, a rather different point, can they be dealt with in the proverbial last chapter of the ethnography. There is a locally specific set of narratives with their own archaeologies, and of course, of counter-narratives.

For this reason it seems right to open not with 'the thing itself', but with a representation of one of the many ways of receiving it, or of narrating it. This is the Baton as a discursive representation, illustrated for a Company report, with all that that connotes. The Baton project, its commissioning, its extensions and its reception, 'draws attention not towards a totality such as a culture, nor to a period that can be defined independently of people's perceptions and strategies, but rather to a socially transformative endeavour that is localized, politicized and partial, yet also engendered by longer historical developments and ways of narrating them' (Thomas 1994: 105). The word 'transformative' imputes action, appropriately in terms of the nexus, to such a 'project'.

'It is not only art', announced the Chairman of the Board of the Vancouver Art Gallery at the opening, in 1994, of *Down from the Shimmering Sky: Masks of the Northwest Coast*, the most comprehensive exhibition of Northwest Coast masks ever brought together in one place and, significantly, shown in an *art* institution. The label art, the nominalist definition, still vacillates between kudos and curse. At this staged public event in the post-Delgamuukw period, Michael Audain's comments, developed with the advice of the exhibition's curators, were listened to carefully. 'Does that mean that it's more than art or less than art?' someone beside me whispered. (If it isn't art then oven gloves and the whole range of items bearing aboriginal imagery, whatever else they may be, are not a degradation of art.) And yet substituting the term 'material culture' may be too deliberately overlooking what is properly spiritual culture for people for whom both 'art' and 'material culture' are no more than deliberate misnomers.

It is now necessary to return to the Queen's Baton and consider it as a social being, both active and passive, within the four terms of the art nexus. In doing so, there will be reference to some parts of the aforementioned conflicts. One prototype for the Baton is readily found in an historical aboriginal object – the soul-catcher. Soul-catchers are shares or parts of that 'distributed object' – Gell's term – that is commonly termed 'Northwest Coast art'. To some people, the most salient features of soul-catchers are those which make them autonomous, immanent art works, belonging in an international museum of the world's great art; for others, they are so dependent on context that they will always be misunderstood by non-natives. Neither position, nor others between them on some putative spectrum, makes a cultural representation such as the Queen's Baton into an empty signifier, a symptom of postmodernism's evacuation of meaning. It is part of an energetic local process where old meaning is debated and contested and, simultaneously, new meaning announced and contested. This characteristic vacillation can be fixed, temporarily, by the organizing power of the nexus.

The Baton in fact has a number of prototypes, of which the soul-catcher, part of the shaman's repertoire, is but one. Another is the representation of wolf, kolus and other ancestral creatures engraved thereon. A third is the class of Queen's Batons, devised to play a role at every meeting of the Commonwealth Games. The nexus enables them to be distinguished in terms of the differential agency they exert over artists, recipients and index.

At each Games the design of the Baton makes some reference to the host country. In New Zealand/Aotearoa, the use of greenstone and a fern motif had been intended to index New Zealand's native roots in nature – a precise instance of the cultural artefact type of a colonized aboriginal people being used, by the coloniser, in the process of nation-building and the creation of national identity (Dawn 1985; Wallis 1991; Blundell 1994; Keesing 1994). As such the Baton prototype exerted agency over Art Thompson, one of the artists of the index considered here. At the Royal British Columbia Provincial Museum in Victoria, Thompson had worked on a 40-foot pole, a gift to aboriginal peoples assembled for the 1990 Games in New Zealand. As payment, he was invited to Auckland, where he observed their version of the Queen's Baton in action, and saw that its action was limited by virtue of being a Maori design not made by a Maori. Admitting to being impressed by the ceremonial but determined to do things differently in Canada, he resolved that the Baton should be a fully aboriginal production. His agency over the Games Baton prototype amounted to a reassertion of native rights over native images as national representations.

The prototypical shaman's soul-catcher was fashioned from bone, most commonly the femur of a bear which is one of the more potent intermediaries between human and spirit realms. (According to Thompson, the Tsimshian have erroneously been designated as the originators of this form of soul-catcher on the coast.) It was used by a shaman as part of a soul-curing method designed to reunite the sick or errant soul with the body. The soul-catcher is the temporary domain of the soul in this procedure. Subsequently it is worn around the neck from a cedar bark or hide string. The soul-catcher has no characteristic resting place from which to be contemplated, it has no base; as an object it cannot be fixed in situ, except when hung around the neck as part of the curing process. It is made to be in action. This state is approximated as the runners carry the Baton in its canvas and hide carrying case slung on their backs. The soul-catcher prototype, then, exerted its agency over the Baton's carrying form.

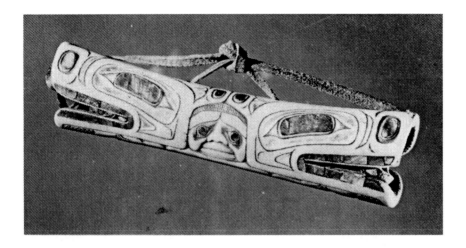

Figure 11.2 Tsimshian soul catcher, 19th. Century, 20cm. (bone and haliotis shell) Photo: Charlotte Townsend-Gault

Commissioned by the Native Participation Committee of the 15th Commonwealth Games on behalf of BC Hydro, each of the artists was required to represent his own people in some way. Artists worked with crests to which they had personal or family rights or prerogatives, or, in other words, they were passive with respect to these prototypical representations. Charles Elliot is a member of the Tsartlip Band of the Coast Salish Nations on whose ancestral territory the Games took place. For the Salish the frog is a herald, 'one who announces', while the wolf is invoked as a protector spirit to protect all who took part in the Games. Art Thompson, a Ditidaht of the Nuu-chah-nulth (formerly Nootka) is an initiate in the Tlu-kwalla or Wolf Society, chose his own wolf to represent his people. Richard Hunt, from the Fort Rupert band of the Kwakwaka'wakw (formerly Kwakiutl) used the raven, the main crest of his family, with a frog in its mouth, in combination with his personal crest the Kolos (immature Thunderbird). Collectively Elliot, Hunt and Thompson acted in such a way that the Baton, with the integration of the spirits and animals, would index the salved historical enmity between the Island's three tribes.

The politics of First Nations reconstruction of identity is accompanied by arguments, both within and outside native communities and in those they share, as to how they have been represented and thus about a struggle for power over a body of knowledge. Art Thompson refers to his mother's generation to whom the situation looks different. As far as she is concerned the so-called 'Cook collection', for example – the beginning of the 'vacuuming up' of the coast – now in the British Museum, belongs to the Nuu-chah-nulth. This is a fact unalterable by any

Figure 11.3 Page from the official programme for the Commonwealth Games showing the Baton and explanatory text

transactions involving money, loans, documents or speeches. As her son sees it: 'I understand her, but I know that we can make our own, we don't need that stuff. As far as my children are concerned, they think of museums as education'.

In deciding to make an object that is in certain respects a copy of the soul-catcher, it might appear that the artists surrendered any agency they might have had, and that, as passive with respect to a classical artefact, they were conforming to the stereotype of traditional anonymous tribal artist perpetuating a comparison with the freedoms enjoyed by the individualist of the Western tradition. Nevertheless, there are several ways in which the three artists, from the three tribes of Vancouver Island, were active rather than passive with respect to the prototype. They made a generic form their own. However, only the shape, and that an approximation, and the fact that some design is engraved on it, is carried over. The scale is much enlarged, the material is different, the bilateral symmetry has been forfeited in favour of an unprecedented, tripartite re-arrangement of the design field, and the purpose commandeered. In a further sense the artists had agency with respect to the prototype inasmuch as their aim was to perpetuate the action of the soul-catcher, its agency as medicine: 'We firmly believed it would be medicine for our people. It is the issue of wellness – it's there in our stories of soul-catchers, of healing, medicine.' In this respect each of the artists attributes agency both to the Baton and to what they refer to as the 'symbols' of their own design.

In assuming representational rights to a soul-catcher the artists Elliott, Thompson and Hunt, puncturing the pieties of authenticity, exercised agency with respect to the prototype. Thompson, speaking for all three, in answer to the anthropologist's question based on the received notion that the soul-catcher derives from the Tsimshian and that therefore the tribes of Vancouver Island cannot properly be said to have them, or (implicitly) have rights to them, says 'Well, we do now'. He points out, speaking for all Northwest Coast people, 'We *all* had our own

Figure 11.4 The artists; Arthur Thompson (Nuu-chah-nulth) R; George Hunt (Kwakwaka'wakw) Centre; Charles Elliott (Coast Salish) L. Photo: B.C. Hydro

medicines.' And then, for the Nuu-chah-nulth in particular: 'Soul catchers are every bit as much a part of our culture. We had our own soul-catcher-type objects and I have seen some that have been decorated up'.

The question 'How Haida/Kwakwaka'wakw/Nuu-chah-nulth is it?', the essentialist question that has been crucial for contemporary 'identity projects', is increasingly modulated. Most recent scholarship devoted to establishing distinguishing tribal and sub-tribal styles on the Coast has, in the process of doing so, uncovered further evidence for inter-tribal contact, trade, warfare and marriage. Furthermore, the interrogation of social memory, as well as museum scholarship, are identifying the work of individuals – part of the effort to counteract anonymity and generic labelling that has been a discursive constant.

In another instance of assertion of agency working on and modifying a prototype as implicated in contemporary shifting social relations, a painting by the Coast Salish artist, Lawrence Paul Yuxweluptun – *Scorched Earth Policy - Clear-cut Logging on Native Sovereign Land - Shaman Coming to Fix* – might be considered. The shaman figure on the left is holding a power board. The artist is both patient and agent with respect to power boards. Some maintain that these things are not to be represented. There are some early photographs, but in recent literature where they are being discussed they will appear as schematic sketches. Coast Salish groups have jealously and successfully guarded the privacy of their ceremonial practices. They have watched while the northern coastal cultures, with their more spectacular and public group displays, have become paradigmatic Northern style – promoted as ur-Northwest and favoured by connoisseurs. From this the Salish perceive themselves to have both gained and lost. Yuxweluptun specifically declines to translate this board clearly, or indeed other masks and dances he represents in his paintings. What he does make clear is that he is not at liberty to disclose all that he knows. Many Salish people subscribe to the notion that knowledge withheld is greater power.

A further, comparable, instance of prototype as agent, and in which the artist is both active and passive, occurred when Bill Reid was supervising the construction, to his own design, of the first Haida ocean-going canoe to be built in about fifty years. In order for the new canoe to be as 'Haida' as its prototype, Reid's expert, but non-Haida, assistant had to leave the *Lootas* (*Wave Eater*) project. (This was the version of the canoe that television audiences could see paddling up the Seine from Rouen to Paris where it took its place in the exhibition of native North American art in the Musée de l'Homme honouring Claude Lévi-Strauss in 1989.) Subsequently Reid experimented with a non-traditional form of cedar strip construction, and then further versions, with mass-marketing potential, in fibreglass. These were named *Looplex* with Reid's characteristic and caustic disregard for what he perceived to be the pieties of authenticity. Elliot, Hunt and Thompson are similarly unrestricted by such boundary patrols. The artists' agency is not seen to be compromised by their passivity to the prototype and need to respect certain aspects combined with the ability to adapt others freely.

The three prototypes are incorporated into a new composite prototype. This is the solid, 16-inch, wooden object carved by the hands of the three artists. From it resulted the index, embodying all other retensions, the Queen's Baton itself, a hollow form in sterling silver, that was created by Jeffrey Miller and then engraved with the three artists' designs by Don Yeomans (Haida). In turn, the silver index itself became prototype for a hierarchy of protensions, of decreasing monetary value, for a hierarchy of recipients, each one embodying a material and technical transformation. Among them: the 'running version', that actually figured in the enactment of passing on the Baton in relay, was made in silver-painted resin, much lighter and more practical for the 1000 or so runners. Both index and 'running version' made the trans-Canada journey, in the care of a BC Hydro agent, the former appearing wherever ceremony, that is to say, the recipients, dictated. A limited number, in silver-plated pewter, were made for presentation to such notable recipients as the Queen and Prince Andrew, to the Lieutenant-Governors and Territorial Commissioners of each province and territory, and to the CEOs of each participating power utility across Canada, as they became involved in the cere-monies surrounding the relay. It became the prototype for an edition of 1994 – the year of the Games – in pewter. This version, a few inches smaller but engraved with the artists' signatures and the edition number, was mounted on a laminated cedar wood stand, to which a dedication plaque could be affixed for presentation and display. This was made available, in the first instance, to sponsors of the Games with the remainder sold in Henry J. Birks and Sons retail stores. Finally a miniature cast resin version was made in the thousands and sold, for about $20.00, at the Games where it became the souvenir of choice – its cream colour close to the bone of the prototypical soul-catcher.

All of these protensions were managed, under licence to the Games' Native Participation Committee, by Birks, Canada's longest-established jewellers, and manufactured by Boma. This Vancouver-based company, which describes itself as 'a supplier of good-quality giftware with a Canadian theme', specializes in the production of native-style work, designed by both natives and non-natives, bearing the label 'Hand made in Canada'. Although this distinguishes Boma products from anything similar manufactured in China, Korea, etc. the company's General Manager explained that he is not concerned with the ethnicity of makers but with the quality of the work. The Company was started in the late 1950s by his father who had been inspired by the work of the nineteenth-century Haida artist Charles Edenshaw, with the aim of extending its reach through the reproduction of goods 'that respect the art form', at a time when Northwest Coast art was little known in the wider society.

In the context of conflicting ideas, about what artists do, what they are supposed to do and whether they should be thought of as 'artists' at all, lie the discussions about the most publicly visible parts of colonialism's cultures. That is to say, about artistic freedom and commissions, about copies, originality and aboriginality, about individuality and working collectively, about their designation as carvers or artists, about art used as advertising and commercial design. In what is often referred to as 'ethnographic art', artists or carvers have been taken to be passive in relation to a tradition or style. That they have agency is part of the current argument, as is the fact that they are the ones who set the line between where their agency begins and ends with reference to tribal prototypes and recipients, native and non-native.

If there is a sense in which the ethnological project has passed into native hands, it is in matters concerning cultural knowledge, its translation or the secrecy surrounding it, that ethno-ethnology is at work. The native demand for privacy, for limitations placed on research, polling, etc. dictates reticence, if not avoidance. In consequence, the social relations of reception are more accessible to the researcher than, say, the production of cultural representations. This is where the objects diffuse into imagery, and where the imagery operates publicly. It is where struggles over authorization, authenticity and ownership are articulated through social relations.

The Baton was named for the Queen whose agency with respect to it lies not in its making but in the use of her name and office and the accompanying narrative of its journey. It is essential that it be in her hands at two separate moments. Protocol might suggest that the Queen be mentioned first among recipients, but as far as Hydro's official line is concerned there is only one recipient: 'We have one target audience – the aboriginal community'. In 1993 Hydro took action to repair deteriorating relations with many aboriginal communities, whose territory is traversed by power lines, or flooded by dams, and established an Aboriginal Relations Department. In 1994 the Squamish Nation hosted a potlatch at which they and the Coast Salish Elders' Council presented Hydro executives with a Talking Stick in recognition of their intent to establish mutually beneficial relationships. This kind of cross-cultural diplomacy is less evident in other provinces. In July 1998 a deputation of First Nations from the prairie provinces of Canada was in the central US arguing against the policies of Manitoba Hydro and trying to deter American customers for its generated electricity. Similar strategies have succeeded against Hydro Quebec as the James Bay Cree fought the flooding of their territory for the production of hydro-electric power intended for the lucrative New England market. According to the Royal Bank's projection of settlements through the BC Treaty Commission, somewhere between $3 and $6 billion of business will be generated. It comes as no surprise to find Scotiabank, the only one of Canada's five major banks not to have established an aboriginal banking department, contributing $200,000 to sponsor *Down from the Shimmering Sky*. The Royal Bank has recently been working with the Museum of Anthropology, at the University of British Columbia, to rectify the conspicuous absence of Musqueam monuments on the grounds of the museum – Musqueam territory. BC Hydro's sponsorship of the Games was promoted through what they termed The Power Smart Queen's Baton Relay. Their Power Smart programme advocates conservation and the economical use of a resource. As its commissioning recipient, a response to Hydro's agency over the Baton as opportunistic and manipulative would not be surprising.

In this context, the Baton fights back. In Gell's terms it is here that the agency of this index emerges, in various forms – artists' statements, speeches, labels, video and film footage, promotional copy. It is described as 'a unique work of art'. It indexes an artistic and cultural collaboration among aboriginal artists from the three First Nations of Vancouver Island, better known for their competition than for their collaboration. Its agency dominated the ceremonial trans-Canada run on its public trajectory, between the Queen in London and the Queen in Victoria, being dipped in the Atlantic and eventually the Pacific Ocean, carried on the backs of the relay runners through aboriginal communities across Canada. The Baton appeared throughout British Columbia at local festivals, and before the mass audiences for the Games, where its agency as a 'sacrosanct' object – as it was coming to be seen – determined events. The gold, silver and bronze medals, each bearing one artist's design, can be thought of as the Baton's protensions. The Games over, it continues to demand, and to receive, the customary reverential attention, given to such treasured valuables as masks and ceremonial regalia which are kept hidden, in all Northwest Coast communities, when not actually in use. Accordingly, at present it is kept, wrapped in a woollen blanket knitted, for the purpose, with Cowichan motifs, in BC Hydro's headquarters, a large postmodern office block dominating downtown Vancouver. Arrangements are being made for it to be appropriately displayed on the Executive eighteenth floor of the building, where it will be shown alongside the Talking Stick.

The Baton with its protensions seems to bear out Gell's reiteration of the notion that '"things" with their thing-ly causal properties are as essential to the exercise of agency as states of mind' (1998: 20). The abduction of this index's agency cannot be adequately specified without recourse to a much fuller account of the social relations of its reception than can be attempted here. In broad terms it can be said to be indexing aboriginality, the relationship between native people and a utility company, Northwest Coast art, and the rights, both old and new, of native artists over their production and the responses of a range of recipients. The prototypical soul-catcher is both art and not-art. The Baton has agency in this contest inasmuch as it indexes not-art, values of a different kind, for its aboriginal recipients and many non-natives too. So it can be said to have agency in this conflict inasmuch as it indexes the conflicted social relations implicated in the term

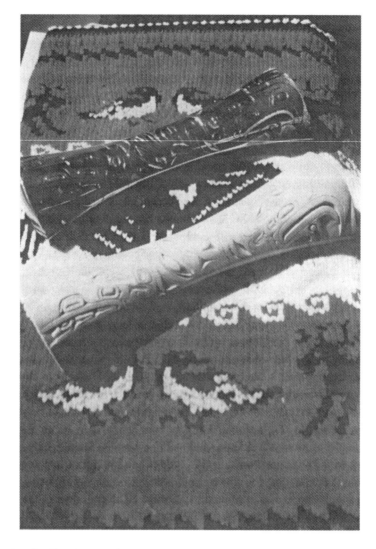

Figure 11.5 The silver Baton, with its carved alder wood prototype, resting on a knitted Cowichan blanket. Photo: Charlotte Townsend-Gault

Northwest Coast art. Like the display of native canoes in Victoria's inner harbour, the Talking Stick on the Executive floor, and the Welcome Figures, implicated with anti-logging rallies and corporate sponsorship, outside the Museum of Anthropology, these are not adequately understood as emollient gestures of reconciliation. Can it now be said to be indexing the heterogeneous status of cross-cultural relations? Working on their self-representation in the public realm is, for Northwest Coast societies and their descendant communities, continuous with a tradition of arguing status identity through public representation.

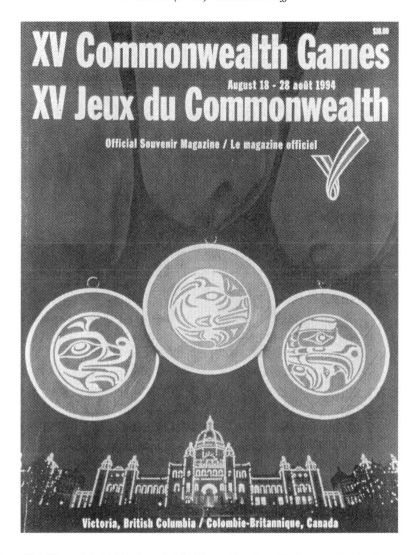

Figure 11.6 The medals: Gold – Coast Salish; Silver – Nuu-cha-nulth; Bronze – Kwakwaka'wakw

So what has this exercise demonstrated about this object that is both art and not-art, that is both tribute to a past and a travesty of it, that is public-relations exercise and token of partnership, where the power of an original has been trivialized in its copies, but where those copies have carried the power where it has never been before? I do not mean to suggest that it is a question of old singularity/new pluralism. The first is probably a delusion and the second is certainly too easy. It can perhaps be seen that certain conglomerations of ideas, substances, images are transformed in the course of negotiations over identity. They are transformed from

Figure 11.7 The pewter version (#499 from an edition of 1994) boxed for presentation, in the home of Gary and Kelly Wharton, West Vancouver. The two plaques read: 'The Queen's Baton, XV Commonwealth Games, August 18–28, 1994, Victoria, British Columbia, Canada'; 'Westcoast Energy Inc. $125,000,000. 6.90% First Preferred Shares Series 4, July, 1994'. Photo: Kelly Wharton

being carriers of one type of message to carriers of another type. The subject of such transformations is persons and relations, so the messages are about relationships between persons or groups of persons, or between persons and some aspect of the external world. Marilyn Strathern has accounted for this kind of explanation as 'theorizing things *and* persons according to a political economy model, as opposed to the neo-classical model of "economics" which takes things as they are

Figure 11.8 Cheryl Rivers (Squamish) carries the Queen's Baton into Cowichan, B.C. Photo: David Neel (reproduced with permission)

subjectively apprehended by Europeans, viz. as inanimate "objects" or artefacts' (1995).

Globalizing accounts are frequently moralizing accounts of one sort or another. They can miss local specifics, local amoralities. It seems necessary to avoid the kind of discourse deconstruction that I take Gell to have been critiquing, that is equipped with 20:20 hindsight and perfect moral acuity. Any anthropological study of art-like indices around here, this place full of fractal things and discursive palimpsests, has to be able to take the diversity, the disputes and the absolute contraries into account. Daily, the confrontation is with what Thomas, in his introduction to *Art and Agency,* calls 'a certain cognitive indecipherability' (Gell 1998: x). The art nexus allows for empirical research and provides a device for deciphering ineffable as well as discursive components. As such it indicates a way in which, and a place where, the social relations of reception can again legitimately be studied because they are enacted by objects in public.

Acknowledgements

With thanks to Charles Elliott, Art Thompson, Richard Hunt, Michael Mange (General Manager, BOMA); Ian Tait (BCHydro, Aboriginal Relations); Matt Vickers (Royal Bank, Aboriginal Department); Michael Audain (President, Vancouver Art Gallery); Ron Hamilton; Marcel Lacasse (Director of Sales, Western Division, Henry Birks & Sons); Yuxweluptun; Deborah Spence (Scotiabank); Kelly Wharton; Angela Rout.

References

Appadurai, A. (ed.). 1986. *The Social Life of Things: Commodities in Cultural Perspective*. Cambridge: Cambridge University Press.

Barrell, J. 1992. *The Birth of Pandora and the Division of Knowledge*. Oxford: Oxford University Press.

Blundell, V. 1994. '"Take Home Canada": Representations of Aboriginal Peoples as Tourist Souvenirs', in S.H. Riggins (ed.), *The Socialness of Things: Essays on the Socio-Semiotics of Objects*. Berlin/New York: Mouton de Gruyter.

Bourdieu, P. and H. Haake. 1995. *Free Exchange*. Stanford: Stanford University Press.

Bracken, C. 1997. *The Potlatch Papers: A Colonial Case History*. Chicago: University of Chicago Press.

Brown, S. 1998. *Native Visions: Evolution in Northwest Coast Art from the Eighteenth through the Twentieth Century*. Seattle: Seattle Art Museum/ University of Washington Press.

Crosby, M. 1991. 'Construction of the Imaginary Indian', in S. Douglas (ed.), *Vancouver Anthology: The Institutional Politics of Art*. Vancouver: Talonbooks.

—— 1995. *Nations in Urban Landscapes*. Vancouver: Contemporary Art Gallery.

Danto, A. 1988. 'Artifact and Art', in S. Vogel (ed.), *ART/Artifact: African Art in Anthropology Collections*, pp. 18–32. New York: Center for African Art.

Davidson, R. and U. Steltzer. 1994. *Eagle Transforming: The Art of Robert Davidson*. Vancouver: Douglas & McIntyre.

Dawn, L. 1976. *'Ksan: Museum, Cultural and Artistic Activity Among the Gitksan Indians of the Upper Skeena, 1920–1973*. Unpublished MA Thesis, University of Victoria.

Douglas, M. and B. Isherwood. 1978. *The World of Goods*. London: Allan Lane.

Empson, W. 1930. *Seven Types of Ambiguity*. London: Chatto & Windus.

Foster, H. 1995. 'The Artist as Ethnographer?', in G.E. Marcus and F.R. Myers (eds), *The Traffic in Culture: Refiguring Art and Anthropology*. Berkeley: University of California Press.

Freedberg, D. 1989. *The Power of Images: Studies in the History and Theory of Response*. Chicago: University of Chicago Press.

Gell, A. 1998. *Art and Agency: An Anthropological Theory*. Oxford: Oxford University Press.

Gell, A. 'Vogel's Net: Traps as Artworks and Artworks as Traps'. *Journal of Material Culture* 1(1): 15–38.

Gisday Wa and Delgam Uukw. 1992. *The Spirit in the Land: Statements of the Gitksan and Wet'suweten Hereditary Chiefs in the Supreme Court of British Columbia 1987–1990*. Reflections: Gabriola, B.C.

Holm, B. 1965. *Northwest Coast Indian Art: An Analysis of Form*. Seattle: University of Washington Press.

Holm, B. and B. Reid. 1975. *Indian Art of the Northwest Coast: A Dialogue on Craftsmanship and Aesthetics*. Houston: Institute of the Arts, Rice University.

Jensen, D. and C. Brooks (eds). 1991. *In Celebration of Our Survival*. Special Issue, *B.C. Studies* 89.

Jonaitis, A. 1993. 'Traders of Tradition: The History of Haida Art', in I. Thom (ed.) *Robert Davidson: Eagle of the Dawn*. Seattle: University of Washington Press.

Keesing, R. 1994. 'Colonial and Counter-colonial Discourse in Melanesia'. *Critique of Anthropology* 4(1): 41–58.

Kirschenblatt-Gimblett, B. 1995. 'Confusing Pleasures', in G.E. Marcus and F.R. Myers (eds) *The Traffic in Culture: Refiguring Art and Anthropology*. Berkeley: University of California Press.

Lévi-Strauss, C. 1943. 'Art of the Northwest Coast at the American Museum of Natural History'. *Gazette des Beaux Arts* 24: 175–83.

Lincoln, B. 1989. *Discourse and the Construction of Society: Comparative Studies of Myth, Ritual and Classification*. Oxford: Oxford University Press.

MacDonald, J. 1995. 'Building a Moral Community: Tsimshian Potlatching, Implicit Knowledge and Everyday Experiences'. *Cultural Studies* 1: 125–44.

Macnair, P., B. Grenville and Chief R. Joseph (eds). 1998. *Down from the Shimmering Sky: Masks of the Northwest Coast*. Vancouver: Douglas & McIntyre/Seattle: University of Washington Press.

Manuel, G. 1977. *Indian Sovereignty: The Indian Bible of British Columbia*. Vancouver: Union of B.C. Indian Chiefs.

Marcus, G.E. and F. Myers. 1995. *The Traffic in Culture: Refiguring Art and Anthropology* Berkeley: University of California Press.

Michaels, E. 1994. *Bad Aboriginal Art*. Minneapolis: University of Minnesota Press.

Miller, D. (ed.). 1998. *Material Cultures: Why Some Things Matter*. Chicago: University of Chicago Press.

Morris, R.C. 1994. *New Worlds from Fragments: Film, Ethnography and the Representation of Northwest Coast Cultures*. Boulder: Westview Press.

Muckle, R.J. 1998. *The First Nations of British Columbia*. Vancouver: University of British Columbia Press.

Neel, D. 1992. *Our Chiefs and Elders: Words and Photographs of Native Leaders*. Vancouver: University of British Columbia Press.

Newman, B. 1946–7. 'Northwest Coast Indian Painting' in J.P. O'Neill (ed.). 1990. *Barnett Newman: Selected Writings and Interviews*. New York, Knopf.

Poignton, M. 1991. *History of Art: A Student's Handbook.* London: Routledge.

Shadbolt, D. 1998. *Bill Reid*. Vancouver: Douglas & McIntyre.

Strathern, M. 1995. *The Relation: Issues in Complexity and Scale*. Pamphlet No. 6. Cambridge: Prickly Pear Press.

Thomas, N. 1994. *Colonialism's Culture: Anthropology, Travel and Government*. Princeton: Princeton University Press.

Townsend-Gault, C. 1988. 'Kwakiutl Ready-Mades?' in J. Bradley and L. Johnstone (eds), *Sightlines: Reading Contemporary Canadian Art*. 1994. Montreal: Artextes editions.

—— 1997. 'Art, Argument and Anger on the Northwest Coast', in J. MacClancy (ed.), *Contesting Art: Art, Politics and Identity in the Modern World*. Oxford: Berg.

Wallis, B. 1991. 'Selling Nations'. *Art in America* 79: 84–92.

Wardwell, A. 1996. *Tangible Visions: Northwest Coast Indian Shamanism and its Art*. New York: The Monacelli Press.

Yuxweluptun, C.Townsend-Gault, and S. Watson. 1995. *Yuxweluptun: Born to Live and Die on Your Colonialist Reservations*. Vancouver: Belkin Art Gallery, UBC.

12

The Patent and the Malanggan
Marilyn Strathern

The perception that Technology is 'everywhere' – within and around us – comes among other things from the way modern people describe themselves. We (moderns of the Euro-American sort) run together all kinds of devices, examples of ingenuity and aids to living as though together they had an existence more powerful than any particular contraption could hold by itself. The conglomerate is glued together by two major assumptions. In everyday parlance 'technology' points to what is contemporary and innovative about modernity; it also points to the creative inventiveness which brings itself into being. A substantial corpus of intellectual property rights, for instance, concerns itself with the producers of contraptions when the producers can also show that they were the original innovators and inventors. I wish to take advantage of the prevalent discourse of technology and the (increasingly prevalent) discourse of intellectual property in order to describe a part of our world not ordinarily brought within the range of these constructs. It creates an interesting context for a question. If we are interested in how we make ourselves at home in technology, then how do we make technology strange to ourselves in the first place? My toolkit is a couple of textbooks on intellectual property rights, an art catalogue from an exhibition of wooden sculptures, and some anthropological reflections on enchantment.

Introducing the Body

New Ireland, off the coast of Papua New Guinea, is famous for its intricately carved and coloured sculptures called Malanggan. Indeed the possibilities of their travelling beyond these islands is written into the technology. They are by and large both portable and durable, while in the minds of the producers they are also supremely ephemeral. Malanggan are produced to be discarded. Created with great care, they may be displayed for no more than a few days, hours even, before they have to be destroyed or thrown away. One mode of destruction is to put them into the hands of European traders: they are one of the most collectible types of art object from any ethnographic region of the world.

Malanggan come from northern New Ireland where they circulate across several distinct language groups.[1] We may imagine them as bodies, although the body appears in many different shapes and forms. The most familiar (most portable) take on the shapes of human and animal beings. Figure 3.2, illustrated by Susanne Küchler, shows a mask with the general appearance of a head, made up of numerous smaller figures, snakes, birds, fish, parrot wings. Its purpose is to contain the life force of a deceased person: New Irelanders say it provides the deceased with 'body' or 'skin', now that their other body no longer exists.[2] Present bodies may at once substitute for absent bodies (New Ireland exegesis on the carving as a body for the deceased), and (exegesis mine) may be presented as composed of other bodies, as this head is composed of birds and fish. It is an open question whether we should see the smaller bodies as inside the larger or as attached to its surface – from either perspective, visually speaking, images are composed of images. So what kind of space for dwelling is being created here?

Imagining entities 'containing' entities is one way of making notions of habitation and dwelling concrete. But of course such a strategy literalizes[3] the basic phenomenological understanding that one cannot describe the world as it appears to people without describing the character of people's being which makes the world what it is.[4] It follows that people are as much within it as the world is within them. Alongside this formulation come the questions. Rather than being surprised that there is anything special about 'inhabiting technology', the arresting issue is why we think technology requires special techniques of habitation, and thus why in effect we distance it from us.[5] From that point of view, different cultural perceptions of worlds within worlds start to become interesting. This mask is not the dead person's spirit, it is a skin or body *for* that person's spirit. The spirit is about to become an ancestor, and the body is carved into a form recognizable as ancestral to the person's clan. A transient container for ancestral power to be, it is also contained by ancestral power. So what is so special about the working of this power that it must be placed within a body before it can be released? Why, like Euro-Americans thinking about technology, do New Irelanders go to such lengths to *separate* something of themselves[6] from what they see as otherwise enveloping them? We shall come back to this.

No doubt a Euro-American observer would comment on the technical skill that goes into making Malanggan.[7] They might also be tempted to read the animal motifs as referring to 'nature', apposite for Euro-American sensibilities which would place seemingly non-modern peoples closer to their environment than themselves because they lack the intervening devices of high technology. However, for New Irelanders, that cannot be what the birds and the fish are about.[8] These people would no more think that they were in 'nature' or 'nature' in them[9] than they would think there was some kind of opposition between nature and the application of knowledge that Euro-Americans call technology.

Enchantment

Exactly this distinction is, on the other hand, thoroughly embedded in Euro-American ways of thinking and is (re-)invented over and again, just as one of its partners, the distinction between the social and the biological, is constantly reinvented (Pottage 1998: 741).

Consider how 'technology' inhabits the English language. By pointing to a substantive entity, it gathers numerous things together under the one rubric so that English-speakers show to themselves the products of technology everywhere and distinguish them from other products. In common parlance, a dishwasher is an artefact of a technological world in a way the kitchen sink simply is not. Technology, in the culturally pervasive sense in which it inhabits this language, does not just reify effort or production; it reifies, gives tangible form to, a creativity regarded as (re)juvenating. So technology embodies more than the recognition of the techniques of human handiwork – it is evidence of the continually creative mind that seeks to enlarge society's capacities.[10] Moreover, it mobilizes agents whose efforts are socially extended, not just as a tool extends human effort but as innovations substitute for old travails (the dishwasher purportedly releasing the washer-upper for other ways of spending time, an altogether friendlier image than Alfred Gell's (1998) devastating depiction of landmines as the dispersed agency of a military commander). Put these together and we have enumerated some of the values attendant on that particular kind of creativity that Euro-Americans recognize in an 'invention'. For, of all the products of human creativity, inventions are defined by the power which 'technology' has to give them life.[11] Thinking about its foundation in inventiveness, we might say that technology lives among us in an enchanted state.

Here I take liberties with Gell's (1999: chapter 5) disquisition on the enchantment of technology. The enchantment of technology lies in 'the power that technical processes have of casting a spell over us' (1999: 163),[12] the way artefacts are construed as having come into being, and thus what makes us marvel at the very ability to translate an idea into an invention and an invention into a device which works. Power seems to end up in the artefacts themselves, harnessing the human energy they augment.[13] Above all, they are physical manifestations of the technical virtuosity and creativity of the maker. In an industrial world such makers may be known through trademarks which weave their own spells (Coombe 1998) – but they may equally well be lost in anonymity. These nameless inventors *could* be named but, importantly, when they are not known they can reflect back a diffuse or generalized aura of capacity, enhancing people's sense that they are all heirs to a collective creativity.[14] This is one way in which technology inhabits us, we inhabit technology.

Enchantment lies in a further dimension, the enlargement of social agency. And here we encounter the technology of enchantment. An essential technique for creating an enchanted space is separation. I said that rather than being surprised that there is anything special about 'inhabiting' technology, the interesting questions are about how we distance it. One obvious way is by dividing 'technology' off from other aspects of life. The magico-purificatory effect of conceptual separation (Latour 1993) suggests there is something special about the inventiveness of human agency; access to technology is in turn prized as extending such general capacities for the individual. How does the purificatory divide work? If technology inhabits the English language as a substantive entity, it can also evoke other entities in opposition – sometimes Society,[15] sometimes Nature. When it is nature that is counterposed, technology and society may roll together as jointly enlarging the sphere of human endeavour at nature's expense. Nature puts technology at a distance from its own world. Thus whatever is categorized as 'nature' simult-aneously provides a measure of the effectiveness of the technology; it reflects degrees of human activity. Moreover, the magic of zero-sum logic makes measure-ment appear to work automatically: the more human activity there is, the less untouched nature or fewer natural processes there must be in the world. You can see it in every medical advance or diminished bird count. Nature in this sense is the ultimate envelope, containing technology and society within.

There are many ways in which English-speakers in particular and Euro-Americans in general make all this obvious to themselves.[16] I note one: Euro-Americans may claim for their culture the special capacity of globalization, the ability which their information technology (IT) gives them to be in several places at once,[17] a spatially unmatched reach of efficacy. The world shrinking through communications and the retreat of untouched (natural) spaces are measures of it. Euro-Americans may even describe themselves as inhabiting a space enabled by technology which they alone are capable of making. In this authorial claim, by a kind of reverse logic which assumes that people without the adjuncts of IT must live in a less expanded world, they may assume that other peoples do a different kind of 'inhabiting'. Think of all their stereotypes of societies as communities. Like the people of Papua New Guinea: perhaps Papua New Guineans have no idea of nature, but surely they have ideas of community, localities that stay put, of a kind of dwelling which yields stable identities, roots, and all the rest of it?

Return to New Ireland – 1

The stereotype would be misleading for New Ireland. This is not just because of the frequency of contact with European navigators, traders and labour recruiters over the last 150–200 years[18] but because they have long had their own ways of moving around, and in a dimension at once spatial, temporal and virtual. Living people are never in just one place. And any one person lives within a stream of persons who move from place to place over time, remembered in some detail. Here the techniques of constructing Malanggan bodies start taking on the characteristics of a technology.

Malanggan do not only take the form of masks; they may be poles, friezes or standing displays.[19] Nor do they only appear at death, although all Malanggan involve the embodiment of deceased persons.[20] What is constant is that such artefacts are briefly displayed for the duration of ceremonies – days, hours – before being deliberately disposed of. The life force of the dead person is then released from its container. But, as Gell remarks (1998: 226), we might as well say the 'life' of the person, for what is held momentarily in one place is an identity which is composed of the person's associations with many others, whether through the garden lands which they worked, or the groups into which they and their relatives have married. Moreover the identity in question is not just of the deceased but of the living owner of the Malanggan who has had it made in a particular way. The owner will produce the designs to which his membership of a clan, and/or of a localized unit of the clan, entitles him.[21] But designs also travel, just as people do.

Malanggan are manufactured in such a way as to suggest multiple identities. Lincoln (1987) shows a Malanggan (catalogue number 40) composed of two chickens, and a frigate bird holding the tail of a snake that undulates through stylized foliage, as the catalogue description has it. In another constellation of elements (13) one sees clearly distinguishable snakes and birds – also chickens – and foliage garlands topped by a hornbill. Variation is necessary if people are not to trespass on one another's designs, and no two figures are identical. In certain Malanggan traditions, acceptable variation may involve as little as two or three centimetres of carving (Gunn 1987: 81). Motifs travel between these figures, then, and each new Malanggan is a composite of elements drawn from other Malanggan. It is a 'place' which gathers places from elsewhere to itself, a 'person' (to which Malanggan are likened) who gathers the interests of other persons into him- or herself.[22]

The social space being modelled here is one of movement over time and distance.[23] For at death a person's attachments are still scattered in several locations.

> The gardens and plantations of the deceased, scattered here and there, are still in production, their wealth is held by various exchange-partners, their houses are still standing . . . The process of making the carving coincides with the [subsequent] process of reorganisation and adjustment (Gell 1998: 225).

At the same time the social space is a virtual one in which the deceased is enveloped in the larger persona of clan connections. The clan is an always present environment.[24] If, however, we say that there is a sense in which a person inhabits a clan and the clan inhabits the person, then we must include those relationships beyond the clan which clanship also brings. Everyone has active relationships with other groups, and a living person's actions are oriented in diverse directions. Gathering these in, Malanggan have been spoken of as bringing together an otherwise dispersed agency.[25] The crucial point about the destruction of the mortuary Malanggan is that the gathered agency of the deceased has then to be *re*dispersed, whether to revitalize old relationships in new form or to return the deceased's powers in a more general way to the clan.[26] When a figure is assembled, it may recapitulate figures created for past clan members, then, containing elements that have travelled down the generations, while other motifs may have travelled across local groups so that elements also come from figures originating elsewhere.[27] The dimensions are of both time and space, and here we stumble across what can only be called a *technology of enchantment*. For the figures are constructed in such a way as to bring together in one place simultaneous reference to the past, present and future.

The moment when the Malanggan is discarded is also the moment at which it or its components may be dispersed to others, the moment people from other localities looking at the sculpture pay for the ability to reproduce the parts of the designs at some time in the future. Küchler (1992: 101–2) argues that Malaggan designs anticipate this – they are planned with the future owners in mind. The past has already become the future. So what is the technology which weaves such enchantment?

There are two distinct axes to the Malaggan figure (as in the example shown as Figure 3.2). Overlaying the wooden three-dimensional framework with its carved motifs is a two-dimensional surface integrated through the painted designs.

> The carved planes refer to the exchange history of the sculptured image, or its 'outer' or 'public' identity, whereas the painted pattern signifies the present ownership of the image, or its 'inner' identity . . . [These] together constitute what is called the 'skin' (or *tak*) of the sculpture' (Küchler 1992: 101).

Strategic relationships between groups (above all, through marriage) are created by ties of 'skin'. The container of the life force is also a map on which participants in a Malanggan ceremony inscribe their anticipated alliances. For the present owners already know who will want to make claims on the designs, and the Malanggan is carved in such a way as to acknowledge the owners-to-be.[28] The carved container as a repository of social effectiveness (Gell's phrase) through time is then covered by the painted 'inside' of current relationships now rendered on the 'outside'. Enchantment is achieved through the technique by which the form simultaneously extends into past and future while holding it all at a single moment in time and space. It is not just that the present encapsulates the past: the future is projected as a remembering of the present. For while the new relationships move into operation straight away, it will be many years before the motifs reappear in daylight; then they will emerge as components dispersed among other Malanggan. They will be brought to life in new sculptures *looking back* to this moment of acquisition. The conjunction of paint and carving does that – each form carries the other into and away from the present.[29]

What the future owners receive is, they say, 'knowledge' of the Malanggan (along with the rearrangements of social relations which gives them land rights and so forth). That knowledge makes them effective in the future, and this is what turns Malanggans into a kind of technology. To use a phrase from Sykes (n.d.; cf also Küchler 1992: 101), they are transmitters or conduits (rather than memorials or representations). They do not just work to make things work or extend people's reach; a Malanggan converts existing relationships into virtual ones, matter into energy, and living into ancestral agency – heralding the reversal of these transformations at a future stage in the reproductive cycle. The technico-ritual process of carving and painting does not produce 'things' as we might think of artistic works – as a thing, the body is not allowed to remain in existence. Rather, like technology which combines knowledge, material form and effectiveness, the reproduction of the Malanggan body makes it possible to capture, condense and then release power back into the world.[30]

One might remark that this happens in social life all the time: we gather the past into our various projects, and then find ways of seeking to influence the future. There is, however, a mode of presenting Euro-American technology which weaves something of a comparable enchantment, enough to make people feel that something momentous might be going on. This is where patents come in.

Patenting Technology

If the very concept 'technology' creates a field of artefacts and expectations, the law runs in parallel: it upholds as a generic category the industrial application of new ideas, so that all such applications come to seem examples of 'human creativity'.[31] How? – through patents. Patents are part of international intellectual property law, which makes

> a vital contribution to mankind's storehouse of technical information. Eighty percent of the existing technical knowledge in the world is estimated to be available in the patent literature, organized in an internationally recognized classification system (Tassy and Dambrine 1997: 196).

The idea of being able to patent something has a double power. First, the patenting procedure requires a body: the initating idea has to be manifest or embodied in some artefact or device, a concrete invention which 'contains' the idea, while at the same time what the patent protects is the idea itself, the creative impetus, minimally an 'inventive step'. Second, patents do not just recognize creativity and originality; they transform creativity into usable knowledge by at once attaching it to and detaching it from the inventor.

That transformative power appeals to the imagination. Indeed, intellectual property systems as a whole have been written about in lyrical terms, as though they were part of a *technology of enchantment*. One writer refers to genetic resources brought under the 'spell' of intellectual property rights (Khalil 1995: 232); another confesses that intellectual property has always seemed 'the Carmen of commercial law' – 'a subject with charm, personality and a force of character' (Phillips in Phillips and Firth 1990: vii). And of all IPR protocols, the patent is paradigmatic – '*the* form of intellectual property *par excellence*' (Bainbridge 1999: 7, my emphasis), for 'intellectual property law reserves a very special and powerful mode of protection for inventions' (1999: 317). That mode is a property right which takes the form of monopoly: the patent attaches the invention exclusively to the inventor. In doing so it also detaches it in the form of knowledge: the patent agreement compels the inventor to yield information to the world about how to re-create the artefact. Patents simultaneously produce private property and public(ly available) information.[32]

As part and parcel of the industrializing project of the West, intellectual property regimes nowadays exert international pressure on countries such as Papua New Guinea which are currently considering the implementation of copyright and patent legislation (in response to WIPO [World Intellectual Property Organization] and under the aegis of TRIPS [Trade Related Aspects of Intellectual Property Rights]).[33] In Britain, specifically, patents began taking their present form at the time of the industrial revolution, with the aim among others of encouraging the development of ideas leading to innovation. They grant a monopoly over the benefits to be gained from an invention, provided it is new, and provided the details are put in the public domain. The philosophy is that inventions in the long run should contribute to a general good. In the interim, however, benefit is channelled through the patent holder who is at liberty to control access to it for a set period (until the patent expires).

Any one invention must build on numerous others:[34]

> all inventions can be regarded as being comprised of units of information [information is composed of information]. Under this view, that which appears to our eyes to be an 'invention', a creation of something new, is no more than a synthesis [a composite] of known bits of information, not really an invention at all (Phillips and Firth 1990: 21, after Michael Pendleton).[35]

Behind these numerous other inventions are of course numerous others involved in the long process of development. At the point of patenting, an invention becomes a 'place' or passage point at which diverse expertise, all the knowledge that went into creating it, is gathered together and condensed into a single entity (cf. Strathern 1996). In turn, precisely because it must meet the specification of being an industrially applicable device, it is through its technological application that the effect of that expertise is extended and dispersed, typically in the form of a manufactured product. Patenting procedures speed up this gathering and dispersal.

I deliberately echo the New Ireland analysis. The fabrication of Malanggan results in a form which condenses a whole history of interactions, and in the process makes it possible to channel clan powers – the clan and its relationships with others – for future benefit; we might say that the patent results in a form – the potency of information made product – through which technological power is also channelled to the future. Depending on the point in the reproductive cycle, Malanggan transform living and ancestral agency, the one into the other. Patents imply a more linear series of conversions, intangible ideas into enforceable property rights. In the place of the enveloping clan with its ancestral potency, at once inside and outside everyone, English-speakers instead accord nature a similar regenerative and recursive potential. Indeed patenting is part of a process which continues to regenerate nature as fast as it appears to consume it. A kind of technology within technology, patents thereby augment the *enchantment of technology*.

First, patents perpetuate the very concept of nature. If technology in general creates 'nature' as a world of materials waiting to be used or of natural processes that carry on without human intervention, then patents create a domain of 'nature' in a very specific sense. For the general rationale is that patents cannot apply to any interpretation or manipulation of natural processes that does not require the specific input of human know-how resulting in things which did not exist before.[36] Invention modifies nature; discovery does not. So objections to patents may be dismissed as the result of 'technical misunderstandings which arise from a wilful refusal to understand the difference between discovery and invention' (Pottage 1998: 750). The rubric is that nature cannot be patented. Ipso facto, anything patentable is already out of the realm of nature. If it can be used as an exclusionary mechanism, the issue then becomes what does or does not count as nature. Many patents deal with refinements of other inventions already in the made world, and there are numerous grounds on which applications for patents may be refused, for example over the degree of innovation which an inventor has brought to materials already worked upon or over how realistic industrial exploitation may be. But excluding anything which exists 'naturally' is a touchstone of patent law that has come into particular prominence with recent developments in biotechnology. '[M]erely to find a hitherto unknown substance which exists in nature is not to make an invention' (Phillips and Firth 1990: 35). Conversely, Bainbridge (1999: 368) quotes Justice Whitford in 1987 [involving recombinant DNA technology, in 'Genetech's patent']: 'you cannot patent a discovery, but if on the basis of that discovery you can tell people how it can be usefully employed then a patent of invention may result'.[37] Nature is redefined, reinvented, over and again by such exclusions.

Second, there is the matter of knowledge about the natural world. Instead of thinking of nature as an axiomatic measure of human endeavour, one may regard it as a source of technological innovation added to as fast as it is taken away. As fast as information is made product, new sources of information about the world are uncovered. And they necessarily point to fresh understandings of natural elements or processes until these are transformed by human ingenuity and lifted out of the natural realm.[38] So nature continues to grow in scope. The more it grows, the more it can be consumed; but the more it is consumed through a patent regime, the more knowledge about it is likely to expand.

Yet why do Euro-Americans sometimes accuse 'scientists' of 'patenting nature'? In biotechnology, the manifestation of nature they dwell on is 'life itself'. So along with objections to patenting 'human beings' or 'individuals' goes 'living things' and 'life' (Strathern 1999: 171–2; Pottage 1998: 744). Yet the very act of patenting seems to reaffirm a strong divide between nature which cannot be patented and artefacts which can. What could be more explicit than the legal exclusion of plants or animal varieties or 'biological processes' (Walden 1995: 182, apropos the European Patent Convention 1973), not to speak of 'the human body' (in the EC 1998 Biotechnology Directive)? So why do people talk as though nature, or life, were being patented? One does not have to look very far for an answer. Patent confers ownership, and there is a (deservedly) long history of suspicion over what people do to one another through asserting ownership.

Patent ownership confers the right to enjoy benefits which arise from the owner's investment in the invention. As with all intellectual property rights, the right is held as private property; although others can seek release of the information (for example under licence), the owner regulates access. But it is not always clear what the property contains. An often voiced concern is about *what is being gathered into the patent*. Let me note several distinct concerns. One has been touched on: truncating the network of scientists behind the invention into those who claim the final inventive step that leads to a patentable product. Second, the breadth of the patent: how much is being claimed over future processes or products.[39] Third, too much modification of what people see as the order of things, and it is here that appeals to 'nature' emerge.[40] When people claim that property ownership has inappropriately extracted items from that world, they go behind the decision as to whether something is an invention to query the process by which the invention came into being in the first place – back to the moment when all the elements were still unmodified (cf Pottage 1998: 753). To assert that 'nature' is being 'patented' is to draw up political or ethical lines in order to curb the extended agency of human interference. Indeed, criticism of property rights may go hand in hand with the disenchantment of technology – it is alleged that the separation between Technology and Nature has been breached since patents which properly apply to technology are now being applied to nature. The phrase 'patenting nature' is part of the politics of disenchantment.

The fourth concern is a very old one. To assert ownership by way of patent inevitably engages with a long Euro-American debate over private property, historically regarded as carved out of what would otherwise be available to all. This may be nature or it may be other human artefacts and knowledge. Critics of current practices have reintroduced the language of 'enclosing the commons'. Phillips and Firth (1990: 21–2) continue their comment on each invention as a permutation of previous inventions thus:

> Correlative to this view [see above], is the asumption that, if each unit of information is a community resource, part of the common heritage of mankind, no edifice constructed from such communal blocks should be able to constitute a privately owned invention. [They then add:] The modern intellectual property lawyer finds it difficult to accept this, unless he can persuade himself that there is no difference between a palace and the pile of bricks from which it is built.

What is claimed for society (common heritage) is then claimed for nature:

> [T]he patentability of discoveries would result in man's expropriation of nature itself, and it is difficult to justify the expropriation by one of what is already the natural legacy of all (Phillips and Firth 1990: 35).

Expropriation implies an exclusion of, the owner's separation from, others. Ownership works as kind of extended agency, an extension of a person's capacity, personal or corporate, with a reach as far as products will travel. If what is owned has the legal character of private property, then technology, in the legal form of a patent as the right to exploit it, is so to speak folded within the individual owner.

This is textbook stuff. Here I have a suggestion. In relation to 'inhabiting', the concept of 'containment' conveys the sense in which parts of our social lives seem to be lived within others, figures within figures, knowledge composed of (other) knowledge(s). With the inflection of dwelling, it implies more than the kind of fit with the world that makes it comfortable and familiar; it points to an existential orientation towards it. Euro-Americans take momentary refuge in Nature or in Technology, either of which seems at once around and part of them, or else in all the dwelling places afforded by notions of community or locality. But there is a further candidate for 'habitation', nothing to do with environment or community, that allows Euro-Americans to dwell in a thoroughly taken-for-granted world, an envelope that allows them to live within themselves.

I take my candidate from the way Euro-American moderns become attached to a world they see full of useful and beautiful things. It is a world they imagine that people desire to appropriate, whether they think of private individuals in exclusive possession of property or of the common people in open possession of its bounty. Ownership. What is not owned exists either to be owned as some future resource not yet exploited or else is notionally owned by humankind in general, including the generations to come. Ownership envelops all. Is 'ownership' a mode of 'habitation'? The manner in which Euro-Americans attach things to themselves makes them at home in the world – whether contained by Technology or by Nature – from which they think of such things as coming. Ownership is a kind of second skin to these two containers, a world through which people are infinitely inter-connected through the inclusions and exclusions of property relations, and in which possession is taken to be at once a natural drive and the just reward of creativity. Property – in rights, in profits – seems comfortably within everyone's grasp, subject only to the limitations of unequal endowment.

It would I think be an enchanted world, created not least by the magico-purificatory divide at the heart of property relations, the cultural sleight of hand that suggests that just as things are intrinsically separate from persons so things intrisically separate persons from one another. Principles of ownership carry their own exclusions and separations. The stereotype is that we would have to go to other cultures to escape that particular enchantment.

Return to New Ireland – 2

For a third time, the stereotype would be misleading for New Ireland. There is much which can be translated as ownership.

We saw that agency or energy located in numerous social places had to be gathered in to one place, focused in the carved and painted Malanggan figure(s) and then re-dispersed. However, that is only half the story. Every gathering together, every recombining of motifs out of motifs, involves a specific claim of title. It is not possible to incorporate designs without permission. That is because only certain people have the 'right' to use the knowledge associated with particular Malanggan.

On the one hand, the authorization to display the image is vested exclusively in the sponsoring clan or local group; on the other hand, expertise is required to carve the figure, and owners of Malanggan must commission an expert carver. Sponsors own not so much rights to the designs as rights to their reproduction, and the subject of reproduction are images retained as memories. It is the right to make bodies, to make material and give physical form to images, which is trans-ferred across the generations and across groups. Transfer is sealed by payment. Now if Malanggan can be considered technology, in the captivating effect of the skill required to reproduce the figure at all we might be tempted to see an *enchantment of technology*. The skill in question is as much intellectual as manual, and requires the work of both owner and carver. Since Malanggan are displayed when the new owner carries off his sighting of the form to which he has acquired rights, and which he holds as a memory for what may be as long as a generation, the would-be sponsor (owner) of a new Malanggan carving will have glimpsed the image long before it is to be reproduced.[41] He must now describe this in detail to an expert carver, who in turn conceives the new form in his own mind, an inspiration assisted by magic and/or by dreaming. What is dazzling to the Euro-American is the ability of the carver to produce a form from a description held by another person (the owner) as the memory of a Malanggan seen years before. What is (one suspects)[42] dazzling to New Irelanders is the way the resulting body emerges from two bodies.

I asked earlier why New Irelanders distance themselves from what they regard as enveloping them. Perhaps one answer lies in the enchantment of this particular technology, the way artefacts are construed as having come into being. Repro-duction requires two persons, and they have to be socially distinct.[43] The techniques by which new Malanggan come into being work only because of the successful joining of quite *separate* efforts (the work of remembering and the work of carving).[44] Indeed it is important that the form which emerges from the clan repertoire is only like its original in some respects: axiomatically, Malanggan do not duplicate one another (cf Küchler 1987: 244), any more than human offspring duplicate one or other parent alone. (We might say that the 'ancestral' Malanggan body is the child's image of the parent body.) What is contained within the 'skin' (body) of the Malanggan must be kept distinct from the container: social difference is conserved at the very point at which the deceased also merges with the ancestors. Similarly, between sponsor and carver, it has to be the work of joining which makes the reproduction a unique and amazing process. 'Work' is perceived to be at the heart of Malanggan (Sykes personal communication).[45]

Now the mode in which these rights are claimed have long prompted compari-sons with intellectual property, and specifically with copyright. Some figures are made with an out-stretched tongue said to have the function of 'threatening all offenders against the owner's copyright' (Heintze 1987: 53). 'Copyright' is of course the ethnographer's gloss.

One could therefore think of the whole figure as an artistic work subject to copyright, a kind of literary text replete with (permitted) quotations from other texts but itself an original form of expression. However, let us take the analogy step by step. What is gained is the right to reproduce the design. And what circulate in transactions are 'not objects, but the images they embody' (Küchler 1987: 629; Harrison 1992: 234).[46] At issue is not the identical text, the form of expression which is key to Euro-American concepts of copyright, but the idea behind it.

For when the license [for a Malanggan] is sold, not the figure itself but the *description of* the form and associated rites are made available to the purchaser (Bodrogi 1987: 21, my emphasis).

When a Malanggan appears, others may challenge the owner's right to reproduce a particular design, and Gunn (1987: 81, 83) talks of people having to 'defend copyright held by another subclan' or of the process of transference being subject to public inspection for 'breaches of copyright'. Yet the challenge comes from those who hold a memory or idea of the image which they claim is theirs, not from being able to compare its expression or realization in material form. The carving no longer exists. Moreover, the owner of the supposed copyright cannot necessarily give permission for others to make copies. He can dispose of the copyright, like property, but in many circumstances another can only make a copy by acquiring the copyright itself. And then,

With the sale of the copyright the earlier owner is deprived of all rights to make the type [now] sold (Bodrogi 1987: 21).[47]

Finally, the design is not 'copied' as such – rather, it is lodged in the memory as an image to be recalled at a later date.[48] Indeed, in respect of certain elements of the Malanggan, we may note that claimants' rights exist only *until* the moment of their realization in material form, the point at which they are transferred to others; people 'own' them most securely as memories still to be realized. Reproduced, not replicated: the analogy with copyright does not seem to go far enough.

If we did indeed think of the Malanggan not only as art or text but also as a piece of technology, then we might refer to the rights in question as being guaranteed by something closer to a patent.[49] Some differences are clear. A patent grants a monopoly to exploit an idea (embodied in some artefact), and is held by one owner at a time; others obtain the idea/artefact through licence or purchase. By contrast, use of Malanggan is (usually) effected only by those who simult-aneously own the 'patent' rights, since one cannot display the product, the embodied image, without having acquired ownership of the idea as well. However, in one respect a Malanggan bears resemblance to an invention under patent. Such an invention gathers together expertise (all the knowledge that went into making it) and then through its application disperses the effect of that expertise (through products widely available). And that gathering together is done for a set period: a patent is made to expire.[50] In the interim it has condensed multiple agencies into itself, reproducing them in the names of the new owners. Of course in the case of expiring patents it is the owner's rights which are extinguished after so many years, and the invention goes on being used, while New Irelanders extinguish the particular invention (the individual Malanggan), and the rights go on being conserved.[51] Nonetheless, we might conclude that Malanggan are not just like a technology in some of their effects but are also like the very patents taken out to protect the application of technology, at once a description of transferable rights and a specification of how they are to be materialized.

Patent applications in the UK run at some 27,000 a year, perhaps 7,000 of these being granted, with some 180,000 renewals (Bainbridge 1999: 336–7). This gives the order of current patents, with upward of some two million, it has been calculated, lying expired in the Patent Office.[52] The reason Malanggan are one of the best represented and collectible types of 'art object', some 5000 now housed within the museums of the world,[53] is precisely because their function as unique habitations for energy and power will have long expired. The rights to reproduction remain active until the image has been properly reproduced, but then it (the image) comes to lodge in a new version whose powers are animated by a new generation.[54] This is technology in a state of perpetual transferral.

Imperfect as the analogy with technology is, it draws attention to the way in which artefacts such as Malanggan work their effects on people, and to the knowledge that is held to be embedded within them. And impossible as the analogy with patenting is, the comparison perhaps enables us to grasp some of the imaginative, and ideological, potential of Euro-American intellectual property concepts, one of the many forms which modern rationalities are given (Rabinow 1996: x).

The recombination of elements of information, the amalgamation of new and existing forms, the minute variations that may be sufficient to demonstrate crucial intervention, channelling past knowledge to future effect, a limited period of efficacy: this could as well describe a Malanggan as it describes a patent. Yet there is a gulf of ideological proportions between them. New Irelanders do not think of Malanggan as inventions (application of technology),[55] nor as describing the original inventive step (patents). Indeed individuals are only regarded as producing original images under certain somewhat risky circumstances. The overriding doctrine is that artefacts are acquired not created, so that the routes of acquisition are a crucial source of their value. Concomitantly, it is not the protection of new forms which New Ireland people seek but the right to reproduce what others have reproduced before them. This representation of their efforts is as much a *mis*representation (Harrison 2000) as are the equally dogmatic assertions by English-speakers of originality and innovation as the basis of technological advance. The Euro-American doctrine is encapsulated of course in the very notion of patent rights. These point to 'inventions' as artefacts created not acquired, and what is protected is not a right to reproduce the original invention but the right to prevent others from freely reproducing the capacity which the invention has created.

We have seen how the concept of nature upholds this doctrine; it underwrites the distinction between discovery (of things in nature) and invention (abstracted from nature through human ingenuity). And it may do so to the point of absurdity. In talking about attempts to patent a cell line and similar biotechnological innovations, Pottage criticizes the way this 'banal doctrinal distinction' (1998: 750) is used to put down political or ethical objections. His own objections to the 'endless permutations of "nature" and "artefact"' (1998: 753) are twofold. First, the distinctions are brought in to truncate arguments concerning the political or ethical implications of what is or is not commodifiable. 'Political oppositions are not a function of [cannot be dismissed as] doctrinal confusion' (1998: 753). Legal doctrine takes, as the basis for decision-making, linguistic and categorical distinctions rather than what is happening to whatever we might want to call nature. Second, there are situations where it is increasingly obscure just how an invention is to be identified. '[T]he production of an immortal cell line demands little more of the "inventor" than the mastery of a routine scientific technique. The "inventive" process seems merely to transcribe a natural code into a new medium' (1998: 752, note omitted). In his view, biotechnology has rendered transparent or implausible the very distinctions that bind the patent law upon which biotechnology so crucially relies (1998: 745).

The question of 'man's expropriation of nature . . . [as] expropriation by one of what is already the natural legacy of all' (see above: Phillips and Firth 1990: 35) is open to debate. But there is a further question in the way the problem is taken care of in the distinction between technology and nature, invention and discovery, and the rest: patent law in effect defines what has *already* been expropriated, that is, is no longer nature. Now New Irelanders remake people out of people, so to speak, bodies out of bodies, and the competition is over claims to ancestral power, that is, making claims to what is already specifically identified as theirs. Patent-holders, on the other hand, deal with people in terms of property claims, and instead make their devices out of things, materials and knowledge ultimately part of a 'commons' belonging to everyone and no one.

When they think of the commons as a natural resource, Euro-Americans may imagine it as a domain free from people's inventiveness, and ideally perhaps even empty of people altogether; at the same time when they think of dwelling, this is the 'location' they often bring to mind, and they would also like to think of the commons as a world which people 'naturally' possess and where people find their 'natural' habitation. It is this flexibility, we could say, making people apparently now relevant and now not relevant to one's perspective (on the world) that has been so enabling of technological 'innovation' in the West (Eric Hirsch personal communication). But I have deliberately ended with an image of nature as a resource – the commons – which points to human interest in it. Is not part of our feeling comfortable with technology, dwelling 'with' it, the fact that it gives us things we can 'own', and thus take possession of, for ourselves? Disquiet when those proprietary extensions of the person seem inappropriate is part of being at home with the techniques and relations of ownership.

By referring to New Irelanders I have wanted to bring a reminder of peoples elsewhere who have been on the receiving end not just of technology, or of intellectual property rights legislation, but of the divide between 'technology' and 'inhabiting' which was problematized at a recent ICA conference (see acknowledgement). They are here as a reminder of the political and ethical debates that surround resource extraction, the extension of property regimes, and so forth. But too often a Euro-American will reinvent the divide (between technology and inhabiting) by investing such peoples with the qualities which his or her own ideas about technology would give to 'nature'. I have tried instead to make them present in a different way – emphasizing the points on which we might draw parallels with ideas about technology in order to put into perspective those on which we we cannot.

Acknowledgement

This chapter was given as a paper under the title 'Patenting Nature', at the conference 'Inhabiting Technology' at the Institute for Contemporary Art organized by the journal *Theory, Culture and Society*; the editors of this volume are grateful to *TCS* for permission to reprint the paper, first published in *TCS*, here. It is not original. I bring together the expertise of several anthropologists dispersed over a range of studies – I am especially grateful to the late Alfred Gell for his anthropological theory of art, and to Susanne Küchler on whose work I draw extensively, as a well as to the compilers of a major catalogue on this art form edited by Louise Lincoln. It will be obvious that my portrait of Malanggan is a composite of features from different ethnographic areas and follows only one track from among many analytical possibilities.

Principal thanks are due to Karen Sykes and the results of her own investigations in New Ireland. I am very grateful for permission to draw on unpublished material and, more than that, on her ideas. [I follow Sykes's spelling and convention of capitalization.] She is part of the Cambridge and Brunel joint research project on 'Property, Transactions and Creations: New Economic Relations in the Pacific' [PTC, funded by the UK Economic and Social Research Council, all of whose members have been an indirect but emphatic inspiration]. Terence Hay-Edie, who has been exploring other enchanted worlds, is also due thanks. The stimulus of the conference at the ICA will be self evident; thanks too to the members of the Summer Institute on World Arts at the University of East Anglia for their several comments.

Notes

1. The basic Malanggan concepts drawn on here are shared across the region (Küchler 1987: 239, who points particularly to Lewis 1969). Matrilineal 'clans' are dispersed across the whole area, being locally concentrated as village-based kin groups and conceptually brought together under a region-wide name. The significance of Küchler's (1987: 249) remark that the 'relationship between localised units of a matrilinal clan is apprehended in terms of places and movements of people between places' will become apparent later.

2. There is only one term here ('skin', *tak,* Küchler 1992: 100); the Malanggan momentarily replaces the rotting body of the deceased, to be one way or another then left to rot itself. An excellent overview of anthropological approaches to 'the body' is found in Csordas 1999.

3. Casey (1996: 39) notes Heidegger's insistence, which I take as a literalism, that it is 'in dwellings that we are most acutely sensitive to the effects of places on our lives' (place here referring to embodiment).

4. I am not sure about borowing terms, notably 'dwelling', from general philosophical arguments about conceptual and bodily orientations which prefigure the perceived world (Heidegger, Merleau Ponty) and then applying them to culturally conceived contexts or environments. The borrowing has some purchase perhaps in the form of a question: how do people fabricate the idea of a world 'containing' things/persons within it?

5. Anthropologists have drawn on 'dwelling' to develop a dialectic not with technology but with 'travelling' (Battaglia 1999: 129, citing Feld and Basso 1996) or, explicitly after Heidegger, 'building' (Ingold 1995). For a full-length ethnography which marvellously explores some of these ideas, see Weiner 1991.

6. I take for granted that what is constructed as contained is thereby constructed as distinct – separate – from its container.

7. Technical virtuosity points to the sheer control necessary to produce these effects out of these materials: light, airy flowing structures from solid wood (though more 'amazing', we shall discover, than the cathedral made of matches: Gell 1999: 167). In pre-steel days much of the work was done by burning.

8. For example, they may be thought of as persons, or they may stand for totemic affiliations to groups.

9. Partly because this is not a concept reified in their thinking, partly because they do not have an environmentalist view of what Euro-Americans call the natural world 'in which' they seems to be situated and thus inhabiting.

10. It is the cultural role which technology has come to play in Euro-American perceptions of their place in the world which has in turn given an impetus to the concept of intellectual property – intellectual property rights (IPR) hold

up a mirror to the dazzle of creativity. For 'intellectual property' points simultaneously to an item or technique made available to knowledge, authorizing its use and circulation, and to the knowledge, on which claims are made, which has made it into an item or technique. Knowledge embedded in technology has already been productive in the manner that labour is productive, while knowledge rendered as a subject of property rights can be put into productive circulation as commodities are (Strathern 1999: 20–1).

11. Inventions are impotent if there is too great a 'technology gap' between the idea and its application (Phillips and Firth 1990: 42).

12. His own subject is the place of art, and he starts with the idea of technologies of enchantment, to which art belongs, as magic and ritual also do. But an important part in the production of their effects is the dazzle of technical virtuosity (the enchantment of technology). His terms are deliberately recursive. Apropos art and magic: '[i]t seems to me that the efficacy of art objects as components of the technology of enchantment . . . is itself the result of the enchantment of technology, the fact that the technical process, such as carving canoe boards [which have magical properties], are [known to be] construed magically so that, by enchanting us, they make the products of these technical processes seem enchanted vessels of magical power' (Gell 1999: 166). Apropos the matchstick model of Salisbury Cathedral which awed him as a boy: '[t]he matchstick model, functioning essentially as an advertisement, is part of the technology of enchantment, but it achieves its effect by the enchantment cast by its technical means, the manner of its coming into being, or, rather, the idea which one forms of its coming into being' (1999: 167).

13. As a concept, technology 'essentially refers to the rational principles [*logos*] governing the construction of artifacts and indicates a move away from artisan or craft production [*techne*] to the possibilities of embedding skills in machines which can then be "operated" by relatively non-skilled workers' (Harvey 1997: 6, after Ingold 1988, 1997). As Ingold (1997: 131) observes, the creative part of manufacture ceases to be found in the application of the craftsman's skills and becomes instead found 'in the element of design or planning' by which the machine itself was conceived and produced.

14. On the empowerment of anonymity, see Konrad 1998. Creativity might be thought individual and idiosyncratic, thereby deserving of personal reward (cf Khalil 1995: 243), but Euro-Americans also imagine their civilization to be characterized by technical innovation at large.

15. In the arena of the once-called new reproductive technologies, arguments are frequently heard that Technology supplies a means, and it is for for Society to sort out the ends to which it will be put (see for example Edwards et al. 1999).

16. For example: by dividing technology off from other things, we create the 'materials' on which 'technology' gets to work. A language which divides off technology as a marked form of human industry from everything else is consonant with one which divides the scientific observer from the observed, culture from nature, and modernity from tradition, not to speak of the mechanical from the organic, human intervention from the self-reproducing, and so forth. There is no end to the number of conceptual supports by which each division is held up through related but distinct divisions (cf Pottage 1998: 745). Bits of this ancient enchantment of the Euro-American world are endlessly destroyed (by critics) only to spring up again (in new contexts).

17. Wherever it is actually operated from; cf Miller on Trinidadian websites. These can be understood as creating 'aesthetic traps that express the social efficacy of their creators and attempt to draw others into social or commercial exchange with those who have objectified themselves through the internet. [As in Melanesian exchange] . . . these websites attempt to expand their creators through casting themselves out into a larger world of exchange with distant places' (see Miller's Chapter Seven: pp. 137–155, this volume).

18. Whalers, labour recruiters and traders followed Carteret's 1767 determination that New Ireland was an island, and encounters with New Ireland people were frequent. After 1885, colonization by Germany added intensive commercial and misionary activity (Bodrogi 1987: 17; Lincoln 1987: 35). But the area had been known since Tasman's voyage of 1643, and carvings (not Malanggan in this case) were recorded from that earliest moment in the seventeenth century (Gunn 1987: 74).

19. Küchler (1987) explains that vertical and horizontal Malanggan may act as 'tree' and 'branch' in relation to one another, while in some areas (Tabar island) 'houses' take over from 'trees'. These structures are at the basis of mnemonic techniques required (as we shall see) for the recall of designs.

20. For Tabar, Gunn (1987: 75) gives a list of diverse occasions which provide the immediate reason for display, but the logic of the display is based on the same premise: that a person honours the dead of his spouse's kin group (from the opposite moiety) when he deploys Malanggan in an appropriate context. Across the Malanggan-making region, occasions include intitiation, cere-monies to renconcile parties after quarrelling, validating land transactions, removing social prohibitions, as well as a host of new events (Sykes, personal communication). I am abbreviating and eliding information and analysis from several distinct social traditions; my principal published source is Küchler (1987, 1992), and Gell's (1998) rendering of her data, along with the examples described in Lincoln 1987.

21. Malanggan may be made for deceased men or women but, regardless of the sex of the deceased, are sponsored and made by men. Küchler (1987: 240)

says that the owner in question will be someone who shared rights in the Malanggan with the deceased person.

22. Rather like the Hagen headdress (Strathern 1999: chapter 2), every such figure, every construction of identity, is an amalgamation of figures, of social identities derived from others. On places as events rather than things, or as location rather than geography, and on the general significance of emplacement as the gathering together of perceptions, see Casey 1996. A hierarchy of Malanggan designations indicates relative mobility. Thus, according to Küchler (1987: 252), each scultpure has three names. One name denotes its original template and place of innovation, and this remains constant throughout its history of transmission; a second name denotes its general shape and its position or stage in transmisson, and is altered only when the transmission involves the trans-ference of rights from one localized group to another within the dispersed matriclan; finally a third-level name refers to the unique combination of elements, all the particular motifs, that is specific to each individual sculpture, and changes every time a Malanggan is reproduced.

23. Weiner (1991: 71) comments on an early anthropological observer of Melanesian languages who said that habits of speaking (through locatives, etc.) implied that everybody or everything was either coming or going, now in one place now in another.

24. As a virtual body, the clan contains all the persons and actions, past and future, that constitute it, and clanship means for any one individual both the possibility of living through all these others and the possibility of benefiting from its numerous connections: not the clan as a discrete unit, but the clan and its relationships with others is what envelops persons (Wagner 1991). Note that, for simplicity's sake, I argue through the concept of 'clanship' in order to summon the collective dimension in rights to produce Malanggan. The reality is complicated by the identities of and interrelations between localised subclans or clan segments. (Küchler 1987: 251 suggests that the transactions over and sharing in Malanaggan across the northern New Ireland region offer their own sources of sociality connected to but separate from the organizational role played by the dispersed matrilineal clans as such.)

25. The phrase is from Gell (1998: 225): 'On death the agency of a [deceased] person is in a dispersed state', and through the Malanggan the dispersed social effectiveness of the person becomes 'something to which a single material index may be attached'. See Hirsch (1995) for a cogent discussion of such processes elsewhere.

26. 'Absorbed into the artistic system, this life-force is rechannelled to the living in the form of power. This power constitutes political authority and is derived from the control over the re-embodiment of the memorised imagery into new sculptures' (Küchler 1987: 240). This is highly pertinent to relations between

land-holding units, whose claims relative to one another are mapped out through their rights to reproduce particular Malanggan.

27. There are both inter-place and inter-clan relations here, not distinguished in this account. The right to reproduce Malanggan may be transferred between parts of the same matrilineal clan living in different localities, or between affinal clans linked in a history of intermarriage and co-residence (Küchler 1987: 240).

28. Thereby (for example) ratifying new claims to landholdings after the person's death: in the area where she worked, recently settled by immigrants from elsewhere in the region and where land was very short, Küchler notes particular emphasis on the readjustment of land claims. It is the anticipated claims which the Malanggan records.

29. Gell (1998: 226, original emphasis) puts it beautifully: the Malanggan is 'a *temporally dispersed object*, an object *at* no specific time or place, but moving through time and place, like a thunderstorm'.

30. On gathering and dispersal as a recurrent template to social arrangements in PNG, see Hirsch 1995. From the perspective of Actor Network Theory (Law and Hassard 1999) the Malanggan can be described as a temporary passage point (e.g. Callon 1986).

31. Tassy and Dambrine (1997: 193) make explicit note of creativity: 'Intellectual property is a generic term which refers to the rights attached to the products of human creativity'. Patent law is 'inherently designed to cope with new technology' (Phillips and Firth 1990: 273).

32. Specifications of the invention must be of a detail to be intelligible to anyone in the position to exploit it. Disclosure must be total, with nothing of substance withheld, otherwise no one could make use of the invention when the patent expires (Bainbridge 1999: 317). I refer to 'inventor', but the eventual patent-holder and owner of economic rights in the invention may be other social entities as well, for example an industrial sponsor.

33. See Kalinoe n.d. The TRIPS agreement requires that patent protection must be provided for products and processes in all areas of technology.

34. Recent impetus is given to this perspective by what is perceived as the galloping rate of technologization, the size of commercial investment, the emergence of biotechnology as a major player, and the accelerated pace at which scientific research is becoming subject to proprietary interests (cf. Nelkin 1984).

35. Bainbridge (1999: 349) quotes two commentators, the first to the effect that inventions are either new ways of producing something old or old ways of producing something new; the second to the effect that every invention is a 'new combination of pre-existing knowledge'. In itself, a single 'invention' may also consist of several (sub)inventions which are allowed together under the one patent as a substantive package.

36. It is not just that raw materials are available to all, but that they have no 'technical effect' (Bainbridge 1999: 368).
37. Pottage (1998: 752) objects to the narrowness of such a technical or doctrinal response. In this case the answer to the objection that a particular recombinant DNA process could not be repeated, because it was unique to an individual, lay in the the claim that it was the very [design of the] process used to transform various genetic materials which was the invention.
38. 'The fact that [certain] material previously occurred in nature does not prevent it from being patented if it is isolated from its natural environment or produced by means of a technical process' (Bainbridge 1999: 378), interpretingArticle 2 of the 1998 European Parliament and Council Directive on the legal protection of biotechnological inventions. There are differences here between European and American patent rights. Thus in the United States it is possible to obtain a patent for a new breed of animal (Bainbridge 1999: 377).
39. A matter of controversy, especially in relation to gene patenting where patents may be taken out on technical processes whose future application is unpredictable. In 1999 the journal *Nature* called on the World Science conference to focus on the implications of the breadth of patents currently being issued.
40. See for instance chapter 1 (esp. 1.32–1.40) of the Nuffield Council on Bioethics, 'Report on genetically modified crops: the ethical and social issues', London, 1999.
41. Among those with whom Küchler worked, the carver will have inherited his skill of carving along with knowledge of the magic to induce a vision of the image to be carved. He has already had the image described to him by the person in the clan responsible for producing the sculpture and what he is told will include not only this memory but all the modifications which current transactions require (1992: 103). Gunn (1987: 74) says it might be thirty years between acquiring rights and passing them on to be reproduced again by the next generation.
42. To follow the non-productionist locations of 'technology' in Weiner's (1995) and Leach's (forthcoming) debates with Gell.
43. Categorically true of marriage relationships, which have to be across moieties; my interpretations here draw on other well documented interpretations of Papua New Guinean materials in the anthropological literature.
44. This can be read as referring to an owner and carver; to a procreative couple who bear a child, or to a localized kin grouping where spouses will always have distinct indentity from one another so no set of siblings replicates any other.
45. I am compressing here all the kinds of work involved in the many ceremonials involving many people that bring Malanggan to fruition; see Powdermaker's observations about work cited by Lincoln (1987: 33).

46. This contributes to Harrison's (1992: 235) general argument about what is owned as intellectual property – not things, but classes of things ('their images or typification').

47. Lincoln (1987: 34) puts this altogether more positively. A clan depleting its wealth when it pays for Malanggan is in effect converting money and labour into enduring prestige. Moreover, she adds, the ownership rights it has acquired, which 'will likely be resold, constitute a sort of semiliquid asset'.

48. However, Gunn (1987: 79–80) distinguishes two modi operandi on the Tabar Islands. Once a major series of Malanggan have been shown and transferred, the original owner cannot display that Malaggan again. This applies to Malanggan transferred across generations within the same clan or subclan. However when rights to a single sculpture or motifs from a sculpture are transferred across group (for example from father to son in this matrilineal system), it is possible to allocate usage and reproductive rights alone, with the owner retaining rights to his own ceremonies. Here we can say that the Malanggan is 'copied'. I should add that I am much stimulated by Gunn's analogy with this form of intellectual property – not criticizing it.

49. Unlike copyright (and design right) which comes into effect automatically on publication, patents have to be registered (designs may be), and there is no equivalent to such a process in this case. If one pursues these analogies, however, then more appropriate forms of intellectual property protection might be found in performers' rights or in the relatively new concept of design rights.

50. A point that is held to perplex some legal commentors: the law has brought a thing into existence and then at the end of a set term the thing winks out of existence (cf. Phillips and Firth 1990: 24). Euro-Americans are also alleged to be mystified by the way in which so much effort goes into producing Malanggan when they are then so quickly destroyed or otherwise discarded.

51. The unique item made on an individual occasion with its particular combination of motifs is the effective materialization essential for transfer to the next generation; the conceptual template held by the clan is not extinguished but neither can it be activated without being embodied in a specific Malanggan form.

52. The Patent Office holds specifications and abstracts for every British patent dating from 1617, over 2 million inventions, and 23 million patent publications from overseas (Bainbridge 1999: 335). Population for population, it is conceivable that there have been almost as many northern New Ireland Malanggan as there have been British patents.

53. The figure of 5000 comes from Kuchler (1992: 97) with reference to the period approximately 1870–1990; it is not the whole output of course, since many more will have been burnt or buried away from sight with the dead in caves (Gunn 1987: 74). Lincoln (1987: 40) gives the figure of 15,000 for all kinds

of material culture objects from New Ireland (principally masks and sculptures) finding their way into European and American museums from the 1885–1914 German period alone. Some of this prodigious production, she speculates, must have been in response to outside demand. There have no doubt been cycles of productivity. Lincoln (1987: 39) suggests that the use of metal introduced into carving in the 1850s, and the experience of colonization in general, stimulated the production of Malanggan.

54. This does not mean to say that different kinds of right might not be subsequently enacted, for example, as 'cultural property' rights. The term 'Malanggan' always included ceremonial and other events surrounding the revelation of the carving and these days New Irelanders may extend the term across a range of customary practices. 'Indeed, New Irelanders claim Malanggan as a distinctive feature of their modern and customary cultural life' (Sykes n.d.).

55. As Harrison (2000) reminds us; the dialectical relationship between invention and convention in Melanesian life, and how we attribute these values, is complicated (Wagner 1975). In the end, however, the Malanggan is an invention without innovation. Although each recombination is freshly inspired, each individual element is also recalled from some other, the creation of entirely new images (through dreaming) being regarded as hazardous; there has been immense stability in the repertoire of forms over the years (Küchler 1987: 239).

References

Bainbridge, D. 1999. *Intellectual Property* (4th edn). Financial Times Management & Pitman Publishing.

Battaglia, D. 1999. 'Towards an Ethics of the Open Subject: Writing Culture in Good Conscience', in H. Moore (ed.) *Anthropological Theory Today*. Cambridge: Polity Press, pp. 114–50.

Bodrogi, T. 1987. 'New Ireland Art in Cultural Context', in L. Lincoln (ed.), *Assemblage of Spirits: Idea and Image in New Ireland*. New York: George Braziller, in association with the Minneapolis Institute of Arts, pp. 17–32.

Callon, M. 1986. 'Some Elements of a Sociology of Translation: Domestication of the Scallops and the Fishermen of St Brieuc Bay', in J. Law (ed.), *Power, Action and Belief: a New Sociology of Knowledge*. London: Routledge.

Casey, E. 1996. 'How to Get from Space to Place a Fairly Short Stretch of Time: Phenomenological Prolegomena', in S. Feld & K. Basso (eds), *Sense of Place*. Santa Fe: School of American Research Press.

Coombe, R. 1998. *The Cultural Life of Intellectual Properties: Authorship, Appropriation and the Law*. Durham, NC.: Duke University Press.

Csordas, T. 1999. 'The Body's Career in Anthropology', in H. Moore (ed.), *Anthropological Theory Today*. Cambridge: Polity Press, pp. 172–205.

Edwards, J., Hirsch, E., Franklin, S., Pine, F., Strathern, M. 1999 [1993]. *Technologies of Procreation: Kinship in the Age of Assisted Conception*. London: Routledge.

Feld, S. and K. Basso (eds). 1996. *Sense of Place*. Santa Fe: School of American Research Press.

Gell, A. 1998. *Art and Agency: An Anthropological Theory*. Oxford: Clarendon Press.

—— 1999 [1992]. 'The Technology of Enchantment and the Enchantment of Technology', in A. Gell, *The Art of Anthropology: Essays and Diagrams*, ed. by E. Hirsch. London: The Athlone Press, pp. 159–86.

Gunn, M. 1987. 'The Transfer of Malagan Ownership on Tabar', in L. Lincoln (ed.), *Assemblage of Spirits: Idea and Image in New Ireland*. New York: George Braziller, in association with the Minneapolis Institute of Arts, pp. 74–83.

Harrison, S. 1992. 'Ritual as Intellectual Property', *Man* (ns) 27: 225–44.

—— 2000. 'From Prestige Goods to Legacies: Property and the Objectification of Culture in Melanesia', *Comparative Studies in Society and History* 42: 662–679.

Harvey, P. 1997. 'Introduction: Technology as Skilled Practice', Special issue *Social Analysis* (*Technology as Skilled Practice*, ed. P. Harvey), no. 41, pp. 3–14.

Heintze, D. 1987. 'On Trying to Understand some Malaggans', in L. Lincoln (ed.), *Assemblage of Spirits: Idea and Image in New Ireland*. New York: George Braziller, in association with the Minneapolis Institute of Arts, pp. 42–55.

Hirsch, E. 1995. 'The "Holding Together" of Ritual: Ancestrality and Achievement in the Papua Highlands', in D. de Coppet and A. Iteanu (eds), *Society and Cosmos: Their Interrelation or Their Coalescence in Melanesia*. Oxford: Berg.

Ingold, T. 1988. 'Tools, Minds and Machines: An Excursion into the Philosophy of Technology', *Techniques et Culture*, 12: 151–76.

—— 1995. 'Building, Dwelling, Living; How Animals and People make Themselves at Home in the World', in M. Stathern (ed.), *Shifting Contexts: Transformations in Anthropological Knowledge*. ASA Decennial Conference series, London: Routledge, pp. 57–80.

—— 1997. 'Eight Themes in the Anthropology of Technology', in Special issue *Social Analysis* (*Technology as Skilled Practice*, ed. P. Harvey), no. 41, pp. 106–138.

Kalinoe, L. n.d. 'Ascertaining the Nature of Indigenous Intellectual and Cultural Property and Traditional Knowedge and the search for Legal Options in Regulating Access in Papua New Guinea: Case Studies'. Discussion paper for PTC Colloquium II, Cambridge 2000.

Khalil, M. 1995. 'Biodiversity and the Conservation of Medicinal Plants: Issues from the Perspective of the Developing World', in T. Swanson, (ed.), *Intellectual*

Property Right and Biodiversity Conservation: an Interdisciplinary Analysis of the Values of Medicinal Plants. Cambridge: Cambridge University Press, pp. 232–53.

Konrad, M. 1998. 'Ova Donation and Symbols of Substance: Some Variations in the Theme of Sex, Gender and the Partible Person', *Journal of the Royal Anthropological Institute* (ns) 4: 643–67.

Küchler, S. 1987. 'Malangan: Art and Memory in a Melanesian Society', *Man* (n.s.) 22: 238–55.

—— 1992. 'Making Skins: Malangan and the Idiom of Kinship in New Ireland', in J. Coote & A. Shelton (eds), *Anthropology, Art and Aesthetics.* Oxford: Clarendon Press, pp. 94–112.

Latour, B. 1993. *We Have Never Been Modern.* Translated by Catherine Porter. London: Prentice Hall.

Law, J. and J. Hassard (eds). 1999. *Actor Network Theory and After.* London: Routledge.

Leach, J. (forthcoming). 'Drum and Voice. Aesthetics, Technology, and Political Relations in a Rai coast (Papua New Guinea) Society', J.B. Donne prize essay, *Journal of the Royal Anthropological Institute.*

Lewis, P. 1969. 'The Social Context of Art in Northern New Ireland', *Fieldiana: Anthropology* 58. Chicago: Field Museum of Natural History.

Lincoln, L. 1987. 'Art and Money in New Ireland', in L. Lincoln (ed), *Assemblage of Spirits: Idea and Image in New Ireland.* New York: George Braziller, in association with the Minneapolis Institute of Arts, pp. 33–41.

Nelkin, D. 1984. *Science as Intellectual Property.* New York: Macmillan Publishing Co.

Phillips, J. and A. Firth. 1990. *Introduction to Intellectual Property Law* (2nd edn), London: Butterworths.

Pottage, A. 1998. 'The Inscription of Life in Law: Genes, Parents, and Bio-politics', *Modern Law Review* 61: 740–65.

Rabinow, P. 1996, *Essays on the Anthropology of Reason*, Princeton, NJ: Princeton University Press.

Strathern, M. 1992. *After Nature; English Kinship in the Late Twentieth Century.* Cambridge: Cambridge University Press.

—— 1996. 'Cutting the Network', *Journal of the Royal Anthropological Institute* (ns) 2: 517–35.

—— 1999 *Property, Substance and Effect: Anthropological Essays on Persons and Things.* London: Athlone.

Swanson, T. (ed.). 1995. *Intellectual Property Right and Biodiversity Conservation: An Interdisciplinary Analysis of the Values of Medicinal Plants.* Cambridge: Cambridge University Press.

Sykes, K. n.d. Outline of proposed research, PTC Workshop 6, Cambridge 1999; '"Losing Interest": the devaluation of Malanggan', Field Report, PTC workshop, Cambridge 2000.

Tassy, J and C. Dambrine. 1997. 'Intellectual Property Rights in Support of Scientific Research', *European Review* 5: 193–204.

Wagner, R. 1975. *The Invention of Culture*. Englewood Cliffs: Prentice Hall.

—— 1991. 'The Fractal Person', in M. Godelier and M. Strathern (eds), *Big Men and Great Men: Personifications of Power in Melanesia*. Cambridge: Cambridge University Press.

Walden, I. 1995. 'Preserving Biodiversity: The Role of Property Rights', in T. Swanson, (ed.), *Intellectual Property Right and Biodiversity Conservation: An Interdisciplinary Analysis of the Values of Medicinal Plants*. Cambridge: Cambridge University Press, pp. 176–97.

Weiner, J. 1991. *The Empty Place: Poetry, Space and Being Among the Foi of Papua New Guinea*. Bloomington: Indiana University Press.

—— 1995. 'Technology and Techne in Trobriand and Yolngu art'. *Social Analysis* 38: 32–46.

Index